C000259973

SRI
SARWARTHACHINTAMANI

Sri
Sarwarthachintamani

ENGLISH TRANSLATION

B. Suryanarain Rao

PART II

MOTILAL BANARSIDASS PUBLISHERS
PRIVATE LIMITED ● DELHI

Reprint Delhi: 1997, 2002, 2007
Second Edition: Bangalore, 1933
Third Revised Edition: Delhi, 1996

ISBN: 81-208-1353-7 (Vol II)
ISBN: 81-208-1351-0 (Set)

MOTILAL BANARSIDASS

41 U.A. Bungalow Road, Jawahar Nagar, Delhi 110 007
8 Mahalaxmi Chamber, 22 Bhulabhai Desai Road, Mumbai 400 026
236, 9th Main III Block, Jayanagar, Bangalore 560 011
203 Royapettah High Road, Mylapore, Chennai 600 004
Sanas Plaza, 1302 Baji Rao Road, Pune 411 002
8 Camac Street, Kolkata 700 017
Ashok Rajpath, Patna 800 004
Chowk, Varanasi 221 001

Printed in India
BY JAINENDRA PRAKASH JAIN AT SHRI JAINENDRA PRESS,
A-45 NARAINA, PHASE-I, NEW DELHI 110 028
AND PUBLISHED BY NARENDRA PRAKASH JAIN FOR
MOTILAL BANARSIDASS PUBLISHERS PRIVATE LIMITED,
BUNGALOW ROAD, DELHI 110 007

If there is friendship between the lord of Lagna and the lord of the 3rd house, there will be cordiality between the brothers. If they are unfriendly, the relationship between the two brothers will be hateful. 426.

If the lord of brothers and the lord of the 3rd house join odd signs and are aspected by Guru, Ravi and Kuja, and if the 3rd house happens to be an odd sign, there will be brothers (males). 427.

If the third house, its lord and the lord of brothers, fall in even signs or amsas, there will be sisters. If these fall in the amsas of eunuch planets those born with the person will become impotent or eunuchs. 428.

The number of brothers and sisters may be determined by the Navamsa the third house falls in, or by the number of the Navamsa, into which the lord of the third house or the lord of brothers, falls— 429.

The number may be determined by the Navamsa occupied by the planets who join the 3rd house, or by the number of the Amsa joined by the lord of the Navamsa occupied by the lord of the 3rd house. 430.

Or the number may be determined by the Navamsa occupied by the planet who is in conjunction with the lord of the brothers or the lord of the 3rd house. The destruction of brothers and sisters must be predicted, when these planets are in combust or in evil conjunctions. 431.

48

Notes.

I have already referred to this question of the possession of brothers in my notes on the previous stanzas.

However much the questions of property and personal aggrandisement may influence a few narrow-minded or narrow-hearted people to have no brothers or sisters to bother them, the overwhelming majority are in favour of this possession and sharing with them the joys and sorrows of their lives. The authors of the Astrological works have viewed the destruction of brothers and sisters as a misfortune and mankind in general holds this view as perfectly correct. There are some wretches who would kill their parents or children for the sake of money but sciences in general of course, view them as miserable mortals.

There are three factors to be considered with reference to brothers and sisters, and the strength or weakness of these three determines the prosperity or danger to brothers. The third house represents brothers in general while the eleventh indicates the elder born. The term brothers includes sisters and therefore the word brothers is generally used in these explanations. The lord of brothers is Kuja and the lord of the 3rd house has also considerable influence. The intermediate complications are many and tedious and I shall give the main principles enunciated by Venkatesa Daivagna. If there is a benefic in the 3rd house, or it possesses beneficial aspect or the lord of the 3rd house is powerful there will be prosperity to brothers. The house becomes powerful, when a benefic occupies it, or when it is hemmed in by two benefics, or when its lord is exalted or is in good conjunction or aspect. The lord of the 3rd house will be powerful when he possesses the six sources of strength already named, or when he occupies favourable divisions or when he shines well on account of beneficial influences or conjunctions 416.

There seems to be some repetition of the ideas or combinations. If the lord of the 3rd house, or the lord of the brothers Kuja, or the 3rd house has beneficial aspects or conjunctions and is powerful, there will be prosperity to brothers. The words "*and is powerful*" will have to be carefully noted. The lord of the third house or Kuja or the 3rd house may be aspected by or may be in conjunction with, benefics but may not be powerful. This means that they may be wanting in Shadbalas or Shadvergas and may be in combustion or otherwise debilitated.

Take an example. Lagna is Meena. The third house is

Lagna	Sani Buda	Ravi Chandra	Sukra Rahu
			Kuja
	Rasi		
Kethu		Guru	

Vrishabha. The lord of the third house is Sukra and the lord of brothers is Kuja. The third house is occupied by two evil planets Ravi and Kshina-Chandra or weak Moon. It is encompassed on both sides by Sani and Rahu and also by Buda and Sukra. The lord of the brothers Kuja is in debilitation in Kataka. The lord of the 3rd house Sukra occupies a friendly house with an evil planet Rahu but powerfully aspected by Guru. Chandra is exalted but is really a helpless one as he is in an Amavasya day or close to the Sun. Under these circumstances the prosperity of the brothers and sisters will be mixed as the influences are mixed. Take another case.

Here the lord of the 3rd house is Ravi and he is in con-

	Kethu		Lagna Sukra
			Buda
	Rasi		Ravi Guru
Kuja		Rahu	Chandra
Sani			

junction with Guru. The third house is occupied by its own lord and is encompassed between two good planets Chandra and Buda and Guru is occupying it. The lord of brothers is Kuja and he occupies an exaltation house aspected by a benefic Buda. Under these situations there will be great prosperity to the brothers and sisters of this horoscope. 417.

Now the author goes to determine the question of having brothers or not. If the lord of the third house or Kuja is found in Kendras or Konas *viz.*, 1—4—5—7—9—10, or if any of them is exalted, or occupies his own division or that of a friendly planet there will be brothers. The number of these brothers will be determined later on. If both the lords of the third house and brothers are occupying Kendras or Konas or their own houses of exaltations or divisions or friendly divisions then there will certainly be a greater number of brothers. The divisions referred to here are the Shadvergas. 418.

If the lord of the third house or Kuja is exalted, or occupies his own house or Navamsa or the Navamsas of benefics there will be increase among brothers. 419.

If the lord of the third house joins a Gopuramsa—four good divisions—or if Kuja is located in Simhasanamsa—·five good divisions—or if a benefic or the lord of the 3rd joins any of the above good amsas there will be increase to brothers' (See p. 39 for explanation of Amsas).

He has already stated that the lord of the 3rd must be in Gopuramsa and I fail to see why he should repeat again the same idea in the latter part of this verse. But he only spoke of Gopuramsa and here he also refers to Simhasanamsa. In this conjunction there will be increase to brothers or he will have many brothers—420.

If the lord of the third house possesses Paravatamsa—six good vergas—or if he occupies a Kendra or if the lord of the third joins a benefic, or a benefical Rasi or Navamsa, there will be many brothers. In the stanza a mistake has occurred through the printer's devils. Instead, "or a benefic occupies a Kendra " it should read " or a benefic or occupies a Kendra." That is, the lord of the third house should join a benefic, or a beneficial sign or Navamsa, or be in Paravatamsa or a Kendra to produce many brothers—421

If the lord of the 3rd house occupies his own deep exaltation cr such good vergas or Mulathrikona, or if the third house
is powerful there will be many brothers. This idea has already
been repeated in the previous stanzas. A slight modification is
indicated. Exaltation is different from deep exaltation and I
shall show the difference. Ravi is exalted in Mesha. Mesha
extends over 30 degrees or Bhagas. His power over these thirty
divisions of the sign cannot be and is not, the same. When he is in
the 10th degree he is in deep exaltation or *Swathunga* or *Swocha*.
In other degrees he is only *Thunga* or in exaltation. Suppose he
is in Meshamsa. This division extends over 3⅓ and he will be
only exalted in the whole, but will be in deep exaltation in a
particular degree of it. 422.

If the lord of the third joins Mridwamsa with beneficial
planets or if he has beneficial aspects there will be increase to
brothers. The 19th and 46th Amsas of the Shashtiamsas
(60 divisions) are called Mridwamsas and the lord of the 3rd
must be placed in these amsas with the conjunction of benefics
or their aspects to produce increase among the brothers—423.

If the lord of the third occupies Viseshika—all the 13 good
vergas or divisions aspected by benefics or is in Mridwamsa etc,
there will be increase among brothers. The lord of the 3rd
may occupy the good vergas but may not have beneficial aspects. This aspect is made necessary in this conjunction.
About Mridwamsa he has already said in the previous sloka but
by the use of the word *adi* meaning etc., he intends that the
lord of the 3rd may occupy any good Shastiamsa with beneficial
aspects and produce many brothers. Amritamsa, Indramsa,
Lakshmiamsa, etc., are good Amsas (See p. 34)—424.

If the lord of the 3rd is in Iravatamsa or if he is powerfully
aspected by or conjoined with Guru, Chandra & Sukra there
will be many brothers. The combination of nine good vergas
is called Iravata. Guru powerfully aspects in the 5th and 9th
and mildly in the 7th. Chandra and Sukra powerfully aspect
in the 7th. When their aspects give brothers their conjunction
must necessarily be higher in efficacy and will produce a larger
number of brothers.—425.

Now the author proceeds to explain the relationship among the brothers and sisters. The lord of the birth indicates the physical and mental side of the person and if he is in friendship with the lord of the third house there will be cordiality among the brothers. Otherwise there will be enemity. Take an example.

Aries or Mesha is Lagna. The lord of Lagna is Mars and the lord of the third is Mercury. There is no friendship between them Take Taurus as Lagna. Its lord is Venus and the lord of the third from it is Moon. There is no friendship between them. Take Gemini, its lord is Mercury and the lord of the third from it is the Sun and they are not friends. Take Cancer. Its lord is Moon. There is no

Pisces	Aries	Taurus	Gemini
Acqua-rius			Cancer
Capricor			Leo
Sagitt-arius	Scorpio	Libra	Virgo

friendship between Moon and the lord of the third from it viz., Mercury. Then between Leo and Libra and their lords the Sun and Venus there is enemity. Between Virgo and Scorpio and their lords Mercury and Mars there is no friendship. Between Libra and Sagittarius, and their lords Venus and Jupiter there is no friendship. Take Scorpio and Capricornus. Their lords Mars and Saturn are not friends. Take Sagittarius and Aquarius. There is no friendship between their lords Jupiter and Saturn. Take Capricornus and Pisces and their lords Saturn and Jupiter are not friends. Take Aquarius and Aries, their lords Saturn and Mars are enemies. Take Pisces and Taurus and their lords Jupiter and Venus are enemies. How then did Venkatesa say that when "there is friendship between the lord of birth and the lord of the third, there will be friendship among the brothers. I have shown by the example given above, that in all the twelve Zodiacal signs, there cannot be any friendship between the lord of any house and the lord of the third house from it. On the other hand, the lord of every third house from any particular house will be his bitter enemy or an enemy. This is an unpardonable mistake committed by a great writer like the author under notice. The Stanza reads clearly like this. Probably this was an oversight on his part or the word should have been referring to lord of brothers, viz., Kuja when it would make some sense. It is absured to think that all the brothers in this world are enemies or all of them are friends. But anyhow I have given the Stanza as I find it in all the copies I possess and all of them read like this. There are, as it were, two sets of planets, one set hating the other or inimicable to the other. The Sun, Moon, Mars and Jupiter form No. I party while Mercury, Venus and Saturn form No. II party. The houses of these planets are also arranged in such a way as to give support to their friendship or enmity.—426.

If Kuja and the lord of the third house are in odd houses, possessing the aspect of masculine planets Ravi, Kuja and Guru and if the third house is an odd house the person will have brothers. Ravi, Kuja and Guru are masculine. Chandra, Sukra, and Rahu are feminine. Buda, Sani and Kethu are eunuchs. Odd signs are Mesha, Mithuna, Simha and so forth. Even signs are Vrishabha, Kataka &c,

The lord of brothers is Kuja and he is masculine. If he occupies odd signs, he produces males ; if he joins even signs, he gives sisters.—427.

If Kuja, lord of the third house and the third house fall in even signs Amsas (Navamsas) the man will have many sisters. If these happen to be in the Navamsas of eunuch planets Sani and Buda, the person will have eunuchs born with him,

Mercury and Sani will influence these conditions a great deal.— 428.

Now, Venkatesa gives some rules by which the number of brothers and sisters can be determined.

As the Lagna falls into a Navamsa, all the other Bhavas have also their Navamsas. This has been previously explained by me in the notes. The third house falls into a Navamsa. This Navamsa possesses a certain number either from its start or from Mesha as we take it to be.

Take the second Navamsa of Vrishabha. It will be placed in Kumbha as the Navamsas for Vrishabha have to be commenced from Makara. This point deserves clearer explanation. The second Navamsa in Vrishabha for example—, will, say, be the Navamsa of third Bhava, when a person is born in Meena Lagna. Are we now to count the number of brothers and sisters as to the number of Navamsa in Vrishabha or as eleventh Navamsa from Mesha in which case the number ot brothers will be eleven? Any how, the number of Navamsas will be nine when we confine ourselves to the divisions of a Rasi or twelve when we count them from Mesha.

Here is another difficulty. A man may have and some have really more than 15 or 16 brothers and sisters, while others have none at all. If the number is to be fixed by the Navamsas alone then we should never get more than twelve in number. But as in the case of Ayurdaya and other processes, their number either increases or decreases as the Navamsas are well or ill occupied or aspected. Suppose, the Navamsa falls in Meena with Sukra in it aspected by Guru. Then the man will have a very large number of sisters and brothers, the latter in smaller proportions. But suppose the Navamsa is Makara with Sani in it aspected by Kuja in Kataka. The number will be less. The lord of the 3rd house as well as the lord of the brothers Kuja must fall into some Navamsa. So far as I have been able to gather the information, the number of the Navamsa must be taken from Mesha and not from the commencement of that particular Rasi. Take a horoscope.

	Chandra Rahu	Lagna	Sani
Ravi Buda Guru	Rasi		
Sukra		Kuja Ketbu	

	Lagna Guru	Rahu	
	Navamsa		
Buda	Kethu	Ravi Sani Sukra Kuja	Chandra

Number of Brothers.

Lagna is Vrishabha and the Navamsa is Mesha or the 4th from Makara. The 18th Navamsa from the Lagna Navamsa will commence the third Bhava, and it will be Thula Navamsa. This may be taken as the 4th Navamsa of the 3rd Bhava or Kataka, and that will also be Thula. Thula is the 7th from Mesha and the person must have 6 brothers and sisters. Take the lord of the 3rd house Moon, and he is found in the Kanya Navamsa, which gives the figure 6 from Mesha. Take the lord of brothers viz Kuja. He is in Thula, which is 7 from Mesha. Therefore, whether we take it from the Navamsa of the 3rd Bhava, or the Navamsa which is occupied by the lord of the 3rd house Chandra or the lord of brothers Kuja we get the figures 6 or 7 and the number of brothers and sisters must be estimated at 6 or 7. In these Navamsas, evil planets, and their aspects, give danger and losses to brothers, while benefics and their aspects, give prosperity and long life to them. As a matter of fact the person has 6 brothers and sisters, out of whom two died early in life. It must be borne as a principle in astrology, that when three or four planets or house lords become governors of any event in life their accumulated and individual energies will have to be carefully weighed and the results must be determined as per their strength. The number is determined by this method but what about the sexes. This has been already explained in the previous verse, but a few notes may also be given here. Suppose the Navamsa representing brothers is feminine, the planets occupying are feminine and masculine conjunction and aspects are wanting, then sisters should be predicted in abundance. But if all these are masculine, preponderance of brothers should be predicted. If a mixture, then the sexes will be equal. Malefics kill them and benefics give them increase and prosperity. Third house represents brothers. Its lord governs them. The planet or planets who occupy the house have power to modify the results. The lord of brothers Kuja must also be taken into special consideration. This procedure must also be adopted in the Navamsa and in all Bhavas and events signified by them. For instance in horoscope given above consider the Navamsa diagram. The Lagna falls in the Mesha and the lord of the 3rd is Budha and he aspects it. The lord of brothers Kuja occupies the 7th Maraka, with Ravi, Sani and Sukra. There is no planet in the 3rd. The same thing will also have to be taken from Chandra Lagna. To foretell the future correctly has been the greatest ambition of man and the greatest achievements in life will always be attended by the most difficult processes and labours. This holds good in the physical as well as in the intellectual planes and must be particularly noticed and weighed by the expert astrologer in his future predictions. The cases of brothers and sisters are curious and various. One man will have a dozen of them   One of them attains to a good position while the rest remain ordinary. One or two sisters will be happily situated while others will be in want and misery. Many of them will be lucky. Most of them will be miserable. All of them will be fortunate or all of them will be unfortunate. All such cases have to be carefully predicted by the astrologer with reference to the above principles laid down by Venkatasa Daivagnya and also by recognised authors who have laboured in its cause and who have propounded the principles in various methods.   429.

The number of brothers may be determined by the Navamsas occupied by the planets in the 3rd house or it may also be found out by tbe Navamsa occupied by the lord of the Navamsa occupied by the planet in the 3rd house. This requires a little further explanation. Take a horoscope.

Girl born at 10—10 p. m. on 1st April 1911.

Sun. Mercu.	Moon. Venus. Saturn. Rahu.		
	RASI DIAGRAM.		
Mars.			
	Birth.	Jupitr. Kethu.	

Mercu. Kethu.	Jupitr.		
	NAVAMSA.		Mars. Saturn.
			Moon.
Sun. Birth.			Venus. Rahu.

She is the daughter of a rich man. This stanza applies only in cases where there are planets in the 3rd house. Here the 3rd house is occupied by Kuja (who happens to be also lord of brothers.) Venkatasa says, the number of brothers may be found out by the Navamsa occupied by the planet in the 3rd house. Kuja occupies the Navamsa of Kataka and it is 4 from Mesha. This is one method. Take another. Mars occupies the 3rd. He occupies the Kataka Navamsa. The lord of that Kataka is Chandra and he occupies the Navamsa of Simha or the 5th from Mesha. Therefore the number of brothers will be four or five. Where different numbers are gained the largest may be predicted with the modification that the difference in numbers of the lowest from the highest were abortions or brothers and sisters who died soon after their birth.   430.

Here we have another conjunction to predict the number of brothers. Lord of brothers is Kuja. If there is any other planet in conjunction with him, then find out in what Navamsa this planet is and determine the figure accordingly or by the number of the Navamsa occupied by the planet who is in conjunction with the lord of the 3rd house. In all the above cases destruction or loss will have to be predicted if these planets are in combustion or in evil conjunctions. But if they are in beneficial conjunctions prosperity and long life should be predicted.   431.

The resultant of the various forms of influences exercised by the planets concerned relating to the 3rd house, will have to be predicted after due deliberations of the above named principles of astrology. 432.

Here the author summarises his arguments and directs the readers to carefully consider the various sources of power and weakness, which the third house, its lord. the lord of brothers Kuja the planets in conjunction with the 3rd house, and the lord of the 3rd house, and with the lord of brothers, possess. Practically we have to take into consideration (1) the power of the 3rd house, (2) the strength of its lord, (3) the potency of the lord of brothers Kuja, (4) the capabilities of the planet who joins the 3rd house, (5) the strength of the planet who occupies the sign joined by Kuja, (6) the lords of the Navamsas occupied by the lord of the 3rd house and the lord of brothers. All these have shadvergas and shadbalas, and the student has to carefully weigh the *bros* and *cons* and then come to a conclusion as regards brothers and sisters, their number, living and dead, and the prosperity or adversity which overtakes them, and when and how they are affected. To form a sound judgment on the merits of any case submitted to a man is no joke and much more so, when the results have to be predicted on the subtilities of mental discoveries. The student must have a good memory, ready powers of analyses, strong and capable mind to grasp the various conflicting evidence presented before his mind, and draw proper and reasonable conclusions. I have made these notes as clear as possible and trust that my readers will understand the principles of astrology well, analyse facts given and draw proper conclusions. The brevity and sublimity of the original Sanskrit texts can never be approached in any English translation, nor the comprehensive *Sutras* be ever adequately translated into any foreign language. This is my humble opinion. In the course of my Indian travels, lectures, conversations and writings, I have never come across a scholar who could do full justice to the task of English translation from original Sanskrit works, and whose translations have correctly expressed the ideas in the original. Sanskrit is a language of the highest constructive capacity, and the facilities for brevity, comprehensiveness and lucidity in the original are sadly wanting in the nonconstructive English language. 432.

If the powerful sun occupies Simhasanamsa, or if the lord of Vikrama or the lord of the 3rd house is powerful, the person will be courageous. 433.

NOTES.

Vikrama implies courage or warlike spirit. Ravi is the lord of courage, some attribute this to Kuja also. The author now suddenly changes the subject to courage. He is going to give us the several combinations which make a man bold and adventurous or cowardly and weakminded. Courage may be defined as " that quality of mind which prepares one to encounter danger and difficulty, with firmness and possess a calmness of temper at the most critical periods by which he is able to act with vigor and decision." It is derived from the Latin word *cor* = heart. Literally it means one whose heart is strong, and who does not shrink from facing any critical and dangerous situation in the world Mankind have been unanimous in their eulogies about people who are courageous, and who have used such courage in the right direction. All the greatest national heroes of all ages and climes have been courageous in defending the innocent and the right and redressing the wrongs of the oppressed and the poor. When a person is rightly courageous and uses it to the best advantage of the innocent and the oppressed classes, he becomes a real hero and deserves the worship of his fellow beings. Some may show this courage in mental planes, while others may exhibit it in physical feats. But all the same there must be the intrepid mind. A man who speaks *Truth* and nothing but *Truth* under all trying circumstances and cruel persecutions is certainly a courageous man, for he is prepared to sacrifice his life and its prospects for the sake of Truth. He commands the admiration of his country men and the moralists of all climes and ages treat him with great respect. Shastras admire real courage and hold out religious merit and salvation to him, who dies in the cause of justice and religion. Third house from Lagna and Chandra denotes Vikrama or courage and the lord of courage is Ravi. Pure *Kshetryas* are represented by the sun, and a true Kshetrya has never been known to fly from the field of danger or death. When Ravi occupies Simhasanamsa, (see page 39) the person becomes courageous. If the lord of the 3rd house or the lord of Vikrama becomes powerful, the person will be bold. If they are not powerful, the man becomes timid, and cowardly. If any one of them is powerful and is well situated and combined, he will be bold. But if all of them are equally strong and occupy good Vergas, his courage will be commendable, and he will be classed as a military genius. Real courage in man makes him sacrifice his life for good. He will be calm in the midst of the greatest dangers, and collected in the midst of the most trying situations. 433.

If the lord of the 3rd is powerful, and joins exaltation, Kendra or Thrikona possessing beneficial aspects, or if he is in Moolathrikona, his own or friendly house, joining Vaiseshikamsa the man becomes brave. 434.

NOTES.

Any one of these combinations is quite enough to make a person brave. The exaltations of the lord of the 3rd, or his occupation of 1st, 4th, 7th, 10th, 5th or 9th with beneficial aspects, will give him great courage, or if the lord of the 3rd is in his Moolathrikona, his own house, or in his friendly sign, the person will be brave. He must also have beneficial aspects, and must be in Vaiseshikamsa. Whatever may be the abstract philosophic view of courage as a quality in man, there is no doubt whatever,

that one who possesses it is honoured by mankind, specially when
he displays it in the interests of a righteous cause and does not
fear death in its defence. But the courage will be characterised
as brutal or tyrannical, when the man employs it in an unjust
cause, or claim, or in the advancement of his own personal and
selfish interests. Courage need not be in battle alone, although the
author seems to incline to such a view indirectly, whether
in battle or outside it, a man may display courage, calmness, timidity, excitement, or cowardice. A really brave man
will hold his honor more valuable than his life and will be prepared to sacrifice everything for defending the oppressed and
redressing the wronged. There are, of course, different cannons
for judging of courage from different standpoints. But really
good and brave man fights for justice, religion and the interests
of the poorer and oppressed classes, as against the tyranny and
injustice of highhanded rulers. In courage, there is rashness at
well as prudence. A General sees that a battle is lost, that is
would be prudent to beat a retreat, and then recover his lost
advantages by strategem and circumspection. He is not afraid
of his life and there is no idea of cowardice, but he sees that no
advantage will be gained by the sacrifice of his life and much
may be gained by its preservation. There is on the other hand,
a general who rushes madly into the thickest of fight and sells
his life as dear as possible. When benefics powerfully aspect the
house of courage, its lord or the lord of courage, the man will be
courageous but prudent and endowed with foresight. But when
malefics predominate and exercise their influences, the man rushes
madly into dangers and perishes without achieving great things.
The greatest Generals of the world since its commencement
have shown various forms of courage. Haninbal as well as his
brother Hasdrubal were courageous Generals. Hasdrubal
lost his life by rushing into the midst of thick fight while. Haninbal
managed to escape out of danger. Napolean was brave like a
lion, but in the end ignominiously delivered himself into the hands
of his bitter enemies. The standard of treatment by the successful

Generals given to the bravemen who made stout defences of their positions, is also curious and instructive. Some conquerors have shamefully butchered bravemen, while noble hearted conquerors, treated their brave enemies with a respect and consideration, which deserve our highest admiration

The question of brothers and sisters, and their value in the determination of property varies with various nations. Among the English and European nations a man may have any number of brothers, and still be unaffected by their large number, only by the law of Primogeniture the eldest gets the ancestral property and the rest will have to shift for themselves without any recognised shares in the property. But in the case of the Hindu the question of the number of brothers, becomes very grave, when the claims of the brothers is taken into consideration. Say a man is worth a million sterling or 10 lacs of rupees worth of property and gets only one son. The fellow is very lucky and he inherits the whole property But suppose he gets 10 sons, then each of the sons gets one lac and the estate therefore undergoes tenfold division and loses much of its value. Suppose one of these sons gets in turn 10 sons, then each of these fellows gets only 10,000 rupees, a very small sum compared with ten lacs the estate of his grandfather and the comforts of the family must be greatly affected by such divisions and smallness of property. Venkatesa has not given how to find out the elder brothers and how to find out the younger brothers and also their numbers, prosperity, long life, and mutual help. Much light however is thrown upon this point by the famous Kalidasa in his *Oottarakalamrita* and I shall explain the method here with some illustrations so that the readers may understand this question well, and predict the number of elder and younger brothers a man may have by consulting his horoscope. All signs have what are called Bhavas and Bhavasandhies must be carefully calculated by the astronomical portion. Take the horoscope given on p. 384 The Navamsa Lagna falls in the 4th or Mesha and for Vrishabha we have to count Navamsas from Makara. Each Navamsa represents $3\frac{1}{3}$ degrees or 200 minutes or *liptas* and so the Lagna having fallen in the 4th Navamsa has gone over 10 degrees in Vrishabha, and must be within 13⅓ degrees. We shall take it as having fallen, in 2 degree 10 minutes in Mesha Navamsa in Vrishabha Lagna. This means that each Amsa gets 200 liptas or a Rasi has 1800 liptas. In the Mesha Navamsa of Vrishabha Lagna the birth has fallen in the 130th minute or *lipta* and this is but proper. To find out the elder brothers we have to go to the 3rd house in the reverse order or the 11th house from Lagna; for younger brothers we have to go to the 3rd house in the proper order from the birth. Thus fixing the Lagna in the 130th lipta in Mesha Navamsa in Vrishabha Lagna, the third Bhava in the reverse order will be the 130th Lipta in the Makara Navamsa in Kumbha Lagna. Counting in the usual order the 3rd Bhava comes in the 4th Navamsa of Kataka or the 130th Lipta in the Navamsa of Thula, as we have to count for Kataka from Kataka alone. From the Navamsa diagram it will be seen that the lord of Makara, Sani is in Tula with Kuja, Ravi and Sukra. Here there are four planets, a most undesirable combination. Ravi is in debilitation while Sani is exalted. Kuja is in an unfriendly Navamsa with Sani and Sukra, while Sukra is in the conjunction of Sani, Ravi and Kuja. Therefore, Thula is thus spoiled, and the person had one elder brother and one elder sister. Makara is aspected by Kuja and there is no beneficial aspect. He had 3 younger sisters born, one of whom died very early after birth, the other after living 4 or five years and his elder sister died when he was about 12 years. His elder brother died 4 years ago and he has one younger sister. Brothers and sisters have to be determined by the number of Navamsas, past for elder ones, and Navamsas remaining for the younger. In the case of Kataka as the 3rd Bhava, there are still five Navamsas to pass and the person should have had 5 younger ones.

But the 3rd Bhava is afflicted by a heterogeneous conjunction of Ravi, in debilitation, Sukra in his own house, Sani in exaltation and Kuja in a bitter enemy's house. Though he had 3 younger

a

sisters, two of them died early. In the case of the elder, the
Navamsa of Makara in Kumbharasi represents the elder brothers
and its lord is powerless though in exaltation as his conjunction
with Ravi and Kuja is injurious and has taken away much of his
vitality. Makaramsa is aspected by Kuja and has no beneficial
aspects.

Therefore though 3 Navamsas have passed he had only one
elder brother and one elder sister, as Sukra, female, Sani impotent,
Ravi and Kuja male planets occupy the first Navamsa of
Kumbha. Since there are only nine Navamsas it may be-asked,
whether, there could not be more than 8 elder brothers or younger
ones. Suppose a Navamsa is occupied by a benefic, it is a
beneficial sign and a benefic aspects it, then the number should
be multiplied by 3 and for one Navamsa three elder or younger
brothers should be predicted.

Suppose the Navamsa is occupied in addition by an exalted
planet, then the number may be multiplied by four or five. In
this way the number of younger and elder brothers and sisters,
may become very great or very small, or there may be none at all.
Another important method has also been recommended in the
Astrological works and I shall explain what it is. As this is a
very important point in the examination of horoscopes, and as it
has to be applied for all Bhavas, it becomes extremely valuable
and should be carefully studied.

We have already referred to Lagna as the starting point,
and there is another and more important one called *Pada*
Lagna. The Sutra runs thus—*Lagnadhipo yavat Thavat Padam.*
Fully explained it means thus—Take the lord of birth and find out
where he is located. A similar house in number will be its *Padam.*
Take the horoscope on p. 384. The lord of birth is Sukra, and
he occupies Dhanus or the 8th from it. The 8th from this 8th
will be Pada Lagna. The 8th from Sukra in Dhanus is Kataka
and therefore for this horoscope Pada Lagna will be the 3rd from

Lagna or Kataka. The lord of Kataka is Chandra and he is in Mesha with Rahu and has Kuja's and Kethu's aspect. The second from this Pada Lagna is Simha, and its lord Ravi aspects it as also Sani, and therefore the person will have disturbed wealth. But this 2nd house is aspected by four planets and some of them good while others are evil. Sani aspects Simha, Ravi, Budha and Guru aspect it also These four aspects of good and evil planets give him disturbed education, money, family and speeches. But the lord of Simha, *viz*. Ravi aspects his own house with two beautiful benefics Budha and Guru and hence they give him wealth, charming eyes, good speech and agreeable conversational powers. Take the 3rd Bhava. Its lord Chandra is in the 10th from it or in Mesha. The 10th from Mesha is Makara and its lord is Sani who is in second Maraka. Hence with reference to brothers and sisters he should have no prosperity but for the fact that Sani is being aspected by the benefics Guru and Sukra. For every Bhava, there is this Pada Lagna, and though Varaha Mihira and Venkatasa have made no reference to it, other eminent writers have largely dwelt upon this subject at considerable length and have given special results for combinations based upon this Lagna. The generality of mankind are, however fond of having brothers and sisters, and the peculiar happiness arising out of a large number of brothers and sisters in a harmonious home, is one over which much could be written with interest. Temperaments of men and women, though different and widely separated from each other, can be harmonised and made to act in unison by pure and simple moral discipline. In these matters the Hindu mind by the fact of living in an undivided family undergoes greater discipline, and shows greater capacity to live in harmony with brothers and sisters than the European, who is accustomed to think that living in company is incompatible with the ideas of personal and individual comforts and conveniences.

Modern civilisation has weakened the beautiful bonds of brotherly and sisterly love and the idea that a man earns for the benefit of his whole family, and not for himself and his wife. Even with reference to wife and marital relations, the Hindu idea seems to make the marriage indissoluble, and therefore more permanent than the European idea of marriage as a pure civil contract, which could be set at nought whenever there is any omission or commission on the part of the joining couple, which have a mutual distaste or disadvantage. A religious notion and sanctity, afforded by the Vedic laws for all work to be done by man for his comfort or for that of his community or nation are matters foriegn to the European taste and his genius, and therefore, customs and manners, radically differ between the Asiatic and the European nations, and their usefulness and advantages can be safely judged by a deep thinking man. In order to determine the prosperity and longevity of the brothers and sisters we have to look to the powers of the planets who occupy the 3rd house, who are lords of the 3rd house, and who aspect and combine in the 3rd house, its lord and the lord of brothers Kuja   The position and powers of Kuja from the 3rd house and its lord becomes important. If an exalted planet, and a benefic join the 3rd house and its lord is exalted and is combined with benefics of great prosperity accrues to brothers and sisters and some of them will attain to very eminent positions. But if debilitated planet, combined with a combust or cruelly situated planet is found in the 3rd, its lord joins a debilitated Rasi and Navamsa, and has other evil associations, the person will lose a large number of brothers and sisters and those who survive will be mendicants or in very distressed state.

Brothers and sisters make the life of a person in young age lively, enjoyable and pleasant. Man cannot have better companions, both for play and for sympathy than his own kith and kin. Whatever may be their relations after they grow up, they will be very cordial in the earlier stages, as then their friendship and relationship will be characterised by great disinterestedness and simplicity and they enjoy their time with great and sincere pleasure. Friendship with others in the earlier stages will not be so very agreeable. Therefore the 3rd Bhava, indicating brothers and sisters, will be

very important, and it must be read very carefully. It also indicates courage and warlike nature, and timid men have never
added any romance to human life and its comforts. Brave men
have done much and are capable of doing a great deal for human
comforts. 434.

STANZAS 435 to 440 inclusive.

If the lord of the third occupies a beneficial amsa or joins a
benefic or the lord of courage Kuja is similarly situated, the
person becomes courageous. 435.

If the lord of the amsa occupied by the lord of the amsa,
occupied by the lord of the 3rd, joins his own house or good
divisions, the person will become courageous and skillful in
war. 436.

If the lord of the 3rd occupies his exaltation with malefics,
and joins movable signs or amsas, or the house of movable
planets, the person will be bold before the battle. 437.

If the lord of the 3rd joins fixed sign or amsa, the man's
courage increases after the battle commences. If the lord of the
3rd occupies cruel shastyamsas or becomes debilitated, or combines with malefics or has evil aspects, the person becomes stupid
or dull in war. If the lord of the 3rd is exalted and occupies
12th he will be defeated in battle. If the lord of courage is
powerless and joins cruel shastyamsas, the person suffers defeat
in battle. If the lord of the 3rd is similarly stationed, the
person becomes dull in war. 438-39-40.

NOTES.

If the lord of the 3rd is in a good sign or division or combines with a benefic or the lord of courage does so, the person
becomes bold. Courage has always been considered a great

qualification in a man, and when he employs it in all righteous work he will be entitled to great respect in his community and his nation. The lord of courage is Kuja as he represents military profession. Whenever the word amsa occurs without any other qualification it refers to Navamsa unless, by the context, some other division is denoted. The next stanza 436 requires an illustration to make it clear.

Take a Horoscope.

	Chand Rahu	Lagna.	Sani.			Lagna Guru.	Rahu.
Ravi. Budha. Guru.	RASI.				NAVAMSA.		
Sukra.		Kuja. Kethu.		Budha.	Kethu	Ravi. Sani. Sukra. Kuja.	Chan

In sanskrit the verse is intelligible enough but in its English garb it may become obscure. The lord of the 3rd is Chandra and he occupies Kanya Navamsa. The lord of Kanya is Budha, and he occupies the Navamsa Dhanas owned by Guru. The lord of the Amsa occupied by Budha is Guru, and if Guru joins his own house or favourable divisions like Hora, Drakkana, Navamsa, Dwadasamsa, Thrimsamsa or Shastiamsa the person will become courageous in battle. In the horoscope given here Guru has not occupied his own house or beneficial divisions and so the person is ordinary.

In Verse 437 the meaning seems to be, that the person will be courageous before the battle, but loses his heart in actual warfare. There are many heroes in words, but when the battle actually begins, they may lose heart and run away. If the 3rd lord in conjunction with malefics joins movable houses or divisions, the person is said to lose heart when fighting begins, but if he joins fixed signs or amsas, his courage increases with the commencement of the battle.   And as difficulties and dangers threaten there are some who lose heart while there are others who gain heart and become very bold.

Many dull and apparently useless persons become intelligent and resourceful when actual war begins, while there are as many, who, intelligent before, become dull and stupid during the progress of the war.   Difficulties and dangers sharpen some intellects while they make others dull and stupid.   Then combinations are given to mark defeat in battle.

If the lord of the 3rd is exalted and occupies the 12th, the person suffers defeat.   If the lord of the 3rd is powerless and occupies cruel Shastiamsas, he will be defeated in the battle. The lord of courage is Mars, and if he is similarly situated he inflicts defeat.   These combinations are extremely useful for persons entering upon their military careers and when the planets. point to defeat, it is better to give up that profession.   The biographies of great men furnish invaluable lessons and when their horoscopes are carefully examined good combinations are sure to be found in them.   As the Sun changes his position and with him all his solar dependents, so also change the horoscopes of nations and the characteristics of their leaders and Kings. About a century ago and much earlier than that, we had a set of warlike monarchs, who always led their generals and armies and either gained countries or lost these as they obtained victories or defeats. But now, in the latter part of the 19th century and the beginning of the 20th century many monarchs have lost those brilliant military characteristics and have hardly known what actual war is.   In fact they have become cardboard kings and shew their regal qualities amidst a round of festivities and revels. The students of astrology, in the national branch of predictions.

must try and make out why the rulers of the present day are thoroughly unmilitary in character.

STANZAS 441 to 445 inclusive.

If the lord of the 3rd joins Simhasana, Paravata, Gopura or Mridwamsa and aspected by benefics, he will be skilful and fond of war. 441.

If the lord of the 3rd combines with benefics and occupies exaltation or Vyseshika or Mridwamsa, and is powerful, the person becomes an expert and courageous general, if otherwise the con-trary results must be predicted. 442.

If the lord of the 3rd combines with Ravi the person be-comes cowardly; if with Chandra he is bold in mind, but looks indifferent outside; if with Kuja he becomes furious and power-ful; if with Budha he becomes just and chivalrous; if with Guru he will be bold and well versed in the science of diplomacy and and negotiation; if with Sukra he will be passionate and engage himself in those quarrels; if with Sani he becomes dull and stupid; if with Rahu, Kethu or Mandi the person looks bold and martial outside, but will have a timid heart and weak mind. 443-44-45.

NOTES.

The amsas in verse 441 are those of the Shastiamsas and they are all good. If the lord of the 3rd joins benefics and occupies any one of these good amsas the person becomes not only fond of war, but also in skilfully waging it.

In 442, the lord of the 3rd must be in exaltation or Vis-hesha or Mridwamsa, he must be powerful and must have beneficial conjunction to make a man an expert and bold com-mander. If these conditions are reversed, he becomes an useless and timid leader. If the lord of the 3rd joins debilitation or evil amsas and has conjunction with malefics, the person becomes an unskilful and timid leader of troops   The next three verses give special conjunctions. If the lord of the 3rd joins Ravi the man will be cowardly, if with Chandra he becomes bold in mind, which means good, if Kuja joins the lord of the 3rd the person becomes a headlong and furious soldièr. Budha makes him cautious and chivalrous. The science of diplomacy and negotiation require not only mere mental or physical boldness, but a great deal of ready tact and shrewdness, which are the characteristics of higher forms of intellectual development. All good and bold warriors are not diplomats of the first water and many of them are even quite unfit to enter into those arts, which refer to the deeper recesses of the human passions. Guru's conjunction with the lord of the 3rd gives a man courage and shrewdness of the mind which will form an incalculable boon to any person who may be engaged in diplomatic and political work. World has produced many bold warriors and statesmen. But very few conquerors were also really successful statesmen and rulers of countries thus conquered. This conjunction of the lord of the 3rd with Jupiter makes a man not only a bold warrior, but also a successful diplomatist and statesman. Of course every person who has this combination of the lord of the third with Jupiter should not expect to lead armies and enter on successful diplomatic relations. There must be higher combinations of planets to give the person Raja Yoga or Senapathi Yoga and then, if this combination also prevails, he may hope to become what has been indicated in these stanzas.

If the 3rd lord joins Sukra, the man becomes passionate and enters upon those quarrels which arise out of his passion for women. If he joins with Sani he becomes dull and stupid in his engagements.

STANZAS 446 to 448.

If the lord of the 3rd joins Guru and occupies Lagna there is danger from quadrupeds or cows. If this Lagna happens to be a watery sign, there will be danger from water. 446.

If the lord of the house occupied by the lord of the 3rd joins Lagna with Rahu there will be danger from a serpent.

If the lord of the 3rd combines with Budha, there will be neck-disease. 447,

If the planet occupying the 3rd is debilitated there or it is in an unfriendly sign, or he is combust or has evil aspects, there will be diseases in the neck by poison administered by others or taken by himself. If these are not present there will be no danger. 448.

NOTES.

In Sanskrit the difficulties of translation are increased by the substitution of words, which without upsetting true meatre or the melody so considerably change the meaning as to be utterly irreconcilable with one another. As the foreign government takes no interest in Aryan sciences, specially Astrology, the abuse has been simply damaging. The indifference of our aristocracy is very lamentable concerning our sciences. The lord of the 3rd occupies some house and this lord must, in conjunction with Rahu, be placed in Lagna to produce danger from snake-bite. Very few cases there are where men and animals have been swallowed by huge snakes. Deaths from snake-bites are frequent and so also deaths from administration of poisons or some substances which, when chemically combined, produce poisonous gases and cause the death of men. Stanza 448 is very peculiar and can also be interpreted as follows. If the 3rd is occupied by a debilitated planet, the 6th by a combust planet and both of these have evil aspects, then neck disease breaks out and causes danger. But if that does not come on, the man takes poison and suffers or has poison administered to him by others. But according to my interpretatien it means that a debilitated planet must be in the 3rd or he must find that house an unfriendly sign or be in combust there with evil aspects, to get the neckdisease through poison or poisonous drugs being administered to him. A planet will be in combust when he is close to the Sun and occupies the same sign.

STANZAS 449 to 452 inclusive.

If powerful Sukra or Chandra has beneficial aspect or joins benefics or occupies exaltation or joins the friendly house or divisions of the planet who owns his house of exaltation, the person will take food in good vessels and have luxurious meals. 449.

If the 3rd house is occupied by a malefic there will be neck disease, if he joins ' Mandi' the disease will be of a virulent type. If Mars joins the 3rd and joins Pratapurisha there will be ear disease. 450.

If the lord of the house occupied by Rahu or Kethu joins Budha with the lord of the 3rd there will be neck disease. 451.

If Saturn joins the 3rd house combined with Gulika unaspected by benefics the person has danger from winds. If the lord of the house occupied by the lord of the third, joins the 8th house, there is danger from winds. 452.

NOTES.

The favourable or unfavourable positions of Venus and the Moon have much to do with the vessels and the luxurious meals a person takes. Venus and the Moon are both white and pure planets. Venus is the most luxurious and highly refined in his tastes. Those horoscopes which have Venus in the 4th or 10th or 11th will have very fine tastes and will be scrupulously clean.

Therefore where Venus or Moon joins benefics or has their aspects or occupies exaltation, or joins the divisions of the planet who is a friend of the lord of the house, where he happens to be exalted, the person gets luxurious meals and takes them in clean and costly vessels. The last portion may be a little unintelligible. Venus is exalted in Pisces. The lord of Pisces (*Meena*) is Jupiter. The friends of Jupiter are the Sun, the Moon and Mars. The author asks us to understand that when Venus is in a horoscope with any one of the planets above named, *viz.,* the Sun, Moon or Mars, hee nables the person to have good vessels and luxurious meals. Mankind have an inordinate desire for rich and luxurious meals and therefore many will be anxious to know what sort of meals they get. Wealth or poverty does not seem to much affect this portion of man's fortune. There are really some rich men who take very miserable meals for various reasons and there are others who are in poor circumstances, but who, somehow, manage to get always clean and well prepared food. Wealthy man must never be confounded with a happy man. The study of mankind is a wonderful intellectual treat and can be only relished by the higher and more godly kinds of intellects. If Sukra or Chandra joins his friendly house or joins the good Vergas of Guru, the food and vessels will be good. 449,

If there is a malefic occupying the 3rd house, there will be neck disease. If such a planet joins *Mandi* the disease will be of a very virulent type. This means that if an evil planet and Maudi are in conjunction with the third house, the neck disease will be of a very serious nature. If the third house is occupied by Kuja, occupying the Pratapurisamsa, there will be ear disease. The 12th Amsa of the 60 divisions (*Shastiamsa*) is called the Pratapurisa which is evil in its nature. For finding out and fixing *Mandi* see p. 49 and my Notes thereon. 450.

Another combination is given here to indicate the neck disease. Rahu and Kethu must necessarily be in some house. The lord of this house should not join Budha in conjunction with the lord of the 3rd. It means that if the lord of the 3rd house, lord of the house occupied by Rahu or Kethu and Budha join together, neck disease should be predicted. There are various forms of neck diseases, and their intensity and extent depend upon the weakness and malefic influences of these three. If Rahu is in Meena then its lord will be Guru. If Simha is the Lagna then the lord of the 3rd will be Sukra. If these two, Guru and Sukra, join Budha wherever he may be, there will be neck disease. Its virulence or mildness depends upon their sources of weakness or strength. Take examples.

Here there is a conjunction of the lord of the house occupied by Rahu, the lord of the 3rd house and Budha. But Budha is exalted, while Sukra is debilitated and all these three planets are benefics.

Rahu.			
	No. I RASI.		
			Lagna.
			Budha. Kethu. Sukra. Guru.

The Lagna is Mithuna. The lord
of the house occupied by Rahu is
Sani. Lord of the 3rd house is Ravi.
These two planets are in conjunction
with Budha. If an astrologer is asked
as to which of these two cases is
worse, then, certainly the second con-

	Kuja.		Lagna.
Rahu.		No. II. RASI.	
			Kethu.
		Budha. Sani. Ravi.	

junction is worse than the first and the form of the neck disease
will be more serious in the second case. 451.

The compiler now gives two sets of combinations which
produce windy complaints. Among the Sanskrit Ayurvedic
Principles there are mentioned *Sapta Dhatus* and *Three Gunas*.
The last are (1) Vata (wind), (2) Pittha (bile) and (3) Sleshma
(Phlegm) Each of these is equally formidable, when it begins
to work out its mischief Vata or wind causes excruciating
pains and rheumatic pains are called in Sanskrit *Vatha Doshas*.
Foods are classified as animal, mineral and vegetable and many
of these food stuffs have the power of setting afloat much wind
in the shape of powerful internal gases, which working in the
human economy produce most painful and horrible diseases.
Paralyses is called Parswa Vayu. When bile increases it produces Vayu, and these two in turn give room for phlegm and its
confounding complications. If Saturn is placed in the 3rd house
in conjunction with Maudi, there will be windy complaints. In
the original, the word is Maudi and not Gulika, and by an oversight Gulika has been used in the translation. (See page 69.)

The second half of this stanza wants a clearer explanation. The brevity of Sanskrit Sutras is not expressable in any other language. Take first the lord of the 3rd house and find out where he is. Then take the lord of this house and find out where he is. Then if the lord of this house occupies the 8th house from Lagna, the person will suffer from powerful ear complaints. Take a living example. A girl born on the 20th September 1911 on Wednesday at 5-30 p. m.

Take first the lord of the 3rd from Lagna and he is the lord of Mesha or Kuja. Kuja is placed in Vrishabha. Then take the lord of the house occupied by Kuja and he is Sukra. Sukra is located in Kanya whose lord is Budha. Find out where Budha is placed, and take its lord. Budha

	Sani. Rahu,	Kuja.	
Birth.		RASEE.	
			Chandra. Buda.
		Guru. Kethu,	Ravi. Sukra.

occupies Simha, and its lord is Ravi. If this Ravi occupies the 8th house from Lagna —as he is occupying, Kanya the 8th from Kumbha Lagna, then predict ear complaints. The girl will therefore be subjected to serious ear complaints. There will be no confusion if a little diligence and patience are brought to bear upon the interpretation of these stanzas. This latter portion of the stanza runs on to the first half of the next verse, and therefore its continuation will be sketched under that stanza 452. Stanza 453.

If such a planet is in conjunction with, or is aspected by malefics the person will have ear diseases. If the lord of the 3rd house joins cruel Shastiamsas there will be ear complaints.

NOTES.

In stanza 452 it has been found out that if the lord of the house occupied by the lord of the house joined by the lord of the 3rd joins the 8th house from Lagna, he will give ear complaints. This he does only when he is subjected to evil conjunctions and aspects. But when he possesses good conjunctions and aspects the complaints will be nil or of a very mild nature. If the lord of the 3rd house joins unfavourable Shastiamsas, like Kala, Pratapurisha, Vishadagdha, Yama, *etc.*, he will give ear complaints to the person. 453.

Stanzas 454 to 457 inclusive.

If the third is joined or aspected by benefics or if its lord is combined with good planets, the person will have ear ornaments 454.

If the Sun is in the 3rd, the ear ornament will be red, if Saturn is there it will be blue. If Jupiter is in the 3rd, it will be composed of gold, and if Venus occupies it, it will be of pearls. 455.

If Moon joins 3rd there will be many ornaments, if Mercury is there, the ear ornaments will be of green color, if Mars occupies it, it will be composed of many colors and if these are aspected by evil planets, there will be loss to these ear ornaments. 456.

If the 3rd is occupied by benefics or if it falls in a *Shubhamsa*, there will be pleasant and virtuous conversation. But if the third is owned by malefics there will be unpleasant news always. 457·

NOTES.

The 3rd house denotes courage, ears, the neck, etc., and therefore all events connected with such phenomena must be referred to the lord of the 3rd, the position of that house, and their combinations and aspects. If a benefic occupies or aspects the 3rd house, or the lord of the 3rd has beneficial conjunction, the ears of the person will not only be well formed but will be adorned by ear ornaments. These ornaments are of various kinds and their description is briefly given in the next two stanzas. Suppose the lord of the 3rd house is subjected to beneficial aspects, the results will also be favourable, though this is not particularly mentioned by the author.   454.

If the third house happens to be occupied by the Sun, the ear-ornaments will be of red color or composed of rubies, if Saturn occupies the house the ornaments will be of blue or black color, if Jupiter occupies the 3rd, the ornaments will be made of gold, and if Venus is there they will be composed of pearls. The original text contains *Sambanda*, and if any meaning is to be given to it, then it means, that if the 3rd house falls in the Sun's house (Simha) or if the Sun is there the result above predicted must be attributed. This expression *Sambanda* must be extended to all the planets. Thus if the 3rd house falls in Makara or Kumba, or if Sani is there, the earrings or jewels will have blue or black stone, and so on for the rest of the planets mentioned in this and the following Verse.   455.

Moon in the 3rd house denotes many ornaments or those which have been acquired as presents for various reasons· Mercury in the 3rd house gives sapphires or gems of green color. Mars indicates ornaments containing many colored stones. If these planets in the 3rd house have evil aspects or conjunctions, or occupy evil sub-divisions, they will cause loss or damage to these ornaments. Suppose Sani and Kuja occupy the 3rd house or have mutual aspects in the 3rd house ? What would be the result. As per instructions given here the ear ornaments

3

will be destroyed or lost. Suppose Vrishabha is Lagna with Kuja in Kataka or 3rd and Vrischika is Lagna with Kuja in Makara In the former he is Neecha and in the latter he is Oocha. Would he make any difference in the value of the ear ornaments ? Of course he does by the general principles of astrology. Exalted planets give exalted articles and debilitated planets give dirty and worthless stuffs. Can a jaded and ugly looking horse be compared to a spirited and splendid looking arab, or a lustreless gem to a lustreful diamond. All these states have to be guessed. 456.

Now the author gives a general hint as to the kind of conversation or the kind of language one often has or hears in his career. It must be admitted whether we like it or not that it is the lot of some to be born and brought up in the midst of disagreeable and quarrelsome surroundings and thus constantly hear unpleasant and unpalatable language, while there are some whose good luck, as we say, always makes them to enjoy agreeable, witty and pleasant conversation and move in the midst of very fine surroundings. If the 3rd house or its lord has unfavourable sub-divisions or Amsas, he will have unpleasant conversation, but if they occupy good *Amsas*, the language will be pleasant and smooth.

Some are extremely fond of all sorts of scandals and always go in search of such sinful company. Some on the other hand, would not tolerate the slightest attempt at sinful or scandalous language and would endeavour to have godly and elevating conversation. The degrees of men and their intellects between the extreme good and extreme evil are many and complicated and the student in astrology will have no light work to unravel all hese mysteries and come to conclusions which tally with facts in the life of man. 457.

The End of the third Bhava.

Close of CHAPTER IV.

———

Stanza 458.

From the fourth house have to be predicted, the relations, houses, mother, waters, self-prosperity or progress, enjoyments, conveyances, heart, the neck and shoulders, seats, beds, happiness, education, etc.

NOTES.

The fourth house from Lagna covers a large variety of events connected with human life, and some of them are very important. It represents mother, relations, happiness, education or self-progress, houses and landed property, articles of enjoyment, furniture and other conveniences, morality and passions for women; the different kinds of waters the person may have to use, the strength or weakness of the heart, the power of the neck and the shoulders, and so forth. To begin with man's fortune entirely depends upon the kind of mother he possesses and is born of. If the mother is moral, well built, happy tempered, intelligent, healthy, and well disposed to her husband, children, relations and friends, the boy necessarily will have a bright environment and the first nursing and instructions will all be that are desirable. If the reverse holds good the mother being unclean, sickly, immoral, irritable and peevish, dull, badly connected, unkind and rascally, the child's surroundings will be unwholesome and the strength of unfavourable and immoral earlier impressions and training will have a permanent jarring effect upon the growth of the tender mind, and make the future man inherit and remember these unpleasant characteristics. If the mother dies early, look at the misery of the child and the changes effected in his temperament. Similarly houses are of great significance. Clean and tidy houses bring up clean and healthy people and make their minds also clean and healthy. Relations exercise a potent influence upon the infantile understanding and temperament.

Where these are endearing, loveable and well bred, the child takes its early lessons from the relations with whom he is surrounded. Many men suffer cruel miseries from bad and

unsympathetic relations and sometimes their whole life careers
are wrecked by the machinations of hateful and undesirable
rascally relations.   In fact it has been observed often that families
suffer great miseries by possessing bad and envious relations.
Man has comfort or misery by conveyances. Education exercises
the greatest influence upon man and this well known question
requires no further explanations. Lands are equally important, and
their possession or non-possession makes a great deal of difference
in man's social status and general credit. If the lands are profitable he will thrive well and if they are nonproductive then
they will ruin him entirely. People apparently attach little
significance to the strength or weakness of the heart. They will
be committing grand blunders. It is the heart which makes a
man what he is. The heart must be good and strong, then alone his
health will be good. If that is rotten not only will he suffer
general misery but will also be subjected to excruciating pains
and sudden dangers. Waters affect his body, his mind and his
health. Some live near healthy waters while it is the misfortune
of others to live close to dirty or bad waters and be compelled
to drink them and suffer the consequent miseries and ill-health.

Accidents from carriages are indicated by the fourth house,
and uncleanly sexual connections are also signified. Therefore
the author proposes to deal in this chapter, with all these and
many other questions and the readers are required to be careful
and diligent in their calculations and inferences. It may be
asked that if all these and many more events are signified or
indicated by the fourth house, then a man must possess all of
these events well or ill as the fourth house, and its lord are in
good conjunctions and aspects or subjected to evil combinations
and aspects. Here the readers are warned to be careful. For
instance while the 4th house represents mother, the lord of
mother will be the moon. According to Brihatjataka there are
as it were two lords for mother. The moon is one, and Sukra
and Sani become lords of the mother as the person is born
during the day or the night respectively. In order to find out

therefore the position, complexion, health, longevity, character and love of the mother, we have to take into consideration not only the fourth house and its lord but have also to consider the position of Chandra, Sukra or Sani as the case may be. Take education. This is indicated by the fourth house and its lord, but the lord of education Guru has also to be carefully considered. Take horses and carriages.

The fourth house represent these as well as its lord, and we have to note also the influences of the lord of conveyances *via* Sukra. In this way different planets become lords of different events and their sources of strength and weakness, considerably affect the events indicated by any Bhava. In fact we have to find the variety of Phmomena by the variety of combinations and permutations of the planets, houses, constellations, their sub-divisions and other minute details which have been elaborately sketched out in the pages of the voluminous astrological literature.

Of the 6 Angas or limbs enumerated for the interpretation and comprehension of the Vedic secrets, Jyotisha possesses the most extensive literature, and its volume can be guaged when we remember that there are 400,000 sutras for its explanation. Man here and hereafter can be advantageously moulded if he remembers the principles of astrology and regulates his conduct in its light. It is really a very grand, comprehensive, and most sublime science man can conceive of and only occupies a secondary position by the side of Vedantha and Yoga. Even for these sciences astrological principles are necessary.

Maha Rishis were sages of a high psychic development, and examined terrestrial and celestial phenomena by their divine sight or *Divya Drishti*. We would hardly be justified in attributing any mean motives for those Sages who have left great names in the landmarks of Time. They saw many phenomena which we could hardly hope to see with our contracted souls and hence contracted and diminished willpower; our minds are

mean and are almost exclusively engaged in studying and pro-
curing worldly comforts. Though at the height of mental and
yougic development they scorned to utilise such knowledge for
any worldly concerns, and solely used such knowledge for the
benefit of mankind and the numberless succeeding generations.
Can such a science be ever untrue?

Stanzas 459 to 467 inclusive.

If the lords of Lagna and 7th conjointly occupy the Lagna or
the 4th house, there will be many houses. If in such a combination,
there is beneficial conjunction or aspect, and if the lord of Lagna
or 7th is exalted, occupies his own or friendly house or otherwise is
powerful, the person gets houses without any attempts on his
part. 459.

If the lord of the 4th joins a Kendra and is powerful, and possesses beneficial aspect, he will get houses. If the lord of the 4th
joins his Paramocha Navamsa, and occupies Visashikamsa, he will
get houses. 460.

If the lord of the Navamsa, occupied by the lord of the Rasi,
occupied by the lord of the Navamsa, occupied by the lord of the
4th is found in any one of the Kendras from the Lagna in the
Rasi, the person will possess houses. 461.

If the lord of the 9th occupies any Kendra, the lord of the
4th is joined in exaltation or friendly house and if the planet
occupying the 4th house is exalted, the person will possess
excellent and artistic houses. 462.

If the 3rd house is occupied by a benefic, the lord of the 4th
is powerful, and the lord of the 3rd is very powerful, the person
will have splendid upstair houses with beautiful compounds. 463.

If the lord of the 4th house is found in Simhasana or
Gopuramsa, occupying Mridwamsa etc. among the Snastiamsas,
the house will have nice upstairs. 464.

If the lord of the 4th joins Paravatamsa or Gopuaramsa etc., and is aspected by Guru and Chandra, the person will have a *Daivika* house. 465.

If the lords of the 4th and 10th join together and occupy a Kendra and Sani also is found in a Kendra, the person will have grand, artistic, and extensive houses with large compounds

If the lord of the 4th occupies *Nasasthana*, aspected by evil planets, the house will be ruined.

If the lord of the Navamsa occupied by the lord of the 4th is found in the *Nasasthana* from Lagna, there will be loss of house 467.

NOTES.

In the treatment of houses, there are any number and any variety. From a straggling hut of the veriest beggar to the most grandly furnished and picturesque palaces of the mightiest Emperors, we have various grades of houses, and all these have to be predicted by the conjunctions which are enumerated in these stanzas. There are many people who never own houses, and who always live in houses built by others, while there are people who have never lived out of their ancestral houses. All these differences have to be identified by the conjunctions of planets according to their strength and the strength of other planets which join or aspect them.

There are many fashions. Some primitive people in fact never live in houses, but spend their lives with their families under the shades of trees, in caves or under the cover of rocks. Some are extremely fond of house building and the mania extends so far as to land them in incurable debts, and make their lives most miserable. Some are extremely wealthy, but are quite content to live in very ordinary or even squalid houses inconsistant with their pecuniary means of the social dignity. We have to take the world as it is and analyse it in the light shed by the planetary influences,

If the lord of Lagna and the lord of the 7th in conjunction occupy the Lagna or the 4th house the person will have many houses. If they are exalted, well aspected, and occupy good vergas we have to infer that the houses of the person will be on a grand scale. A person may possess several huts, ordinary houses, decent houses or palatial buildings, some entirely live upon the rents realised by their house property, and they will have no other means. World presents a great problem for study and investigation. When these lords of the 1st and 7th are exalted, occupy their own or friendly houses and are otherwise powerful, the person gets house property without any exertions on his part or seeking for them. That is somebody bequeaths houses to him or he gets them for nominal values without seeking for their acquisitions.

The words "*otherwise powerful*" require a little explanation. In each stanza, the author certainly is not expected to give all the details of strength and weakness. He names some and asks the readers to use their brains and find out other sources of strength. In this sloka, he says that the lords of the 1st and 7th may be exalted or occupy their own or friendly houses. But this is not exhaustive. A planet may have good conjunction or aspect, may occupy beneficial signs, may be hemmed in by two benefics, may occupy beneficial amsas with beneficial conjunctions or aspects, may be in exalted or friendly Navamsas and so forth. All such things should be particularly remembered by the astrological readers before they venture to enter into the fields of prediction. 459.

If the powerful lord of the 4th occupies a Kendra *viz* 1—4—7 or 10 possessing good aspects, the person will have houses. He will also get houses if the lord of the 4th house occupies his paramochcha and possesses Viseshikamsa. The reader must remember that *paramochicha* is different from oocha. The latter means exaltation and the former means deep or highest exaltation. Take an example. The sun is exalted in the 30 degrees of Aries (Mesha) but he is *paramocha* in the 10th degree of Mesha. 460.

Now comes in a stanza expressed in a very pithy but complicated way and the meaning becomes only clear by one or two practical illustrations. Take a living horoscope. Born 4th May 1903 at 2 A.M., on Monday the 22nd of the solar month Aries in Shobakritu.

Kethu.	Ravi.	Buda. Sukra.	
Birth. Guru.	RASI.		Chundra.
Sani.			
			Kuja. Rahu.

Kuja. Buda.	Guru. Sani.		
Birth. Chundra. Kethu.	NAVAMSA.		Rahu.
		Ravi.	Sukra.

Take the the Lord of the 4th house from Lagna, and he is Sukra. He occupies the Kanya Navamsa, and its lord is Budha. Budha occupies in Rasi Vrishabha, and its lord is Sukra, and take again the lord of the Navamsa occupied by Sukra and he is Budha. If this Budha occupies any one of the Kendras from Lagna in the Rasi, (and he is found in the 4th house) the person will have houses. Take another living example. Born on the 24th October 1871 Tuesday at 55 ghatis after sun rise. This falls on the 9th day of the solar month Thula.

			Rahu.
Chundra.	RASI.		Guru.
Sani. Kethu.	Kuja.	Ravi. Buda.	Sukra. Lagna.

Kuja.	Kethu.		Lagna. Chundra.
	NAVAMSA.		Sani.
Sukra.			
Ravi.		Buda. Rahu.	Guru.

The lord of the 4th is Guru and he occupies Kanya Navamsa. The lord of Kanya is Budha. Budha is in Thula in the Rasi and its lord is Sukra. Sukra occupies the Navamsa of

4

Makara and its lord is Sani. If this Sani is in one of the Kendras from Lagna in the Rasi (as he is in 4th house) the person will have houses. I think by these two practical illustrations, the meaning has been made clear to the readers. 461.

Here the author gives conjunctions of planets for possessing artistic and fine houses. There are some who spend a lot of money on artistic decorations on their houses. The lord of the 9th should occupy any one of the Kendras. The lord of the 4th must be in exaltation or friendly house, and there must be an exalted planet occupying the 4th house. Then the person will have grand and decorated houses or mansions. Here the lord of the 4th must be in exaltation and there must be an exalted planet in the 4th, while the lord of the 9th (*Shubhasthana*) should be located in one of the Kendras. All these conditions must be existing. It is not enough if one or two of them are found in a horoscope. 462.

We now come to storied houses. There are some grand— very grand houses, but without upstairs, while there are some mud or squalid looking houses with upstairs. Much depends upon the taste and liking of the man and he will be guided in these matters by the inclinations his *Poorva Janmakarma* (his actions in the previous states of existence) gives him.

There should be a benefic in the 3rd house. The lord of the 4th must be powerful, and the lord of the 3rd must be completely powerful, to give the man storied houses possessing good and ornamental compounds. The benefic in the 3rd house may be exalted, debilitated, in an unfriendly, friendly or his own house All these different states produce different effects.

The skill of the astrologer consists in the interpretation and right comprehension of these minutes. Suppose Vrishabha is Lagna and Guru is in Kataka. This is the 3rd house and he is exalted there. Suppose the other two conditions are present. Then the person will have excellent houses. But suppose

Vrischika is Lagna and Guru is in Makara. He is debilitated there and the houses though artistic will present marks of neglect or want of repairs. Suppose Guru in Kataka is aspected by Sani in Makara, then, as there is an evil aspect for an exalted benefic in the third, the person will repair an old house and keep art with neglect or dilapidation side by side. There are some who keep front rooms neat, and back rooms old and in ruins. These varieties are too numerous to be exhaustively related. The astrologer must have a sharp eye on all such complexities. 463.

The lord of the 4th house must be occupying Simhasana or Gopuramsa, and join good Shastiamsas like Mridvamsas etc., then the person will have nice upstair houses. All good Shastiamsas should be considered as favourable. 464.

If Guru and Chandra aspect the lord of the 4th, when he gets Paravatamsa, Gopuramsa, etc., the person will have Daivika houses. I cannot exactly understand what Daivika means, probably it means that he will get houses close to the temples or churches or houses attached to places of worship, such as quarters arranged for priests, missionaries, etc., in some cases. 465.

When the lords of the 10th and 4th conjoin and occupy any of the Kendras, and Sani also is located in a Kendra, the person will have grand, artistic and extensive houses and these will have large compounds. There are some ruined palaces or aristocratic mansions occupied by their unworthy descendants. When the planets in the above conjunction are weak or powerless or debilitated, etc., then the mansions will be in ruins or without repairs, and quite uncouth in appearance. But when these planets are exalted and are not otherwise subjected to evil conjunctions or aspects they give excellent, up-to-date, and picturesque mansions and smiling gardens and artistic compound walls. 466.

When the lord of the 4th joins *Nasasthana* possessing evil aspects, the houses will be ruined or lost. These losses may be due

to various causes. They may be destroyed by fire, rain or earth-
quakes, or by litigation, debts, or sold in time of need or may be
forsaken for their evil reputation. The word used in the original
texts is *Nasasthana*. This means both the 8th and 12th houses
from Lagna. When the lord of the 4th joins the 8th or 12th
house from Lagna, there will be loss to houses. I would however prefer to interpret it as the 12th house while there are some
writers who explain it as the 8th house. Both are acceptable.

Take the lord of the 4th and find out in which Navamsa he is

Take the lord of this Navamsa and if he is in the Nasasthana
from the Lagna in the Rasi, then there will be destruction to
houses. Some acquire lands and houses, others sell them.
These currents are constantly kept up by dame fortune as indicated by the planetary conjunctions at the time of birth. Take
an example.

	Chun-dra. Rahu.	Lagna.	Sani.
Ravi. Buda. Guru.	RASI.		—
Sukra.	Kuja. Kethu.		

	Lagna Guru.	Rahu.	
	NAVAMSA.		—
Buda.	Kethu	Ravi. Sani. Kuja. Sukra.	Chun-dra.

Here take the lord of the 4th and he is Ravi. Find out the
Navamsa he occupies. It is Thulamsa. Take its lord Sukra,
and if this Sukra is found in a Nasasthana, there will be loss to
houses. Sukra is found in the 8th house from Lagna and therefore there will be loss to them. 467.

Stanzas 468 to 478 inclusive.

If the lord of the 4th is a benefic, aspected by a benefic,
and if the lord of the *Bandhus* is powerful, the person will be
respected by his relations. 468.

If the lord of the 4th occupies a Kendra, or Kona, or the
11th house, joining Viseshikamsa and not in conjunction with or

aspected by evil planets; the person becomes a helper of his relations. 469.

If Jupiter occupies the 4th house, or if the lord of the 4th is in conjunction with Guru, or is aspected by him, the person wiil become a leader of his relations. 470.

If the 4th house is conjoined by Guru, Budha and Chandra or is aspected by them and joins Mridwamsa etc. he will be a great helper of his relations. 471.

If the lord of the 4th is in conjunction with malefics joining cruel Shastiamsas or occupies debilitation or unfriendly houses the person will be rejected by relations. 472.

If the lord of the 4th house is in conjunction with many evil planets, he will be rejected by relations.

If the lord of *Bandhus* (Guru) is similarly conjoined, he will become a hater of relations or one who does mischief to them. 473.

If the lord of the Navamsa occupied by the lord of the 4th house or lord of Bandhus joins Neecha, or unfriendly, combustion houses, the person will be guilty of despicable or unpardonable deeds to his relations. 474.

If the lord of the 4th house joins a Kendra, aspected by a benefic and occupies Gopuramsa or Mridwamsa etc⁻ he will have good enjoyment with his relations. 475.

If the lord of the 4th occupies2nd, 11th, 5th or 9th aspected by benefics or joins beneficial Navamsa, he will help his relations. 476.

If the 4th house is occupied by a malefic, in conjunction with or aspected by Neecha or Asta planets, the person will be ever hating his relations. 477.

If any one of the planets occupies the 4th house, in exaltation or friendly or own house, aspected by Guru the person will be highly respected by his relations. 478.

NOTES.

The lord of *Bandhus* or relations is Guru. The house of the relations is the 4th from Birth or Lagna. It may be remarked here, that in consultation of the different Bhavas or houses, we have not only to look to them from the *Birth* (Lagna) house but also from that of the house which is occupied by the Moon. There is the Lagna or the ascendant. There is Chandra Lagna or the house which is occupied by Chandra at the time of birth. Sometime it happens that Lagna and Chandra Lagna fall in one and the same house. Then this difficulty is obviated. When Chandra and Lagna fall in different houses it may be asked as to which of these two should be preferred. I have already explained in the earlier stanzas that Chandra represents mind and Lagna represents the Physique. The intimated connection between these two is very complicated and this is not the place for me to take my readers into the Psychological puzzles and its confusing problems.

If Chandra is stronger, then it would be safer to take the different Bhavas (significations) from him, but if Lagna is stronger the latter should be preferred—one or two illustrations would make this point clearer. Take a horoscope.

		Kethu.	
Guru.			Kuja.
	RASI.		Buda. Lagna. Ravi.
	Rahu. Chandra. Sani.		Sukra

Here it is desired to ascertain who is stronger of the two, *viz* Lagna or Chandra.

Take a rough argument. Chandra is Neecha, there are two evil planets with him *viz* Sani and Rahu. He has no beneficial aspects or conjunctions and he is therefore very weak. The lord of the Chandra Lagna is Kuja and he is occupying his Neecha Rasi or house of debilitation.

Take Lagna. Its lord is Ravi and he is in it aspected by a powerful benefic Guru and conjoined with another benefic

Budha. It possesses no malevolent aspects or conjunctions and therefore it is stronger than Chandra Lagna. Therefore the readers are advised to take all such planets into consideration and analyse the positions of the planets carefully before they attempt to make predictions. When the lord of the 4th is a benefic, possessing beneficial aspect and when Guru is powerful the person will command the respect of his relataions. There are many classes of persons. Some love animals better than men. Some love relations better than others. Some love friends better than relations. Some love servants better than others. In fact there is such surprising variety of tastes and likes and dislikes that volumes can be written upon them with great interest and advantage. To command respect among the relations requires greater ability and tact, than to get respect from others. The reasons are not far to seek. Relations know the man closer, watch his actions more keenly and pass criticisms of a more poignant nature because of their greater knowledge and familiarity with him. One who has the knack to steer clear of these dangerous shoals, certainly shows a better head than one who begins to hate them and be hated by them. There are only six signs in which there is the possibility of the lord of the 4th becoming a Soumya or benefic and they are Kumbha, Meena, Mithuna, Kataka, Kanya and Dhanas.

The 4th houses from these are owned by benefics. For the rest of the signs the 4th houses will be owned by malefics. With reference to Kataka when the moon is full, it becomes beneficial, but when he is weak it becomes malefic. But the same argument may be advanced against Mithuna and Kanya, as they are owned by Budha and he becomes bad in bad company and good in good company. This argument however, is negatived by the astrological writers as they have expressly designated Mithuna and Kanya as Shubha Rasis. 468.

When the lord of the 4th joins a Kendra or Kona (5th and 9th) or 11th house from Lagna, occupying Viseshikamsa, and does not possess the conjunction or aspect of evil planets, the person

becomes a helper of his relations.   There are some people who
hate their relations and try to injure their interests whenever they
get an opportunity.   There are others who create opportunities
to help their relations.   There are any number of grades between
these two extreme classes of people.   The help or respect or
hatred or mischief depends upon the intensity or power of the
good or evil planets who represent the interests of the relations.
469.

If the lord of the 4th house joins Jupiter or Jupiter occupies
the 4th house, the person becomes a leader of his relations.   This
position varies with the strength of Jupiter and the lord of the 4th
house.   Suppose Mesha falls as Lagna, and Jupiter and the Moon
are in Cancer, then the position is very favourable as Jupiter is
exalted, and Chandra occupies his own house and also is in conjunction with the lord of relations.   Under these conjunctions the
person becomes a powerful leader of a powerful community where
many of his relations will be influential and rich men and he will
have the good luck of leading them.   470.

When the 4th house is occupied by Guru, Budha and
Chundra or possesses their aspect, and the house falls in good
Shastiamsa like Mridwamsa, Devalokamsa, Kinnaramsa, etc., he
will be helping his relations.   The extent of the help depends
upon the power of these planets, and their conjunction and
aspects.   471.

Now the author gives some combinations where the person
will be hating his relations and where they would reject him.
If the lord of the 4th joins evil planets, and occupies cruel
Shastiamsas like Ghora, Rakshasa, Agnighatha, etc., or if he is
in debilitation or unfriendly houses, he will be rejected by his
relations.   This rejection is certainly a misery.   472.

If the lord of the 4th joins many evil planets, he will be
rejected or disowned by his relations.   If Guru joins evil planets
he will hate his relations, and try to do mischief to them.   473.

The lord of the 4th house and Guru lord [of relations, must join some Navamsa.

When the lord of this Navamsa occupies house of debilitation or enemy or becomes combust the person will commit evil deeds prejudicial to his relations, or despicable to him and to them. If lords of both the Navamsas occupied by the lord of the 4th and lord of relations Guru are unfavourable, the mischief will be greater. 474.

There are some people who enjoy comforts at the cost of their relations. There are some who are comfortably maintained by friends. There are some who make enjoyment at the cost of their enemies. There are so many varieties among human careers. If the lord of the 4th joins a Kendra, possessing beneficial aspect and joining Gopuramsa or Mridwamsa, etc., the person will live comfortably with his relations and enjoy his life well. This means that he will be a dependent upon his relations without feeling so, and enjoy well his life. 475.

When the lord of the 4th house occupies 2nd, 5th, 9th or 11th houses aspected by benefics, or when he joins beneficial Navamsas, the person will help his relations. 476.

Neecha means debilitation.

Asta means combustion or in close conjunction with the sun.

When a malefic occupies the 4th house joining with or aspected by debilitated or combust planets, the person becomes an inveterate hater of his relations. 477.

Any planet may occupy the 4th house. If such a planet is in exaltation, or the 4th house becomes his own house or that of his friend possessing the aspect of Guru, the person will command the high respect of his relations. Leading them, helping them and respected by them are different in results and must not be confounded. 478.

5

Stanzas 479 to 482 inclusive.

If the 4th house, its lord and the lord of houses (Karaka) occupy movable signs, the person will have houses in many places.   479.

If the 4th house, its lord, and the Karaka join fixed signs or if the lord of the 4th occupies good Shastiamsas the person will have permanent house.   480.

The number of houses destroyed will be determined by the number of evil planets, which are in conjunction with the lords of the 2nd, 12th and 4th houses. If these are subjected to beneficial aspects, there will be no loss or destruction.   481.

If the lord of the 2nd, 12th and 4th houses occupy Kendras, Konas, etc., all the houses belonging to the person will be prosperous or in good condition.   482.

NOTES.

These combinations are sketched out to show the possession or loss of houses for a person.

There are 3 sets of houses, *viz*, movable (*chara*), fixed (*sthira*) and double bodied or common (*dwiswabhava or dwidha*) The lord or Karaka of houses is Sukra. The 4th house, its lord and Sukra, occupying chara Rasis produce houses to the man in many places. Some interpret this stanza as meaning that the person will be constantly removing the materials of one house and use them in the building of other houses in other places. This idea seems to me to be far fetched and strained from the original. On the other hand, I am tempted to put the meaning in a different light altogether. Movable signs have been referred to in the relation of various events of human life. If these named above occupy movable signs, the person may be

frequently changing his houses. There are some who never stick
up to anything like permanent. They own some house, sell it
away or mortgage it or gift it away and take to another. Then
again change that for another and so on. On the other hand
there are some people, who tenant permanently one house, and
take their birth and death there. This often obtains good even in
cases of tenancy. Some rent houses and keep them without
changing. For classifications of these movable signs etc., see
page 58 It is also possible to imagine by such conjunction,
the possession of houses in different places. There is also a
hint by the conjunctions given in the next verse that these
houses are not permanent and may slip away from his ownership, 479.

If the 4th house, its lord and the Karaka occupy fixed signs
like Vrishabha, Simha etc , or if the lord of the 4th house joins
good *Shastiamsas*, the houses will be permanent. In all these
cases Venkatesa expects the readers to look to the other sources
of strength of the planets and then predict the possession or
non-possession of the houses and the state in which they are
kept by the person. Even small houses may be kept very clean
or very dirty, and so also about grand and upstair houses.
Neatness has nothing to do with the extent of the house or
means of the proprietor or tenant. It depends upon his
temperament as indicated by the planetary conjunctions at birth.
If Sukra is well situated, aspected by powerful benefics and
unaspected by and un-conjoined with malefic planets, the person
will have very fashionable houses, well furnished and very tidily
kept. A man may buy costly clothing, but may keep them in a
dirty or unwashed condition. Another may buy a very ordinary
cloth, and keep it scrupulously clean. Similarly in all human
dealings. Even in mental planes these points are well observed
and illustrated. A person for example, may read many works,
may possess great knowledge, but the intellectual plane may be

kept very dirty by doubts, suspicions and uncalled for difficulties. On the other hand a man may possess ordinary training but may manage to keep his mind in perfect cleanliness. 480.

If the lords of the 2nd, 11th and 4th are in conjunction with evil planets then the number of these evil planets gives an idea of the number of houses which will be destroyed. Here a question naturally arises, as to the number of evil planets and its disparity with the large numbers of houses possesed by many rich or influential people. Venkatesa has given hints elsewhere as to its proper solutions. This difficulty arises in judging of brothers, wives, branches of learning, and possession of properties. Where the planets are exalted they give a very large number, when they are debilitated they destroy a very large number. At the utmost we get only 7 evil planets and at the best we get only four good planets. Evil planets are—Ravi, Kuja, Kshina Chandra, evil Budha, Sani, Rahu and Kethu. Good planets are Guru, Sukra, good Budha and Purna Chandra. A man may have hundreds of houses and these may be predicted by the strength of the lords of the 4th, lord of houses, and of the 4th house itself. The destructions of the houses happens when evil conjunctions predominate and if they are subjected to beneficial aspects, no loss to house property should be predited. 481.

The house property will prosper and increase, when the lord of the 2nd, 12th and 4th houses occupy *Kendras* or *Konas*. The word *Adi* is used after *Kendrakona* and the author wishes the readers to understand that if the lords of these houses are exalted, occupy their own or friendly houses, or otherwise get powerful by joining good Vergas and Amsas, there will be increase to house property. It is a well known fact that when a man buys a new house, he may either fare better or worse or die or remain ordinary. Certain houses, when purchased, will bring on others to their proprietor, while others cause ruination to their masters. Houses are constructed out of various materials and these necessarily generate a series of invisible electrical currents. When they are attractive the person prospers well but where they are repulsive they induce a lot of misery to the owners. These interesting facts are within my humble knowledge and my readers cannot be unaware of such circumstances. With a view to find out these conditions the horoscope is examined and when the 4th Bhava is well combined the person may be assured of success in this line. But when it is unfavourable he must be very careful in buying houses and causing directly his own ruination, and if he wants to succeed well there, he must generate a neutralising set of electrical vibrations which would nullify the evil effects indicated by the planets and thus improve his prosperity and happiness. All Sastras are meant for man's well being and happiness, and astrology becomes supremely important on this account. 482.

Stanzas 483 to 497A inclusive.

If the lords of the 4th and 10th exchange their houses, and if Kuja is powerful the person will have many lands. 483.

If the 10th and 4th lords are friends and are powerful he will have many lands. 484.

If the 4th, its lord, and Karaka (Mars) join benefics, he will have many lands and much money, 485.

If the lord of the 4th occupies 11th and joins Gopura or Mridwamsa etc he will have many lands. 486.

If the the 4th or its lord has conjunction with the Karaka of brothers or has the aspect of the lord of the 3rd, he will have lands through brothers. 487.

If the lord of the Navamsa occupied by the lord of the 4th joins the Karma or other Kendras and has Martian conjunction or aspect, the person gets money and lands through brothers. 488

If the powerful lords of the 1st and 4th exchange their places, aspected by or in conjunction with benefics, the person gets self-aquired lands.   489

If the Karaka of Kalatra is in 4th, or if the lord of the 4th is in the 7th, or if the lords of the 4th and 7th are friends, he gets lands through his wife.   490.

If the powerful lord of the 6th occupies the 4th or if he occupies his own house, with the lord of the 4th joining Parava-tamsa he gets lands from enemies.   491.

If the lord of the 4th is in *Aroha*, possessing beneficial conjunctions or aspects, the person will have many lands.   If the lord of the 4th or lord of lands joins the lord of 2nd or 11th occupying Visashikamsa, possessing mutual aspects or conjunctions, the person will have many lands.   492.

If the lord of the 4th is neecha or Mhoodha, or between evil planets or subjected to evil aspects, or occupies a sign between two evil planets, destruction to landed property has been predicted by the learned in Astrology.   493

If the 4th house is between evil planets, or has evil conjunctions or aspects or falls into evil signs or joins cruel Amsas, the person will have his lands destroyed.   494.

Though the lord of the 4th is in his own house, if he is in conjunction with evil planets and occupies cruel shastiamsas, or if he joins Dusthanas, occupying Ati Bhishanamsa, the landed property of the person will be destroyed.   495.

If the lord of the 4th joins malefics and occupies the 2nd house in neecha or unfriendly state, the lands will be lost. If the, lord of the 4th is exalted in conjunction with a malefic, he will sell his landed estate.   496.

If the lord of the 10th in conjunction with a malefic occupying an evil navamsa and joining Pitru, Yama etc., shastiamsas conjoins the 4th house, the person will lose lands by want of command. The same may be predicted when the lord of the 4th joins 10th under similar planetary state or conjunctions. 497.

If the lord of the 4th, Rajyakaraka and the lord of the 4th join cruel amsas or occupy *Avaroha*, joining the Nasasthana, in cruel Shastiamsas like Mrityu, Yama etc., the lands will be lost by Government order. 497. A.

NOTES.

The possession of lands, the sources from which they are obtained, their prosperty and the means or ways by which a person loses them are all sketched in these stanzas. These are important as giving beforehand, an estimate of the landed property and the consequent status the man has in his society and the country he lives in. *Bhumi Karaka* is Kuja and this word in Sanskrit signifies *Ku* Bhoomi or earth and *ja* that which is born of it and the ancient scientists have clearly stated that Mars is a miniature of the earth and possesses similar properties or characteristics. Compare the present day groping knowledge with the definite information the Maha Rishis have included in the names of planets. Wherever Mars is powerful, because, he is physical in nature, the person gets lands in abundance. Here we must have the lord of the 4th in the 10th and the lord of the 10th in the 4th and Kuja must be powerful to enable the person to have many lands. Much landed property gives a man a status in society and a position under the Government he lives. 483.

If the lord of the 4th and 10th are friends and are otherwise powerful they will give many lands. The possession of entensive lands while giving much respect and comfort will also produce its own cares and anxieties and unless they are yielding they will eat away the fortune of man. What is meant by *powerful* has been explained clearly in my notes on Brihatjataka English Translation (*See Statement 19 Ch. II*). Who are friends and who are enemies, have been clearly detailed in the same work (*See Statement 15 Ch. II*). See also my notes to Statement 105 of this work. 484.

If the 4th house, its lord and Mars have beneficial conjunctions the person will have many lands and much wealth. If all these three have beneficial conjunctions, the wealth in lands will be very great, if two of these have beneficial conjunctions then he will have something less, but if only one of these three has beneficial conjunction, then he will have a few lands. This is not explicitly stated by Venkatasa, but we can easily apply our experience and make the meaning clear in this way. 485.

If the lord of the 4th joins the 11th and also is in Gopura or Mridwamsa etc-, he will have many lands. The author has a weakness often to confound shadvergas and such others divisions with the repetition of shastiamsas in the same breath No other writer in Astrology, so far as my hnmble reading goes in this branch, confounds himself or his readers in this awkward fashion. His repetition of amsas is simply deplorable. His cruel amsas may refer to Navamsas of cruel planets, or the evil divisions of the Shastiamsas. Why he should run away so often to shastiamsas, and what authority he has for these statements is not clear to me. 486.

The Karaka of brothers is Kuja and he is also Karaka of Bhumi or lands. But the place or sign of brothers is the 3rd house. If Mars aspects or joins the lord of the 4th or the third lord joins or aspects the lord of the 4th, the person gets lands through brothers. There are some lucky fellows who are given landed property by brothers' brothers-in-law, wives' grandmothers and even by distant cousins and friends. All these can easily be guessed by a clear astrologer. 487.

The lord of the 4th joins some Navamsa. If the lord of this Navamsa is found in the 10th house (*Karma*) or any other Kendra with the aspect or conjunction of Mars, the person gets money and lands through his brothers. 488.

If the lord of the birth occupies the 4th and the lord of the 4th is in the 1st having beneficial conjunctions or aspects, he will have self-acquired lands. The lord of the 1st denotes one's own person and personal exertions. Suppose these join with or have the aspect of malefics, contrary results must naturally be predicted. 489.

The lord of wife is Sukra and he is called *Kalatra Karaka*. If Sukra occupies the 4th or if the lord of the 4th occupies the 7th (house of wife) or if the lords of the 4th and 7th are friends, the person gets lands through his wife. Friendship is of two kinds: *Nisergika* or parmanent and *Tatkalika* or temporary The term *Mitra* used in the original includes both these states. Getting lands through wife or being benefited by her may be classified under various headings. A person may marry in a very rich house, and may get a valuable dowry of cash, jewels and lands. She may have inherited valuable property or may be heiress to such and any one who marries her, necessarily gets her property. She may be presented by rich and influential relations and friends valuable lands. She may be earning honestly and thus be in a position to procure property. She may commit adultery and get him lands or he may fall in love with rich widows or husbandless women and get lands or he may be taken care of by a prostitute and she may give all her property to him. All these different states of acquisitions of property can be analysed by clearheaded and clever astrologer. 490.

Of their enemies and the acquisition of their wealth. Such a combination is furnished by 489A. The sixth lord must be powerful, and join the 4th or Paravata, or his own house in

company with the lord of the 4th, he gets wealth through destruction of his enemies or from their victory. 491.

Aroha and *Avaroha* are names given in Sanskrit for ascending and descending planets. A planet is *Aroha* when he moves
from his debilitation to his exaltation. He acquires power
gradually till he gets the highest in the deepest exaltation.
Avaroha is the state of a planet when he moves from his exaltation to his debilitation. The Sun for example, will be an *Aroha*
planet from the 10th degree of Libra to the 10th degree of Aries.
But from the 10th degree of Aries he will be *Avarohi* till he
reaches the 10th degree of Libra. (*See my notes on Eng.
Trans. of Brihatjataka St. 6 Ch. VIII.*) If the lord of the 4th
is an Arohi planet and has beneficial conjunction or aspect, the
person gets many lands. If the 4th house, or its lord or Kuja
has conjunction with the lord of the 2nd or 11th the person gets
much landed property or if any of these is in Viseshika or have
mutual aspects or conjunctions, the person will have many lands.
For example, if the lord of the 2nd joins or aspects the 4th, its
lord or Mars or if the lord of the 4th joins the 11th, or the 2nd or
if Kuja does so. the person will have many lands. 492.

If the fourth lord is debilitated, or in combust or between
malefics, or in evil signs or has their conjunctions or aspects,
or is in unfriendly houses, the person loses landed property. 493.

If the fourth is between malefics, or has evil aspects or conjunctions or if it falls in evil signs or amsas, the person loses
lands. " *Between malefics*," must not be interpreted very liberally. If the evil planets on both sides of the 4th or its lord is far
away, I doubt very much the evil of the combination lasts at all.
The evil planets must be close to the lord of the fourth or the
fourth house or Verga to make the person lose his lands. 494.

There is great confusion and repetition of Venkatasa's
Amsas. He begins with cruel shastiamsas (one sixtieth divisions)

and then again makes mention of a particular Shastiamsa by name *Bheeshana* or the 1st Shastiamsa in odd and the 60th Amsa in the even signs. This is called in the original by the word *Ghora* which is synonym for Bheeshana. If the lord of the 4th is in evil Shastiamsas, (like Rakshasa, Kulaghna, Garala, Agnighata) or combines in debilitated or evil house, or is in 6th, 8th or 12th or in unfriendly sign the person loses lands. 495.

Repetition there is much in Venkatasa. Again Venkatasa declares that if the fourth lord combines with a malefic, and occupies the second house or is found in Neecha or enemy's house, the lands will be lost. If on the other hand the fourth lord is in exaltation in company with a malefic, he will sell the lands. The difference between the two seems to be that in the first case the lands will be lost in litigation or carelessness or by other causes and in the second case they will be sold by him and he will get the money value. 496.

The lord of the 10th must be in conjunction with a malefic, and join an evil Navamsa and also be found in bad shastiamsas as *Pitru, Yema* etc. If such lord of the 10th occupies the 4th house, the person loses lands by want of *Agnya*. This word means command or order and the 10th house is called *Agnya sthna*. The lands may be separated from his command by his own mismanagement as by being sold in auction for realisation of Government rents or creditors' demands or they may slip away for want of supervision or personal neglect which may give rise to adverse possession and right.

The same result will happen when the lord of the 4th with evil planet in conjunction joining bad Navamsa and cruel Shastiamsas occupy the 10th house. 497.

Take the lord of the 10th, take Pujyakaraka or the Sun. Take also the lord of the 4th. If these are in *Avaroha* (falling) joining cruel amsas or sub-divisions and occupy the *Nasasthana*

or the 12th house from Lagna, the property will be lost by Government orders. Sub-divisions are Navamsas and Shasti-amsas and I am inclined to include all evil *amsas* or divisions. Government orders are many and various. The lands of a person may be removed from the possession of a person, and his enjoyment for fines, penalties, confiscation for State or heinous offences, land revenue, or under the provisions of the Land Acquisition Act. They may be sold for Civil liabilities, or for some other causes by Government. The degradation in the loss of lands varies with the intensity of the evil indicated by the planetary positions. All phases of human transactions are well pourtrayed in the astrological works, and the gigantic intellects of the remotest times comprehended the details of political and civil administration which are even to-day astonish-ing the intellectual world. These niceties of conception can only proceed from a highly developed civilisation and no better proof can be required or given than these valuable details of human existence. Whether rightly or wrongly the Government of all enlightened nations from the remotest anti-quity to the present day, have thought that they possess power to deprive a man of his landed property for certain offences or state exigencies. Such power to resume the lands is, also supposed to act powerfully on the minds of the criminal classes as not only they suffer for their faults, but also their innocent progeny and these thoughts act as deterrents upon some think-ing minds among the criminally inclined persons. These are very important and should be carefully perused. 497A.
Stanzas 498 to 508 inclusive.

If the lord of the Navamsa occupied by the lord of the Navamsa occupied by the lord of the second with a malefic joins the lord of the fourth, the person loses lands through Govern-ment. If the lord of the 4th is aspected by Jupeter or joins Mridwamsa, the person will be happy and wealthy. 498.

If Guru or some benefic occupies 4th and if the 4th is between two benefics or if it is a beneficial sign and if Guru is more powerful than the lord of the 4th the person will be a leader among his relations. 499.

If Guru is in the 4th combining Gopuramsa etc., and if the lord of the 4th occupies 2nd, 11th, 5th, or 7th houses, the person will be happy. 500.

If the 4th is combined by malefics when Guru is weak and if the powerless lord of the 4th joins a malefic, the person will be miserable although he is wealthy. 501.

If a Neecha planet occupies 2nd, 4th or 5th and if the lord of the 4th occupies the 4th, with malefic or joins cruel Amsas the person will be miserable. 502.

If the lord of the 4th joins Ravi and Kuja, occupying cruel amsas without beneficial aspect and if he be in other than *Aroha*, the person will be constantly sick. 503.

If Ravi or Kuja joins Neecha or unfriendly amsa occupying the 4th with malefics, or if the lord of the 4th is in cruel Amsas, the person will be travelling with sickness. 504.

If the 4th or its lord is with malefics or has their aspect or lies between evil planets and joins cruel *Sasttamsas*, the person becomes sinful though there are beneficial aspects. 505.

If many malefics join the 4th or if its lord conjoins unfriendly houses or is in combustion or with a malefic or with *Yamasunu,* the person becomes extremely sinful. 506.

If the fourth house falls in the signs of Sukra, Chandra, Budha or Guru and the 4th is combined with or aspected by benefics, the person will be very happy. 507.

If Sukra occupies the 4th aspected by Budha, or if Sukra is between benefics and joins Gopura etc. amsas, the person will be meritorious. 508.

NOTES.

The lord of the 2nd occupies some Navamsa. Its lord occupies again some other Navamsa. The lord of this Navamsa must join the lord of the fourth with a malefic to make the person lose lands through Government. I have already shown the various sources through which Governments contrive to take away the lands of its unfortunate people.

	Birth Guru.	Rahu.			Chand Rahu.	Birth.	Sani.
	AMSA.			Ravi. Budha. Guru.	RASI.		
Budha.	Kethu	Ravi. Kuja. Sani. Sukra.	Chan	Sukra.		Kuja. Kethu.	

The lord of the 2nd is Budha. He joins the Navamsa of Dhanas. The lord of this is Guru and he joins the Navamsa of Mesha. The lord of Mesha is Kuja, if this Kuja combined with a malefic had joined the lord of the 4th Ravi in the Rasi, the person would lose lands through Government displeasure. Take another example. A man was born on the 30th of July 1859 Saturday at 36-15 ghatis after sunrise.

			Guru. Sukra	Kethu	Guru.		Sukra
Birth.	RASI.		Ravi Chandra Kuja Sani Kathu	Chandra Sani	NAVAMSA		Budha
Rahu			Buda				
				Birth	Ravi	Kuja	Rahu

The lord of the 2nd is Guru and he occupies Mesha Navamsa. The lord of Mesha is Kuja and Kuja joins the

Navamsa of Thula. The lord of Thula is Sukra. The lord of the 4th is also Sukra, and if he is in conjunction with an evil planet, the result predicted would happen. But here Sukra is with a benefic, and confiscation or Government bother would not come. These illustrations make the points clear and intelligible. Now from confiscation or loss of lands Venkatasa Daivagnya takes the reader to happiness and wealth. Those who are happy are few and far between. The wealthy are not always happy nor the poor always miserable. When the beneficial influences in any horoscope predominate the person will be wealthy and also happy. When the evil influences are predominent misery of various descriptions attacks the man and makes him unhappy although he may be rich.

If the lord of the 4th is aspected by Guru, or if he joins Mridwamsa, the person will be happy and wealthy. If the lord of the 4th joins any other good Shastiamsa happiness and wealth must also be prodicted by suggestion. Here aspect of Guru is stated. If he conjoins the lord of the 4th, certainly the result will be even more beneficial. 498.

In the comparison of Guru and lord of the fourth as regards strength, the sources of power arising from various causes should be clearly ascertained as per principles enunciated in the first chapter of this work.

If the fourth house is between two benefics or if a good planet is in the fourth, and if Guru is stronger than the lord of the 4th, the person will not only be happy but will also be a leader among his men. This leadeship and its concomittant influences will be according to the intensity of the planet and its position and power. Leadership of anybody of men or community or class or society is both a blessing and a curse as the person exercises his influence for the good or bad of its members. Anyhow it confers a power on a man and gives him a position which men envy for the influence it weilds among the followers and for the advantages and respect which it confers upon the man. There is also much pride attached to such leadership, and it is considered to be a fortune to be the leader of his men, or society. Therefore those who become leaders should particularly remember that the power and influence thus conferred upon them by this previous good *Karma* should not be misused or turned to selfish pupposes. 499.

If Guru is in the 4th house joining Gopuraṃsa etc., when the lord of the 4th is in the 2nd, 11th, 5th or 7th houses, the person will command happiness. Here Guru should not only be in the 4th but must also occupy Gopuramsa or such other good *shadvergas* and the lord of the 4th house must occupy any one of the following Bhavas *viz.* 2nd, 5th, 7th, or 11th houses. There are some who enjoy happiness at the cost of others, and without any appreciable wealth with them. With some there is contentment and these are generally happy, while there are others who are exceedingly rich but whose avarice and ambition make them discontented and miserable. God's creation is most wonderful and affords inexhaustible food for contemplative minds. 500.

Guru seems to play an important part in causing happiness or misery. He represents *Ganan Sukha* or philosophical wisdom and when a person commands such a noble disposition, happiness will certainly court him. The strength or weakness of Guru, should be carefully considered. (See my Notes on St. 1. Chap. II of Brihatjataka and Note on St. 69 of this work.)

If Guru is powerless and if the 4th has evil planets in it, or if the weak lord of the fourth joins a bad planet, the person will be miserable, although he may have much wealth. The possession of happiness or misery largely depends upon his mental composition and training. But other conditions of life also add or take away from pleasurable feelings. 501.

If a man possesses good houses, decent carriages, fine horses, loving children, enviable wealth, rich furniture, obedient wife and grateful relations and enjoys them, then the world will at once say that he is happy without going deep into the workings of his inner mood. Wealth secures many of these objects and a tactful behaviour with a charitable disposition, may give him other comforts. But a developed mind will see that all these are fleeting pleasures, and become the sources of sorrow and misery. It is here that the vulgar minds are incapable of judging the true value of these so-called sources of happiness. The love after Brahma, the renunciation of transient and unreal pleasures, the contemplation on the Sublime and the everlasting, the feeling of happiness at the sight of God's glorious creation in all its phases of existence and display, and the determination to evolve himself into the final Bliss, where the gross worldly concerns appear as utterly unreal, all these give his mind sources of pleasure which are constant and highly refreshing. 502.

The author now changes the subject to general health and sickness. A wealthy man may be sickly while a poor man may be quite healthy. Although the doctors, for the sake of increasing their medical emoluments, may propound any number of theories, health and sickness certainly depend upon other conditions than hygenic. If this were not so, then all the rich men having fine and clean houses would be healthy while all the poor people would be sickly. On the other hand the reverse holds good. Poor men in the midst of their dirtiest sanitary conditions manage to keep better health than the rich. When the lord of the 4th in conjunction with Ravi and Kuja, occupies cruel Amsas without beneficial aspects, joining *Avaroha* the person will be constantly sick. Other than *Aroha* means *Avaroha*. *Aroha* means that the planet is going from debilitation to exaltation. *Avaroha* means the planets march from exaltation to debilitation. Three conditions are here laid down. (1) the

7

lord of the 4th should be in conjunction with Ravi and Kuja.
(2) He should be in cruel Amsas without beneficial aspects and
(3) he should be moving towards his house of *fall* or Neecha,
when all these are present, he will be constantly sick. But when
one of the conditions is absent, the sickness will be less and when
two of the conditions are absent the sickness will be still less and
when two of the conditions are absent the sickness will be
nominal or least harmful. 503.

If Ravi or Kuja occupies the 4th with a malefic joining
Neecha or unfriendly Navamsa and the lord of the 4th joins cruel
Amsas, the person will not only be sick but will also be compelled
to travel. Sickness is itself miserable and to travel at such
times will certainly be more miserable. 504.

Some combinations will now be given indicating sin and
virtue.

The fourth house and its lord must be taken. If the 4th is
occupied with or aspected by evil planets, or if it is between two
evil planets occupying cruel shastiamsas the person becomes
sinful though there are beneficial aspects. Similarly with the lord
of the 4th house. If he is with an evil planet or is aspected by an
evil planet combining in bad shastiamsas the person becomes
sinful even though there be beneficial aspects. The last portion
is a little puzzling. The expression is *Shubha Dristi Yuktay*
with beneficial aspects. But instead of Yuktay, it may also be
read as *Hinay* which means without beneficial aspects. It is
really difficult to say what could have been the original. Both
may be accepted. The general principles are sometimes violated
by special combinations and we have many such instances.
Properly speaking, beneficial aspects and conjunctions always
modify the evil nature of the conjunctions. But here it is possible that beneficial aspects will have no mitigating power over
the sinful nature of the conjunction. 505.

If there are many evil planets in the 4th house, or if the lord
of the 4th is in combustion, or unfriendly house with a malefic or

Yamasunu the person becomes very sinful. For Yamatmaja or Yama sunu see P. 69. There are some persons who are fond of sinful deeds and this disposition and inclination for sin is indicated by evil planets in the 4th or the lord of 4th occupying unfriendly house or being in combustion and combination with evil planet or Yamatmaja. The latter is thoroughly evil and Venkatasa's language looks repetition. 506.

If the 4th house falls in the signs of Sukra (Vrishabha and Thula) Chandra (Kataka) Budha (Mithuna and Kanya) and Guru (Dhanus and Meena) and it is combined with or aspected by benefics, the man will be very happy. This means that it the fourth is a beneficial sign and has beneficial conjunction or aspect, there will be much happiness. 507.

Sukra must be in the 4th house possessing the aspect of Budha, or if Sukra, joining Gopuramsa, etc, is between two good planets, the person will be meritorious. He will be noble, generous, moral and god-fearing. These combinations are clearly stated by the author and I have made them as clear and simple as possible. What is *sin*, what is *merit* and what is happiness and what is misery, these are relative terms which cannot be easily explained in short notes. But in all these matters we have to interpret the stanzas in the popular language and with reference to general moral and religious principles. Take different nations. Their varied training from the earlier days, gives them turns of mind which cannot be easily reconciled. If a Pariah is asked he says it is quite meritorious to kill a cow and offer it to his Goddess. A Brahmin on the other hand would shudder at the idea of killing a cow. A Christian would consider it a moral deed if he could murder pagans in the name of Christianity, and introduce the name of his God Christ into their midst. Europeans would relish pork and seek for it while the Mahomedans would hate it as if it is their satan. Instances can be quoted of such radical differences in the development of human ideas, that it would look almost impossible to classify sin and merit. But all sciences have application in places where they are most prevalent. When applying these stanzas to a Mahomedan, to a Christian, to a Buddhist and to a Brahmin, the astrological adopt, like the learned medical expert must take the time, circumstances, history and temperament of the individual, and the traditions of his family and community in determining the events and classifying them as sinful or meritorious. 508.

Stanzas 509 to 521 inclusive.

If a Neecha planet joins the 4th house with an evil planet, or combines in the 6th house, a jala Rasi, and the lord of the 4th is weak, the person will fall into a well, tank or other watery place. 509.

If the powerless lord of Lagna joins the 4th, or if he in conjunction with a malefic, joins his house of debilitation, with the sun, and the weak lord of the 4th joins a watery planet, the man will be drowned in large watery places. 510.

If the lord of *Saristhana* (7th house) joins the lord of birth, and occupies the 4th aspected by the lord of the 10th, the person will fall into a well, tank or river. 511.

If the lord of the Navamsa occupied by the lord of the 4th has the conjunction or aspect of the lord of the 7th or 4th, the person will fall into a well, tank or river. 512.

If the lord of the 7th house is Sani and the 4th is occupied by Ravi and Kuja, combined with or aspected by the lord of the 10th, the person will be stoned to death or will fall on rocks. 513.

If the lord of the 4th combines with Rahu and Sani, aspected by Kuja, without beneficial aspects, the person will have stone cuts. 514.

If the Moon or Venus joins a Kendra combined with or aspected by malefics, and occupies cruel shastiamsas or Ava

Roha position, the person will be guilty of criminal intercourse with his own mother. 515.

If the 4th is occupied by malefics, aspected by evil planets, the person will be guilty of sensual intercourse with his mother.

If the lord of the 4th in combination with a malefic, is aspected by evil planets, without beneficial aspects, the person will commit criminal intercourse with his mother. 516.

If the lord of the birth is weaker than the lord of the 7th, the person will be guilty of sensual intercourse with motherly relations.

If the lord of the 7th in conjunction with cruel planets occupies the 4th and has combination with or is aspected by malefics or joins cruel shastiamsas, the man will have cohabitation with his own sisters. Or if Sani occupies the 4th with evil planets or possesses evil aspects, the person will commit adultery with his own sister. 517 & 518.

If the 4th house is an evil sign and falls in cruel shastiamsas, the person will have connection with his sister.

If Chandra joins Kuja and the lord of the 4th aspected by malefics occupies the 4th house, the person will be guilty of sexual intercourse with his mother. 519.

If the lord of the Navamsa occupied by Chandra joins Kuja and the lord of the 6th occupies the 4th aspected by evil planets, the person will have criminal intercourse with his mother.

If the lord of the 4th joins Rahu with another malefic aspected by Kuja or Rahu, he will commit adultery among other women than his mother. (*Matanyasakta*.) 520.

If the lord of the Navamsa occupied by the Rasi in which the lord of the 4th joins has evil conjunctions and aspects or has combination with Mandi, etc., the person will have connection with some other women than the mother. 521.

NOTES.

Now the reader is taken to some misfortunes which happen to man in the shape of drowning or water danger. If there is a Neecha planet combined with a malefic in the 4th, or if the Neecha planet with a malefic joins the 6th house which falls in a Jala Rasi (watery sign) like Kataka or Meena, when the lord of the fourth is weak, the person will fall into a well, tank or oth·r watery place. This is a danger indicated by evil conjunctions of the planets. The author does not say whether the man dies or is saved from such a fall. He leaves the readers to judge the seriousness of the result by the intensity of the evil indicated by the planets. Take Thula as Lagna then Makara will be the fourth. Suppose Kuja is there with Guru Guru is Neecha and joins an evil planet Kuja who is in exultation and if the lord of the 4th Sani is in combustion or unfriendly house, the person will fall into a well or tank, but will be saved Suppose Kataka is Lagna with Kuja and Ravi in the 4th Thula, and its lord Sukra is in Kanya, then as Ravi is Neecha and has joined Kuja in an unfriendly house, with the lord of 4th Sukra in Neecha, the person will fall into a watery place and will die by its effects or drowning. 509.

If the lord of birth is weak and joins the 4th, or if in conjunction with a malefic he occupies his house of debilitation in combination with the Sun, when the weak lord of the 4th conjoins a watery planet, the person will be drowned in large watery places. Watery planets are the Moon and Venus. 510.

The lord of *Sarithina* is the lord of the 7th. (See. St. 1 of Ch. on *Katatra Bhava*) Sarit—a river. that which flows— (Sec. St. 264 I Kanda, Amara.)

If the lords of the 7th and 1st join and occupy the 4th aspected by the lord of the 10th house, the person will fall into a well, tank or river. The death by drowning or escape from it must be predicted by the extent of the evil they indicate. 511.

The lord of the 4th occupies some Navamsa. If the lord of this Navamsa has the conjunction or aspect of the lord of the 4th or 7th, the person will be drowned in a well or tank or river. 512

From water danger the reader is now taken to stone danger to the man. Dangers arise from various causes, such as sickness of many descriptions, water danger, danger from wild animals, danger from conveyances and horses, danger from falls from high elevations, danger from murder or violence, danger from reptile bites, danger from inclemencies of weather, thunder, lightning, rain, cold, sun, electricity and from many other causes.

The lord of the 7th must be Sani and the 4th must be occupied by Ravi and Kuja possessing the combination or aspect of the lord of the 10th to make the man die by being stoned or by falling on a rock or a stone falling on him. If the planets are favourable, there will be injuries, but he will escape death, but if they are powerfully evil, the person will die by such injuries. 513.

If Sani and Rahu conjoin the lord of the 4th house, possessing the aspect of Kuja but without beneficial aspects, the person will have stone cuts, proving fatal or otherwise according to the intensity of the planetary evils Kuja is Martial and adventurous and he will always influence a man to enter into dangerous enterprises. 514.

If the Kendras are occupied by Chandra or Sukra with malefic conjunctions or aspects and joining cruel shastiamsas or found in Avaroha position, the person will be guilty of sexual intercourse with his own mother. The question is a very delicate and difficult one, and it may be doubted whether there are any men in this world who could be guilty of such abominable acts. Men with strong passions and uncontrollable minds, are not only brutes but worse than brutes. Animals make no distinction between mothers, sisters, and other females of their species. There are instances of men wherein they have been found guilty of even worse sins, unnatural offences have been not only noticed by laws of all Governments, but cruel punishments are ordained by them. Do not these clearly show the depth of the depravity in human nature. Medical Jurisprudence and criminal cases show how far man can degrade himself in such matters. When the moral and religious cultivation are neglected, the mental depravity would condescend to do any abominable act. Ethnology of different nations has shown cases of remarkable degradation which immoral humanity is capable of doing. If the higher moral culture and reverence to time-honored customs, are neglected, the mind can do anything it pleases. A man kills another, kills his father or mother, his children and his benefactors and commits horrible indecencies on the opposite sex and sometimes on his own sex, and even on beasts. To such depraved men, connection with their mother may not appear very unpalatable. 515.

When there is an evil planet in the 4th aspected by another evil planet, the person will be guilty of such mean acts. The evil planet in the 4th and the evil planet which aspects it must be very malicious to produce such criminal intimacy with his mother. If they are not very bad he may think of such evil deeds, but may not be guilty of actual commission. If there are beneficial aspects, then such evil results should not be predicted. 516.

When the lord of the birth is weaker than the lord of the 7th, the person will commit adultery with motherly relations. The sources of strength such as, Sthanabala (Positional), (Kalabala timely), Digbala (directional), etc., would determine which planet is weaker and which is stronger. Motherly relations are, aunts, paternal and maternal, elder sisters-in-law, mothers-in-law, grandmothers and aunts, wives of preceptors and benefactors, and so forth. Here the lord of birth must decidedly be weaker than the lord of the 7th. In each case, one of these generally will be weaker. That is not enough,

Both must be bad and then the worst must be the birth lord. Suppose Makara is Lagna and Sani is in the 2nd Kumbha. The lord of the 7th is Chandra and he is exalted in Vrishabha. Here the lord of 7th is exalted and therefore stronger than the lord of birth Sani who is in his own house Here this unfavourable result must not be predicted, although there will be some passing thoughts in his mind to that immoral effect. But suppose Chandra is in Vrischika and Sani is in Mesha, then, if by other sources of power Sani is weaker than Chandra, the result abovementioned may be predicted as both the planets are evil and the lord of the Lagna Sani is much weaker than the lord of the 7th. If the lord of the 7th with cruel planets occupies 4th and possesses evil aspects or joins cruel shastiamsas, the man commits adultery with his own sisters. There are some low-minded men who are guilty of such abominable offences. If Sani occupies 4th house with evil con junctions or aspects he will be guilty of such offences 517 & 518.

The 4th house necessarily falls into some sub-divisions. If it falls into cruel shastiamsas, the person will sexually correspond with his sisters.

If the lord of the 4th aspected by malefics occupies 4th while Chandra joins Kuja, the man commits adultery with his mother. Chandra is the lord of mother. 519.

Chandra occupies some navamsa If the lord of this Navamsa combines with Kuja, while the lord of the 6th occupies he 4th aspected by evil planets, there will be adultery with his own mother. If the lord of the 4th joins Rahu with another evil planet aspected by Ravi or Kuja, he will commit adultery among other women than his mother. The original runs as *Matanya-sukta* other than his mother.

This may mean also that his mother will have liking for other men than his father. But the author seems to convey the idea that he will commit adultery among other women. 520.

The lord of the 4th joins some Rasi. He may be in his
own house or in the house of another planet. The lord of this
Rasi ·occupies some Navamsa. If the lord of this Navamsa
joins with evil planets or has their aspects or combines with
Mandi, etc , the person will commit adultery with other women
This means that he will not be guilty of any criminal maternal
intercourse, but will be guilty of sexual correspondence with
women whom he ought to respect as his own mother. 521.

Stanzas 522 to 533 inclusive·

If the powerful lord of the 4th occupies birth, aspected by
Guru, Chandra, Buda and Sukra or if he joins Viseshika and has
beneficial aspects the mother of the person will be chaste. 522·

If Chandra occupies birth with Rahu or Kethu, the mother
will be fond of low men, if Moon joins Saturn, then she will be
fond of Sudras, if Mercury joins Chandra in Lagna, she will be
fond of Vaisyas. 523.

If Moon joins Lagna with the Sun, she will be fond of
Kshetryas, if Moon conjoins Jupiter or Venus in birth, the mother
will be fond of holy Brahmins, if the Moon joins in Lagna with
Kuja she will be fond of low class men. 524

If the lord of the 6th joins the lord of the 4th and occupies
the 9th house, the father of the person will be adulterous, or if the
lord of the 9th and 4th combined together in the 4th house, the
father will be fond of other women. 525.

If the lord of the 6th joins with the lords of the birth, 4th and
9th houses, the person will be born of adultery.

If the lord of the Navamsa occupied by the lord of the 6th
combines with the lord of the 4th aspected by malefics, the
person takes his birth from adultery. 526.

When the 4th house is between malefics, if the lord of that house or the lord of the mother has malefic aspects and if the lord of the 9th is weaker than the lord of birth the person will be born of adultery. 527.

If the birth or Moon is not aspected by Jupiter, or if the Sun and Moon joined together, have no jovian aspect, or if the Sun and the Moon in conjunction with each other, join with evil planet, the person will be born of adultery. 528

If an evil planet joins the 9th while another evil planet occupies the 4th, and the weak lord of the Lagna joins a malefic and the 4th house occupies other Navamsa, the person will take his birth in adultery. 529

If there is a benefic in the 4th, if the lord of mother joins a good planet and if the lord of the 4th is powerful, the mother will be long lived. 530.

If Chandra or Sukra is powerful occupying good Amsas and aspected by benefics and in any of the Kendras, while the 4th house has beneficial conjunctions or aspect, the mother will live long. 531.

If the lord of the Navamsa occupied by the lord of the 4th joins Kendras or is in Kendras from the powerful Moon, the mother will have a long life   532.

If the Moon is between malefics combined with or aspected by evil planets, the mother will die soon. If Sani occupies an evil sign aspected by malefics. the mother will die soon. 533.

NOTES.

If the fourth lord is powerful and is in Lagna aspected by Guru, Chandra, Buda or Sukra or if the fourth lord combines in Viseshika, with beneficial aspects, the mother of the person will be chaste. There is always a great credit attached to birth and surroundings of a man, and to be born in adultery will take away a great deal of the reputation from a native's honor. A chaste mother, a chaste wife or sister, or daughter will be an object of worship and the possession of such relations will be a great blessing for the man. 522.

If Moon combines in Lagna with Rahu or Kethu, the mother will be fond of low men, if such Moon joins Saturn, she would co-habit with Sudras, if with Buda, Visyas, if with Ravi, military classes, if Moon joins Guru or Sukra she will be fond of holy Brahmins ; if with Kuja she will'be guilty of adultery among low classes. 523-524.

If the lord of the 4th and 6th combine in the 9th house or if the lords of the 9th and 4th occupy the 4th house, the father of the person will be a *Vita* or paramour, one fond of other women. *Vita* in Sanskrit means a lover. 525.

When the lords of the 6th, 1st, 4th and 9th join together in any house, the person will be born of adultery. The author makes no mention of any house for their junction and therefore they may be found in any house The lord of the 6th occupies some Navamsa. If the lord of this Navamsa joins with the lord of the 4th aspected by malefics, the person will take an adulterous birth. 526.

The 4th house must be lying between evil planets, with the lord of the 4th house and lord of mother (moon) possessing malefic aspects, and the lord of the 9th must be weaker than the lord of the birth. In such conjunction, the person will be born in adultery. 527.

Moon and birth must possess the aspect of Jupiter. The conjunction will of course, be more favourable. When the Sun and the Moon join, they must have jovian aspects. This conjunction of the Sun and the Moon happens only on an Amavasya day. If Jupiter does not aspect in these conjunctions, the person will be born of adultery. If the conjoined Moon and the Sun, combine with evil planet, the person will be born of adultery. Who is the other evil planet who must join the Sun and the Moon. Some commentators refer to Sani or Kuja. This is very reason-able. But I may here suggest that suppose such a conjunction of the Sun and the Moon has the combination of Rahu or Kethu, evil results may also safely be predicted.

If such Moon occupies any of the divisions of Guru, the person will have a clean birth. Predictions in such cases must be made with great care and ability.

These are very important Yogas or combinations which are likely to disturb the equanimity of many individuals, whose birth and parentage do not brook much examination and search. It would be useless to sleep over certain facts, when they are world widely known, recognised, talked of, but at the same time pretended to be unnoticed. The ratio of pure and chaste women to impure and adulterous females is very small indeed. Men and women are more given to sexual indulgence than its absti-nence and when we compare the opportunities asked and given by men and women respectively, we need not be surprised at such indulgences prevailing to an enormous extent, among all times and all nations Therefore such plain facts as adultery, are an admission of the loose morals under which men and women are being trained In all the cases above quoted, the combinations are sketched, but with great reserve. Even when Moon joins with Jupiter and Venus, the woman is credited with fondness for holy Brahmins or ecclesiasts, with due deference to Venkatasa, his statements here must be accepted with great reserve and are not absolutely true. If Moon is in the fourth aspected by Jupiter or Venus, the mother of the person will be thoroughly chaste, and Venkatasa is completely wrong. Adultery among any classes is prohibited, and although the licentiousness of the sin may be great or less according to circumstances, it still forms an item of crime and sin. When benefics aspect the 4th, its lord or its Karaha moon, there should be cast no imputation against the mother of such

a person.   Even when evil planets aspect the fourth if they are
exalted or occupy good divisions and have beneficial aspects or
conjunctions there should be no imputations against the honor of
the mother.   When the fourth, its lord, and Moon are thoroughly
bad, the person may claim safely an adulterous birth. Venkatasa's
combinations about the adultery of women are opposed to the
spirit of great men like Varaha Mihira, Yavanaswara and Maha-
rishi Garge *see Ch. V t 6 and my notes on their translation in
Bhat Jataka*.) Venkatasa is only a recent compiler and as
such can claim no originality and cannot be placed in the same
scale as the abovenamed great authors.   Bagavan Gargi observes
on this most important question of a man's good or adulterous
birth thus. " If Chandra combines in Guru's Rasi, or joins him
in any Rasi, or joins Drekkana, or his Navamsa, the person will
not be born of adultery." This authoritative quotation must at
once silence men of Venkatasa's stamp once and for ever.
Throughout the length and breadth of the astrological   sciences,
the conjunction and aspect of Jupiter in every direction have
been considered as extremely wholesome, and if Guru does not
give good character and noble birth, then, Venkatasa can think of
no other planet who would be able to do so and astrology must run
rank with evil influences   528.

There must be one evil planet in the 9th and another evil
planet in the 4th, the weak lord of Lagna joins a malefic, whilst
the 4th house occupies other Navamsa, the person will have
adulterous birth   In this conjunction if the 4th joins its own
Navamsa, the evil should not be predicted. Suppose Mesha is the
4th and it joins Mesha Navamsa   Here it falls in Vargottama
and this has the power of neutralising the evil.   529.

Venkatasa now comes to deal with combinations which
indicate longevity to mother or her early death.   There must be
a benefic in the 4th, the lord of mother Chandra must also have
beneficial conjunction and if the lord of the 4th is powerful,
the mother of the person will live long.   It is a great blessing to

have a long lived mother and every good man should do his best
to prolong the life of his mother.   530.

Chandra or Sukra must be powerful, must occupy good
Amsas, must have beneficial aspects, must be in Kendras from
Lagna and the 4th house must have beneficial conjunction or
aspect, to give long life to the mother   Sukra represents mother
for those who are born during the day and Sani governs mother
for those who take their birth during the night time   Chandra is
the general lord governing mother.   The strength of all these
must be taken into consideration   531

The lord of the 4th occupies some Navamsa.   Take the
lord of this Navamsa and see which Amsa he occupies.   Then
take the lord of that Navamsa and see if he is in Kendras to
Lagna or to the powerfully situated Chandra.   This combination gives long life to the mother.   532

If Chandra combines with a malefic and is hemmed in by
two evil planets, the mother will die soon.   If Sani occupies an
evil sign aspected by a malefic, the mother will die early.   Sani is
an evil planet and he may occupy his own Rasi   Could the
result be foretold ?   The author apparently refers to other evil
planetary houses and not his own.   A planet occupying his own
good or evil house cannot be so very bad and the evil must be
predicted in a considerably modified form.   533.

Stanzas 534 to 540 inclusive.

If Sani combines with an evil planet, the mother dies early,
but if such Sani has beneficial aspects, the learned Maharishis in
astrology say that the mother's life will be considerably prolonged.
534.

If the lord of the Navamsa occupied by the lord of the
Navamsa occupied by the lord of the *Matrusthana* joins *Dusthas*,
the mother dies early.   535.

If the Moon in combustion joins an evil house or occupies a
Neecha Rasi and Amsa, there will be early death to mother.   If

the Moon is between two evil planets, in conjunction with or aspected by a malefic, the person gets sorrow through the loss of his mother. 536.

The loss of mother has been predicted by the ancient learned Maha Rishis, when the lord of the 4th, the Moon, and Venus, occupy evil houses, have evil conjunction or when they are subjected to malefic aspects. 537.

The time of the mother's death should be determined by the rays of the lord of the Navamsa occupied by the lord of the 4th house. Finding which is the strongest among the lord of the 4th house and the lord of the mother, take the Navamsa occupied by the strongest of the three, calculate the numbers of the Navamsa it occupies from Mesha and fix the period of the mother's death in that year. If the lord of this Navamsa is in retrograde, the year of life must be doubled, if he is in *Ativakra*, the figure must be trebled, if this lord is in his own house or Navamsa, or in *Vargatama* the figure must be trebled. If such a retrograde planet is aspected by benefics, the figure must be quadrupled. 538-39-40.

NOTES.

If Saturn combines with an evil planet, the mother dies early. but if he has beneficial aspects, she lives long. Here it is understood that Saturn must be in any of the evil houses owned by evil planets. If he occupies Capricorn or Aquarius, he occupies evil signs, although in this case a little longer life may be predicted for the mother from the fact of his occupying his own Rasis or houses. It looks as if the conjunction mentioned in St. 453 must be present in a horoscope along with the position named here for Saturn to produce early death to mother, otherwise the Stanza has to be strained a great deal. Saturn is not in any way related, to mother and does not control her. On the other hand for those who are born during the night he becomes the lord of father, (*see my notes on Eng. Trans. of Brih at Jataka sh* 5, *Ch. IV*).

When Moon is between malefics, and Saturn occupies cruel houses with malefic aspects, he cuts short the mother's life, because Moon represents mother and Saturn denotes, longevity, death and means of general livelihood. 534.

The lord of the 4th joins some Navamsa. Take the lord of this Navamsa and find out which Navamsa he occupies. If the lord of the latter Navamsa occupies 6th, 8th or 12th, the mother will die early. Take an example of a real horoscope.

	Rahu Chandra	Birth	Sani
Ravi Buda Guru	RASI		
Sukra		Kuja Kethu	

	Birth Guru	Rahu	
	NAVAMSA.		
Buda	Kethu.	Ravi Kuja Sani Sukra	Chandra

Take the lord of the 4th from Lagna and he is Ravi. Find out the Navamsa joined by Ravi and it is Thula. Take the lord of Thula and he is Sukra. Find out who is the lord of the Navamsa occupied by Sukra. Here we find he himself is the lord If this Sukra is found occupying *Dusthas* or 6th, 8th or 12th houses from Lagna and Sukra is found in the 8th house from Lagna in the Rasi—the person will lose his mother early and this is a fact as he lost his mother in his 14th year. 535.

If Chandra in *Moodha* (combust) occupies an evil house or joins a debilitated Rasi and Navamsa, the mother dies early. If Chandra is between two malefics and has evil combination or aspect, sorrow comes to him through the loss of his mother. Many ordinary astrologers are labouring under the belief that Chandra has no *Asta* or *M. oda* (combustion.) This is a great

mistake.   If we refer to Suryasiddhanta p. 209 Grahuyutij St. 1,
with Ranganath's commentaries it is plainly stated that *Kujadi,
Tara Grahas*, viz., Kuja, Buda, Guru, Sukra, and Sani as well
as Chandra get into Asta (combustion) when they are close to
Ravi (see also st. 20 Ch. II Brihatjataka.)   Chandra has therefore a clear state of combustion as well as any other planet when
he gets close to the Sun.   This state goes under the technical
name of Amavasya,   when any good act should not be performed.   Planets get into combustion when they are within ten
degrees or Bhagas of the Sun, and the greatest *Asta* will be
when they are in the same degree with the Sun.   This state
makes them lustreless or without rays and therefore they produce
positive evil.   Chandra must both be in *Moodha* and also occupy
an evil house. Houses owned by evil planets become evil or cruel
houses. 536.

This stanza is a general summary of what has already
been stated by the author in the previous verses.   The
lord of the 4th, the lord of mother, *viz*, Moon, and Sukra,
should not occupy evil houses, should have no evil conjunctions
or aspects and should not live between evil planets.   A
planet is said to be between two evil or good planets, when
he has any planets, within 30 degrees on both sides of him.
Say Chandra is in Mesha in the 10th degree.   Thirty degrees on
either side, must be clean, *i. e.,* from the 11th degree in Mesha to
the 10th degree in Vrishabha there should be no evil planet. This
is in front.   There should also be no evil planet from the 10th
degree of Meena to the 9th degree of Mesha. Suppose Chandra is
in the 1st degree of Meena and Kuja is in the 30th degree of
Mesha The distance is nearly 59 degrees. Similarly if Sani is in
the 2nd degree of Makara, then there are 59 degrees between him
and Chandra, but still he may be said to lie between two evil
planets Here there will be almost no evil result. These
different positions should be carefully considered by the student
when he ventures into the fields of actual prediction.   Now he

takes the reader to ascertain the time when the mother is likely to die. Astrologers would be committing a great blunder if they simply confine themselves to Dasas and Bhuktis. 537.

The author now refers to Kiranas which he has not explained in the earlier portions of his work. Kirana means a ray. It may be questioned that when the planet shines, his rays are countless and therefore we have no methods by which we can count them. Bhoutikakala *sutras* also say *Kiranah Paramko ayaha* meaning that the rays of the Sun are numberless crores. *Kirana* here is used in a technical way and denotes the concentrated energy which a planet is able to exercise by virtue of its position, state, etc. This question is well illustrated in Jataka Parijata (Ch. V, St. 22 Benarese Edition Vikramasaka 1191 or 1886 A. D.) The exalted Sun gets 10 rays, the Moon gets one, Mars has five, Mercury has five, Jupiter seven, Venus eight and Saturn five. The lord of the fourth occupies some Navamsa. The lord of this Amsa has some rays (*Kiranas*), which determine the longevity of the mother. Find out who is the strongest of the lot, *viz*, the fourth house, its lord and the Moon. Find out in which Navamsa, the most powerful of these three, *viz.*, fourth house, its lord, and the Moon, falls. Then count that Navamsa from Mesha, the figure so obtained represents the term of years the mother of the person lives. The time so obtained has to be doubled if the lord of that Navamsa is retrograde or *Vakra*. If this lord is *Ativakra*, the time has to be trebled. When the lord of that Navamsa occupies his own house, or Navamsa, or Vargottama, the time must be trebled. If a benefic aspects such a retrograde lord, then the number of years must be quadrapled Venkatesa has made no reference to exaltation or Mula-thrikona. By general principles they will also produce a quadraple of age indicated by the Navamsa gained. Take an example. Suppose the 4th house is the strongest amongst the Rasi, the lord of the 4th and the lord of mother Moon·

Then ascertain in what Navamsa it falls. Say it falls in Vrischika Navamsa; Vrischika is the 8th from Mesha. The lord of
this is Kuja. If Kuja is Vakra (retrograde) then the mother gets
double the number of years indicated by the Navamsa that is
8x2 = 16 years. If Kuja is *Ativakra* deep retrograde, then it
must be multiplied by 3. Thus we shall have $8 \times 3 = 24$ years
If this Vakra Kuja possesses the aspect of benefics, the mother will
live up to 8x4 = 32 years. Similarly other results must be ascertained. The Sun and Moon have no Vakra state. The other five
planets have Vakra. There are 8 varieties of Vakra movements
mentioned in Suryasiddhanta (see St 12, in Sphutadhi Kara
Suryasiddhanta with Ranganatha's commentaries P. 64).

They are (1), Vakra (2) Anuvakra, (3) Kutila. These three
states are classed as retrograde.

(4) Manda (5) Manda Tara (6) Sama (7) Sighra and (8)
Sighra Tara. Thus we have no mention of the *Ativakra* in it
The last five states are classified as falling under *Rujugate.*
This means that the planet is freed from Vakra state, turns back
again and begins to move in the usual direction. It is difficult
to see why Venkatesa should use a word which is not found in the
revered work of Suryasiddhanta. When so many complications
are given in the valuable texts by eminent authors, it is really
very funny to see the common run of Astrologers making
predictions without the slightest knowledge of these advanced
principles. Combination and proper Government and public
encouragement and patronage should be given. These have
become things of the past and so also profundity of knowledge
in the astrological sciences.

The mathematical portion of astrology should not be
neglected. When predictions are made without exactly knowing
the real sources of strength of the planets, constellations and
Zodiacal signs or houses, there can never be a certainty as to
the correctness of the inferences. Care and prudence coupled

with intelligence and devotion will enable a man to achieve success in any Department. 538-539-540.

Stanzas 541 to 550 inclusive.

If the 4th is combined with a malefic, or its lord has evil aspect, or if it lies between malefics, the person will be a cheat. 541.

If the 4th is combined with Sani, Kuja or Rahu, without benefics, and if the lord of the 10th is an evil planet and occupies the 4th with evil aspects, the person will be dishonest. 542.

If the lord of the 4th joins Sani, Mandi, or Rahu, and is conjoined with or aspected by malefics, the heart will be rotten. 543.

If the lord of the 8th with a malefic joins the 4th aspected by evil planet and if the 4th is unaspected by benefics, and combined with a malefic, the person will be a dissimilator. 544.

If the 4th is occupied by the Sun and weak Moon, the person will have dishonesty for a short time but will be alright afterwards. 545.

If the 4th happens to be in exaltation or friendly house for a benefic, or if it is a beneficial sign, the person will be straight-forward. 546

If the lord of the 4th is powerful and joins Gopura etc., or occupies his own or friendly Amsa, the person will be clean hearted. 547.

If the lord of the birth is in the 4th, or joins with or aspected by benefics and is in Paravata, etc., the heart will be clean. 548.

If the birth is combined with Guru and Sukra, or if a benefic is in the 4th and its lord joins a good planet, the person will have a clean mind. 549.

If the 4th house is occupied by Rahu having evil aspects, the person will put on an outer appearance of purity of heart, but it will be rotten within. If the evil planets occupy the 4th as a beneficial sign, the honesty will be external   550.

NOTES.

If a bad planet joins the 4th house or the lord of the 4th has evil aspect or if the 4th house is hemmed in between two evil planets, the person will have *Hrit Kapatya   Hrit* in Sanskrit means heart and *Kapatya* means deception   The person will feel one thing at heart and will do or speak out another thing with a view to deceive people or take undue advantage of their position. This means in plain language that he will have a bad heart and will be a cheat, or dishonest fellow. When the lord of the 4th produces rottenness of heart by the aspect of an evil planet he will certainly produce this in a more intensified form when an evil planet conjoins him. Degrees of rottenness of heart must be guaged by the evil nature of the planet, and the house. Suppose Makara happens to be the 4th house and two evil planets Sani and Kuja are in Kumbha and Dhanus respectively, and Meena happens to be the 4th house, and Sani and Kuja occupy Kumbha and Mesha respectively, the reader must make a difference in these two sets of conjunctions. Makara is an evil sign, and Kuja falls in the 12th (*Dhanas*) and San occupies the 2nd Kumbha. But Meena is an auspicious house and Kuja in Mesha and Sani in Kumbha, are in their Moolathrekonas. The first conjunction produces more rottenness of heart than the 2nd and all these shades of differences should be particularly noted. A man with a bad heart is an undesirable person from every point of view. 541.

If Sani, Rahu or Kuja occupy the 4th without beneficial conjunctions, and if the lord of the 10th being an evil planet occupies the 4th with evil aspects, the person will have a rotten' or unclean heart. Suppose there are beneficial conjunctions or aspects, then the evil will he minimised. Suppose the evil planets are exalted, or debililated, it may be questioned whether they make any difference.

The exalted evil planets, will not produce such bad hearts as the delibilated evil planets. Evil planets in their own houses will decrease the evil while they increase it when they are in unfriendly houses. Position, conjunction and aspect increase or decrease the efficacy of planets influence and these sources of strength and weakness should never be lost sight of Suppose the lord of the 10th is a benefic, and occupies the 4th aspected be evil planets, then there will be some dissimulation or badness of heart. 542.

Mandi is the son of Manda or Sani and is considered to be even more malicious than his father, who is the most inauspicious among the seven planets. If the lord of the 4th is in conjunction with Sani, Mandi or Rahu and other malefics aspect or join him, the person will have a bad heart. (See notes on p. p. 69—70). Mandi is made by Venkatasa to be quite a different planet from Sanisuta who is called Gulika. The names of Mandi given in stanza 75 are Mandi, Yamatmaja, Prana Hora, and Atipapi. I shall try to deal with this question in my Appendix. The details as regards finding out and fixing Mandi on each day are given in my notes on Stanza 45, Page 49. Not only should the lord of the 4th join any one of these evil planets but that he must also have the conjunction or aspect of other malefic planets. The lord of the 4th may join Rahu and be aspected by Sani, Kuja or Kshina Chandra, and produce unclean heart.

The heart exerts the greatest influence on the whole body and the enclosed nervous system, and where it is bad, the whole range of thought in man takes a perverted and selfish turn which is very prejudicial to society and business and which takes away happiness from its surroundings. Where you do not know the heart of man or where it is bad, then he becomes a dangerous person and society suffers from his evil deeds and evil example. **543.**

When the 4th house is combined by the lord of the 8th with another malefic possessing malefic aspect or if the 4th is combined by a malefic, without beneficial aspects, the person will be guilty of dissimulation. Dissimulation in a man is a dangerous quality and leads to very serious consequences.

These smooth faced villains can do more mischief by ingratiating themselves into the favours of innocent and confiding people, then those bad characters who openly say so and put the other men on their guard. The lords of the 6th, 8th and 12th are always bad and these houses themselves are called *Dusthanas* or evil houses. Even here some nice distinctions must be made, and ordinary intelligence prompts men to see to these delicate differences. Suppose the lord of 8th is a benefic, in conjunction with a matefic in exaltation and aspected by another evil planet and combines in the 4th and suppose the lord of the 8th is a malefic, combined with another malefic in debilitation and aspected by malefic in unfriendly house, would there be any difference between these two sets of combinations? Certainly there must be some differences and the reader should note all such conjunctions and conditions of planets. 544.

When the 4th house is occupied by the Sun and weak Moon, the badness of the heart will be for a short time. This apparently means that the man will be bad for a short time and afterwards will repent for his rottenness of heart and think and act better. There are many men like this. If the Sun is exalted even this temporary badness must not be predicted. When the Moon is exalted, evil should not be predicted on any large scale. When the Moon joins the Sun he must be always weak 545.

Planets, constellations and Zodiacal signs add to or take

away from the strength of the combined influences and these should be carefully noted. If the 4th house happens to be the friendly sign or sign of exaltation for a benefic or if it happens to be a beneficial sign, the person will be straightforward. Take Dhanas as Lagna. The 4th is Meena, and it is a beneficial sign and also the house of exaltation for Venus or Sukra, and therefore, has a tendency to make the man straightforward. If Mesha is Lagna, then the 4th is Kataka. This is also the house of exaltation for Guru and therefore is good for making the heart pure But suppose the lord of Kataka, Chandra is in debilitation or weak state, then it may be presumed that he will be treated as a bad planet and the house also as bad as it belongs to a malefic. But as it invariably happens to be the house of exaltation for Guru, it produces moral strength to heart.

It is a great blessing for a man to be honest and straightforward and if he really possesses these admirable qualities, he will approach the Divine in proportion to the extent to which he puts them into action. 546.

The original says *Hridayasay Balanvilay*. This means that the lord of the 4th must be powerful. I have already hinted that the lord of the 4th even when he happens to be a bad planet, will produce good if he is well situated, exalted, or joins good Amsas and Vergas. His joining Gopura, or Paravata or Parijata Amsas is good. Even when the lord of the 4th occupies friendly or his own Amsas, he produces goodness of heart. A clean heart is a great blessing and every one should try to secure this blessing by steady practice and moral reading. 547.

When the 4th house is combined by the lord of the birth, or when the lord of the birth has the conjunction or the aspect of benefics or when he joins Paravatamsa, etc., the heart of the person will be pure. Here the strength of the birth lord has much influence in giving a good *heart* to the person. 548.

Clean mind must always be attributed to good heart. But

it is possible to make some distinction between heart and mind. A man may have good heart but may be weak-minded. Mental strength is apparently different. Take a man who is very sympathetic, charitable and generous, but his mind may be unclean by being engaged in adultery, drinking or gambling. Many drunkards are known to be very charitaole people and so also many adulterers, male and female. But if a man possesses a clean mind he must invariably possess a good heart. Cleanliness is next to godliness and a really clean moral mind will be a great boon to society and to the person who possesses it. The author introduces the readers to combinations productive of clean minds. If Guru and Sukra join birth or if a benefic occupies the 4th house, or if the lord of the 4th has beneficial conjunction, the person will have a clean mind. Mental purity is a difficult thing and all Shastras and Vedas give injunctions to achieve this purity.

Yogasastra leads to mental purity and then to final emancipation. *Yogaschitta Vritti Nirodhahu.* The object of Yoga is to attach the mind to Godly essence and purge it from all worldly grossness and concerns. 549.

If Rahu combines in the 4th house aspected by evil planets, it will make the man put on an external appearance of purity in heart, but he will be really bad inside.

If the 4th happens to be a beneficial sign and is occupied by evil planet, the honesty will be external. There are many belonging to this section and their professions of charity and religiousness are all meshes to gain their selfish ends. Suppose the 4th is an evil sign and a benefic is in it, then the result must be similar. 550.

Men are seen in great varieties, in their physical, educational, mental, intellectual, moral and religious planes. Their development in these phases furnish endless lessons for an observant mind. The student of human life is ever baffled in his attempts to systematise human frauds or human generosities. The most valuable, the most instructive, the most interesting and the most difficult study for man is his own self and the lives of human creatures who are surrounding him. In his pride and ignorance, he often deceives himself, cheats others and is often deceived by others. This chapter gives invaluable hints to find out the human heart, and how it will be inclined towards the terrestrial and celestial phenomena at the time of its birth. These suggestions will be of immense benefit to the student of psychology, physiology, law, politics, and morality, and will enable mankind to find out their defects and improve their minds and hence directly improve their position here, and evolution into a higher state hereafter. When we find a boy inclined to do evil or be dishonest by the planetary conjunctions at the time of his birth, it should be the duty of every person interested in the welfare and progress of that child, to do his best and make him adopt a course which would completely combat the evil and eventually produce good.

Stanzas 551 to 560 inclusive.

If the lords of the 1st and 4th are friendly, having beneficial conjunctions or aspects, there will be maternal love and friendship 551.

If the lord of the 4th aspected by the birth lord, conjoins a Kendra, combined with or aspected by a benefic, the person will have maternal love. 552.

If Buda becomes the lord of the 1st and 4th, having malefic conjunction or aspect, there will be enmity between the mother and the person. 553.

If the lord of the 4th is powerful and the 4th is strong and aspected by a benefic, there will be conveyances. 554.

Sweet scents, fine clothes, ornaments, and conveyances must

be ascertained with reference to Sukra or by the strength of the 4th house. If the lord of the 4th with Chandra and the lord of the birth combines in Lagna, the person will have horses. 555.

If the lord of the 4th joins Sukra and occupies Lagna. he will have conveyances carried on the shoulders of men. If the lord of the 4th joins Guru and occupies the birth, the person will have *Chaturanga yanas,* 556.

If the birth or the lord of the 4th is combined with Chandra Sukra and Guru when these three planets are not in debilitation, unfriendly houses, combustion, etc., the person will have three conveyances. 557.

When the lord of the 4th occupies the 9th, Guru and Sukra combined in the 4th and the lord of the 9th joins Konas, or Kendras, tbe person will have ornaments, clothes, conveyances and other articles of comfort from many countries. 558.

If the lord of the 4th combines with the lord of the 9th, possesses good sources of power, aspected by Guru, joins the birth or his own house, or house of exaltation, or houses of thrikona, the person will get conveyances, wealth and other com- forts through the royal favour or through his dependency on the palace. 559.

If the lords of the 1st, 4th and 9th are not in combustion, etc., and occupy the 10th house, and the lord of the 10th com- bines in the birth, the person will have political power which secures him a throne or Simhasana. 560.

NOTES.

These Stanzas are not very difficult and can easily be understood with a little patience. The lord of the 1st and 4th must be friendly to ensure love and friendship with the mother. There are some Lagnas whcse 4th lords are friendly to the lords

of the birth while others are not so. This is Nisargika or permanent friendship. Take Mesha as Lagna. The 4th is Kataka
and the lords of Mesha and Kataka, *viz*, Kuja and Chandra are
friends. Take Vrisbabha. The 4th is Simha. The lords of these
two, *viz*. Sukra and Ravi are bitter enemies. But the reader must
also look to the temporary friendship (See notes on Brihatjataka ch. II Sts 15-16-17, see also Sts 105 of P 91 of this
book). The lords of the 1st and 4th must not only be friendly but
must also have beneficial conjunctions or aspects to ensure love
between the man and his mother. 551.

The lord of the 4th possessing the aspect of the lord of
birth, joins any Kendra having beneficial conjunctions or aspects,
there will be maternal love.

The lord of the 4th must be in a Kendra, have the aspect of
the lord of birth and also beneficial conjunction or aspect to give
love and friendship with mother. 552.

Buda must become lord of the birth and 4th and be can become so only for Mitheena Lagna, and if such Buda has malefic
conjunction or aspect, there will be enmity between the man and
his mother. Generally mother is the most lovable object in
nature and mother's love to children is proverbial. But as the
children grow older and have personal and marital interests to
look after, they grow indifferent to their mother. Sometimes
this maternal attachment dies and gives rise to great bitterness
of feeling and even open acts of hostility and injury. 553.

Now the author takes the reader to the possession of conveyances, horses and other ornaments and furniture. The 4th
house as well as its lord must be powerful, possessing beneficial
aspects to get the man conveyances. Majority of the people are
without these luxuries. But there are many and some of them
develop a taste and hankering for conveyances and horses, camels,
elephants, etc., that they will spend any amount for such
purposes. 554.

The strength of Sukra or the strength of the 4th house furnishes clue to the possession of scents, ornaments, furniture, clothing and other objects of necessity and luxury. When Sukra is well situated and when the 4th house is powerful, the man will possess all these objects· Where he is bad and the 4th house is weak, these objects go away from him and the man will be without them. The possession of horses has been considered to be a fortune, which is generally envied by mankind. The lord of the 4th, birth and Chandra, must join together in Lagna to give the man horses, Suppose these are debilitated or weak, the person will have jaded or dying horses. But if they are strong and exalted, possessing beneficial conjunctions or aspects, the person will have spirited, lovely and splendid horses! There is much difference in all such matters. 555.

Naravahana means one who gets palanquins, tomjons, etc., usually carried by men on their shoulders. Dholies are carried by men and so also some baskets by the hill tribes· There are some who take pleasure in such means of conveyances. There are some people who would like to be carried on the shoulders of men. Lord of the 4th and Sukra must be combined in Lagna to get him palanquins, etc. But if the lord of the 4th joins Guru and occupies Lagna, the person will have conveyances carried by *Chaturanya* or the men, camels, horses and elephants. Some ride on these in suitable devices· There are howdas on elephants, palanquins for men, saddles, etc., for horses, and some sort of saddle for camels. 556.

When Chandra, Sukra and Guru are not in debilitation or unfriendly houses, or in combustion, and join the birth or the lord of the 4th, there will be three conveyances. A planet may not be in debilitation but be may not be in exaltation· But suppose one of these is exalted, and the other is in his own house as in Kataka, there will be more than three carriages or conveyances. 557.

There are some people who are fond of indigenous manu. factures while there are others who are extremely fond of foreign articles. They spend a lot of money and take great pains to collect articles of value from the remotest parts of the world. There must be Guru and Sukra in the 4th, the lord of 4th must be in the 9th and the lord of the 9th must join a Kona or 5th or 9th or a Kendra, 1-4-7-10, to enable a person to get ornaments, clothes, conveyances, furniture, and other articles of comfort and luxury from foreign countries. 558.

There are some who would never condescend to work under a King or a ruler, and whose independent spirit keeps them away from the royal personages, while there are many who are willing to sell their principles, liberty, wives or sisters to get royal favour and the favour of the richer clssses. There must be a conjunction of the lord of the 4th and 9th. They must be powerful and aspected by Guru. These must be in the birth or the house of the lord of the 4th, or in his house of exaltation, or thrikona. Then the person will get wealth, ornaments, houses, etc.· from royal patronage, or by his dependency upon the palace, That is he will be a dependent or servant in the palace and by his conduct or attraction to the royalry, he will get these advant. ages. 559.

The lords of the birth, 4th and 9th should have no combus. tion and must occupy the 10th house while the lord of the 10th must be in the birth, to enable the person to sit on a throne and wield political power, making him a throned monarch or ruler. The strength and value of the throne depends upon the strength of these three lords and the exaltations and beneficial conjunctions and aspects they possess. The throne is called simhasana, for it is made to resemble a seat, born on the heads of lions. 560.

Stanzas 561 to 570.

If the lords of the 4th and 9th join the 4th house or aspect it, combining in Viseshikamsa or being powerful, the person will possess carriages fitted up with all sorts of luxuries and also have many other desirable objects. 561.

If the lord of the 4th being a benefic occupies 6th, 8th or 12th or is in deep combustion aspected by the lord of the 9th, the person will have undesirable carriages or ricketty ones. 562.

If the lord of Lagna occupies the 11th from the lord of the 9th and the lord of the 4th joins the 9th house, the person will command many troops and possess, wealth, ornaments, conveyances and other articles from different parts of the world and many countries. 563.

If the lord of Lagna occupies the 4th, 9th or 11th, the person will have numberless carriages and become a famous man. If the lord of the 4th joins any Kendra from Lagna and the lord of that Kendra occupies the 11th from Lagna, the person will have many conveyances. 564.

If the lord of the Lagna is in the 10th and the lord of the 10th is in Lagna, the person will command many carriages.

When the lord of the 4th occupies the 10th, and more than two planets join the 9th house, the person will be master or lord of weapons, horses and treasure houses. 565.

If the lord of the 4th being powerful joins the 11th house, or joins the 4th house with Kuja, or if the lord of the 4th occupies the signs of Kuja, the person will have Rajya, wealth, happiness, jewels, conveyances and other objects. 566.

When the powerful lord of the 4th occupies the 4th or the Lagna, there is a benefic in exaltation in the 9th, and the lord of the 2nd combines in a Kendra, the person will ascend a throne. 567.

When all the benefics are in Kendras and all the malefics occupy the 3rd, 6th and 11th houses, the person will have a high position. If the lord of Lagna occupies the 12th, the person will live in a foreign country. 568.

If the lords of the 4th joins the 8th, the person will acquire a house himself. When the lords of the 4th and 10th occupy the 2nd and the lord of *Vahanas* joins exaltation, the person will be commander of conveyances or horses. 569.

If the lord of the 11th joins the 4th aspected by the lord of the 10th or birth, the person will be commander of Vahanas. 570.

NOTES.

The powerful lords of the 4th and 9th should occupy the 4th, joining Viseshikamsa, or aspecting the 4th to make the person possess the latest fashionable carriages and other desirable articles of comfort. 561.

When the lord of the 4th becomes a benefic, and occupies 6th, 8th or 12th or is in deep combustion possessing the aspect of the lord of the 9th, the person will possess shaky or useless carriages. Deep combustion means any planet within 10 degrees of the sun. 562.

The lord of the 9th joins some house. The lord of Lagna must be in the 11th house from him. The lord of the 4th houses must be in the 9th house. Then the person will command many troops, wealth, ornaments, conveyances and lands. This means a Rajayoga to make the man master of many countries or districts. 563.

When the 4th, 9th or 11th is occupied by the birth lord, the person will have numberless carriages. The reader must not make mistakes. To possess numberless carriages the person must be a king or a big millionaire. When the lord of Lagna is exalted and is otherwise powerful in occupying any of these houses, he will give many carriages. The lord of the 4th must be in a Kendra from Lagna, and the lord of this Kendra must be in the 11th house from Lagna to give the man many carriages and horses. 564.

The lords of 1st and 10th must exchange their houses to give him many carriages.

There must be more than two planets in the 9th, and the lord of the 4th should occupy the 10th to make the person master or commander of weapons, horses and treasure houses. 565.

The powerful lord of the 4th should be in the 11th house, or if he joins the 4th house with Kuja or combines in the houses of Kuja, *vis.*, Mesha or Vrischika, to give the man territory, wealth, happiness, etc.

This means that he becomes a king or kinglike personage. 566.

If the lord of 4th is in it or in Lagna and the 9th is occupied by a benefic in exaltation, with the lord of the 2nd in Kendra, the person will ascend a throne. He becomes a throned monarch. 567.

If all the benefics, Guru, Sukra and Buda are in Kendras and all the malefics occupy 3rd, 6th and 11th, they will raise the man to great position, politically and financially. 568.

If the lord of the 4th occupies the 8th, the houses will be self-acquired. If the lords of the 4th and 10th are in the 2nd house, and Sukra (lord of carriages) is exalted, the person will be commander of carriages and horses. 569.

If the lord of the 11th and the 4th are in conjunction aspected by the lord of 10th or birth, the person will be commander of carriages and horses.

The dignity of this office varies with the power of the planets and the strength of the houses mentioned by the author. Beneficial aspects and conjunctions will add a great deal to increase the position while malevolent conjunctions and aspects take away from their efficiency. 570.

Stanzas 571 to 588 inclusive.

If the lords of the 1st, 4th, and 9th occupy mutually Kendras from each other, when the lord of Lagna is powerful, the person will be master or commander of vehicles. 571.

If the powerful lord of the 4th joining Gopuramsa, etc., is aspected by the lords of the 11th, 10th and 9th, the person will command many conveyances. 572.

When the lord of the 9th, joining Kendras, occupies exaltation Amsa, etc., and two other planets are in exaltation, the person will command or possess many countries and conveyances. 573.

If the lord of the 12th joins the lord of the 2nd occupying his exaltation and aspected by the lord of the 9th, the person will be master of many conveyances. 574.

If the lord of the 10th with the lord of the 11th occupies the 4th or if he combines with the lord of the 9th, the person will have many carriages and countries. 575.

It the 10th is occupied by an exalted planet aspected by the lord of the birth or the 9th, the person will be master of many conveyances. 576.

If the lords of the 10th and the 4th joining Simhasanamsa are aspected by the lord of the birth, the person will have many lands and carriages. 577.

If the lords of the 9th, 10th and 4th are found in the 4th, 2nd and 3rd houses, with a benefic in the 8th house, the person will have strength, wealth, and *Vahanams.* 578.

If the lord of the 4th joins exaltation and the lord of *that* house is in Kendras or Konas, and an exalted planet is in the 4th house, without any planet in the 12th, the person will have 8 carriages. 579.

If Sukra joins Paramocha Navamsa and the lord of the 10th occupies the 4th, the person will have music and other appurtenances in his house *(Vadyaghoshadi).* 580.

When the lord of the 9th is in 4th and the lord of a Kendra occupies a Kona, while the lord of the 10th joins the 4th, the person will have four kinds of music in the house *Sankhadi Chaturvidha Vadyas.* 581.

When the lord of the 10th with Chandra joins a Kendra in conjunction with a benefic, while the lord of Lagna is found in an *upachveya*, there will be music of *Panavadi*. 582.

If exalted evil planets occupy the 10th, 9th, and the 1st, aspected by the lord of Lagna, the person will have sorrow in the end from carriages 583.

If the lords of the 7th, 6th, 3rd, 4th, 9th, 1st and 12th houses join the lord of the 5th, he will have countless *Ghosha Desa* 584.

When the 4th house is combined with a benefic, the lord of the 4th joins a Kendra or Kona from Lagna or his exaltation, and the lord of the 9th joins his deep exaltation Amsa, the person will have happiness, agreeable music and other works of opulence. 585.

When the lords of the 10th and 11th occupy 4th, and Lagna is aspected by a benefic, the person will have many kinds of musical appurtenances. 586.

The person who is born in Rajayoga and the person whose lord of the 10th occupies the 4th, will have all sorts of music appertaining to royalty or aristocracy. 587.

Srivenkatasa has explained the Bhavas of the 3rd and 4th houses with a careful consideration of the strength and weakness of the planets and the sources of power or influence arising from beneficial conjunctions and aspects in accordance with the principles of Astrology propounded by the ancient Maha Rishis. 588.

NOTES.

When the lords of the 1st, 4th and 9th are mutually occupying Kendras from each other, and the lord of birth is strong, the man will be lord of vehicles. Vahana in Sanskrit means any convey-ance and this includes, Aswa Vahana, horse, Gajee Vahana elephant, Vrishbha Vahana, bull, Yana or conveyance carried by men, and carts and carriages of any other description. He will possess many of these carriages or will be a commander over them. 571.

The lords of the 9th, 10th and 11th must aspect the powerful lord of the 4th, when he joins Gopuramsa, etc., to make him master of many carriages. The carriages may be his own or he may be commander of them for the benefit of another King or Prince under whom he may be an officer, Civil or Military. As *Adi* is used after Gopura any other good vergas will confer the same good luck. 572.

The lord of the 9th must be in a Kendra from Lagna, and must occupy an exalted Navamsa, and if two more planets are in exaltation, the person will be master of many countries and carriages. This can only happen when the person is a King or a Ruler. 573.

The lord of the 12th, being in exaltation must join the lord of the 2nd and possess the aspect of the lord of the 9th to give the man many conveyances. 574.

If the lords of the 10th and 11th occupy the 4th in conjunction, or if the lord of the 10th conjoins the lord of the 9th, the person will have many countries and carriages The possession of various sorts of conveyances always give the man a high social and political status and if they are very large in number, they would make him a monarch or ruler. Kings alone possess many carriages and horses and they will wield good political power. 575.

When an exalted planet occupies the 10th aspected by the lord of Lagna or by the lord of the 9th, the person will command many carriages and horses Among the ancients, the possession of Rathas (chariots,) padatties (infantry) Aswas horses and Gajas elephants, gave them high rank and Kings or Ministers and commanders of high rank kept these in their establishments. 576.

The lords of the 4th and 10th should join Simhasanamsa aspected by the lord of the birth to give the man many lands and carriages.

If they are very strong and possess beneficial conjunctions and aspects, the person will be a ruler or King and will have several countries under him and possess also many conveyances. 577.

Here the verse must be properly understood. The author seems to mean that the lord of the 9th must be in the 4th, the lord of the 10th must be in the 2nd, and the lord of the 4th must be in the 3rd, and a benefic occupy the 8th house, the person will be strong, rich, and possessor of many conveyances. This seems to be a special conjunction and all the conditions laid down here must be present. But even when the planets are so, there are differences in their power. They may be exalted, debilitated, in friendly or unfriendly houses and so forth. All these make differences in the number of carriages as well as their condition and value. 578.

The lord of the 4th must be in exaltation, there must be an exalted planet in the 4th. and the lord of the house of exaltation of the 4th lord must be in a Kendra or Kona from the Lagna and there must be no planet in the 12th, then the person will possess many carriages Take an illustration. Here Lagna is Mesha and the lord of the 4th is Chandra and he is exalted in Vrishabha. The 4th house is occupied by Guru in exaltation The lord of the house of exaltation of the 4th lord Chandra is Sukra.

Lagna	Chandra	
		Guru
	RASI	
		Sukra
Kuja	Sani	Ravi Buda

Chandra is exalted in Vrishabha and Sukra is its lord. Sukra now must be in Kendras or Konas and here he is in the 5th from Lagna, a Kona. The 12th house is without any planet. This conjunction gives the man many conveyances. 579.

Sukra must be in his Navamsa of deep exaltation, and the lord of the 10th occupies 4th house from Lagna, there will be a musical department attached to his house. Among the ancient Monarchs, Statesmen, Matadhipatties and other men of political or religious distinction, there invariably existed many musicians and drummers who had to play on their instruments at stated hour s. This holds good even unto this day among the rulers and religious heads in India. Such instruments are *Mela, Nagara, Bhuri, Dakna, Nowbit, Kihila, Sankhi, Panava, Gomakha, etc.* "The musical instruments are classified under 4 varieties, *viz., Tanti* (strings) *Annidha* (drums, etc., having skins) *Sushira* (pipes, flutes and other instruments having holes) and *Ghana* (cymbols, etc., made of metals.) (See Amara Kosa Natyaverga 1st Canto. Sts. 185 to 189.) The classification is highly comprehensive. *Tanti* means a string and all such instruments where strings are used come under this head. *Annatha* means a hide or skin and all such musical instruments which have skins in them come under this head. *Sushira* means holes and such instruments as pipes, bugles, flutes, clarionets fall under this heading *Gana* comprises metals, silver, bell metal, etc., and all such instruments which are made of metals come under this classification.

The possession of these Vadyas or musical instruments indicates high rank and political or religious distinction and the students should be careful in making their predictions about them. 580.

In the Bhagavadgita we find *Sankhas,* conch shells playing an important part in giving signals about the commencement of the war and also of the presence of particular warriors. These must have been huge conch shells of particular descriptions, and producing terrific sounds which had the effect of intimidating and causing fear among the opposing army. *Panchijinya* was the Sankha used by Sri Krishna while Deva Datta was the bugle

Sankha of Arjuna.   Even in the softer music of the present day,
these conch shells are often used by special experts in the mani-
pulations of Krities and Pallavies and have their own value.

In all parts of India *Sankha Dhvani* or the sounds emanating from conch shell are considered necessary in religious worship
and religious processions, and there are very clever experts in
using them and producing good musical effects from them.   The
lord of the 9th must be in the 4th and the lord of a Kendra must
be in a Kona.   The lord of the 10th must also be in the 4th.
Then the person will have the four kinds of musical instruments
which have already been mentioned in the previous notes.

The development of music in India from the remotest times,
has been of a very high standard and the Goddess of learning
Saraswati is painted and described with a Veena (Lute) in her
hand. A more perfect musical instrument has yet to be invented
Those who are familiar with this wonderful instrumental music
can bear undoubted testimony both as regards its completeness
as an instrument and also as regards its capacity to produce the
softest musical touches which man can conceive of.   581.

When the lord of the 10th, with Chandra and another benefic
joins a Kendra while the lord of Lagna is in an Oopachaya, he
will have musical instruments.   Oopachayas are 3, 6, 10 and 11,
Panava seems to be a variety among the bugles.   582.

The 1st, 9th and 10th must be occupied by exalted evil
planets aspected by the lord of
Lagna to produce sorrow in the
end from carriages. This can
happen only in a few cases· Take
an example, Venkatasa seems to
be entirely wrong in this conjunction as it never can happen. He
wants 3 evil planets to be exalted
and their houses of exaltation
will be Mesha, Thula and Makara, for Ravi, Sani and Kuja

respectively. Kshina Chandra and weak Buda may also be considered as evil for certain purposes. If Mesha is Lagna, then Ravi can be there and Kuja can be in Makara and being Lagnadhipathi, he aspects both Lagna and the evil planet Ravi there. But how can we get an evil planet exalted in the 9th. Take Thula, Sani can be in Lagna, but there can be no exaltations for Kuja and Ravi in the 9th and 10th houses. Take Makara as I have given here. Then there are 3 evil planets exalted in 1st, 9th and 10th, v'z., Kuja, Buda and Sani respectively but you cannot get the lord of Lagna Sani to aspect the other planets. As the verse stands, the author wants three evil planets to be exalted in the 1st, 9th and 10th aspected by the lord of Lagna, and I fail to see how such a conjunction could ever be conceived. This is a clear mistake. Probably the author might have meant that any one of the three evil planets, occupying any one of these houses aspected by the lord of Lagna, would produce the evil result he has predicted. The students are requested to carefully consider this conjunction and its possibility. 583.

When the lords of the 1st, 3rd, 4th, 7th, 6th, 9th and 12th join the lord of the 5th, the person will have countless Ghosha Desas. *Ghosha* means a cowherd and a shepherd; also it means Simshasana. The person may have a throne which commands many countries or he may command many districts where cowherds and shepherds are plentiful. This in simple language means he will be a ruler over many provinces. 584.

There must be a benefic in the 4th house, its lord must be in a Kendra or Kona from Lagna, or he must be in his exaltation and the lord of the 9th must be in his exalted Navamsa, to enable the person to secure happiness, agreeable music, and other appurtenances which mark the royal or aristocratic positions. 585.

When the lords of the 10th and 11th occupy the 4th house, with a beneficial aspect for the Lagna, the person will have many kinds of musical departments. Suppose the lords of the 10th

and 11th are weak and the 4th happens to be an evil sign, then
the value of the combination is considerably lessened. If they
are exalted or beneficially conjoined or aspected they give high
value to these objects.   Combustion, unfriendly houses, evil conjunctions and aspects take away a great deal from their effici·
ency. 586.

There are many Rajayogas mentioned in this work and if one
is born under them, other conjunctions need not be consulted.
Political power gives the possession of certain articles or objects
without which the power can never exist. A man cannot be called
a ruler unless he has a Kingdom to rule. A person cannot be
called wealthy unless he has plenty of money. The author therefore directs the reader to remember these facts. If a person is
born in a Rajayoga and becomes a King, then it is unnecessary
to examine, whether he will have a palace, troops, servants, carriages, horses, money, etc., as without them he could not become a
real ruler. Some kings may have a great love for certain articles
while others may not have. But all the same, some parapharnalia necessary for royalty must be there·

When the lord of the 10th occupies the 4th, the person will
have all paraphernalia belonging
to high personages. Here the
lord of the 10th is Chandra and
he occupies the 4th and the lord
of the 4th Sani occupies the 10th.
This gave the person·great position and he had all the paraphernalia of distinguished position. 587.

The author now concludes the
3rd and 4th *Bhavas* (houses with

Sukra	Guru		
Ravi Buda			Sani
Chandra			Kethu
	Kuja	Lagna	

signification) by a few remarks. He says that he has carefully
studied the ancient works left by the Maha Rishis, has compared
all the sources of strength and weakness for planets, and houses

by beneficial conjunctions and aspects and by evil conjunctions and aspects, has analysed the principles of astrology and has composed this work for the benefit of his fellow subjects. He does not claim any originality and he is modest enough to say that he has compared carefully all the astrological works available during his time. The reader will certainly agree with his statement and feels that Venkatasa has done his best in epitomising the grand works of ancient writers, and put the principles of astrology in as concise and clear a form as an intelligent and learned scholar can do. His language is happy and he is never confused in the explanations he gives for the benefit of his readers. 588.

End of Chapter IV.

Suta Bhava

HOUSE OF CHILDREN, ETC.

From the 5th house, the prosperity of children, *Mantras*, intelligence of father, *Atmavidya Hridayodara Pradasa* and discriminating power will have to be determined by the clever Astrologers. 589.

The prosperity or otherwise of Children will have to be determined from the lord of the 7th, 5th and 9th and also from Guru lord of children. Intelligence has to be examined with reference to Buda and Chandra. For the father and his intelligence and position, etc., it has to be determined from the 5th and 9th houses and also from Ravi 590.

If the Sun occupies the 5th house, the father will die, and if the Moon occupies the 5th, the mother will die. If the lord of the 5th or the 5th house, joins a benefic and has beneficial conjunctions or aspects, the man will have issues. 591.

If the 5th house, or its lord or Guru (lord of Children or Putrakaraka) has beneficial conjunction or aspect, there will be children. 592.

If the lord of Lagna joins the 5th house, if the lord of the 5th is strong, and Guru is all powerful. the man will undoubtedly get children. 593.

If Guru becomes the lord of the 5th house, being all powerful, aspected by the lord of Lagna, the person will certainly have children. 594.

If the lord of the 1st and 5th join in one house, or have mutual aspects or join their own, friendly or exalted houses, the person will have children. 595.

If the lords of the 1st and 5th with a benefic combine in a Kendra when the lord of 2nd is strong, there will be children. 596.

If the lord of the Navamsa falling in the Bhava occupied by the lord of the 7th is aspected by the lords of the 9th, 1st and 2nd, the person will have progeny. 597.

If the lord of the Navamsa occupied by the lord of the 5th joins a benefic, or joins the 5th house with a benefic there will certainly be children. 598.

If the lord of Lagna joins the 7th house, and the lord of the 9th also joins the 7th, and if the lord of the 2nd combines in Lagna, the man will have children. 599.

NOTES.

Conjunctions of planets which give children and prosperity to them have been named in the above 9 stanzas, and these must be read with the greatest care. Each Bhava is useful and important in its own way and no one should be neglected. But there are some Bhavas apparently more important than others and the whole world is agreed in the proposition that man must have children and without them his life will be dreary and useless. There is the same difference between European ideas of possessing children and the notions entertained by the Aryans of India. The former looks at his children, not as a necessity, but as luxury and even some of the recognised leaders of Society and thought have published some dirty books, like fruits of Philosophy Malthusian theories and Appliances, etc , condemning the begetting of children and recommending hateful methods for their non-possession and removal.   Among the Aryans of India, the possession of children is a religious necessity and a duty, and those who have no children will be looked on with pity and contempt   Remedies are advised for begetting children.   Among the higher classes of Hindus the barren women become unfit for even preparing meals and serving food as the religiously inclined will not accept food at their hands and the meals prepared by them cannot be offered to the household gods. *Put* is a Naraka or place of punishment after death and one who Saves a man from this hell is called *Putra*   There is no salvation without a *Putra* or son and the religious significance is indeed very great. Female c h i l d r e n are equally valuable.   A real and sincere *Kanyadanam* or gift of a daughter to a holy man is said to add much merit to the family of the man, and the merit extends even to his dead ancestors.   These holy institutions have been greatly abused and people are now beginning to sell not only their daughters but there are many in the southern districts of India where without the slightest shame or degradation they sell their sons at certain rates proportionate to their educational qualifications.   These educated youths, with degrees attached to them, must be ashamed to dictate monetary terms and accept them as fees for marrying the girls.   There was formerly *Kunyasulcu,* but now there is also sprung up among certain even rich families *Varasulka.*   These practices are much to be regretted and are hateful.

Mantras are sacred hymns, taught by only qualified masters, and when practiced in the approved methods are able to give great psychic power to the practiser, and enable him to perform wonders.   These are composed of indestructable forms of sound vibrations modulated to conserve mental energy and give the man a great deal of power for good or bad as he may use it.

Atma Vidya is the knowledge which a person has to get from his Guru and by practising which he attains to final emancipation from his grosser environments. This *Vidya* or knowledge and practice will elevate the *Atma* or soul and make it to be finally incorporated in the universal Intelligence.

Hridaya means heart, Oodara means stomach or belly and Pradasa means the space. From the conjunctions mentioned in this chapter on Putra Bhava we have to find out the prospects of children, the man's intelligence, the intelligence of his father, his strength in the Mantra Vidya, the health or defects in heart and stomach, his discriminating power, his counselling or *Mantralochana* and so forth. These are important and the learned Astrologers have to consider all combinations, sources of strength and weakness and aspects of planets and houses, to make correct predictions in this Bhava. At the end of this work under *Karakateva* of Rasis, the 5th also represents Harsha or Jollity of temper, wisdom or gnana, speech, counselling or ministering power, skill or dexterity, learning, mechanical skill, and these have also to be judged from this house. 589.

To determine the prosperity and adversity of children, the author wants the reader to look to the lord of the 7th, 9th and 5th houses. Guru must also be consulted as he is the lord of children. 9th is the 5th house from the 5th from Lagna, and 7th house is the house of wife. The wife's character, disposition, wealth and education must necessarily affect her children and the author therefore refers to the lord of the 5th, 5th from the 5th and the 7th representing the wife.

Buda is the lord of intelligence and Chandra represents mind and he has to be taken into consideration in determining the intelligence of the person. Some may be highly educated but may not be intelligent, while others may be extremely intelligent without any pretentions to learning. 9th represents the house of father and the 9th from the 9th is the 5th from Lagna. Both these houses, as well as the lord of father Ravi should be considered to find out the intelligence and positions of the father. 590.

Ravi in the 5th house kills the father and Chandra in the, 5th house endangers mother's life· This is a very vague statement and must be cautiously interpreted. Suppose Mithuna is Lagna and Ravi is in Thula, 5th house· Dhanas is Lagna and Ravi is in Mesha 5th house. The same results cannot be and ought not to be predicted. When a man is born with a Ravi in the 5th in exaltation without evil aspects, the danger to the father is averted· But when Ravi is in debilitation in the 5th without beneficial aspects or conjunctions, there is danger to the father. In many cases, Ravi with malefics remains in the 5th house and the father does not die. Father means and includes only he from whose seed the child has sprung. If the mother is adulterous and the child is born to another man, while there is a nominal father, and when the 5th house is badly occupied and aspected, the paramour of the mother dies as the child is born to him leaving the registered father quite unhurt· If the 5th is occupied by Kshina Chandra or in debilitation, the mother will die. Makara is Lagna and Chandra is in Vrishabha. There will be no danger to mother.

If the lord of the 5th or the 5th house has beneficial conjunction or aspect, the person will have issues. If both of them have beneficial aspects and conjunctions there will be many issues. If Guru is also powerful, the person will have a very large number of children. There are some people who have as many as forty or fifty, and Drutharastra had one hundred and one sons by his wife Gaudhari. I have seen as many as 25 or 26 children by one wife, and special cases are recorded where as many as 47 children have been born to one man by one wife. These are remarkable cases of fecundity and are well worth examination from an Astrological point of view. 591.

When there is beneficial conjunction in the 5th house, or with the lord of the 5th or with the lord of issues, Guru, the man will get children. If there is only one conjunction, say 5th is occupied by a benefic, then he will have a few issues, if the lord of the 5th and the 5th house are beneficially combined, the children will be greater in number, and when in addition to these two, Guru is also beneficially conjoined, he will have the greatest number of children possible to have.   592.

The 5th must be combined by the lord of Lagna, and the lord of the 5th house and Guru are all powerful, the man will have children without any doubt.   593.

If strong Guru becomes the lord of the 5th house, possessing the aspect of the lord of birth, there will certainly be children. This applies only for two Lagnas, *viz.*, for Simha and Vrischika. The lords of these two houses, *viz.*, Ravi and Kuja are Gurus friends and their aspect under this special condition becomes good. Otherwise Martian conjunction or aspect is prejudicial to begetting children.   594.

If the lords of the 1st and 5th combine in one house or aspect each other, or if they join their own houses, friendly signs or exaltations, the person will beget children. The lord of the birth may also be the lord of the 2nd or lord of the 12th as in Makara and Kumbha, 1st and 10th as in Meena and Kanya, or 1st and 6th as in Vrischika and Vrishabha or 1st and 8th as in Thula and Mesha, or 1st and 4th as in Dhanas and Mithuna. The lord of the 1st and 5th may combine in any house. Their conjunction is productive of children. But the results must vary. Take the lords of Vrischika and Meena, *viz.*, Kuja and Guru. They may be in any house. Say they are in Dhanas. This is good, say they are in Makara, this is bad as Guru is debilitated, and it is good for Kuja, say they are in Vrishabha, this is bad as both of them are in unfriendly houses. In aspects the same thing holds. Suppose they occupy exaltations or debilitations. There is great difference in results.   595.

In the lords of the birth and 5th with a benefic join a Kendra from Lagna and the lord of the 2nd is powerful they will give children. 596.

The lord of the 7th occupies some Bhava. This Bhava falls necessarily in some Navamsa, as Lagna does.

If the lord of this Navamsa possesses the aspects of the 1st, 2nd and 9th, the person will have progeny. The readers must be familiar with the mathematical portions of astrology. The Bhava differs from the Rasi or sign. Take a horoscope.

The planets are roughly given in degrees. Vrishabha extends over 30° degrees, but the Lagna has fallen in the 11th degree. 15 degrees on either side will compose the Lagna and therefore, the beginning of the Lagna commences in the 26th degree in Mesha and continues up to 26th degree of Vrishabha. After the 26th

Chandra 20º Rahu 3º	Lagna 11º	Sani 2º
Ravi 3º Buda 6º Guru 22º	RASI	
Sukra 22º	Kuja 2º Kethu 3º	

degree in Vrishabha, the 2nd Bhava commences, although the Rasi extends to the 30th degree The distance between Lagna and Chandra is 21 degrees, while the distance between Lagna and Rahu is 38° degrees. This practically places Rahu in the 11th Bhava and he has given the results from that Bhava. The Lagna has fallen in the 4th Navamsa and therefore the 7th is Bhava also falls in the 4th Navamsa. The lord of the 7th Kuja and he occupies the 6th Bhava. This Bhava falls in the 4th Navamsa and it would be for Thula the 4th from it or Makara. The lord of that is Sani and if Sani is aspected by the lord of the birth, 9th and 2nd there will be children. 597.

The lord of the 5th joins some Navamsa. Take the above horoscope. The lord of the 5th is Buda and he joins Dhanur

Amsa. Its lord is Guru and he is with a benefic Buda in the Rasi diagram and he has given children, or if this lord of the Navamsa joins the 5th with a benefic, the person will have children.   598.

If the lords of the Lagna and 9th join the 7th house, or if the Lagna is combined by the lord of 2nd, the person will have children.   599.

In all these cases, the student should make a careful survey of all the forces working to produce the result and the correctness of his predictions depends upon the analysis he makes and the value he attaches to each source of strength or weakness and the cleverness with which he draws his inferences from the facts marshalled out by the astrological sciences.

Stanzas 600 to 608.

When the 5th is aspected by a malefic, the lord of the 5th combines with an evil planet and the lord of children joins the 5th house, the person will lose children.   600.

If both the lords of the two Navamsas occupied by the lords of the 2nd and 7th, are combined with malefics joining evil Navamsas, there will be loss of children.   601.

If the lord of the 5th occupies debilitation or combustion, joining cruel Navamsas, has malefic aspects, or joins Dusthas, there will be loss of children.   602.

If the lord of the Drakkana occupied by the lord of the Navamsa, joined by the lord of the 12th, aspects the lord of the 5th house, there will be sorrow to the man by loss of children. 603.

If the lord of the 5th combines in Dusthas, joining cruel Shastiamsas or possesses cruel aspects, the person will have sorrow from loss of issues.   604.

If the lord of the 5th is strong (Driday) retrograde, etc , and joins good Shastiamsas like Mridwamsa or Gopuramsa, etc., there will be prosperity to children·   605.

If the lord of the Navamsa occupied by the lord of the 5th combines in Lagna, and the lord of the Navamsa occupied by the lord of birth joins the 5th, and the lord of the Navamsa occupied by Guru combines in a Kendra from the Lagna, the Maha Rishis predict children to such a man. 606.

If the lords of the 5th and 9th occupy Paravatamsa, etc., and the lord of Lagna is aspected by a benefic, the person will have children. 607.

The Maha Rishis, highly skilled in the astrological sciences, predict children in these combinations only when there are no conjunctions of planets, which clearly indicate extinction of families or *Vamsa Kshaya Yogas.* Therefore the learned in astrology must carefully consider over these various combinations and proceed to make predictions after thoroughly understanding all the principles. 608.

NOTES.

The reader is now taken to some combinations of planets which indicate destruction to children and they are no doubt very important. It is better not to have children at all than to have them and lose them constantly. The miseries of parents who get and lose their children are simply indescribable and they can only be realised by those who have such sad experiences. There are some who get as many as 10 or 15 children and lose them all one after another. Their lot is most pitiable. Remedies would alleviate these miseries a great deal and add vitality to children, when properly undertaken and completed before the period of danger actually threatens. When the 5th is aspected by a malefic and the lord of the 5th combines with a malefic and Guru, lord of children, occupies the 5th, children will die. Here there must be an aspecting of the 5th by a bad planet, conjunction of its lord with a malefic and occupation of 5th by Guru. Thus both Guru and 5th are aspected by a malefic and the lord of 5th conjoins an evil planet. 600.

The lord of the 2nd and the 7th occupy some Navamsas. If the lords of these two Navamsas combine with an evil planet, and join evil Navamsas, loss of children must be predicted. Take a real horoscope.

	Rahu	Chandra	Sani
Lagna Guru		Rasi.	
			Kuja
	Ravi	Buda Kethu	Sukra

Buda		
		Sukra Rahu
	Navamsa	
Chandra Kethu		
Kuja Sani	Guru	Lagna	Ravi

The lord of the 2nd is Guru and he occupies the Vrischika Navamsa. The lord of Vrischika is Kuja and he is found in Simha in the Rasi, here he is aspected by Sani but not conjoined with a malefic. In the Navamsa he is occupying Dhanus which is not cruel but Sani is with him. The lord of the 7th is Ravi and he occupies the Kanya Navamsa. The lord of Kanya is Buda and he is with Kethu in the Rasi and occupies Meena in debilitation. The conditions laid down here are not satisfied, but I have shown how the conjunctions should be interpreted. 601.

When the lord of the 5th joins debilitation or combustion, occupies; cruel Navamsas, possesses evil aspects or is found in the 6th, 8th or 12th houses, there will be loss of children. 602.

The lord of the 12th occupies some Navamsa. The lord of this Navamsa must necessarily be found in some Drekkana. Take the lord of this Drekkana and if he aspects the lord of the 5th, there will be sorrow on account of the death of children. Drekkanas are fully treated in Brihat Jataka, Ch. XXVII and their uses are also detailed there very well. 603.

When the lord of the 5th is found in 6th, 8th or 12th, joining evil Shastiamsas like Pratapuri, Yama, Kalaghna,

Mrityu, etc., or evil planets aspect him, there will be sorrow from the death of children These combinations give the man children and then kill them also bringing sorrow and misery upon the parents 604·

Driday is interpreted by some commentators as retrograde and it seems to be right Vakra or retrograde is also called *Bali* or one who possesses strength. Four good Vergas or sub-divisions of the sign form Gopuramsa. The lord of the 5th must be retrograde, must be in good Shastiamsas or must join the Gopuramsa to give prosperity to children. When the lord of the 5th joins good sub-divisions, the children will be long-lived and will also be prosperous. 605·

The lord of the 5th joins some Navamsa and the lord of this Navamsa should join Lagna· The lord of the birth joins some Navamsa and the lord of this Navamsa should be in the 5th house, Guru combines in some Navamsa, Take the lord of this Navamsa and if he is in a Kendra from the Lagna, the Maha Rishis predict children to such a person. Here we have to take three points into consideration. Take the lords of the birth and 5th and see what Navamsas they occupy. Take then the lords of these two Navamsas and see that these lords occupy the birth and the 5th That is the lord of the Navamsa occupied by the lord of the 5th must be in birth while the lord of the Navamsa occupied by the lord of the birth should be in the 5th. There is thus a mutual exchange. Then the third point is that the lord of the Navamsa, occupied by Guru should be in a Kendra Then the person will have children, 606.

The lords of the 5th and 9th must be in Paravatamsa, etc. The word *Adi* used in the text means any good Shadvergas. The lord of the birth must also have the aspect of a benefic to give children to the person. Suppose the lord of birth instead of having the aspect as is given here joins that planet then will such a conjunction be productive of children ? Certainly, when a good effect can be produced by aspect, the conjunction must necessarily produce it in a more tangible form. 607.

The author here offers a few suggestions which the readers should particularly remember   There are several sets of combinations and some of them are more powerful than others. Gains and losses for a man should be carefully analysed.   When one set of conjunctions are prejudicial and these are stronger and there is another set of conjunctions which are helpful but not so strong as the first set, then the evil predominates and the astrological adept should be cautious in making his predictions good or bad as the case may be.   The author here says that the foregoing conjunctions which give a man children, will only take effect when the other set of combinations which he is going to treat in the next stanzas about the loss of children and extinction of families are not present.   If both of these are present, then the evil predominates, and the man will not beget children and even when they are born they will die and bring him sorrow and misery.   *Vamsa* means a family and *Kshaya* means loss or destruction.   The proper meaning is extinction. Suppose a father has four children and three of them are blessed with offspring while the 4th has no issues·   Then the branch represented by the fourth will become extinct from the family tree and it stops away with him.   In all these cases, the strength of the houses, planets, and the lords of the events should be carefully compared.   Rash or ill-considered and ill-digested conclusions will prove incorrect and will do harm both to the Professors of Astrology and also to the dignity of astrology as a science.   Venkatasa requires the readers to master the principles of Astrology well and then attempt to make predictions·   608.

Stanzas 609 to 618.

If Chandra, Sukra, and evil planets occupy the 10th, 7th and 4th respectively while the lord of Lagna joins with Buda, the persons family becomes extinct.   609.

If the evil planets occupy the 12th, 5th and 8th, the person's family becomes extinct and he becomes also poor·   610.

If Chandra and Guru occupy Lagna and if the lord of Lagna and Sani join the 7th house from Lagna, when all the evil planets are in the 4th, while Chandra occupies the 5th, the person will have all his children dead and family extinct. 611.

If Buda with Sukra, combines in the 7th, malefics in the 4th, Guru in the 5th, and evil planets are in the 8th from Chandra, the family becomes extinct. 612.

If a malefic combines in Lagna, Chandra in the 4th, the lord of Lagna in the 5th, and the lord of the 5th is powerless, the family becomes extinct· 613.

If weak Moon joins Lagna, if Jupiter in combustion occupies the 8th and if all the malefics join the 5th and 9th, the person dies before he can enjoy the happiness of children. 614·

If Buda occupies the 5th, if an evil planet occupy the birth or the 4th, and the other evil planets occupy the 5th and the 9th, the man will never see the face of children. 615.

If one of the houses of Kuja, becomes the Lagna, and if Ravi and Sani occupy the 5th and 8th respectively in conjunction with or aspected by a benefic, the person will have children at the latter stage of his existence. 616·

If the lord of the 5th joins the 5th in conjunction with Rahu, unaspected by a benefic, the children of this man will die by snake bite· 617.

If the 5th house falls in the houses of Buda or Sani and combines with Sani and Mandi, he will have an adopted son, etc. 618.

NOTES.

Chandra should be in the 10th, Sukra in the 7th, and the evil planets in the 4th, while the lord of Lagna is in conjunction with Buda, to destroy all the issues of the man before he dies and make him the last of his family, so that the family may become extinct with him. Here also the readers should not rush blindly into the regions of prediction. The junction of the lord of Lagna with Buda an impotent planet, also tends to the extinction of a man's family. Among the Hindus, this extinction of family is considered to be a very heavy misfortune, and with such misfortune the man's life here and hereafter is said to suffer a great deal. A real Yogi, of course, has no concern with this. But all are not real Yogis. Here the author seems to hint that in all these conjunctions the person gets issues and they all die before him, making him the last of his race and family. Each individual develops a new family and where he does not do so, he gets the stigma of stopping that branch of the family with him. If Chandra is exalted or Sukra is exalted, then, even if the other conjunctions are present, the reader must be careful in his predictions. Chandra and Sukra both cannot be exalted and occupy the 10th and 7th. For Simha Lagna Chandra will be exalted in Vrishabha or 10th, but Sukra then will be in Kumbha the 7th without exaltation. Beneficial aspects and conjunctions mitigate the evil a great deal. 609.

Evil planets should not be in the 5th, 8th and 12th, as they produce loss of children and make the man also poor. Take the following horoscope and examine the conjunctions given here.

Here Sani is in the 5th but exalted, Kuja is in the 8th in exaltation and Chandra is in the 12th, in combustion (weak) but exalted. Can we say that the person becomes poor or all his issues will die. Exaltation takes away the sting of evil planets a great deal, and I should certainly predict a

		Chandra Ravi	Lagna Buda
			Sukra
	Rasi.		
Kuja			
Guru		Sani	

child to the man. Of course the conditions would be reversed where these are evil. Take Meena as Lagna.

Here the 5th and 8th are occupied by Kuja and Ravi, both evil planets but in debilitation. The 12th is occupied by Sani, though he is in his own house and Moolathrikona. He will have an extinction of his family. 610.

Lagna		Guru	
Sani	Rasi		Kuja
	Buda	Ravi	Sukra

When Chandra and Guru are in Lagna, how can Chandra be again in the 5th. The Verse seems to have been miscopied or misinterpreted. This point will be considered later on. The lord of birth or Sani should be in the 7th, and all the evil planets should be in the 4th, his children will die and family becomes extinct. The expression used in the last portion of the Verse is *Sutay Abjay, i.e.*, while Chandra occupies the 5th. It would be absurd to expect Chandra to be both with Guru in Lagna and again occupy the 5th in the same combination. Probably it may have been *Abjay*, that is within a year the person will lose his son. It is now extremely difficult to guess what the author might have written in the original, I am sure, he could never have meant that Chandra would occupy two houses, *Lagna* and *Punchima* in the same conjunction. All the evil planets here contemplated are Ravi, Kuja and Sani. 611.

The conjunction of Buda and Sukra in the 7th house, evil planets, Ravi, Kuja or Sani in the 4th, Guru in the 5th, with an evil planet in the 8th house from Chandra cause the extinction of family. There are some points here which should be well discussed. When Buda and Sukra are in the 7th, they powerfully aspect the Lagna and occupy Kendra which is good for benefics. Guru in the 5th necessarily aspects Lagna from the 9th and this triple beneficial aspect of Buda, Sukra and Guru

for Lagna must certainly produce good results and the family
extinction, considered as a severe punishment, should be averted.
An evil planet in the 8th from Chandra is bad, and evil planet
or planets in the 4th equally so.   I am not however thoroughly
convinced of the evil nature of this conjunction where Lagna
becomes the most powerful by virtue of the full beneficial
aspects of the best benefics, and where such a serious misfortune,
even when indicated by other planetary conjunctions should be
averted.   I have pointed out the line of my argument and leave
the readers to draw their own inferences.   When Lagna is
powerfully aspected by the three benefics, and when the best
benefic Guru, also the lord of children, occupies the 5th, I would
not be tempted to predict the extinction of a man's family.   612.

There must be an evil planet in the Lagna, Chandra should
be in the 4th house, lord of Lagna must occupy the 5th house,
and if the lord of the 5th is powerless, the person   will lose his
children and his family becomes extinct.   If the lord of children
Guru is powerful and there are beneficial conjunctions for the evil
planets, he may lose children, but the family extinction should
not be predicted as one or two issues may survive and continue
his family.   613.

Kshina Chandra should be in Lagna and when he is there
necessarily Ravi must be close to him.   If Chandra in combus·
tion occupies Lagna, how can Guru be in combustion and occupy
8th from Lagna.   The text seems to be perfectly wrong as such
a conjunction of planets, Chandra and Guru occupying Lagna
and Astama in combustion, would be an impossibility under the
present conditions of planetary movements.   A planet will be
in deep combustion within 10 degrees of the Sun on either side.
If we take even Moudhya in a most liberal sense, and give the
elongation even to 30 degrees from the Sun on either side, for
combustion, here too, the conjunction becomes impossible.
Chandra must be in Lagna.   This means he must occupy the

degree the Lagna joins or be within 15 degrees on either side
from it. Thus when Chandra occupies Lagna in Moudhya or
comb ustion, Guru can never have Moudhya and occupy the 8th
This is therefore a mistake and it is difficult to say what the
original expression could have been. Again he wants the readers
to believe that all the malefics should be in the 5th and 9th,
quite an absurd proposition. When Chandra gets Kshina, he
does so when he is very close to the Sun, and therefore when
Chandra occupies the Lagna, Ravi must be say at least in the
2nd or 12th houses. How can then all the planets occupy the
5th and 9th. The author could have stated that the evil planets
Kuja and Sani should be in the Thrikonas. This conjunction
in my humble opinion may not happen for the reasons given
above. If such a combination is possible, then the man will die
before he sees his sons. In this case he may not see the face
of the son, but all the same a posthumous child may be
born. 614.

The impotent planet Buda must be in the 5th, there must
be a malefic in the birth, and the other evil planets should be
in the 5th and 9th. Here the
person will never have the
happiness of seeing the face of
his children. He will get no
children. T h i s combination
will be thus:—An evil planet
may be in birth or fourth, and
I have simply given the two here
for ready reference. 615.

Kuja owns two houses, *viz*, Mesha and Vrischika. One
of these houses should become the Lagna. Ravi must be in the
5th and Sani should be in the 8th house and these two should
have the conjunction or aspect of a benefic to make the man
get children about the end of his life, or at a later period of his
life. Children are born in a most surprising variety. Some get

children within a year of their nuptials, and they go on getting every year a child up to a certain age. Others get a child every alternate year. Some get children once in three years, while others have them once in 4 or 5 or 6 or 7 or 8 years. The regularity is most perplexing and cannot be explained. Some will have no children for 30 years after marriage and nuptials and then get one child before closing their chapter. Some get only males. Others get only daughters. Some get a son and a daughter alternately, while the others get a daughter and a son alternately. Some get two sons and then two daughters while others get 3 sons and 3 daughters. There are some who get consecutively five or six sons or daughters and then the sex is changed. The wonders of creation are mysterious and Mahatmas alone can read them satisfactorily. 616.

The lord of the 5th house must be in the 5th and Rahu must join him there. If these two planets are not aspected by a benefic, he will lose his child or children by snake bite. Rahu represents snake. Beneficial aspect or conjunction averts this danger. A child may be bitten by a snake but it may recover from the bite and live. This may be predicted if the lord of the 5th is exalted or occupies good Amsas. 617.

The houses of Buda are Mithuna and Kanya and Buda is impotent as also Sani.

The houses of Sani are Makara and Kumbha. The fifth house should not fall into anyone of these four houses. If Sani and Mandi combine there when the 5th house falls in one of these four, the person will have an adopted son. The word *Adi* used in the original includes such kinds of children. Among the Hindus, according to Hindu Law, there exist fourteen varieties of sons and they range from *Aurasa Putra* legitimate son to *Swayam Datta* one who gifts himself away for the sake of convenience or money. Some of the varieties are *Aurasa* natural born, *Datta Putra* or adopted, *Palaka Putra* or foster child, *Kanina* or daughter's son, etc. All such are included in such conjunctions and the reader has to carefully consider all these cases according to the strength of the planets and their conjunctions.

Now the author takes the reader to the intelligence of man, his sincerity, his tact, knowledge, wisdom, counselling power, foresight, prudence, etc.

These are very important and they must be read with care and devotion.

5th house is the house of intelligence, lord of education is Guru and lord of intelligence is Buda. Wherever there is a conjunction of Buda and Guru in a horoscope there will be both education and intelligence.   There is often a wide gulf between the two Vidya and Buddhi.   The real Vidya of course comprises in telligence.   Sometimes we see men are highly educated but betraying want of equal intelligence.   Their heads will be full of booklore or education taught to them by teachers and colleges, but they want intelligence to digest and apply them to other c onditions of life.   On the other hand some are extremely intelligent but often remain without even the rudiments of education.   A happy junction of these two will, not only make the man a leader, but will also enable him to do much in a practical way.   Genius, of course is a different capacity and men of real genius are always few and far between. 618.

Stanzas 619 to 634 inclusive.

If the lord of the 5th is a benefic, and has beneficial con-junction or aspect, or occupies a beneficial house, the person will become an intelligent and straightforward man.   619.

If the lord of the 5th joins a Paramocha Navamsa,has bene-ficial aspect and lies between two benefics, the person will be extremely intelligent. 620.

If the lord of the Navamsa occupied by the lord of the 5th, has beneficial aspect and the lord of the 5th becomes a benefic, he will be very intelligent. 621.

If the lord of the Navamsa rising in the *Bhava* occupied by the lord of Buddhi, occupies Kendra or Thrikona from Lagna, aspected by the lord of the 5th, the intellect will be comprehensive and piercing. 622.

If the lord of the Navamsa occupied by the lord of intelligence, joins a Kendra or Kona, and has the aspect of the Karaka, he will be able to grasp the thoughts of others and will be highly intelligent. 623.

If the lord of the Drakkana, occupied by either the lord of the 5th or the lord of intelligence, being a benefic, occupies a Kendra or Kona, aspected by a benefic, the person will be very shrewd and be able to read the thoughts of others. 624.

If the 5th is occupied by a malefic and if the lord of the 5th combines with a malefic or joins cruel Shastiamsas, the person will be devoid of intelligence. 625.

If the lord of the 5th is debilitated, in combust, or in unfriendly house, aspected by a malefic occupying a cruel Shastiamsa, the person will be devoid of intelligence. 626.

When Sani is in the 5th, and aspects the lord of Lagna, and the lord of the 5th is combined with a malefic, the person will be dull and stupid. 627.

If Sani, Mandi and Rahu join the 5th unaspected by or uncombined with a benefic, and the lord of the 5th has the aspect of a malefic, the person will generally be forgetful or unmindful of events. 628.

If the lord of intelligence joins a malefic, and the lord of the 5th house combines with a malefic or joins cruel Shastiamsa the person though intelligent will be often forgetful. 629.

If Buda combines in the 5th house, aspected by Guru and Sukra or if the lord of the 5th is in the 5th aspected by Guru and Sukra, he will be able to explain to all others the facts he grasps. 630

If the lord of the 5th joins Gopuramsa and the lord of the house occupied by the lord of intelligence is aspected by the lord of birth, the person will be far-sighted and intelligent. 631.

If the powerful Guru is aspected by the lord of the 5th or occupies Gopura, etc., Amsas, such a person will become a Prime Minister or Raja Mantri. 632.

If the lord of intelligence, occupies a Kendra or Kona combined with Sukra and Buda, or possesses their aspect, in conjunction with a benefic, the person will be a minister who will be able to foretell the future events from his intelligence. 633.

If Guru occupies his own Navamsa joining Mridwamsa or if he joins a beneficial Navamsa aspected by a benefic and occupying Gopuramsa, etc., the person will be able to read the past, present and the future or a Thrikalagna. 634.

NOTES

The lord of the 5th should be a benefic and should possess beneficial conjunction or aspect, or he should occupy a beneficial sign to make the person not only intelligent, but also moral or straightforward. A straightforward man need not necessarily be a moral man in its fullest sense. Moral course enjoins so many restrictions upon the actions of the individual that only very strong-minded and great men alone can become moral. A man may be an adulterer or drunkard, but still may be a straightforward man. But strict principles of morality will exclude him from its province. Intelligence is often combined with humbug and self-interest, and it becomes a dangerous weapon unless strongly curbed by the noble principles of moral behaviour. If

Simha is Lagna, then the lord of the 5th is Guru and he is a
benefic. He may be combined with Buda or Sukra, or possess
their aspect or may occupy a beneficial house like Vrishabha or
Mithuna. Chandra's house becomes beneficial only when he is
full or deeply exalted without evil associations. 619.

The lord of the 5th must join his Paramocha Navamsa,
must possess beneficial aspect and should lie between two benefics to give the man high intelligence. Good intelligence is a
ready passport for success and influence and if to this the man
brings devotion and honesty, his prosperity here and hereafter
will certainly be secured. What is a Paramocha Navamsa has
not been explained by the author or by any of the Commentators.
In fact this noble work of *Sarwartha Chintamani* has had no
commentaries worthy of that name and one or two Sastrys who
have tried to give some Telugu notes, have made a mess of the
whole by confounding one principle of Astrology with another and
giving a lot of misinterpretations. An able Sanskrit commentary
is still wanted. I have already explained what is meant by a
planet being between two other planets. The Sun is Paramocha
in the 10th degree of Mesha and naturally he occupies the end
of the 3rd Navamsa from Mesha indicated by the 3rd *Padam* or
quarter of the constellation Aswini. When a planet is in the 3rd
of Aswini he is placed in the Navamsa of Mithuna and this is not
his Oocha even   In order to remain in Paramocha he must be
in the 10th degree, but that does not fall in the Mesha Navamsa.
If he is within 200 liptas or 3⅓rd degrees, he will fall in Mesha
Navamsa, but then he will not be in Paramocha. What then
could be the meaning of Paramocha Navamsa. Take the Moon.
He is Paramocha in the 3rd degree of Vrishabha. When he is
here, he will be in the 2nd padam of Krithika and this necessarily
falls in Makara Navamsa Similarly for other planets. Here
the readers have to understand that he means by Paramocha,
the Navamsa of his exaltation. It is not necessary that a planet
must be in exaltation in the Rasi to occupy a Oocha Navamsa.

For instance the Sun occupies Thula, his house of debilitation. But even here he may occupy a Paramocha Navamsa, as when he is in the 1st padam of Visakha. Here, apparently the author seems to make no difference when he refers to Navamsas as Oocha and Paramocha. These terms are used to fill up the metre conveniently. But when they are used with reference to planets in the Rasis, there is a difference which should not be lost sight of by the readers. Such a combination as the above will give the man extreme intelligence. It is a good luck to possess high order of intelligence, and much more it would be so if he uses it in proper and beneficial ways to himself and to the fellow-beings who surround him. 620.

The lord of the 5th occupies some Navamsa. Take the lord of this Navamsa and if he has beneficial aspect, and if the lord of the 5th also becomes a benefic, the man will be very intelligent. Here the lord of the 5th must be a benefic and the lord of the Navamsa occupied by this benefic must have the aspect of a good planet to make the man very intelligent. When the aspect gives the person intelligence, much more will be the result for good by a beneficial conjunction. In some cases a peculiar efficacy is attached to conjunction and in others, this is done for aspect. 621.

There is a great confusion as to who is the lord of Buddhi. When the Lexicons or Nighantus are examined, the confusion is not cleared. A careful perusal of this work itself has led to some uncertainty. Some commentators have taken lord of Buddhi as Guru. The author uses, in all these conjunctions on intelligence and stupidity, the words Buddhi, Buddhisthana, Buddhi Natha or Karaka and so forth. There seems to be some difference between Buddhi and Pragna. The former probably means less than the latter. The lord of intelligence is Budha. But Buda is called Budha, because he causes or gives Buddhi. In this work in the end the Karakas of planets and Rasis are given, and Buda governs Buddhi and Pragnya. Guru governs Medha. Panchama is governing Buddhi, Sachivya, Gnyana, etc. In Muhurtha Dipika under Bhava Nighantu, Chandra is made Karaka of Menas and Buddhi. Guru also is made to govern Buddhi. Buda is made to govern Pragnya. A clue however is given by the author in stanza 634, where the Karaka or lord of Buddhi is made to be aspected or conjoined by Sukra and Budha to produce great intelligence, as to whom he considers as lord of Buddhi. Here he means Guru, and we have to interpret by the Karaka of Buddhi Guru and not Budha.

The Karaka or lord of Buddhi is Guru. He occupies some Bhava or house and a certain Navamsa must rise in this Bhava, as it does in the Lagna.

	Chandra Rahu	Lagna	Sani
Ravi Buda Guru		Rasi	
Sukra		Kuja Kethu	

	Lagna Guru	Rahu	
		Navamsa	
Buda	Kethu	Sani Ravi Sukra Kuja	Chundra

Take a living horoscope. The lord of Buddhi is Guru and he occupies the 10th house. In the Lagna the Navamsa which rises at birth is the 4th and therefore the fourth Navamsa also rises in the 10th Bhava. The fourth Navamsa for Kumbha is Makara and its lord is Sani. If in this horoscope Sani had occupied any Kendra or Kona (he does not do so) and possessed the aspect of the lord of the 5th, *viz.*, Budha, then the intellect will be comprehensive. 622.

The lord of intelligence is Guru and he occupies some Navamsa. If the lord of this joins a Kendra or Kona, possessing the aspect of Guru, the Karaka, the person will be able to grasp the thoughts of others and be very intelligent 623.

The lord of the 5th house occupies some Drekkona. So also does the lord of intelligence Guru. The lord of one of these Drekkonas should be a benefic, occupy a Kendra or Kona, and should possess the aspect of a benefic to make the man a clever thoughtreader or one who is able to guess the thoughts of other men. There are some people who are remarkably gifted with this power of knowing others thoughts and by this superior knowledge they will become leaders and command great respect among their fellow men. Hitherto the author gave several conjunctions to show the possession of great intelligence and foresight. Now he takes his readers to some combinations which show want of intelligence or stupidity. There must be a bad planet in the 5th, the lord of the 5th must have malefic conjunctions, and he must join some cruel shastiamsas, such as Ghora, Mrityu, etc., This conjunction will make the man dull. Here the fifth as well as its lord are with malefic conjunctions and the lord of the 5th joins evil shastiamsa. This combination takes away the intelligence from the man. 625.

When the lord of the 5th is in debilitation, or in combustion, or in an unfriendly house, joins a cruel shastiamsa, and possesses malefic aspect, the person will be devoid of intelligence. 626.

If Sani occupies the 5th and the lord of Lagna is aspected by him, while the lord of the 5th has evil combination, the person will be stupid. Here the 5th should have conjunction with Sani as also the lord of birth and the lord of the 5th must have evil conjunction. Sani in the 5th and 9th houses will be bad for various purposes. 627.

When Sani, Mandi and Rahu are in the 5th, and they have no beneficial conjunctions or aspects and the lord of the 5th is aspected by an evil planet, the conjunction produces forgetfulness. Some people are intelligent but very forgetful. There are others who are dull but very tenacious in their memory. Forgetfulness will be a great misfortune in many cases as the people forgetful lose many advantages and many profitable bargains. 628.

If Guru joins a bad planet, as also the lord of the 5th, or if the lord of 5th combines in a cruel Shastiamsa the person will be often forgetful. 629.

When Buda occupies the 5th house, aspected by Guru and Sukra, or when the lord of the 5th is in the 5th aspected by Guru and Sukra, the person will become a very intelligent man and will be able to explain what he knows, in a very clear and convincing style to others. This power is a splendid fortune and very few persons possess this. There are some who are very learned, but who have not the knack or power to explain to others what they know or learn. Some possess ordinary powers of imparting instruction. There are few who explain facts in such a nice and convincing way that their hearers always go away highly enriched in knowledge and wisdom. This is called teaching power or Bodhana Sakli and will be a very valuable adjunct to a man in this life. 630.

The lord of the 5th must be in Gopuramsa, while the lord of the sign occupied by Guru should be aspected by the lord of birth to make the man intelligent and farsighted. Some are intelligent, but are hasty, while others are intelligent and deeply foresighted. They can judge from the present circumstances how the future results would be. 631.

Guru, lord of Buddhi, must be powerful, and should be aspected by the lord of the 5th, or if the powerful Guru occupies Gopuramsa, etc., the person will become a Rajamantri or Prime Minister to a ruler or king. In order to produce this desirable conjunction and result, Guru should be really powerful, and must be aspected by the lord of the 5th. Suppose Guru is powerful and the lord of the 5th aspects him (1) in a debilitated condition (2) in an exalted condition and (3) from an unfriendly or friendly house. The rank of the minister will vary according to the strength of these planets. There are various grades of ministers and these can be judged by the power of these combinations. 632.

If Guru is in a Kendra or Kona, with Buda and Sukra, or is aspected by them, and also in conjunction with a benefic, the person will be a minister who will be able to read the future by the aid of the present circumstances. This means that Guru, Buda and Sukra must be in a Kendra or Kona with another benefic. The three Benefics are already named and where are we to search for a 4th. Chandra when full, falls in the classification of a benefic, Guru with Chandra may be in a Kendra or Kona possessing the aspect of Buda and Sukra to make him a farsighted statesman. 633.

Guru must be in his own Navamsa, and must also be in Mridwamsa, or he must be in a beneficial Navamsa aspected by a benefic, and also joining Gopuramsa, etc, This conjunction will enable a man to read the past, present and the future Such men are called *Thrikalagnyas*. This may be done by high intelligence or able judgment or by the help of sciences like Yoga, Mantra, and Jyotisha. 634.

Stanzas 635 to 645 inclusive.

The author now gives some conjunctions which indicate the sex of the progeny.

If the lord of the 5th is masculine, joins a masculine sign, and combines a masculine Navamsa, the first born of the man will be a male. 635.

If the lord of the 5th joins a female sign with a feminine planet and combines in a feminine Navamsa, the first born will be a female,

If the lord of the 5th joins an eunuch Navamsa, the first born will be impotent.   636.

The number of children may be determined either by the number of *Bindus* (ciphers) in the 5th sign or by the number of *Bindus* indicated by the sign occupied by the *Putrakaraka* subtracting the Bindus obtained by the Neecha, Moodha, and Satru Rasi planets.   637.

The number of children may be determined by the strongest of the following three, *viz.*, by the Kiranas of the lord of the 5th, by the Navamsa occupied by the Putra Bhava, or by the *Rasmijala* of Guru.   638

The friendliness, neutrality or enmity of the children and the father must be predicted by the friendliness of the lord of the birth and the 5th, their neutrality or enmity.   639.

If the lords of birth and 5th have mutual aspects, cr occupy each others houses or Navamsas, the person will have obedient and dutiful children.   640.

If the lord of the 5th aspects the birth, or occupies the 5th house, or if the lord of the birth combines in the 5th house, the person will have a dutiful son.   641.

If the lord of the 5th joins *Dusthas* and is aspected by the lord of birth Kuja and Rahu, the person will have sons who would be hating and abusing the father every day.   632.

If Buda, Guru and Sukra join the 5th or if the 5th falls in any one of the houses of these benefics, the person will have his sons always with him and will make others enjoy comforts through their earnings.   643.

If the lord of the 3rd is in the 3rd, the lord of the 5th occupies the 4th, and the lord of 4th or the 2nd being exalted, occupies a Kendra, the person will become an *Anna Data*.   644.

If the 5th is occupied by a malefic and the lord of the 5th is between two malefics aspected by a malefic, the person will have heart disease.   645.

NOTES.

The possession of children is a great blessing and specially it is so to possess male children.

To perpetuate the families and to continue to keep the traditions of the family unsullied, children are heartily desired and among the Hindus, the possession of a son is very much coveted, so much so that as soon as a man's wife becomes pregnant there are some Karmas, actions or ceremonials which are ordained not only to avert the evils indicated by the uufavourable planetary positions but also to change the sex of the foetus in the womb to the masculine gender if it happens to be a feminine.   Nuptials are not according to the Vedas beastly acts for the gratification of sexual passions, as many Europeans erroneously think, but are acts of sexual correspondence for the propogation of the species, for the begetting of sons to perform the necessary ceremonies for the benefit of the dead ancestors and for the purpose of helping the aged parents when they need protection from the younger generation.   The European generally has very low ideas about his parents and the duties he has towards them, he seeks gratification of passions, neglects the parents soon after he marries, withdraws his support from them and goes away to any part of the world where he has self-interest and where he could live with his wife.   This arises from the keen competition they have for worldly concerns and the absence of any sanctified idea to serve his helpless parents when they are old and need support.   The parents protect the children when they are young and helpless, but these children grow ungrateful to the highest degree, when they renounce their parents and only seek enjoyment in serving their wives, their children and their grosser material desires.   Among the Hindus, the ideas are quite different and radically opposed to European code of parental ethics. When the Hindu sacred writings, the *Upanishads* say *Malru Devo Bhava, Pitru Devo Bhava Acharya, Devo Bhava Atithi Devo Bhava* the European social codes observe quite the reverse, and we may humorously observe—Kalatra *Devo Bhava*, *Putra Devo Bhava* and *Dhanu Devo Bhava*. When the Hindu holds his mother and father as next to God, and so also his precep- tor and the guest, the European falls on his Knees before his wife, his children and his money God, the Mammon. Therefore the anxiety of the Hindu to get a son, at first, can never be realised, by the average mercenary European mind, and in fact men and women among the Europeans are so supremely indifferent to anything like domestic relationship and family constraints that they always think it would be better for them to remain unmarried rather than to put themselves under the yoke of wedded life. This scandal has grown so loud as to demand notice from Presidents of enlightened governments like America and France and the divorce scandals have become so rampant that a woman is often said to reject as many as half a dozen men in one year, and seek companionship at her sweet will and pleasure. If the lord of the 5th is a male planet, occupies a masculine house, or joins a masculine Navamsa, the first born child will be a son. The author uses masculine, feminine and eunuch or impotent signs, thereby clearly indicating the gender of the lords of the signs rather than the signs themselves. Odd signs are mascu- line and even signs are feminine. No impotent or Napumsaka signs have been enumerated. Mithuna is an odd sign and therefore would be cruel and masculine. But how the author would expect the reader to hold it as an impotent sign as its lord is Mercury and he is classified as an eunuch. These are general instructions. The Dasas and Bhukties exercise a great deal of influence and if at the time of conception and delivery, the major lord is male as also the sub-lord, then a male child may be predicted. All sources of influences should be considered in making a prediction and the

skill of the astrologer depends upon his vast knowledge and the
sound judgment he brings to bear upon any particular Bhava he
is engaged in examining.   Three conditions are laid down here.
The lord of the 5th must be a male, he must join a male sign and
also a male Navamsa to make the man get a male child first.   The
position of the child may also be predicted. Suppose the lord of 5th
is male, and joins an exaltation.   In the Navamsa if he joins an
exaltation or friendly or his own house, the boy will become an
eminent or lucky fellow. If the lord of 5th is debilitated or occupies
unfriendly house and joins an unfriendly or Neecha Navamsa, the
boy will become a beggar or unlucky.   As regards the possibility of
changing the sex in the womb and its development during the nine
months in it see *Charakasamhita.*

English Translation by Avinash Chandra Kavi Ratna, PP. 824-25.
Brihatjataka English Translation by myself. Ch. IV Stanza 16.

Astrological Magazine Vol. XII P. 53.

To get a female child, the lord of the 5th must be in a female
sign, with a feminine planet and join a female Navamsa.   He does
not say here whether the lord of the 5th should be a female.   By
anology with the above stanza it would be better if he is also a
female planet.   In the whole of India, male children are coveted.
While in Malabar, the peculiarity is for craving a female.   If the
lord of the 5th joins an eunuch Navamsa, an impotent child should
be predicted.   Napumsaka is a eunuch.   There is some difference
between impotency and eunuch state.   Impotency may be brought
on by excesses of diseases.   Eunuchism is natural born.   636.

In the Astakaverga Bindushodana, the technicalities connected
with Astakaverga, Bindus, Rephas, etc., are well explained. See
my notes on Brihat Jataka Chap. XI.

When the Astakaverga Bindushodana, is made, each Bhava
gets a certain number of Bindus after all the deductions are made
for Neecha, Asta, Satrus house, etc., The number of Bindus in the
5th Bhava may show the number of issues. The putrakaraka is Guru.

He occupies some house or Bhava.   Take the number of Bindus in this house and say the number of children will be equal to those Bindus.   637.

We have already explained what is meant by *Kiranas* or rays.

Rasmijala also means the same.   The amount of light which Guru will be able to shed.   This is measured by mathematics.   The lord of the 5th has some Kiranas, the putra Bhava occupies some Navamsa and Guru also gets a certain number of Kiranas.   Find which of three is the strongest, and predict the number of children similar to that number which is represented by the strongest of the three.   638.

While it is one thing to beget children, it is everything to get them of good behaviour and love to their parents.   To get bad or unfriendly sons will be courting thorns on our sides.   If the lord of the 5th and the lord of the birth are friends, then there will be friendliness between the man and his sons.   If they are neutral, then the feelings between the father and the son will be indifferent, but if they are enemies there will be hatred.   This looks plausible as a theory, but I show its fallacy by diagrams.   Take the Rasi.   A man born in Mesha has Kuja as the birth lord and the 5th from Mesha is Simha and its lord Rasi is a friend of Kuja.   Take Vrishabha.   Its lord is Sukra and the lord of the 5th from it is Buda and they are friends.   Take Mithuna and its lord Buda is a friend of the lord of the 5th Thula, *vis.*, Sukra so that if you take each of the Lagnas, the lords of the 5th from each will be his friend.   I have written several times on this point in the Astrological Magazine under the heading " Triangular Friendship among planets."   This Sloka is therefore quite inapplicable as we get no enemies between the lord of any Lagna and the lord of the 5th from it.   But by friendship not only the *Nisaga* (Permanent) but *Tatkalika* should also be taken and this makes some difference.   But the wording in the text is quite misleading and I wonder why an eminent astrologer like Venkatasa should have now and then fallen into such unpardonable errors. It is possible that the wording he gave in the original text may have been slightly different but unfortunately the manuscript and the printed copies give this reading. 639.

If the lord of the birth aspects the lord of the 5th and *vice versa* or if they occupy each others houses or Navamsas, the person will have obedient and dutiful sons. 640.

The lord of the 5th must occupy the 5th, or aspect the birth or the lord of the birth joins the 5th the person will have obedient and loving children. 641.

The lord of the 5th should not be in *Dusthas* 6th, 8th or 12th houses and should not possess the aspect of the lord of birth, Kuja and Rahu. When there is this conjunction the person will have issues who would be hating and abusing him. The lord of the 5th must be in the 6th or 8th or 12th and possess the aspect of the three planets, *viz.*, the lord of birth, Kuja and Rahu. 642.

When Buda, Guru and Sukra are in the 5th, it has the best benefics in it and necessarily the children ought to prosper well. If the 5th house falls in any of these planetary houses *viz.*, Vrishabha, Mithuna, Kanya, Thula, Dhanas and Meena, he will have sons through whom he will be able to entertain others. I cannot really understand what this means. It probably means that the sons will be in a flourishing condition and that through their earnings the father may be able to treat others hospitably. Here there may be a limit that his own earnings will be smaller than his sons. The son must always eclipse the father in glory. 643.

The lord of the 3rd must be in the 3rd house, the lord of the 5th should occupy the 4th, and if one of these two lords, *viz.*, 4th and 2nd, is exalted and occupies a Kendra, the person will be an *Anna Data*. This means that he will have an hospitable house where he will ever be ready to give anybody food. Among the

Hindus, food given in charity is considered to be a great merit, and such people are highly respected.   Take an example.

Kanya is the Lagna.   Lord of the 3rd is Kuja and he is there. The lord of the 5th is Sani and he occupies the 4th.   The lord of the 2nd is Sukra and he is in exaltation and also occupies a Kendra (7th) from the Lagna.   This conjunction will make a man very charitable in food giving.   644.

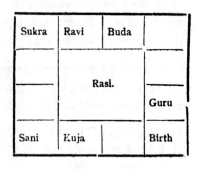

Sukra	Ravi	Buda	
		Rasi.	
			Guru
Sani	Kuja		Birth

When there is an evil planet in the 5th house and the lord of the 5th has two evil planets on either side of him, the person will suffer from heart disease.   Heart disease is always a dangerous complaint and many people die suddenly from this ailment. With this Sloka, the 5th Bhava is completed and from the next stanza the 6th house and its significations will be deleniated. 645.

The end of Fifth Bhava.

SIXTH BHAVA.

Stanzas 646 to 660 inclusive.

We have to find out from the sixth house, about enemies, thieves, wounds or cuts, disappointments, miseries or sorrows, belly and navel, sweet and such other tastes, diseases, pickles, etc.   646.

If the lord of the 6th joins birth with a malefic, or the 8th, the body will be covered with sores or cuts.   There will be also sores or wounds if there is a malefic in the 10th, combined with or aspected by another evil planet.   647.

For father, etc., find the house, its lord and the lord or Karaku of an event, and find out as per principles enunciated in these Slokas, all the good and evil results for father, etc.   648.

Mesha represents head, Vrishabha indicates face, Mithuna shows neck, Karka signifies ears, Simha indicates nose, Kanya private organ, Thula represents *Pani* or hands, Vrischika shows sides, Dhanas signifies eyes, Makara feet, Kumbha, knees and Meena indicates the stomach. 649.

If the lord of Lagna, Kuja and Buda combine in the 4th or 12th house, the man will suffer from any one of the following diseases, *viz.*, *Apana Vyadhi, Pavitra Vyadhi, Pandu Vyadhi* or *Kusti*. 639.

If Chandra, Buda and the birth lord combine with the sun when in conjunction with Rahu, the person will suffer from syphillis whose color will be greenish dark. If the first three planets join the Navamsa of the Sun, there will be similar disease. If these three planets join with Kuja, there will be leprosy. If these join with Sani, the person will suffer from *Nylya Vyadhi*. 615.

If Chandra, Buda and birth lord join Ravi, there will be disease of the blood. These diseases will appear in places or parts of the body indicated by the planets.

If the lords of the birth and 6th join with the Sun there will be fear or danger from fever. If they join with the Moon, there will be danger from water. If they join with Mars there will be danger in battle or *Sphotaka*. 652.

If the lords of 1st and 6th join Mercury, there will be danger from bilious complaints or *Pytya Roga*. If they join with Jupiter he will be free from diseases. If they combine with Venus, the wife of the person will be weak or in sickness. If they join Saturn, he will suffer from low windy complaints. 653.

If the lords of 1st and 6th join Rahu or Kethu, the person suffers dangers from headache or complaints in the head, from thieves, fires or from windy complaints. If the lord of the 6th with Buda, combines in Lagna, the man will suffer diseases in his sexual organ or *Sisna*. 654.

If the lord of the 6th combines with Sani and joins Lagna unaspected by benefics there will be amputation of the sexual organ. 655.

If the lord of the 6th joins Kuja, there will be danger from *Vrana* or *Sphotaka*. If the lord of the 7th with Sukra combines in the 6th house, the wife of the person will be askanda or impotent. 656.

If the lords of the 6th and birth join with Sani and conjoin a Kendra or Thrikona, the person will be imprisoned. If they join Rahu or Kethu and occupy a Kendra or Kona, there will be imprisonment. 657.

The results in the case of father and other relations, must be similarly ascertained by planetary conjunctions, aspects and subdivisions, with reference to the house, its lord, and the lord of the event or Karaka. The times at which results will happen will be the Dasas, Vidasas and other minor periods of the planets concerned in causing such combinations. 658.

If the 9th is combined by Saturn and the 3rd is conjoined by Jupiter or if Saturn is in the 8th, Jupiter is in the 12th house, the person will have his hands cut off. If the Moon is in the 7th or 8th, combined with Mars or Jupiter, the person will have his hands cut off. 659.

If the 10th house is occupied by Rahu, Sani and Euda the person will have his hands cut off. When the lord of the 6th combines with Sukra, and Ravi or Sani joins Rahu, joining cruel Shastiamas, the person will have his head cut off. 660.

NOTES.

A chain can never be stronger than its weakest link. No part of a man's life history is more important than his chapter of misfortunes, and the astrologer must pay particular attention to this division as it deals with enemies, debts and diseases of man. If man has any one of these, his life will be sufficiently miserable, but if he has all these three, then his cup of misfortunes will be full to the brim and his life will be one of the bitterest experiences imaginable for man to endure.   No man is safe from the attacks of any one of these three, and many are assailed often by more than one of these items.   The proudest monarch on the throne, be-decked with costly gems and surrounded by the finest armies and the bravest warriors, is impotent before the stroke of paralysis under which his pride is humbled to the dust and for which his best medical advisers can give no radical relief.   His exalted position, his inexhaustible wealth will be of no avail if he suffers from diabetes or dyspepsia.   His rank and proud family traditions can give him no relief from an attack of fever or a stroke of delirium. The best medicines in the world, the largest quantity of wealth or the highest political position cannot give a man children, cannot make him free from diseases, cannot destroy his constitutional complaints, or cannot give him peace of mind.   Astrology alone helps all classes of men and gives them timely warning and relief to find out their misfortunes.   With the help of Astrology remedies could be adopted by which the evils indicated by the planetary conjunctions at the time of birth can be modified, averted or altogether counteracted.   This is the highest science concievable and the safest for future guidance.   Under the advice of astrology. man will be able to minimise the evil and maximise the good. According to Ayurvedic sciences, diseases are of various kinds and their magnitude and the trouble they give to mankind may be easily conceived by a few quotations from the immortal Charaka-samhita.   There are four kinds of diseases (1) accidental, (2) windy, (3) bilious and (4) phlegmatic.   Though different in classification, their character as diseases is of one kind in conse-quence of the common element being present in all of them of producing affliction or pain.   The second set arising from the three Dhatus of *Vata*, *Pitta* and *Sleshma* may be called consti-tutional.   In their normal status, these three varieties produce good

growth, strength, fair complexion, clearness of senses, good temperament, hope and joy. When they are not in a normal state, they
produce many evil consequences which are usually called diseases.
Windy diseases are of eighty kinds, Bilious diseases are of forty
and those of phlegm are of twenty kinds. (See Lesson XX
Charkasamhita.)

The splendid advancement in the Ayurvedic Sciences in India
in the remotest antiguity is a fact which excites modern admiration
and the aphorism *Agniyeca* lays down as the cause of diseases,
must hold good at all times among all nations and in all conditions
of human and animal life. Charaka observes—" correlation,
adverse, absent or excessive, between time mental faculties, and
objects of the senses constitutes in brief, the threefold causes of
disease, affecting either the body or the mind" my purpose however here is not to expand on the medical theories. The ancient
Maha Rishis not only understood and analysed the causes of
diseases, but traced them to their final causes, the previous Karma
of the person to be affected by changes in the weather. Excessive
heat produces sunstroke but does not affect all or kill all. Change
of weather produces fevers, plague, cholera, etc., but they do not affect
all. Those only are affected whose planetary conjunctions indicate their pliability to such. Some children are born very healthy
from weak and diseased parents, while others are born quite weak and
full of diseases though born of healthy and robust parents. Even
the law of heredity, so much talked of by the modern medical man,
is often disappointing. All these and many more, within our
everyday experience, show clearly that any science which confines
its researches only into the eternal atmospherical conditions will
be a superficial science whose achievements cannot stand the test
of long time or varied experience. Sixth house also indicates
enemies, a source of misery, than which there can be no greater
distractor to the peace of mind or to the body in the world. The
machinations of the enemies are so profuse, so bewildering, so
numerous and so varied that all the bitterest touches of the
world's misery, lie concealed in them.

Debts are another source of misery and wretchedness, whose magnitude could hardly be conceived by the ordinary man. It is easy to get into small debts, but when once a man is fairly in it he can hardly get out of it. "He that goes a borrowing, goes a sorrowing" well said the Proverb. When once a man gets into the clutches of a money-lender or creditor, he can never hope to get out of them and all the horrible forms of misery described in the books can easily be imagined. Sixth house therefore is a significant house and the following combinations of planets should be carefully perused. Thieves, troubles through them, losses and worry, wounds, cuts, burns, or sores, disappointments of all descriptions, miseries of various grades, belly and navel, their health, and disease, the different tastes, *Shadrosas* such as acid, bitter, sour, pungent, sweet and saltish and the various pickles and such other culinary luxuries have all to be found out with reference to the 6th house and the conjunction of planets there. 646.

When the lord of the 6th occupies the Lagna with a bad planet, or is found in the 8th house with a malefic, the body of the man will be covered with sores or cuts. Similarly if the 10th house has one malefic associated with another or possesses malefic aspects there will be wounds or sores over the body. This may be due to internal disease or external causes like cuts or burns or falls. Some are liable to this kind of misery more than others. When the whole body is covered with sores or wounds, it will be a loathsome sight for others to see or associate with. Venkatesa has repeated in several places the idea about finding the good and bad results of father, mother, children, wife, brother, sister, etc., from the horoscope of the man. The general principles enunciated are thus laid down. Take a real horoscope.

From the birth sign, *viz.*, Vrishaba and its lord Sukra, their
conjunctions, aspects, occupations
and other sources of strength,
have to be determined, the complexion, stature and physical
characteristics of the person himself. All the delineations of
character are given for the man,
from the Lagna and the other
Bhavas from it   Now suppose

Chandra Rahu	Birth	Sani
Ravi Buda Guru	RASI Male's Horoscope	
Sukra	Kuja Kethu	

you want to know something about the mother of this man, his
father, his brother, etc. Take the mother first, the fourth house
represents mother, this as well as the lord of the 4th should be
consulted and the lord of mother Chandra should also be examined   The lord of the 4th house is Ravi and he occupies the
10th house with Buda and Guru, two benefics, and all of these
are aspecting the 4th house as also does Sani   The complexion
of the mother must therefore be good and her body well formed
and handsome. Take the 4th house as the Lagna for the mother.
As the lord of Lagna joins good planets and aspects the Lagna
she must be fair and well proportioned. This is the Navamsa
diagram of the horoscope

In the Navamsa, Ravi is debilitated and is in evil conjunction
with Kuja and Sani and also
with Sukra. All these are weak
points for her longevity and
when the Dasa of Ravi came for
the person she died. Take also
the *Matrukaraka* or Chandra. He
is in conjunction with Rahu and
occupies Mesha aspected by
Kuja. The health of the mother

Lagna Guru	Rahu	
	NAVAMSA	
Buda	Kethu	Ravi Kuja Sani Sukra	Chandra

was good. She was fair and graceful and a good wife and

loving mother. Take her mother's place that is the 4th from 4th or Vrischika. The lord of that is Kuja and he occupies the 12th from it but he is in a beneficial sign aspected by Guru in the 9th. Her mother lived to a fairly good age and was in good circumstances as the lord of that house Kuja possess good yoga for this Simha Lagna, and also is aspected by the lord of the 5th Guru in good conjunction. Take the father of the person. This is represented by the 9th house and also by Ravi. The 9th house is Makara and its lord Sani is in the 6th from it and in a friendly house aspected by two benefics Guru and Sukra. This is good for the father and he was in good circumstances. As there are three planets in the 2nd house from Makara, *viz*, Ravi, Buda and Guru he was an educated man and commanded familiarity in half a dozen languages and possessed also sufficient wealth and never was in want of money. This is what the author means by this stanza When we want to consult the good and evil fortunes of a man we have to look to the Lagna in his horoscope and make it the basis for all calculations. If his mothers property, complexion, character longevity, etc., are wanted, the 4th house, its lord and the lord of mother Chandra should be taken as the Lagnas for his mother and then the principles of astrology should be applied. If father's disposition, success, longevity, education, etc., are to be consulted, then the 9th house from the man's Lagna should be taken as the birth sign of his father and also the position of Ravi, the lord of father and also the lord of the 9th house. Then they form the Lagna for the father and his Bhavas should be consulted from that as the basis. 648

In this way the most important relations connected with a person, may be described as regards their characteristics, position, longevity and other details.

Here be gives some information which is quite different from that which is given in stanza 4 of Ch. I. of Brihatjataka.

With a view to find out which part of the body is affected by sores, cuts, diseases or health, a list is given below to show the different organs governed by the different houses of the Zodiac.

This is what Venkatasa observes:—

> Mesha represents head.
> Vrishabha—face.
> Mithuna—neck.
> Kataka—ears.
> Simha—nose.
> Kanya—sexual organs.
> Thula—pair of hands.
> Vrischika—sides.
> Dhanas—eyes.
> Makara—feet.
> Kumbha—knees.
> Meena—kukshi or stomach. 649.

The lord of the 1st, Kuja and Buda should be in the 4th or 12th house, to produce danger from any one of the following diseases *Apana vyadhi—Pavitra vyadhi, Pandu vyadhi, and Kustu vyadhi. Apana* is one of the five *vayoos* or airs which govern different parts of the body inside and they are, (1) Prana, (2) Apana, (3) Vyana, (4) Oodana and (5) Samana. The functions served by these different kinds of airs inside the body are clearly described in several of our ancient works and they are worth studying as showing the profound knowledge of the Maha Rishis in dealing with questions of external and internal human phenomena, both physical and also mental. The derivation of Apana as given by Amara Nighant or lexicon is very interesting. It says *Adho Vinmutraditwa Janadantyana Natya-panaha.* This means that this air works inside the body, facili-tates the removal of foecal and urinary matters from or through the lower organs and enables the people to live in health. When this does not work properly, the dirty matters inside the body are not properly thrown out, and when they are not removed

regularly, the body gets out of order and suffers from various
painful forms of internal and external diseases. The accumulation of wind and bad gases in the internal machinery is always
dangerous and a free motion and a free passage of urine are
always healthy marks in a body. *Panitra vyadhi* probably
refers to waist and round about diseases which are equally painful. *Pandu vyadhi* is jaundice, and this makes the man weak and
powerless. *Ku tu* is leprosy and it is of various description
like black, white, etc. *(See Amara Kosha Kanda I. St 63.)* 650

Chandra, Buda and the lord of the birth combine together with Ravi and Rahu, this means that Chandra, Buda, Ravi
and Rahu should combine with the lord of the birth, he will suffer
from a form of syphillis whose color is shyama or greenish dark.
If Chandra, Buda and the lord of Lagna occupy together the
Navamsa of the Sun, *viz.*, Simha, there will be similar complaint.
If Chandra, Buda and the birth lord combine with Kuja,
the person will suffer from leprosy. When Chandra, Buda
and the lord of the birth conjoin Sani, there will be
Nylya vyadhi which means black leprosy or the whole body
turning out black and ugly. Suppose Chandra is exalted in
Vrishaba, Buda is there in a friendly house, Sani is also there
and the lord of Lagna Sukra is also there, can we predict this
disease. Sukra is in his own house, and Sani and Buda are in
friendly houses while Chandra is exalted, the result will be that
there will be some faint traces of *Nylya vyadhi*. In diseases as
in other human events, there are degrees of difference, and the
worst form will only be produced when the planets are in full
debilitation or possessed of evil sources of strength. 651.

Bloody diseases are dangerous and loathsome and they are
capable of producing serious evil results. Loss of blood will
kill a person in few minutes. Corruption of blood is at the root
of all diseases and is a bitter enemy of human health. If Chandra,
Buda, lord of birth and Ravi are in one house, corruption of
blood is produced and hence all those diseases have it as

their root.   These diseases appear in parts of the body indicated by the planets.   When there is a conjunction of the lords of the birth, sixth and the Sun, danger comes from fevers.

The intensity and danger from such fevers will be proportionate to the extent of the evil indicated by the planetary conjunctions. When the lords of the birth and the 6th join Chandra, there will be danger from drowning.   This also includes watery diseases such as cholera, dropsy, cold, etc.

If the lords of the 1st and 6th combine with Kuja they will bring on danger to the person in battle or *Sphotaka*. *Sphotaka* means small-pox and such hot cutaneous eruptions. 652.

The lords of the 1st and 6th should not join together   The lord of the 1st indicates body and 6th indicates diseases   Their junction means a junction of the body with the disease. If these two join Mercury, there will be bilious complaints, such as distaste for food, vomitting, belching, bad gases in the stomach, weakness, etc.

If there is conjunction of the lords of the 1st and 6th with Guru, there will be no disease and the person will keep excellent health.   If these two lords conjoin with Sukra, the wife of the person will suffer from weakness, or debility.

If they combine with Sani, the person will suffer from Vatha Roga or windy complaints, such as noises in the bowels, accumulation of gases, indigestion, irregular motions.   653.

If the lord of the 1st and 6th combine together with Rahu or Kethu, he suffers dangers from headache or giddiness in the head, from thieves, from fires, or from windy complaints. Thieves may beat him, murder him, rob him of his valuables and make him suffer miseries.   Fire mischief is well known.   The person may get burning· scorching, or destruction from fire.   If the lord of the 6th combines with Buda, and occupies Lagna, there will be diseases in the sexual organs.   Irregularities or diseases in the sexual organs are very painful and many die from the sufferings caused by such complaints 654.

When the lord of the 6th and Sani combine in Lagna, the sexual organ will be amputated on account of incurable and rotten disease. If there is beneficial conjunction or aspect, the result will be considerably modified, and no amputation or cutting should be predicted. If Sani is exalted and the lord of the 6th joins a friendly house, there will be some irregularity in the sexual organ, but no amputation should be predicted 655.

If the lord of the 6th joins Kuja, there will be danger from sores or wounds or small-pox.

Here the author does not say that Kuja and lord of the 6th should be in Lagna. But from the trend of the previous thoughts, I believe they should be in Lagna to produce the danger indicated by this Stanza.

If Sukra and the lord of the 7th join the 6th house, the wife of the person will be *shanda* or impotent. The impotency here refers to her incapacity to sexual correspondence and therefore her unfitness for marriage purposes. 7th house is Kamasthana or house of passions. Sukra represents wife, and when he joins the lord of the 7th and occupies the 12th house from the 7th, *viz.*, 6th house, the Bhava indicated by it will be destroyed or will not prosper. The 7th house represents wife. 656.

Venkatasa now gives some combinations which indicate bodily incarceration. The lord of the birth must combine with the lord of the 6th and Sani and occupy a Kendra or Kona to give imprisonment to the person.

Take an example, the lord of the birth is Buda The lord of the 6th is Sani, and these two are with Sani and occupy a Kendra from Lagna, such a man would get imprisonment.

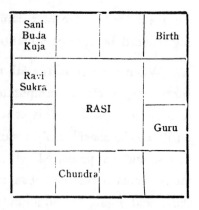

Sani Buda Kuja			Birth
Ravi Sukra	RASI		
			Guru
	Chundra		

If the lord of the birth and the lord of the 6th join with Rahu or Kethu and are found in a Kendra or Kona, he will suffer imprisonment. Various kinds of incarcerations are ordained and these can be determined by the intensity of the evil indicated by the planets. 657.

There is a sort of repetition in this Stanza. About father, mother, etc., he has already given us the directions in Stanza 648 but he gives some more details here. We take the father's house (9th) as the Lagna of the father, and then judge the conjunction from it as we do in the case of any other person from his Lagna in a horoscope. The planetary conjunctions, their aspects, their sources of strength and weakness, their good and evil natures must all be considered. Not only the father's house (9th) but also its lord and the lord of father Ravi should be considered. Results indicated by the planets must and will come, in their periods and sub-periods and other minor divisions. These can be found out by mathematical calculations given for fixing Dasas and Bhukties. 658.

The cutting off of hands as a sort of punishment was in great vogue in the former times. But hands may also be lopped off by weapons, by falls, by amputations, and by breaks.

If Saturn joins the 9th house, and Jupiter is found in the 3rd, the hands will be cut off. If Saturn is in the 8th and Jupiter occupies the 12th house, his hands will be cut off. If the Moon is combined in the 7th or 8th houses, with Mars or Jupiter, the hands will be cut off. How can a junction of the Moon with Jupiter enable a man to have his hands cut off ? 659.

The presence of Rahu, Sani and Buda in the 10th house, causes his hands to be cut of. The verse is simple and does not require much comment. When the lord of the 6th is in conjunction with Sukra, and Ravi or Sani combines with Rahu, and occupies cruel shastiamsas, the person will have his head cut off. This may be in battle or by thieves or by weapons. In the latter portion Sani or Ravi should join Rahu and also occupy cruel shastiamsas like Ghora, Rakshasa, etc. 660.

Stanzas 661 to 669 inclusive.

When Chandra occupies 6th, 8th or 12th, aspected by the lord of Lagna, and conjoined by Sani, Mandi and Rahu, the person dies by accident. 661.

When the Drekkana occupied by the lord of the 8th falls in *Pasa, Sarpa, etc.*, the person will die by imprisonment or by hanging. 662.

If the lord of the Drekkana occupied by the lord of the 8th combines with Sani, Mandi and Rahu, the person dies by hanging. If Sani is similarly situated, he will die by hanging or imprisonment. 663.

If the lord of the 6th or 8th or 'Kuja joins the lord of the 3rd, combines with Sani, Mandi and Rahu and occupies cruel Amsas, the person will die in battle. 664.

If the lord of the Drekkana occupied by Sani combines in the house or Amsa of Kuja, and is aspected by Kuja, the person will meet with his death in battle. 665.

If Ravi and Kuja have mutual aspects, and occupy each others houses, or occupy each others Navamsas, the person will be killed in a duel fight. 666.

When the 8th is occupied by many malefics, and these malefics join the Navamsas of Kuja and combine in cruel shastiamsas,
the person will have *Sangh itik i mar inu.*   667.

When all the benefics are in debilitation, unfriendly houses,
combustion, suffering defeat in the planetary fight, occupying evil
Navamsas, and combining with malefics, the person will be killed
by a *Sungha* or die along with other people.   668.

When Sani, Rahu and Surya are aspected by the lord of the
8th, occupy cruel Amsas, and are in combustion, the person dies
along with many others.   669.

NOTES.

Some of these combinations are preculiar and must be well
analysed.   Various kinds of death are here pourtrayed and the
manner of death known beforehand, will give us time by warning
to avoid such incidents and escape the death by superior knowledge
and suitable remedies.

The Moon is always specially bad in the *Dusthas* or 6th, 8th
and 12th houses.   If he occupies any one of these evil houses in
conjunction with Saturn, Mandi and Rahu and the lord of Lagna
aspects such Moon, the person dies by accident.   The Western
nations are generally indifferent as regards the nature of death.
When death ends all, it is immaterial as to how a man dies.
Whether a man gets an attack of fever, cholera, plague or consumption and dies or whether water, fire, wild beast, fall, battle or
poison claims him as a victim, it is immaterial if there is no future
state of existence after death.   The Hindu religion lays down
a very complicated system for the purification of mind and the
elevation of the soul.   At the time of death, the mind must be
cast into a mould of perfect peace and contemplation upon God.
Accident is called *Dur Marana* or evil kind of death and will
have to be avoided by every sensible man who has his salvation
before him and who wishes to attain to higher states of evolution

till he becomes finally emancipated from the grosser environments of existence and becomes one with the *Supreme Intelligence* or *Para Brahma*

When a man gets seriously sick he will either prepare himself to die or his well-wishers give him ideas to approach God and contemplate upon Him. But when he is engaged in any work or calling, his mind will be grossly engaged in that work, or event, and if he suddenly dies, the mind having been set upon some object, is drawn again towards terrestrial objects and will be clothed in the spirit forms of which there are a large variety according to the Hindu sciences. It is considered, therefore by a man, that to die by accident means the assumption of a devils existence, and these evil spirits, because they are held by grosser ties, are incapable of rising higher into the purer and more moral and saintly planes.

This conjunction requires Chandra, Sani, Mandi and Rahu all (four planets) to be in the 6th, 8th or 12th and possess the aspect of the lord of Lagna. Take a horoscope.

The lord of Lagna is Kuja and he aspects Chandra, Sani, Mandi and Rahu who are occupying the 6th house from Lagna, such a man will meet with *Darmarana* or death by evil accident. 661.

Kethu Kuja	Lagna		Guru
		RASI	Buda Ravi
			Sukra
			Chandra Sani Ravi Mandi

The lord of the 8th naturally occupies some Drekkana, and if this Drekkana becomes *Pasa*, *Sarpa*, etc., the person dies by imprisonment or hanging or gallows.

Sarpa or serpent Drekkanas are—

The third of Kataka

The first of Vrischika

The second of Vrischika, etc.,

The *Pasa* Drekkana is the first of Makara.

The author uses the word, etc., and I suppose he includes the Andajas or Pakshi Drekkanas (birds) (see Brihatjataka Ch. XXVIII. Sts. 9, 12, 13, 23, 24, 28). Death by hanging or imprisonment will entail much degradation on the man when he is condemned to death for some offence. But occasionally such a death entails honor upon the person when he is condemned to death for religious differences in opinion or as a patriot fighting for the cause of his country or for upholding the cause of the innocent people as against the tyranny and oppression of evil rulers or authorities.   662.

The lord of the 8th joins some Drekkana. If the lord of this Drekkana is in conjunction with Sani, Mandi and Rahu, the person dies by hanging.   In the second part of the stanza, the author uses the word *similarly* for Sani and I cannot really understand what he means. He names a conjunction with the lord of the Drekkana (occupied by the lord of the 8th) with Sani, Rahu and Mandi. He says similarly for Sani. What is the similarity I cannot guess.   He means probably, that Sani occupies some Drekkana, and if the lord of this conjoins Sani, Mandi and Rahu, death will result by hanging or imprisonment.   663.

He gives three alternatives, *viz.*, lord of the 6th, lord of the 8th, or Kuja. If any one of these joins with the lord of the 3rd, and also with Sani, Mandi ànd Rahu, and further occupies cruel or evil *Amsas* (*Navamsas*, *Dwadasamsas*, *Shatiamsas*, etc., the person dies in a battle.   Death in a battle is both graceful and disgraceful as the cause for which a man fights is just or unjust. In commenting upon *Vartmapunar Janmanam* it is quoted by Bhatotpala from Bharadwaja Samhita, that those who fight in a just cause and those who are in Pravarajyra or Sanyasa Yoga, go through the Solar globe after their death, and attain to Maksha or final emancipation, (*See my notes on English Translation of Brihatjataka Page* 7. *Stanza* 1 *Chapter I*). But there are many, who in search of aggrandisement and avarice engage themselves in killing business (war) and who are often killed in the battle. Such deaths in selfish pursuits must be held as disgraceful. 664.

Sani occupies some Drekkana and if the lord of that Drekkana is located in the house, or Navamsa of Kuja and is aspected also by him, he will die in a battle. 665.

Ravi and Kuja to have full mutual aspects must be in the 7th house from each other. Kuja aspects 4th and 8th but Ravi does not do so with any effect. Therefore if Ravi is in Mesha, Kuja must be in Thula to have mutual aspects. If Ravi and Kuja occupy each others houses, there will be no aspecting of each other. They may also occupy each others Navamsas. These combinations make the man die in fighting a duel. Ravi represents royalty and Kuja military honor. Their aspecting mutually or occupying each others houses or Navamsas makes man to fight a duel. This is always done in the defence of a man's supposed righteous conduct or political honor. Men may also fight for wealth, wine and women or the three W's and die in such fights. 666.

There must be many malefics in the 8th and these evil planets are Sani, Ravi, Kuja, Rahu and Kethu. Of course Rahu and Kethu do not occupy one house as they are always 180 degrees apart or quite opposite to each other. The zodiacal circle is divided into 360 degrees or equal divisions and Rahu and Kethu are separated from each other by 180°.

All the malefics should be in the Navamsas of Kuja. By malefics Venkatasa recognises only three, viz., Sun, Mars and Saturn. In addition to this, these malefics must be in cruel Shastiamsas. Venkatasa contemplates in this Yoga, a special conjunction which may not easily occur. This produces death in a sangha or crowd or company. A regiment of soldiers is blown up and almost all those who compose that regiment die at the same time. A Titanic drowning takes place and thousands find a watery grave.

An explosion occurs and many are killed. An earthquake happens and thousands are swallowed. A tidal wave sweeps over thousands of dead bodies. Serious epidemics rage and thousands are killed. A company is cut off without a man to tell the tale. Fire destroys thousands at one stretch. Rivers claim many as their victims in a few hours. Big tanks breach and floods carry away thousands. In all these cases, not one man but thousands of men are destroyed simultaneously, and this death is called *Sweghatika* (company) Marana-death or death occurring with many others at a time. A huge building collapses and many are killed. If these evil conjunctions have beneficial aspects or sources of good strength, then the danger comes and the man will be saved. 667.

The benefics are Mercury, Jupiter and Venus and all these must be in Neecha, or unfriendly or combustion houses, and should also suffer defeat in the planetary fight. The Sun and the Moon represent royalty, and Mars denotes military. Planets with th Sun will be in combustion while planets with Mars will be in planetary fight, and get defeated. The stanza does not mean that all the benefics should be in debilitation, and they will never be so. Only two benefics can be in debilitation at a time. Guru s exalted in Karka, and Buda is exalted in Kanya and Sukra is exalted in Meena. *Tna Asta Neechaha.* The 7th house from exaltation will be the house of debilitation. When. Guru is in Neecha in Makara, Buda can be in Neecha in Meena. When Buda is in Meena, under no circumstances could Sukra stay in Kanya. The longest elongation Buda can obtain from Ravi is 29 degrees and the longest elognation Sukra can obtain from Ravi would be 49 degrees. Thus even taking the extremest cases of elongation, Buda from Sukra will be 29 + 49 or 78 degrees, or say about three signs. But the debilitation of Buda in Meena will be 180 degrees from Sukras debilitation in Kanya. Therefore it is clear from this that any one of the benefics may be in debilitation, another may be in combustion, another may be defeated and one may be in unfriendly houses. All may be in combustion or defeated in the planetary

fight, or all may be in unfriendly houses, but all cannot be in debilitation at the same time. In addition to this, these benefics should
be in evil Navamsas and malefic conjunctions. Then the person
will be killed by an excited or enraged crowd, or will die along with
many others as in collisions, shipwrecks, etc. 668.

The author wants Sani, Rahu and Surya to be aspected by the
lord of the 8th, they should occupy cruel Amsas or divisions of
houses, and they should be in combustion. The last sentence is
quite absurd, and a learned author like Venkatasa could not commit such palpable mistakes. Rahu and Kethu eclipse the Sun and
the Moon, and are themselves never affected as they are *Thamo-
grahas* and possess the power of absorbing all vitality from other
globes. The Sun is the planet who causes combustion or *Moodha*
to the other planets excepting Rahu and Kethu by whom he is himself eclipsed. The word Moodha can never be applied to Ravi.
Then the only remaining planet is Sani and he will be in combust
when he is close to the Sun. Therefore to name three planets and
say they should be in combustion when two of them never have
such a state, would show either great ignorance of Astrological
Principles or they show that the manuscript of the author must
have fallen into evil hands who did not know what the author meant
and who might have unconsciously substituted other words. This
conjunction also gives *Sangha Marana* or death in company or by
a gathering of people. 669.

Stanzas 670 to 680 inclusive.

If the Sun occupies the 6th with another evil planet
possesing malefic aspect, the person will suffer from bilious
complaints. 670.

If the Moon occupies the 6th aspected by a malefic and
joining a cruel Navamsa, the person suffers from windy complaints.

If Mars joins the 6th house aspected by an evil planet and

combining a cruel Navamsa, the person suffers from *Rak'a Pitya Vyadhi.* 671.

If Mercury joins the 6th house aspected by a malefic and occupying an evil Navamsa, the person suffers from phlegmatic complaints. 672.

If Sani occupies the 6th aspected by a malefic and joining a cruel Navamsa, the person suffers from Gulma Roga.

If Rahu or Kethu occupy the 6th aspected by a malefic and joining an evil Navamsa, the person suffers from Pisachas or Devils. 673.

If Chandra and Kuja together join the 6th, the person will suffer from Branti, Swetha Pandu, etc.

If the Sun and the Moon join together in the 6th house, he will suffer from *Sarpasula.* 674.

If Buda joins the 6th house with Kuja aspected by Chandra and Sukra, and joining some evil Amsa, the person will suffer from *Kshaya.* 675.

If Saturn and Mars join the 6th aspected by the Sun and Rahu, and unconjoined or unaspected by benefics, the person suffers from Khasha Kshaya. 676.

If the powerless lord of the 6th or Kuja occupies the birth, the man will suffer from Ajirthi, Mukha Roga or Gulmavit. 677.

If the lord of the Navamsa occupied by the lord of the 6th happens to be Ravi or Kuja, the previous rusult must be predicted according to the nature of the planet. 678.

If the 6th house falls in a *Jalarasi* and Chandra occupies it, or if the lord of the 6th combines in *Jalarasi* aspected by Buda, the person will have Moothra Krichra.

If the Moon joins the 6th, Saturn joins the 8th and a malefic combines in the 12th, and the lord of the birth conjoins an evil Navamsa, the man suffers from *Peenasa Roga.* 680.

NOTES.

Bilious complaints assume various forms and some of which turn out very serious also. The Sun excites bile and if he occupies the 6th or house of disease with another evil planet, and possessing also malefic aspect, there will be bilious complaints. Evil planets are considered to be good in the 3rd, 6th and 11th houses, but in all the following stanzas it will be seen that their occupation of the 6th house, gives room to complaints of various kinds This shows the complicated nature of human existence, and how men are situated with reference to the various good and evil effects which they have to enjoy and endure. All the good and all the evil are not possessed by any one man. Dharmasastras say that within certain degrees of good and evil Karma, man takes his existence on this earth and possesses a power to emancipate himself from the grosser surroundings. If his Karma is better, then he rises in the scale of creation and occupies higher *lockus* or spheres of existence. If his Karma is worse, then he gets into the life of lower animals and reptiles and serves his rounds there. All diseases are a sort of punishment and may exist and do exist, side by side, with some of the most coveted objects of life in this world. Sani or Kuja or Ravi in the 6th gives victory over enemies and makes him prosper well. There is nothing inconsistent in the life of an emperor to get news of constant acquisitions of valuable countries and also as constantly get attacks of fever, dysentery, asthma, colic pain or headache and piles. In fact, he may be lying down on a fine bed from pain, and a telegram may reach him or his herald may announce that his enemies have been spoiled and that a large territory has been acquired and added to his extensive empire. He may get an immense quantity of wealth

and may also lose his wife or son or brother or some other dear
relation or friend. The human body is called *Roga Bhogalaya*
or the residence for Roga (diseases) and Bhogas, pleasures. 670.

When the Moon is in the 6th, he increases sickness. He is a
watery planet and diseases are fanned by watery vapours. If
such a Moon is aspected by a bad planet and the Moon also joins
some cruel Navamsa, the man will suffer from windy complaints·
This Vayu or wind results from consumption of wind, increasing
food, or from excessive heat which at an advanced stage will be
termed *Ooshna* (heat) and *Vayu*, air.

If Kuja combines in the 6th aspected by another evil planet
and joining an evil Navamsa, he suffers from Rakta (blood) Pitha
(bile) and Vyadhi (disease). Pitha is bile in one sense and heat
in another sense. There are some stuffs which produce heat in
the body and have blood purifying effect, while there are other
stuffs which increase heat and corrupt the blood. Take a few
ordinary examples. A man consumes almonds. These have
a heating effect, increase the bile to some extent, but they cleanse
the blood and thus invigorate the system. Hence in all *Unani*
or Mahomedan treatment Badam plays an important part.
Suppose a man constantly uses brinjals· These, like almonds,
also heat the body, but have a tendency to corrupt the blood, and
introduce blood irregularities and hence disorders into the system.
When too much of bile joins the blood, various maladies are
engendered and the man suffers from general weakness. Cruel
Navamsas are the Navamsas of evil planets such as Makara,
Kumbha, Mesha, Vrischika, etc. 671.

Phlegmatic disorders are of many kinds and they are often
excruciatingly painful in their effects. Uudesirable bulkiness is
a positive misfortune and those who accumulate much of fat are
often very miserable. When Buda is in the 6th aspected by an
evil planet, and occupying a bad Navamsa, there will be phlegma·
tic disorders. 672.

When Sani, aspected by an evil planet, occupies the 6th join-ing a bad Navamsa, the person will suffer *Gulma Rog i*. *Gulma* is the spleen and its enlargement is always a dangerous one. This is defined in *A mara Kosha* as a fleshy organ near the chest and placed more to the left side. *Pleha* is also a similar one. (See stanza 325. II Canto (Amara.)

If there is Rahu or Kethu in the 6th aspected by a malefic and joining an evil Navamsa, the person will suffer from diseases attributed to devils or spirits. Sani and Rahu represent Pisachas or devils Devils are of two classes Devils or Pisachas as created by God, and having their separate lokas or planes of existence and Pisachas or those departed spirits of human beings, who through foul deeds, or accidental deaths with avarice and sin guiding them in their actions, become Pisachas or devils These are generally mischievous in their tendencies and cause a lot of harm to the unfortunate persons whom they select to tease or hold. Those who are possessed of Pisachas are generally gloomy, weak, suffering from horrible dreams and constant mental fears indigestion, frequent motions, emaciation, and fits. 673.

If the Moon and Mars are combined in the 6th, the person will suffer from *Branti* or mental disturbance and delusion or hor-rible dreams. Some are very uncomfortable on this score, and lose their health and vigour.

Swetha Pandu is white jaundice. This is a terrible disease and will work a lot of mischief. Some jaundice makes the whole body, eyes, tongue. etc., quite green and he sees the world as one green mass Another variety makes the person yellowish and he sees all phenomena yellow. Some variety makes him white and he becomes quite pale and the whole phenomena appear as per-fectly white or colourless. If the Sun and the Moon join together in the 6th, the person suffers from *Sarpashula* or pain from serpents or shooting pains which twist and torture the man like a serpent or this may be the name of a particular disease. 674.

Buda and Kuja should be in the 6th house. Chandra and Sukra should aspect them, Buda should join an evil Navamsa. This combination produces *Kshaya* or consumption. This is a well known disease, and exposes the person to great danger and all sorts of miseries. Loss of appetite, loss of sleep, loss of memory, loss of vigour, expectoration, dry cough, restlessness and emaciation and final death. If there are beneficial conjunctions or aspects, these results should not be predicted. In this combination two benefics, Mercury and Venus are already named. Therefore the only benefic who could avert this dire misfortune will be Jupiter. 675.

The aspects of Rahu and Kethu have not been much commented, and very few authors have referred to such.

Sani and Kuja should be in the 6th and should possess the aspects of Ravi and Rahu. When Rahu aspects the 6th, Kethu must be in conjunction with Sani and Kuja.

The simple conjunction of evil planets is itself harmful and evil results accrue, as a matter of fact, to the native. The above conjunction should have no beneficial combination or aspect. The person will have Asthma and consumption. One of these is quite enough and both of them are quite prejudicial. 676.

The lord of the 6th should be powerless, and so also Kuja. If any one of these occupies the Lagna, the man will have Ajirthi or indigestion, or some facial disease, or enlargement of spleen. If the combination is very bad, then he may have traces of all these. 677.

The lord of the 6th occupies some Navamsa, and if the lord of this Navamsa happens to be Ravi or Kuja, the result foretold in the previous stanza will be according to the nature of the Navamsa lord, *viz.*, Ravi or Kuja. That is the disease they will give will be similar in nature to the Dhatu they govern. In the first chapter in this work, as well as in Brihat Jataka, all these details have been elaborately given. 678.

Jala Rasis or watery signs are Cancer, Pisces, portion of Capricorn and Aquarius. When the 6th house falls in a watery sign and Chandra combines in it, or if the lord of the 6th occupies a Jala Rasi and possesses Mercurial aspect, the person will suffer from urinary diseases, such as stone in the bladder, holes in the sexual organs, difficulty of passing urine, etc. 679.

Peenasa R ga means some peculiar nasal disease, which unfits a man to either speak distinctly or to distingush the smells. The Moon should be in the 6th house, Saturn should be in the 8th house, an evil planet should be in the 12th and that evil planet must be Kuja or Ravi, of whom one must be in the 12th house, and the lord of the birth should go and join an evil Navamsa, to produce this dirty nasal disease. 680.

Stanzas 681 to 690 inclusive.

When the lord of the 6th occupies *Dusthas*, being in Neecha, Moodha, or Satrusthana and the lord of the Lagna is powerful, there will be destruction to enemies. 681.

When the lord of the 6th is aspected by a benefic, occupies a beneficial sign and is in conjunction with a good planet, the person will become a friend of his enemies. 682.

If the lord of Lagna joins the 6th house aspected by the lord of the 6th, or if the lords of the 1st and 6th together occupy the birth, the person will suffer much from the machinations of his cousins. 683.

If the lord of Lagna, Guru and Sukra join with the lord of the 6th aspected by Sani, Kuja and Rahu, the person will suffer much from his cousins. 684.

When the lord of Lagna is powerful, if the 6th is occupied by Chandra or some other benefic and Guru joins in a Kendra or Kona, the person will live with his cousins and make his livelihood. 685.

If the lord of the 6th is Guru, aspected by a benefic and

conjoining a good planet, and Guru combines Mridwamsa, etc., he will have many cousins. 686.

If the lord of the 6th is in conjunction with a malefic, joins combustion or cruel Navamsa, unconjoined or unaspected by a benefic, the person loses his cousins. 687.

If the lord of Lagna joins Paravatamsa, etc., aspected by benefics, and the lord of the 6th becomes weak, he will be a high man among his cousins. 688.

If the lord of the 9th joins the 6th, aspected by the lord of the 6th, and the lord of the 6th possesses the conjunction of Sani and Kuja, the person will suffer much from *Choras* and *Agni*. 689.

If the lord of the 6th conjoins Gopuramsa, etc., aspected by Ravi, and the lord of Lagna becomes completely powerful, the person will be a great helper of his cousins. 690.

NOTES.

The word *Gnati* has no equivalent in the English language, and as we have Hindu Dharma Sastras the Europeans have none similar to them. In the European and other countries there are no restrictions as to births and deaths, and no ceremonies are connected with such important occasions. When a high caste Hindu dies, the death rites enjoined upon the next heir are too many and too complicated for an ordinary European to know or understand. When a man dies in Europe, there is no necessity for a son or anybody else to be near him at the time. I mean there is no religious necessity. The dead body will be taken and buried as suits their convenience. There is no restriction as to its mode of carriage or other disposal. The Hindu is tied down by a lot of *Karma* at every turn in his life and this gives rise to a class of relations who are entirely absent among the European codes of social law. Dharma Sastra and Law have combined effect in this Karma Bhoomi and this should be particularly remembered. *Gnati* means one connected on the paternal side, through his brothers only and who are bound to keep death and birth pollutions for 10 days and who would get the right to perform funeral ceremonies in the absence of direct and immediate heirs. They cannot inter-marry among themselves and they are held to be the children of one parent, and share the civil and religious rights and liabilities.

The lord of the 6th must be in *Dusthas viz.* 6th, 8th or 12th, and if he is in debilitation, in combustion or unfriendly house, while the lord of the birth is powerful, the person's cousins will be destroyed. This is considered by some as a bit of fortune, as with the destruction of the gnathis, the man will have no difficulties in the way of claimants to any ancestral property, Good aspects and conjunctions negative the evil indicated. 681.

Enemies are no doubt a source of trouble and anxiety and the less a man has enemies, the more peaceful he will be in every way. The lord of the 6th must be aspected by a benefic, he must occupy a beneficial sign and when he is in conjunction with a benefic, his enemies will become friends and he will have a smooth sailing in his life. A man without enemies will be a happy man and very few are so. As regards some of the greatest rulers in the world, they seem to be very unlucky in this respect and they deserve to be more pitied than admired. They always think that their lives are uncertain, that they are objects of envy and ill-will and are always hunted down by anarchists, discontented persons and those who have received unjust treatment at their hands and these are usually a large and bewildering number. When enemies become friends, a great relief comes to the man. 682.

The lord of Lagna must be in the 6th aspected by the lord of the 6th, or if the lords of the 1st and 6th occupy the Lagna, the person will suffer much from his cousins. These sufferings will be by carrying tales, fighting for ancestral rights, putting obstacles on the way to the success of the man, degrading him before his equals, etc. In extreme cases they may resort to poison, murder, fire, and other hateful methods. 683.

Here almost all the planets are named in the combination. Take an illustration.

The lord of Lagna is Chandra and he joins with Guru and Sukra and Guru also happens to the lord of the 6th and all these are in one house aspected by Sani, Kuja and Rahu. When these have the aspects of Rahu, they must be necessarily in conjunction with Kethu. This combination is not happily given and for all the Lagnas, the conjunction appears quite inapplic-

Sani Kuja Rahu		
		Lagna
	RASI	
	Guru Sukra Chandra Ketha	Buda Ravi

able, unless the lord of the 6th also becomes Guru or Sukra or the lord of Lagna himself. Take Mesha, the lord of Lagna is Kuja, the 6th is Buda and Guru, and Sukra must be with him, and there must be Kethu, and then they can have only the aspect of Sani and Rahu and not Kuja. In this conjunction cousins give the man much trouble. In some cases Venkatasa gets into confusion, and apparently has not examined the possibility of such conjunctions. 684.

The lord of Lagna must be powerful, Chandra or some other benefic should be in the 6th house, and Guru should be in a quadrant or trine to enable the person to live amicably with his cousins and make his livelihood through them. This means that the person, would be helped by his cousins and he earns money through their support. 685.

Guru must be in Mridwamsa, etc. Any good Shastiamsa will do. He must become the lord of the 6th and he can do so only for two Lagnas, viz., Kataka and Thula. Guru must be in conjunction with a benefic and also have the aspect of a benefic. Thus Guru must be with Sukra or Buda and be also aspected by one of them. The person will have many cousins. As no mention is made of their ill-will or good-will towards the man and as the combination is composed of benefics, we have to draw the inference in favour of good and not in favour of evil. The possession of many cousins will be good if they are well disposed towards the man and bad if they are inimicable. 686.

The lord of the 6th must not be in conjunction with a malefic, should not be in combustion, should not join the Navamsa of evli planets, and should possess the conjunction or aspect of a benefic. Then there is prosperity to cousins. But if these conditions are reversed, his cousins will be destroyed. The lord of the 6th with an evil planet in combustion, joining an evil Navamsa, unaspected by or uncombined with a benefic, will cause loss to cousins. 687.

The lord of the Lagna should join good Vergas like *Paravata*, *Gopura*, *Parijata*, etc., have the aspect of a good planet, and the lord of the 6th must become powerless, then the person will be a leader or a high man among his cousins.

The lord of the 6th (indicating cousins) by becoming powerless, brings his cousins to a lower social level than himself. When the lord of the birth joins good Vergas, and possesses beneficial aspects, the conjunction raises the man above the members of his community, and necessarily his cousins who belong to his own family.

He may hold a higher political rank, or be more wealthy, or educated to a higher extent than his cousins and naturally he will be a bigger man than themselves. This is considered as a special fortune and no doubt it will be so, if he becomes a higher personage than his cousins. 688.

The lord of the 9th from Lagna should be in the 6th and he should be aspected by the lord of the 6th and the lord of the 6th house should possess the conjunction of Sani and Kuja. Persons born in such combination will be very much troubled by *choras*, or thieves, robbers, and other pilferers, and also by *Agni* or fire. The Pancha Mahabhootas, Akasa, Vayoo, Agni, Appu and Prithive or

the mighty compounds, sky, air, fire, water and earth are both constructive and destructive and when they get these two different
moods they form or destroy mighty compounds as they please.   Fire
often destroys tremendous properties and drives thousands and
millions of men homeless and helpless.   The troubles men will have
from thieves, robbers and dacoits are too numerous and too plain to
require any elaboration here.   689.

When the lord of the 6th conjoins good Vergas like Gopura, etc.
possessing the aspect of Ravi, while the lord of Lagna becomes very
strong, the person will help his cousins.   This means that he will
become a greater man than his cousins and also will be inclined to
assist them as far as he could.

This should be considered as a good conjunction and the person will necessarily command much influence among his cousins.
The word used in the original is *enati*, and it should be taken in
the restricted sense in which it has already been explained in the
note to.   681.

The author from cousins, diseases and enemies now changes
the combinations which indicate his tendency to luxurious food and
the appurtenances which accompany its consumption.   690.

Stanzas 691 to 700 inclusive.

Where there is benefic in the 6th aspected by another benefic
if the lord of the 6th combines with a benefic and is placed
between two malefics, the person will be fond of *upadamsa*
(pickles, chutnies, etc.)   691.

If Jupiter and Mercury occupy the 6th or if the 6th falls in
the houses of Jupiter or Mercury, and joins Mridwamsa, etc., the
person will be very fond of pickles, etc.   692.

If Guru joins the 6th or if the lord of the 6th becomes
Sukra, and joins Gopuramsa, etc, the person will be fond of
sweet food.   693.

If the 6th is combined by Sukra or Buda, aspected by a benefic and occupying auspicious Navamsas and becomes powerful, and joins good Shastiamsas, the person will be always fond of sweet food. 694,

If the 6th happens to fall in evil signs, the person becomes a hater of sweet food. If the lord of the 6th aspected by a benefic, combines in a Martian sign, and joins Mars there, he will be eating much ghee. 695.

If the lord of the 6th is aspected by the Sun, the person consumes large quantities of ghee. If the lord of the 6th joins Ravi, Rahu and Kethu, the person will become *Vivadaohourya*. 696.

If the lord of the 6th occupies the house of Kuja, he becomes a *Vivadachourya*.

If Rahu and Kethu occupy the 6th aspected by a malefic, the person becomes a *Vivaduch urya*. 697.

If the lord of the 6th occupies cruel Amsas, the person becomes *Viv id ih ur a*. For father, mother, etc., the results wi l have to be predicted by applying these principles for their Lagnas and Karakas 698.

In this way the results for Putra Bhava and Satru Bhava have been very skilfully explained by the learned Venkatasa. 699.

These principles of the science have been explained for the benefit of the good and god-fearing people, and are not addressed to the *Nastikas*. These must be accepted by the learned Sadhus in Astrology. 700.

NOTES.

The author now gives two or three combinations which show a man's taste for pickles, soups, etc A variety of pickles adds a great relish to the food, and some are so accustomed to the use of pickles, etc., that if these are not available, they will feel miserable and would not relish their food at all.

A benefic in the 6th aspected by another good planet, and the lord of the 6th should join a benefic and must be placed between two malefics to produce much likeness for *Upadamsa* or pickles, etc. This seems to be a big combination of planets for a small event like fondness for pickles. Three benefics are named, one in the 6th, another aspecting it, and another has to join the lord of the 6th. This good conjunction produces only pickles, etc. 691.

When Buda and Guru are in the 6th, or the 6th falls in the houses of these planets, *viz.*, Mithuna, Kanya, Dhanas and Meena, and if the 6th joins Mridwamsa, etc., he will be fond of pickles. 692.

Guru must be in the 6th, or 6th should be owned by Sukra, and if the 6th joins Gopuramsa, Parijata, or other good vergas, the person will be fond of sweets or sweet food. There are 6 tastes or Rasas named by the Hindu Scientists and these are governed by the different planets. 693.

If Buda or Sukra is in the 6th, aspected by a benefic, and the 6th occupies a beneficial Navamsa, becomes powerful, and also joins auspicious Shastiamsas like Mridwamsa, Chandramsa, Kinnaramsa, etc, the person will always be fond of sweet food. 694.

When the 6th house falls in the houses of evil planets, like Mars, Saturn, etc., the man will hate sweet food ; not liking is different from hating. The lord of the 6th should fall in Aries or Scorpio, having beneficial aspect and joining Mars, the person will consume a large quantity of ghee. In all the Vedic Mantras, ghee is specially recommended in all foods and Agnikaryas and the Devatas are said to be highly pleased when the sacrificial rites are performed with copious drafts of ghee. A peculiar energy called *ojah* or *ojas* comes out of ghee and this develops will power, purifies it and enlarges it. Tne ghee prepared out of cow s milk is the best imaginable and this ghee has the energy to increase and cleanse the brain, to purify the blood, to correct the mind and to improve the moral tone of the man. Hence the cow has become such an object of adoration in the eyes of the high caste Hindus. 695.

When the lord of the 6th is aspected by the Sun, the person consumes large quantities of ghee. The consumption of ghee on a reasonable scale will act as a tonic in the system and as the ghee is the essence of *beef*, its regular consumption will act as a great stimulant for keeping the health in a normal and vigorous condition.

If the lord of the 6th joins Ravi and Rahu or Kethu, the person will become a *Vivada* litigation, *Chourva* a thief. This means that in litigation, etc., or in all dealings, he will be acting the part of a thief or perjurer or forgerer. 696.

If the lord of the 6th occupies the house of Kuja, namely Mesha or Vrischika, he becomes a thief in transactions. The same result should be predicted when Rahu or Kethu occupies the 6th aspected by a malefic planet. 697.

Similar results will happen when the lord of the 6th occupies cruel Amsas. This may refer to bad Shastiamsas or the Navamsas of the evil planets. Again he repeats the injunction that the character and peculiarities of father, mother, etc., should be ascertained with reference to these principles, taking as the basis for calculation, the house of father or the lord of father as the Lagna, etc. 698.

The author calls himself as *Dhimati* or one highly educated and intelligent. His name Venkatasa is also mentioned. He read the ancient works very carefully, analysed them properly, collected the principles regulating the prediction of results, and summarised the *Phalain* in a very skillful and clever manner for the two Bhavas, *viz*, the fifth and sixth. 699.

Then comes in a concluding stanza for this chapter which sounds rather curious for non-believers in astrology. The word used is *Nastika* or one who denies the existence of God He says that this work is not addressed to *Nastika*; but *Astikas* and *Sadhus* or believers in God and good people. It may be argued that if this is a science, then it makes no difference whether a *Nastika* or *Astika* studies it, and the results as indicated by the planets must happen. The Sun burns believers in God and also the non-believers. Two and two will make four wh ther a *Nastika* or an *Astika* work out the addition. Why then should the author address this injunction and show some invidious distinction. The answer is not far to seek When the principle of *Aptavakya* or the advice given by good and confidential elders, is violated, no teaching could be imparted to anybody with success; and chaos will be introduced. I shall give one or two terse examples In teaching the elementary mathematics. the teacher says to the boy that when *one* is *added* to another *on*, the result is *two* The non-believing boy says why should that be ?

The teacher can proceed no further and the progress of the boy must be at a stand still. *I mind* in a concrete state of existence is generally incapable of understanding an abstract principle. When Euclid is taught to the boy, the master begins by saying that a " Point is that which has no length or dimensions." The boy asks him why ? There must be an end of Euclid teaching, for the Professor can never show that point which has no length and breadth. A man should have no connection with his mother. If he asks why ? no satisfactory explanation can be given at that stage. No proposition could ever be proved without assumptions and all the grandest theories are based upon premises and suppositions. Similarly, when a man does not believe in God, and is not amenable to reason and conviction, the author observes rightly that his works are addressed to intelligent, good and God believing souls If others read them, they begin to laugh from the very outset, and the shallowness of their brains and their consummate pride prevent them from understanding or following any valuable sciences. 700.

End of Shasta Pshava.

KALATRA BHAVA.

(Seventh House).

Stanzas 701 to 713 inclusive.

From the 7th house, marriage, wife, husband, prosperity, curd, sweetness, milk, Agama, river, cows, urinary organs, and recovery of lost wealth have to be examined. 701.

If Sukra occupies the 7th house, the person will become very passionate, if Buda joins the 7th, he will be fond of other women, if Guru occupies the 7th, he will be fond of his own wife, if Sani joins the 7th, he will go after bad women, if Sani conjoins the lord of the 7th and occupies the 7th, his wife will be good. 702.

If Kuja occupies the 7th, he will be enjoying many women and will cause destruction to his family.

If Ravi occupies the 7th house, he will commit adultery among his own relations. If the lords of the 2nd, 7th and 5th combin e with Sukra in the Lagna, the person will commit adultery among many women and will be a bad man. If these have beneficial aspects there will be no evil. If the lords of the Lagna and 6th are in conjunction with evil planets, the person will be adulterous and bad. 703 & 704.

If the lords of the Lagna, 2nd and 6th have evil conjunctions or occupy the 6th house, or if the lord of the 7th joins the birth, the person will be corrupting females among his own relations. 705.

If the lord of the 7th joins Rahu or Kethu or has malefic

aspects, he will be adulterous. If the lords of the 10th, 2nd and 7th houses occupy the 10th, the person becomes adulterous.   706.

If any one of the lords of the 10th, 2nd and 7th occupies the 4th house, the person will hunt after other women.   If the powerful lords of the 5th aud 7th combine with the lord of the 6th or possess his aspect, the person born will have no issues.   If in such a conjunctions there is beneficial aspect, the person will have issues by his wife from adultery.   If the lord of the 7th combines in the 2nd with a malefic aspected by Kuja, the person will have children born to his wife by adultery.   707 & 708.

If the Dara Bahutwa Yoga appears quite inauspicious, want of issues should be predicted.   If the weak Moon in conjunctoin with a malefic occupies the 7th house, he will join others wives.   709.

If debilitated Sukrà or Chandra occupies the 4th house there will be destruction to wife.   If in this conjunction, the lord of the 7th occupies *Pasa* or *Sarpa* Drekkana, his wife will be hanged. 710.

If the lord of the 7th with Rahu occupies the 10th house, the wife will die by poisoning.   If the lords of the 2nd and 7th occupy their own houses, the person will have one wife.   711.

The number of wives may be predicted by the number of planets who are in conjunction with the lords of the 2nd and 7th houses.   712.

If the lord of the 7th is armed with sources of strength such as exaltation, retrograde, etc., or occupies the Lagna, the person will have many wives.

If in this conjunction the birth occupies *Nasasthana*, the person will be married twice.   713.

NOTES.

Many of these stanzas are very simple and do not require elaborate notes.   The proverb says that with a loving and chaste wife, earth becomes a heaven and with a quarrelsome and unfaithful wife, the home becomes a hell. Whatever may be the formalities of marriage, nature has implanted in man and woman such a strong desire for sexual correspondence that the overwhelming majority of human beings are always seeking sexual company. In some respects man is far superior to beasts, while in other respects he is far behind them. His intellectual development and moral advancement seem to depend directly upon the process of his sense gratifications and the sexual gratification seems to be the strongest, if not one of the strongest, among human desires. Beasts mount their own mothers and sisters and this promiscuous sexual correspondence seems to be one of the mightiest causes for the stagnation we find in their intellectual progress. On other hand, man progresses proportionately to the control he exercises upon his sexual desires and the highest man is he who completely controls his senses. Beasts are possessed of a powerful instinct by which they are prohibited to enjoy excessive sexual indulgence. This instinct rules more supremely among the female animals than among the males. The feminine animals would never permit their opposite sex to mount upon them unless they are in *rut* and this safety valve acts as a strong preventive upon the inordinate desire and sexual irritation of the male animals. In man and woman, this instinct is entirely absent, and in its place God has placed in the human species a *will power*, which, when properly developed and controlled, will be able to stop and control the most powerful and excitable sexual desires. There have been instances of strong-minded men and women, who have never even once enjoyed sexual pleasure in spite of all the voluptuous temptations with which they might have been surrounded. Of course these remarks do not apply to impotent animals or human beings. Among the beasts no such instances could ever be found, simply because animals have no strong controlling will power as men have got. The horoscope of every human being therefore becomes important in the delineation of its 7th house. Marriage plays an important part in the economy of human nature. A man or woman, who is well sexed and whose temperament is in perfect argeement with his opposite mate, will not only possess good health, cheerful disposition, reasonable contentment, but will also produce very strong, healthy, cheerful and loving children. These form excellent citizens and endearing brethren. Therefore, it is very necessary for each person to examine his 7th Bhava and when there are any defects found in it, it must be his first duty to remove the evil by the necessary remedies and rites which are so well organised in the Hindu ritual. From the beginning to the end of a personal career, rites are prescribed, which, on a careful examination, will be found to be full of significant meaning, and these rituals, when properly adjusted and performed, will set afloat a series of electrical and ethereal vibrations which are highly beneficial in their effects and which largely minimise the evil and increase the good. The word *Sampat* in Sanskrit means prosperity or wealth. Tastes are many and sweet tastes are recommended for high moral development. *Agama* means a series of rites ordained by the Hindu Sastras by which the special knowledge needed to make the proper worship to the various forms of deities, is inculcated. Milk, curds, rivers are also indicated by the 7th house. Some have never seen rivers and the comforts which large and holy rivers like the Ganges, the Jamna, the Godavery, can bestow upon the people who live in close quarters to them. The poseession of cows has more than a physical efficiency. Cows milk, butter milk and butter are so peculiarly formed that those who constantly use them, will become better persons both physically and also mentally and morally. These moral tendencies, produced by a free use of cows products, have been understood by the educated Aryans from the remotest times and hence the high place which has been assigned to the cow among the high castes of the Hindu society. Urinary diseases are very painful and they come of course as the result of ill-directed or excessive sexual indulgences. Recovering lost properties or stolen wealth or apparently destroyed objects has a peculiar charm for the mind which can only be conceived and described by those who have had the fortune to recover lost estates or wealth. Thus the seventh house occupies a prominent place in the examination of a horoscope and

Venkatesa now gives an elaborate sketch of some of the events indicated by this Bhava. 701.

There is some difference between action and desire for such an
action. Sukra in the 7th makes a man very passionate. Suppose
Sukra is in the 7th in debilitation with Kuja, this excessive passion
takes an undue hold upon the man's mind and makes him reckless
of honor and commit all sorts of sexual excesses. Suppose Sukra is
in the 7th but duly exalted and beneficially aspected. Then the
passions, though excessive, take a reasonable turn and the man will
have the nobility and strength of mind to control them. Buda exalted
in the 7th, will hardly make a man adulterous. In loving a wife,
there are various degrees and these are to be judged by the different
states of the planets occupying the 7th house. If the lord of the
7th conjoins Sani and both are located in the 7th, the person will
have a good wife.

But if Sani joins the 7th, he will go after bad women. It may
be asked, that when adultery is itself bad, why should the woman
be called bad, as every woman who commits adultery must necessarily be a bad woman. Committing adultery is no doubt bad, but
the nature of the woman may be very good and agreeable excepting
weakness in this direction. When Sani occupies the 7th, the person
will have the misfortune to hunt after dirty and quarellsome
women. 702.

Mars in the 7th makes the man enjoy many women, and also
bring on destruction to his family and surroundings. The Sun in
the 7th house sends the man seeking opportunities for sexual intercourse among women in close relationship. The morality of men
and women is often very curious and conflicting. Even in doing
bad things there are some principles which are appreciated by the
masses. Some men never commit adultery among their relations
even when they have heavy temptations. Some avoid incestuous
intercourses. Some avoid certain classes of females. Some never
condescend to enjoy widows or old women. Some do not care with
whom they have connection provided they satisfy their excited lust.

Some are utterly devoid of principles. Some seek promiscuous intercourse. Some fellows go even to the lowest grades of sexual disgrace and beastial gratification. The phsychology of human mind is often very strange. If Sukra combines with the lords of the 2nd, 7th and 6th and occupies Lagna, the person will be a bad man and will be highly immoral. If the lords of the 2nd, 7th and 6th with Sukra joining in birth, have beneficial aspects, then there will be no evil, that is the person will not commit adultery. Take an illustration.

In Lagna, the lords of the 2nd, *viz.*, Buda, and 6th and 7th Sani, with Sukra are located. But suppose Guru aspects all these from Kumbha or Dhanas or Mesha, then the person will not become adulterous or may go rarely wrong. Bad man means many things and the readers understand easily what is meant by this term. If the lord of the birth and the 6th are in

conjunction with evil planets, the person will be bad and adulterous. Here the meaning seems to be that there is no necessity for the lords of the birth and 6th to join together, but they should be combined with evil planets and may be placed anywhere in the horoscope since no particular house has been named for this. Take the following horoscope.

The lord of Lagna is Chandra and he is with Kuja, an evil planet. The lord of the 6th is Guru and he is in conjunction with Sani.

Where they are posited makes no difference. But suppose Chandra and Guru are both in Simha with Sani or Kuja, then the same evil results must be predicted. 703—704.

If the lords of the 1st, 2nd and 6th combine with evil planets, or if they join the 6th house, or if the lord of the 7th combines in the birth, the man will commit adultery among his relations. This is bad and the man will have greater moral degradation than an adulterer among prostitutes and other women of evil repute. Take an example.

Here the lord of birth is Ravi and he joins Sani. Sani is the lord of the 6th and he joins Ravi. The lord of the 2nd is Buda and he occupies Thula with Kuja an evil planet. Or all these may be in one house with an evil planet to constitute this immoral Yoga. 705.

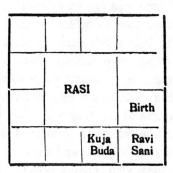

	RASI		
			Birth
		Kuja Buda	Ravi Sani

The conjunction of the lord of the 7th with Rahu or Kethu or his possessing malefic aspect will drive the man to immorality. If the lords of the 10th, 2nd and 7th houses are combined in the 10th house, the person becomes adulterous. 706.

If any one of the lords of the 10th, or 2nd, or 7th combines in the 4th house, the person will become adulterous. With due deference to Venkatasa Daivagnya I may submit that this statement may not altogether be true. Fourth house is the house of morality and within my small experience, only evil planets in the 4th, unaspected by benefics, will cause immorality. Take Kanya as Lagna. Then the lord of the 7th is Guru and if he occupies the 4th house Dhanas, I shall not predict adultery in the man unless he possesses evil associations or aspects. But the author probably means evil planets or auspicious planets who are wanting in power. If the lord of the 6th joins with the powerful lords of the 5th and 7th or aspects them, the person will have no issues. Fifth house represents children and seventh house indicates

Maraka or death. The junction of these two with the lord of the 6th or his aspect for them would destroy children. When the lords of the 5th and 7th join together, combined with or aspected by the lord of the 6th, and possess beneficial aspects, the person will have issues by his wife by her connection with other men. There are men and women of many and varied temperaments. Some men are very sensitive and they would be ready to lay down their lives in defence of their honor. There are others who connive at their wife's adultery while there are some who make up their minds to prostitute their wives and daughters for gain or for pleasure. Among women the same mental characteristics prevail. Some ladies are very sensitive and if they learn of their husbands immorality, they will kill themselves by drowning or poison. Some are quite indifferent as to how their husbands behave in sexual matters and with whom they enjoy and there are some others who actively help in introducing females to their husbands and act the part of pimps and mediators. There are some men who, anxious to get children, submit their wives to other men and get children through them and glory in the possession of such issues. Of course some have children, and believe they are theirs while as a matter of fact they may have heen born to regular adultery. Man's mind is not known to himself

If the lord of the 7th joins the 2nd house in conjunction with a bad planet, the issues will be born for other men and pass off as his children. 707 & 708.

Some combinations will be given hereafter, in which the possession of more than one wife will be predicted. *Dara* (wife) *Bahutwa* (many) *Yoga* (conjunction). If in such conjunctions where many wives are predicted or indicated by the planet, the evil planetary influences predominate, there will be no issues, although the person may have two, three, four or more wives. *Darabahutwayoga* means possession of many wives. Adultery is of many kinds and comprehends a large variety of immoral actions hardly

understood by the common mind. A man may commit adultery
among declared prostitutes, public women, dancing girls or women
who never cared to marry. He may commit sexual sins among
his own relations or among his friendly females. He may commit
immoral deeds among the wives of other men. He may commit
adultery among only widows, or among old and neglected women.
When the Moon is weak and conjoins the 7th house with a malefic,
he will corrupt married women. This is certainly considered to be
a more serious form of sin than the commission of adultery among
public prostitutes. Moon can be weak only when he is close to the
Sun and the conjunction will necessarily be with the Sun and also
with another evil planet. 709.

If *Neecha Sukra* or *Neecha Chandra* occupies the 4th house,
the wife will be destroyed. This can happen only for two Lagnas.
Mithuna and Simha. For Mithuna the fourth house will be Kanya
and Sukra is debilitated there. For Simha, the 4th house is
Vrischika and Chandra is debilitated there. In such a conjunction
if the lord of the 7th joins *Sarpa* or *Pasa* Drekkanas, the wife of
the man will be hanged. For *Sarpa, Pasa, Khaga Drekkanas,*
etc., see Ch. XXVII, Brihat Jataka and my notes thereon.

A difference must be made between *Kshina Chandra* and
Neecha Chandra. The first means combustion or proximity to
the Sun and the second means debilitation. When the Sun is in
Vrishabha, the Moon in the 7th, *viz.,* Scorpio, will be full, but
debilitated. But when the Sun is in Scorpio and the Moon also
is there, then he becomes both *Kshina* and *Neecha*. In the first
instance quoted, the Moon is full or poorna but Neecha. 710.

When the lord of the 7th house in conjunction with Rahu
joins the 10th house, the wife will die by poisoning. The lordship
for poisoning has been ascribed to Mars, but in the results predicted
for the period and sub-period of Rahu, *Visha* or poison is
frequently mentioned when he is in unfavourable or inauspicious
houses. Sani also shares these tendencies to poisoning when he is
unfavourable. The wife may be poisoned by others, she may take

poison herself and die, or she may unwillingly take articles which are poisonous in nature and die from their evil effects. When the lord of the 2nd is in his own house and the lord of the 7th occupies his own house, the person will have only one wife. Second house represents family in general including wife and when the lord of that house is in his own house,. he protects the family concerns. The lord of the 7th represents wife and he becomes powerful by occupying his own house. Here the author's meaning should not be misunderstood. It is not neccessary that the lord of the 2nd or 7th should be in the second or 7th house, but he must be in his own house. Take an example.

The Lagna is Vrishabha and the second lord is Buda. He may be in Mithuna or Kanya. The lord of the 7th is Kuja. He may be in the 7th or 12th, both of which are his houses.

Kuja	Lagna	Buda
	RASI	
Kuja		Buda

It is a great blessing to have one wife, and no sane man, with a grain of common sense in his head, would like to see his wife dead. But suppose the wife is quarrelsome, disagree ableand adulterous, then the question becomes extremely difficult to solve. Her continuance in this life means a constant source of hellish misery and the man need not have any further punishment or sorrow besides this. Then it may be asked whether it is desirable to have one wife, or change her for something better. Her life would be a great burden to him and her death would be a great boon. These are all complications in human affairs which have to be noticed by the psychologist and the philosopher. 711.

Now Venkatasa comes to an important point, viz., to find out the number of wives for a man. Take the lord of the 2nd and see how many planets are with him. Take the lord of the 7th and find out how many planets are with him. The number of wives will be denoted by the number of planets in conjunction with these two lords. There are various phases in marital state which one has to carefully notice. A man may marry several times after the death of each wife, or may marry several and all of them may be living. Along with married women he may also keep a number of concubines or keepers, who may live with him like almost married wives. Such instances are very frequent in human societies. 712.

The lord of the 7th must be powerful, *i. e.*, he must be exalted, retrograde or occupy Mulathrikona, or join good Shadvergas or six sources of strength, Lagna, Hora, Drekkana, Navamsa, Dwadasamsa and Thrimsamsa or if he occupies the Lagna, the person will have many wives. Evil conjunctions and aspects will kill some wives and good conjunctions will give them long life and prosperity. When the lord of the 7th joins the birth and the lord of the birth joins *Nasasthana*, the person will be married twice. *Nasasthana* means house of loss, and the 8th and 12th houses from the Lagna are called *Nasasthanas*. Both are bad and the readers may select their own house out of these two. 713.

Stanzas 714 to 731 inclusive.

If the 7th falls in an evil sign, if the lord of the 7th joins debilitation and if a malefic occupies the 7th, the person will have two marriages. 714.

If the lord of wife combines with a malefic or joins the house or Navamsa of debilitation aspected by a malefic, there will be two marriages. 715.

The previous results must be predicted according to the strongest among the planets, *viz.*, the lord of the 7th Chandra, Buda, Guru and Sukra or Kalatra Karaka. 716.

When the 7th or the 2nd house has evil conjunctions or aspects, and the lord of the 7th or the 2nd is powerless, there will be another wife. 717.

If Kuja occupies the 7th, or the 8th or the 12th without the aspects of the lord of the 7th there will be two marriages *(Kala-trantara).* 718.

If the lord of Lagna or the 7th falls into *Neecha, Mudha,* or *Aribhava* and occupies cruel Shastiamsas, there will be *Kalat-rantara* (death to wife). 719.

If the lord of the Navamsa, occupied by the lord of the 7th falls into debilitation, combustion or unfriendly Navamsa, is placed between two malefics, and is aspected by malefics, there will be loss of wife. 720.

In this way, the loss of wife must be predicted, by the lord of the 2nd, by the lord of the Navamsa occupied by the lord of wife, by the 7th house lying between two malefics, or by the lord of the 7th hemmed in by evil planets. 721.

If powerful Buda is occupying the 10th house from the lord of the Lagna, and Chandra occupies the 3rd or the 7th house, the person will be surrounded by many women. 722.

If there are many malefics in the 2nd or the 7th, and the lord of the 2nd or 7th is aspected by evil planets, the person will have three wives. 723.

If there is an evil planet in the 1st or 2nd or 7th, and the lord of the 7th falls in debilitation or combustion, there will be three wives. 724.

If the lords of the 12th and 2nd occupy the 3rd house aspected by Guru or the lord of the 9th, the person will have many women. 725.

If the lord of the 7th joins a Kendra or Thrikona and this falls in the Vergas of exaltation, own house or friendly sign, or if he joins the lord of the 10th, the person will have many women. 726.

If the lords of the 7th and 11th join together or possess mutual aspects and occupy powerfully a Thrikona, the person will have many wives. 727.

If the lord of the 9th occupies the 7th, the lord of the 7th joins the 4th, and the lord of the Lagna or the 11th occupies a Kendra there will be many wives. 728.

If the lord of the Navamsa, occupied by the lord of the Navamsa, occupied by the lord of the 7th house, conjoins a benefic, occupying powerfully Paravatamsa, etc., the person will have a hundred women 729.

If the lord of the Shastiamsa, occupied by the lord of the house, occupied by the lord of the 2nd, is powerful, and joins Mridwamsa and falls in Gopuramsa, the person will have two hundred wives. 730.

If the lords of the 7th and 10th exchange their houses and the lord of the 2nd occupies any one of the above two houses, the person will have numberless wives. 731.

NOTES.

Marriage institutions differ in different countries and ages, but the spirit remains the same all through these immense cycles of time. There are some men who would only look upon one woman as their consort or companion in life. There are some who possess two or three women under different names. While yet there are others who are notorious for their lustful embraces with any number of women, and who pride themselves on the possession of hundreds of women. This is both a physiological and also a psychological puzzle which requires vast experience to solve. A man sometimes has as many as thousands of women and physiologically speaking, it is next to impossible that he could possess any vitality to enjoy sexually so many healthy and strong women, or much less to give them any real sexual satisfaction. These women are generally guarded and their passions must necessarily be very strong. They require strong sexual action and it is indeed a problem for the expert medical men, for solution, how a single man could have real sexual connection with so many women. Facts are facts and there are men even now whose harems or Zenanas are filled with many women and who are supposed to enjoy them sexually. Evil signs are those which are owned by malefics such as Makara, Mesha, etc. When the 7th *Bhava* falls in an evil sign, the lord of the 7th is in debilitation, and a malefic occupies the 7th, there will be two marriages. The second marriage may be after the death of the 1st wife, or he may marry a second time while the first is living, according to other planetary influences. Beneficial conjunctions and aspects avert these evils. In all these conjunctions the *pros* and *cons* should be carefully analysed, and predictions should not be ventured on rash and ill-digested positions. 714.

Lord of wife is Sukra. Sukra or Sukla means vital essence or sperm, and hence he governs marital relations and passions where the sperm plays the chief actor. If Sukra is in conjunction with a bad planet, or joins his house or Navamsa of debilitation, *viz.*, *Kanya*, with a malefic aspect, he denotes two marriages. As he is the lord of wife, his malefic conjunction or weak state in the Vergas or sub-divisions causes two marriages. 715.

Compare the relative strength of the planets, *viz.*, the lord of the 7th, Chandra, Buda, Guru and Sukra, and specify the above results according to the strongest. The author uses the word *Karaka* in the Text, and also mentions the name of Sukra. This will be certainly a useless repetition, probably the original must have contained the word *Adhipati* or lord of the 7th house. It is difficult to make out what the author means. What have all these planets to do with the double marriages ? The stanza seems quite abrupt and meaningless unless we take it to be that the strongest among all these represent the *Kalatra* and her

prosperity depends upon his strength. In the course of the translation I have found stanzas suddenly introduced in places where
they do not fit or where the context does not justify their inser-
tion. 716

If the 2nd or the 7th has evil conjunctions or aspects and its
lord is powerless, the person will have two marriages. In all these
cases, the author generally indicates the loss of the 1st wife and
the marriage of the 2nd wife. *Powerful* and *lowerle s* have
been often explained in the previous notes. 717

Kalatrantara is the expression used in the original and it
means that the person will lose his wife before him. Does it
signify that he will be married again? There are many men,
who for various domestic, financial, social, religious, devotional or
physiological reasons, remain unmarried after the death of their
first wife, and probably such cases are included in these combinations of planets where Kalatrantara is used. There may also be
two marriages included in this expression. Kuja Dosha is here
referred to. The evil of *Martian* influences is generally recognised and followed in all parts of India. If Kuja in the 7th, 8th or
12th possesses the aspect of the lord of the 7th, the evil should
not be predicted. Beneficial aspects would also mitigate the
evil. 718.

Neech is debilitation, Mudha is combustion, *Ari Bhava* is
unfriendly sign. If the lord of the 1st or the 7th has any of the
above three states, and he also falls into cruel Shastiamsas, there
will be death to wife. 719.

The lord of the 7th occupies some Navamsa. If the lord
of this Navamsa falls into debilitation, combustion or unfriendly
sign, and is placed between two malefics, possessing the aspect of
evil planets, there will be death to wife The word used is
Kalatrantara which has already been explained above. There
are three conditions laid down here. First the lord of the
Navamsa occupied by the lord of the 7th should occupy a

Navamsa which is Neecha, or he should be in combustion or occupy an unfriendly Navamsa, second, he should be placed between two malefics and third, he should be aspected by a malefic. The second part refers to his position in the Rasi and not in the Navamsa. Suppose he is not between two malefics in Rasi, but is so placed in the Navamsa, could loss to wife be predicted? I should certainly do so although the text is not clear on this point. 720.

This is a short summary the author sketches for the readers information. To find out the loss or death to wife, the reader is asked to consult the position of the lord of the 2nd, the situation of the Navamsa occupied by the lord of the 7th, by the 7th house being placed between two malefics, and its lord being hemmed in by two evil planets. A Bhava, may have an evil planet in it, an evil planet may be close to it in the second house or its front when we count from the left to the right as is done in all my publications. an evil planet may be in the 12th house or back of it. or there may be three evil planets one with or in the Bhava, one in the front and one in the 2nd the rear, or there may be two evil planets one in the 2nd and one in the 12th house. All these conjunctions are indicative of evil and the reader should gauge their strength according to the different states named in the astrological works for the planets. 721.

Buda seems to play some part in the aquisition of women and wives. The word used in Sanskrit is *Bahustri samyuta* which means in conjunction with many women or surrounded by many women. A man, innocently, may have many female relations or maid servants, and protect them. Does the author refer to such circumstances.

By the context it seems to be plain that the many women referred to here will be women with whom the man will have sexual correspondence, and not stand simply as an innocent protector or helper of them. Buda should be powerful and occupy the 10th house from Lagna. This should be referred to only .n the Rasi. If Chandra occupies the 3rd or the 7th house from Lagna, the person will have many women. The text simply says 3rd or 7th house and we have to interpret it with reference to the Lagna. 722.

He now gives some conjunctions of planets which indicate three marriages. All the three wives may die before the man or the third may survive him or be may marry thrice, all of them may not only live with him but may even survive him and live long after his death. These complications have to be understood by the positions, conjunctions, sources of strength and aspects of the planets, Many malefics in the 2nd or 7th indicate three marriages. He also mentions that the lord of the 2nd or the 7th should be aspected by evil planets. Beneficial conjunctions and aspects will prevent these miseries to some extent or if they are powerful enough they may avert them altogether. 723.

When the 1st, 2nd or 7th is occupied by an evil planet and the lord of the 7th joins debilitation or combustion, there will be three marriages. The lord of the 7th may both be debilitated and also be in combustion. If he falls into both these states at one and the same time, the danger to wives will be heightened and the wives will die quicker. 724.

The original text records *Bahustri sahita* or one who is connected with many women. This refers clearly to sexual connection and not simple innocent company.

The lords of the 12th and 2nd should be in the 3rd house, and should possess the aspect of Guru or the lord of the 9th, to give the man many women. 725.

When the lord of the 7th occupies a Kendra or Thrikona, and joins exaltation, his own house or friendly sign, or if he combines with the lord of the 10th, the person will have many women. Possessing many women, though sentimentally be a source of pride, cannot be really considered as a practical benefit and such men are generally very unhappy and miserable. 726.

When the lords of the 7th and 11th join together or mutually aspect each other and occupy powerfully a Thrikona, the person will have many wives. Should both the lords of the 7th and 11th be in a Thrikona, or will the position of one be sufficient for the illustration of this principle. Mutual aspect can be only in the 7th house from each other. As both of them should be in conjunction or aspect, other positions cannot be repeated. These many wives may be living together or some of them may die and others may be living or all may die. 727.

The lord of the 1st or 11th must occupy a Kendra, the lord of the 7th must join the 4th and the lord of the 9th should be in the 7th, to make the man get many wives. The word *Kalatra* clearly indicates married wife and *Stri* may or may not refer to a wife. It may simply mean a woman. 728.

There are various kinds of women and hundreds and thousands in a harem or palace may not mean that they are all married. The lord of 7th occupies a Navamsa. The lord of this Navamsa occupies some Navamsa. The lord of that Navamsa should be in conjunction with a benefic joining power-fully Paravatarisa, etc., to give the man a hundred women. Take an example.

	Chandra Rahu	Lagna	Sani
Ravi Buda Guru		RASI.	
Sukra		Kuja Kethu	

	Lagna Guru	Rahu	
		NAVAMSA	
Buda	Kethu	Ravi Kuja Sukra Sani	Chandra

The lord of the 7th is Kuja He occupies the Navamsa of Thula. The lord of that is Sukra. He occupies the Thula

Navamsa and if this Sukra had been in conjunction with a benefic in the Rasi (which he is not) and if he had been occupying
Paravatamsa, etc , then 100 women will be kept by the man. 729

The lord of the 2nd occupies a house. The lord of that house
occupies a Shastiamsa. Take the lord of this Shastiamsa and if
he is powerful and join Mridwamsa and falls in Gopuramsa, the
person will have two hundred wives. Most of these wives will
come under the category of nominal sexual connection and are
generally attached to a person as wives. The stanza is vague
and non-intelligible. In Ch. I. Stanza 22, the order of Shastiamsas is given. When a sign is divided into 60 equal divisions,
i e., when each division gets ½ a degree or 30 minutes, it becomes
a Shastiamsa or $\frac{1}{60}$th of a Zodiacal sign. Take Mesha. It is
odd and the author asks the reader to give the Shastiamsas in
the order in which he has enumerated them. In the *Yugma* or
even signs, the order must be reversed, see my notes on Stanzas
22 to 27. He has, there, given the names of Shastiamsas, but no
where has be given the names of the planets who own them.
Therefore when we take a Shastiamsa, whom are we to take as
its lord? This is not solved anywhere in Sarwartha Chintamani
Brihat Jataka makes no reference to Shastiamsas and therefore
the lords of Shastiamsas are not named therein. In these circumstances, the Stanza must remain as vague and inexplicable.
730.

The lord of the 7th should be in the 10th and the lord of the
10th should be in the 7th with the lord of the 2nd, occupying the
7th or the 10th, the person will have numberless wives. This
means that he will have many. The harems of many of the
Mahomedans and the Hindu Sovereigns contain many women,
call them wives or women. Among the Europeans many
women are kept in different places and adultery prevails to a large
extent. The conjunction gives many wives and if there are
evil aspects, some of these women will die. 731.

Stanzas 732 to 751 inclusive.

In this way the marital relations for father, etc., should be predicted.

If the lord of the 7th combines with a malefic or if a bad planet occupies the 7th house, or if the lord of the Navamsa occupied by the lord of the 7th joins a malefic, or if the lord of the 7th conjoins cruel Shastiamsas, the person will have a *Kustri* or bad wife. 732 and 733.

If the lord of the 7th or the lord of wife, joins a debilitated sign or Navamsa, the person will have a bad wife. If there are beneficial aspects or conjunctions, the evil will be averted. 734.

If the lord of the 7th combines with a benefic, the person will have a good wife· He will also have a good wife if the lord of the 7th joins exaltation, own or friendly house and combines in Gopuramsa, etc. 735.

If the powerful lord of the 7th aspected by Guru, joins Mridwamsa, the wife will be good· 736.

There will be a good wife if powerful Sukra, aspected by Guru, occupies Mridwamsa.

If the lord of the 7th or Sukra is aspected by Guru and Buda, the wife will be chaste. 737·

If Guru joins the 7th house, the wife will be virtuous.

If the lord of the 7th occupies a Kendra, aspected by a benefic, joins a beneficial sign or Navamsa, his wife will be chaste. 738.

If the lord of the 7th or the Sun, occupies a malefic sign or Navamsa, aspected by or in conjunction with a malefic, his wife will be fond of drinking. 739.

If the lord of the 7th occupies a cruel Navamsa, she will be given to drinking. 740.

If the powerful lord of the 7th happens to be the Sun, combines with a benefic and joins a beneficial sign or Navamsa, aspected by a benefic and becomes a friend of the lord of birth, the wife will be dutiful and devoted. 741.

When the lord of the 7th happens to be the Moon, in conjunction with a malefic or being aspected by an evil planet or joining an evil sign and Navamsa, his wife will be crooked, cruel-hearted, and sinful· 742.

If the lord of the 7th (being Moon) and Sukra join beneficial signs or Navamsas, occupying friendly or own houses, or houses of exaltation. joining Mridwamsa, the wife will be charitable and dignified. 743·

If the lord of the 7th happens to be Kuja and joins cruel Shastiamsas, without power or is in debilitation, unfriendly house or combustion, falling in Pakshi or Satru Drekkanas, his wife will be cruel-hearted, adulterous, and mis-behaviug. 744.

If the lord of the 7th Kuja joins friendly house or exaltation, combines with a benefic, aspected by a good planet, and powerfully joins in Paravatamsa, etc., his wife, though cruel-minded will be agreeable and obedient to her husband 745.

If Mercury becomes the lord of the 7th, combines with a malefic, falls in debilitation, unfriendly house, or combustion and occupies the *Nasasthana*, lying between two malefics, and is aspected by malefics, the wife of the man will become a murderer of her husband and destructive to the family. 746·

If Guru becomes the lord of the 7th, is powerful, is in friendly house, exaltation, his own house and occupies Gopuramsa, the wife of the person will bear good children, be pious, charitable and possess a mind purified by religious penances and pious rites. 747.

If the lord of the 7th happens to become Sukra, combining with or aspected by malefics, or joins debilitated or unfriendly

Navamsa, falling in cruel Shastiamsas, his wife will be like a prostitute, cruel-hearted and given to pilfering.   748.

If Sukra is powerful and becomes the lord of the 7th, combined with a benefic, joins a beneficial Navamsa and occupies
friendly, own or exalted Verga and falls in Mridwamsa, his wife
will be eloquent, blessed with children and good character.   749·

If Sani becomes the lord of the 7th, combines with a malefic, joining Neechamsa, or sign, or occupies unfriendly house
with a malefic, aspected by a malefic, and joins evil Navamsa,
the wife will be adulterous, cruel-minded, and will bring disgrace
on her family.   750.

When Sani as lord of 7th, is powerful, and aspected by a
benefic, his wife will be virtuous, good tempered, highly obliging,
helpful to others, and when he is aspected by Guru, she will be
devoted to God and holy Brahmins and will be Philosophic.   751.

If Rahu or Kethu occupies the 7th and combines with or is
aspected by malefics, his wife will be mean-minded.

If such a Rahu or Kethu occupies an evil *Amsa*, his wife
will poison her husband, will court disgrace from the public and
will suffer great miseries.   752.

NOTES.

Venkatasa has often drawn attention to the fact that not
only the results of any person, in his horoscope can be predicted,
but they may also be predicted for the man's father, mother,
brothers, etc.   Take the house of the father for a man.   It is
the 9th from Lagna and Chandra Lagna.   Convert this 9th
house as the Lagna or first house of his father's horoscope and
then predict from the Lagna as the starting point all the Bhavas
or significations as we do for any man.   These facts have already
been pointed out in the notes to the earlier Stanzas, but lucidity
and conviction may often be obtained by a little repetition and
emphasis.

Take an example.

	Moon Rahu	Birth	Saturn
Mercury Jupiter Sun			
	Horoscope of a man		
Venus		Mars Kethu	

The birth is Taurus and the lord of father is the Sun while the house of father is the 9th. Both of these should be taken into consideration.

The 9th from Vrishabha is Makara and that must be taken as his father's Lagna. To find out a father's wife look to the 7th from Makara, *viz.*, Kataka. The lord of Kataka Chandra is in the 4th from Makara *viz.*, Mesha with Rahu. Take the father's wealth. The second from Makara is Kumbha and there are three planets in it. Buda, Ravi and Guru. His father was in good circumstances. The fourth house represents his father's education and its lord Kuja occupies 10th from Lagna and aspects his own house Mesha. This is fairly good. Chandra and Rahu there, having given him some education on a variety of subjects made him intelligent. In this way, all Bhavas should be construed and explained If the lord of the 7th or 7th is occupied by a malefic or if the lord of the Navamsa occupied by the lord of the 7th joins an evil planet, or if the lord of the 7th combines in cruel Shastiamsas, the person will get a bad wife. The original word is *Ku*-bad and *Stree* woman, kustri implies base, crooked and mean-minded woman For every house, good and beneficial rays of planets indicate fortune and success, bad and dark rays denote contrary results. All progressive and moral influences are contained in Light or *Ivoti* and all deteriorating and sorrowful results are contained in dark and opaque rays. Evil planets absorb vitalising influences and good planets give them. 732 & 733.

When the lord of the 7th or the lord of wife (Venus) joins a Neecha sign or Navamsa, the wife will be bad.

Beneficial aspect and conjunctions will avert this evil. Badness of wife will be like a thorn on the side of a man and he can never have peace or enjoyment with such a woman. His home therefore, instead of becoming a real attraction, will become a constant source of misery and unhappiness. 734.

Gopura and the good Vergas indicate prosperity and success. If the lord of the 7th is exalted or joins his own or a friendly sign and occupies good Vergas like Gopura, Simhasana, Parijuta, etc ; the nature of the wife will be good and agreeable. The character of a person will have the greatest influence on his surroundings, and it leads to good or evil associations as it is good or bad in itself. Nature can, to a very large extent, be altered by sound training, but the struggle between natural tendencies and artificial training is very severe and stoutly contested, and it requires very high order of intelligence and mental determination to overcome natural tendencies defects. 735.

The lord of the 7th must be powerful. This means he must possess the six sources of strength enumerated in Brihat Jataka, and also occupy good Shadvergas. If the lord of the 7th is powerful, and joins Mridwamsa, aspected by Guru, the wife will be good. Other good Amsas will produce the same effect. Mridwamsa makes her mind soft and yielding and these are special attractions in a wife which enhance her value as a help-mate in life and make her a great source of domestic comfort and happiness. Sweetness of temper and devotion to her lord are special attractions in a wife. 736.

The same result may be predicted when the lord of wife Sukra joins Mridwamsa aspected by Guru. A man may have a chaste and loving wife and she may be miserly and quarrelsome with others. This takes away much from her value even as a wife, and the surroundings become unpleasant on account of her disposition and uncharitable tendencies. But if the wife is both chaste and charitable, then her value will be immensely raised as a wife and an agreeable and desirable woman in the society she moves in. The aspecting of Guru and Buda, produces good and desirable qualities as both of them are benefics. 737.

Guru in the 7th house produces a good and chaste wife. When the lord of the 7th happens to be in any one of the Kendras, which is a beneficial sign, or occupies a beneficial Navamsa aspected by a good planet, the wife will be chaste and good. Chastity in itself is an admirabie quality, but to have a comfortable home where external miseries have to be forgotten, the wife must also be good and loving. From good wives, the author takes the readers to bad wives, such as drinking, quarrelsome, cruel-hearted, whoring, and otherwise criminally inclined wives. There are wives who murder their husbands, their children, their lovers who become hateful to them after some time, who poison people, whose hearts are as black as the darkest of nights, who run away from their homes with lovers of a very degrading type, who are given to excessive drinking and lying, and who quarrel with their husbands and make their lives most miserable. They certainly form the majority among women, and hence the Chaucerean complaint that the cow which fed on good and obedient wives was lean and dying, while the cow which fed on disobedient and bad wives was bursting with fat foi excess of food. 738.

When the lord of the 7th or the Sun is in an evil sign or Navamsa, aspected or joined by a malefic, the wife will become a drunkard. So far as this vice of drinking goes in the world, it must be said to the credit of the women that they are as a class addicted less to this abominable vice than their male co-partners. If the wife and the husband both drink, the misery, though great, will not be so severely felt at home, as if any one of them is addicted to drinking. Here the author seems to hint that while the man is sober, his wife becomes a drunkard, and thus causes him discomfort and disgrace. For various reasons, into the examination of whose morale we need not enter here, mankind tolerate some vices in men, while the same among women are considered serious. World's ways are curious. 739.

If the lord of the 7th occupies cruel or evil Amsas, she will be given to drinks.

What are these Amsas ? The author generally means by this expression *Shastiamsas* or $\frac{1}{60}$th divisions of a Sign or Rasi. But *Amsa* simply means a division of a Rasi. Navamsa, Dwadasamsa, Shodasamsa, Thrimsamsa, are all Amsas. Suppose the lord of the 7th is in Makara or Mesha Navamsa, these are evil Navamsas, and the reader should not jump into the conclusion that such a man's wife is a drunkard. I believe the lord of the 7th must be in several evil Amsas to produce this undesirable habit in a wife. A woman, may be given to milder drinks, like sherbets, tender cocoanuts, water mixed with sugar and enlivened by limes, cardamoms, etc. When the lord of the 7th is not entirely bad, but gets a cruel Amsa, the habit I believe, will be confined to simple drinks as I have stated above. There are other females who are averse to even such mild drinks, and this aversion arises from the lord of the 7th being good and powerful. 740.

Here a good combination is given. The lord of the 7th house may happen to be any planet, Venkatesa gives the results from the Sun to the other planets. The lord of the 7th should be the Sun, he must be in a beneficial sign or Navamsa and combine with a good planet, he must be aspected by a benefic, and must also be a friend of the lord of the birth to make the wife dutiful, devoted and chaste. Here the author's wordings are not happy. The Sun owns only one house Simha and therefore this combination applies only to those who are born in Kumbha Lagna, here the 7th house is Simha, its lord is Ravi. Take an illustration.

The lord of the 7th is Ravi. He is in Meena, a beneficial sign, with Sukra a good planet and aspected by Guru a benefic. But he does not become a friend of the lord of Lagna. In fact, Venkatesa will be entirely wrong if he said that the Sun should be the lord of the 7th and still be-

Ravi Sukra			Kuja
Buda Lagna	Rasi Illustration		
		Sani	Guru

come a friend of the lord of birth, as that relationship can never be claimed by Ravi and Sani, both of whom are bitter enemies as light and darkness neutralise each other. How then can the stanza be reconciled ? The author apparently means, friendship of the present time or Tatkalika. The planet in the 2nd house becomes a friend at the time of birth though he may be a permanent enemy. This will remove difficulties and reconcile the stanza to facts. 741.

If the lord of the 7th is Moon, aspected by or is in conjunction with malefics, or joins an evil sign or Navamsa, the wife will be crooked or always taking quite perverse views and opposing her husband and relations, she will be hard-hearted or devoid of feminine sympathy, so attractive and graceful in a woman, and will be sinful. The last means, that she will be adulterous, unreligious or fond of sinful deeds and will have unholy thoughts. All religious systems have recognised immorality as a sin, and also irreligious deeds. By this we have to understand that when the lord of the 7th Moon is in evil conjunctions or aspects, or occupies evil Rasis or Navamsas, the wife will not be good. The same applies to the husband, taking the 7th from the Lagna of a woman. Degrees of sinfulness, cruelty and crookedness must be differentiated by the relative strength of the planet, and his associations and aspects and no hasty judgments ought to be pronounced. There will be a great gulf of difference between a woman, who is a regular street prostitute and who is thoroughly reckless of her health and reputation and a modest woman who may once err, in her life under very strong and passionate temptations. So also with a woman who gets cross occasionally with her husband and a woman who glories in bullying her poor husband and making him to drink deep the bitter cup of unhappy marriage. Suppose Moon is the lord of the 7th and joins Saturn in exaltation and again when he is in debilitation ? There is great difference. Suppose Moon is aspected by an exalted planet and a debilitated planet, there will be much difference. Even in joining benefics unalloyed good ought not to be predicted. The conjunction

of Guru in Kataka and in Makara are quite different matters and give
different results. These general observations hold good in all Bhavas
and for all combinations and should ever be carefully remembered
by the readers and Astrologers in predicting any results. In my
capacity of an Astrologer, having had to mingle with all classes and
creeds of people, my observation of women's character may be recorded in several volumes. Some are crooked.to the husband and
quite agreeable to others. Others are crooked to others and quite
agreeable to their husbands. Some are crooked to the relations,
while yet others are crooked both to the husband and to the others.
To summarise the whims and fancies of the fair sex (although many.
of them are quite unfair and extremely ugly, and I do not know
which fool of a philosopher called them as fair sex) it is not easy
to do so in a short note like the present. 742.

The lord of the 7th, Moon and Sukra (lord of wife) must be
in beneficial signs or Navamsas, and they must also occupy their
own, or friendly or exaltation houses, and must further join
Mridwamsa, to make the wife charitable and dignified. The
original words are Punyasila, or fond of virtuous deeds and
Sucharitra or one who bears good character. Both words indicate
chastity, as well as eagerness to do good to others. I have used
dignified, specially with a view to convey the idea, that a dirty or
sinful womau can never be dignified. Adulterous women may be
charitable, as many of them are, but no real dignity can be claimed
by them or given to them. They may have the social gloss but not
the real dignity. 743.

If Kuja, is the lord of the 7th, joins cruel *Shastiamsas* such
as Raksha, Pratapuri, etc., without power and in debilitation, unfriendly house or in combustion, and occupies Pakshi (Bird) or Satru
(enemy) Drekkanna, she will be cruel-hearted, adulterous and given
to misbehaving. Kuja himself is an evil planet, and a strong planet
and when he owns any Bhava he will give it a military turn. Any
one of the evils enumerated above is enough to produce a bad wife,
but if all these evil sources of power accrue to Kuja, he will

produce a wife that would be a terror and a source of misery to the poor husband. Kuja may be in an evil Shastiamsa, a bad sign and Navamsa, may fall in combustion by being close to the Sun (within 10 degrees) and may have also evil conjunctions and aspects. Adulterous wives are of various grades. Husbands may willingly prostitute their wives for money or power, the wives may do so on their own initiation, they, may stand in open adultery, and may even control and murder their husbands. 744.

If Kuja, as lord of the 7th, joins a friendly or exaltation sign, conjoins with a benefic, or aspected by a good planet joining Paravatamsa, etc., the wife, though cruel-minded, will be agreeable to her husband and will be obedient. A person may naturally be inclined to be cruel, but by education or discipline, or with selfish motives, may be acting with agreeableness and obedience, Kujas ownership of the 7th though in good combinations and Vergas, apparently does not seem to be as good as Guru's or Sukra's. By nature Kuja is cruel and imperative and represents military authority. 745.

Buda seems to be more cruel than even Kuja, when he is bad and owns the 7th house. He must be in a bad house or with a bad planet, hemmed in by two malefics, in combustion and occupying the Nasasthana, or fall in debilitation, the wife will not only murder her husband, but will also become the agent, for the destruction of her family. Her family here means the family of her husband. Nasasthana may refer to 12th or 8th us both those houses are equally bad, 12th represents loss and 8th represents danger. Here as lord of the 7th if he occupies the 8th, he will not be so dangerous as when he occupies the 12th sign. Some are apt to put 8th as Nasasthana, but my humble view is it must be 12th rather than 8th. Venkatasa has not given what good Buda will do when he owns the 7th house. This seems to be apparently an omission on his part or on the part of his copyists. But by analogy, we can understand that when Buda is good, in friendly or exaltation sign, or occupies good Vergas or beneficial conjunctions, the wife will be chaste, dignified and honorable. 746.

Now we get combinations for excellent **wives**. When Guru governs the 7th, is in his own, friendly or exaltation sign, with good conjunctions and occupying Gopuramsa, he gives a wife who bears good children, will be pious and charitable and possessing a mind purified by penances and religious rites. Mental currents are purified by devotion, faith in God and elders, and observance of approved religious rites. All religious refer to God, and though his attributes are various as His wide creation, contemplation on Him, in any way will improve the mind, elevate the thoughts, purify the feelings, and ennoble the soul. Such minds are angelic and association with them leads to purity of thoughts, ideals and practices. Venkatasa does not tell his readers what sort of wife will be given by Guru when he is in unfriendly sign, or debilitation, or conjunction with or aspect by evil planets. But these are fairly indicated by the general principles suggested throughout the work and also enunciated by the best Astrological writers. When Guru is bad, he will give a bad, quarrelsome and uncharitable wife. 747.

When Sukra becomes the lord of the 7th, he will possess a double power. He will be lord of wife, as also lord of the house of wife. If such a Sukra, occupies unfriendly, malefic, or debilitated house, possessing malefic conjunctions or aspects, and falling into cruel or evil Shastiamsas, the wife will be like a prostitute, cruel-hearted and given to thieving habits. A prostitute or a woman like that need not be a thief or a cruel one. Some women are adulterous but they are very good otherwise. Some are chaste and obedient to husband, but they will have other evil habits. Bad Sukra gives an undesirable wife, while good Sukra, as the author is going to show, will give a very good wife. 748.

Mridwamsa seems to be good as he often refers to it in preference to many other Shastiamsas. When Venus is the lord of the 7th house, joins friendly, own or exalted Rasis and has the conjunction or aspect of the benefics, falling in Mridwamsa, the wife will bear good children, possess agreeable and lovable manners, and her character will be excellent. Chastity in a woman has been considered the greatest virtue, and all other qualities, however good they may be, fall behind that noble trait. This is a philosophic and scientific view. Chastity secures for a woman, a moral stamina, a saintly nobility and an elevation in ethereal currents which make her morally strong, and those who incur the displeasure of such a woman will pay a very heavy penalty in their lives. She will also be talkative. 749.

When Sani becomes lord of the 7th, joins unfriendly sign or Neecha Navamsa, with a malefic, or joins the Navamsa of evil planets, the wife will become adulterous, heartless, and will cause disgrace to her family. When Sani joins evil Vergas or Shastiamsas, though not named expressly by Venkatasa, the wife will become a bad woman. Sani would inflict a series of miseries, which others are not able to do when he is evil and joins with malefics. 750.

Higher the mountain, greater is the grandeur in landscape, but greater also will be the fall. When Sani is good, powerful, joins benefics in beneficial or exaltation signs, he will give a wife who will be devoted to her husband, virtuous, sweet-tempered, obliging, and helpful to others, and where Sani is aspected by powerful Guru, the wife will be philosophic and devoted to holy Brahmins and God. These are all excellent qualities in a woman, which would make her a model. But Sani will not give her that fine physical appearance, which good Guru or Sukra can give. 751.

Venkataswara now refers to Rahu and Kethu, and the effects they produce on the wives by occupying the 7th, as these planets do not own any houses. With this he closes, as it were, a part of the chapter referring to character of wives. If Rahu or Kethu occupy the 7th in conjunction with evil planets or possess their evil aspects, the wife will be a mean-minded woman. Meanness of mind adds poison to every act of human life and causes miseries to others as well as to the person concerned. If such a Rahu or Kethu joins evil *amsas*, Navamsas or other divisions of the signs

with evil conjunctions or aspects, the wife will poison her husband'
court disgrace, cause and suffer great miseries. Rahu and Kethu
are dark planets and they govern poisons, fires and other cruel
acts when they are evil, but when they are good, the wife will also
be good. 752.

Stanzas 753 to 755 inclusive.

If the lord of the 7th is close to the lord of the Lagna, or if
there is a benefic close to Lagna or the 7th, the person will have
early marriage. 753.

If there is a benefic in the Lagna, 2nd or 7th houses, and
joins a beneficial Verga, and if its lord is in conjunction with or
aspected by a good planet, there will be early marriage. 754.

If the lord of 7th joins Paravatamsa, etc., the lord of the 2nd
is powerful and the lord of the Lagna joins Mridwamsa, the man
will marry early. 755.

NOTES.

Different nations have different views about the ages of
marriages as different conditions and temperaments require early
or later sexual satisfactions. Marriage is a complicated problem
which cannot easily be solved. Old maids are most dangerous as
old bachelors are most deadly. It is not even the development
of the physical constitution and the sexual powers, as the morbid
state of the mind which has to be noted in the person in marriage.
There are some temperaments, like that of *Pluto* the philosopher
where the mind controlled strongly the physical susceptibilities.
Some boys and girls, are prematurely adulterous and such temperaments should not be allowed to run naked without early
marriages, which prove a blessing to them Some persons,
though in good position, marry late in life and their only explanation is that something or other prevented their marriages.
There are some, who, without the slightest move, get marriages
easily accomplished, while with others it will be a wild goose chase.
Here Venkatasa gives some combinations by which we can find

out early marriages. The lord of the 7th must be close to the lord of the Lagna, to have an early marriage. Proximity of the lord, of 1st and 7th gives early marriage. A benefic close to Lagna or 7th indicates early marriage. 753.

A benefic in 1st, 2nd or 7th, joining good Vergas and the lord of the house occupied by this benefic is aspected by or combined with a benefic, early marriage may be predicted. This means that a good planet must be in Lagna or second or 7th, and the lord of any of these three houses where the benefic occupies must be in conjunction with a good planet, or be aspected by him. 754.

The lord of the 7th house should be in Paravatamsa, the lord of the 2nd must be powerful, and the lord of Lagna should be in Mridwamsa to get the man married early. Venkatasa does not define what is meant by early. He uses the word Balya, which generally means before 16, and then comes *Youvana* or youthfulness, and then Koumara or manhood, and then Vardhikya or old age. The ages for these stages are variously defined, and must be taken in a general way. 755.

Stanzas 756 to 760 inclusive.

When Sukra occupies 7th or Oopachayas, the lord of the 2nd is similarly conjoined and the lord of birth is in combination with a benefic, the person will get wealth after marriage. 756

If the lords of wife, 7th, 2nd and 1st join Dusthanas, and join debilitated, unfriendly and combust Navamsas, aspected by evil planets, he will lose wealth after marriage. 757.

If the lords of wife and 7th join cruel Shastiamsas, and possess beneficial conjunctions or aspects, he will lose wealth after marriage, but will get it again. 758.

If a malefic joins the lord of the 7th and occupies a Thrikona and if the lord of wife, or the 2nd house is combined with a malefic, the marriage will take place at a distance. 759.

If the 10th, 2nd or 9th is combined with an evil planet, and the 7th is conjoined with a malefic, and joins a cruel Amsa, or possesses evil aspects, the marriage will be performed at a distance. 760.

NOTES.

There are some people who remain poor till they are married and then get very wealthy. Here the wife seems to bring luck. There are others who are rich before marriage, and become paupers soon after the marriage. The wife seems to bring good or bad fortune. Some get rich, lose it again and then get wealthy. Some marry girls within short distances, which give them great advantage for social funttions. Some get marriages at great distances, and these entail their own inconveniences. Venkatasa seems to think that marriages at great distances are brought about by evil planets, thereby considering them as unfavourable.

I shall not enter into the psychology of these marriages, but give them as Venkatasa has detailed in his noble work, Sukra is the lord of wife. Oopachayas are the 3rd, 6th, 10th and 11th houses from Lagna. *Dusthas* are the 6th, 8th and 12th houses from Lagna. Here there seems to be an astrological difficulty, which very few authors have explained. 6th house represents debt, disease and enemies. It is both an Oopachaya and a Dustha. The former is good, while the latter is injurious. When a principle explains in the same breath, that a certain thing is good, and also as bad, we are at a loss to know what way we have to proceed or judge. Planets in Oopachayas are good, while planets in Dusthas are bad. I leave the readers to solve these problems as best as they could. Like the Thirikonas, the 1st is both a Thrikona and also a Kendra. But generally by Thrikona we take the 5th and 9th and leave the first under the jurisdiction of a Kendra. Similarly 6th may be left to Oopachaya, and 8th and 12th may be taken as Dusthas, but this is simply my humble suggestion and the readers are at liberty to draw their own inferences. To get wealth after marriage, three sets of combinations are named. Sukra should be in the 7th or in Oopachayas, the lord of the second should be in the 7th or Oopachayas and the lord of birth should join a benefic. 756.

Soon after marriage some are unlucky to lose all wealth and become paupers. Sukra, lord of 7th, 2nd and 1st should be in *Dusthas* and join debilitated, unfriendly and cumbust Navamsas aspected by malefics, the person loses wealth after marriage.

Here Venkatasa has given many conjunctions, and the verse signifies the presence of all these combinations. But is it possible to have all these four planets to occupy the evil houses and Navamsas named and also be aspected by malefics. Suppose the lord of the 7th is in the 12th, occupies a bad Navamsa, and possesses evil aspects or conjunctions ? So also about the lord of wife Sukra. Then I should like to predict poverty after marriage. What the author may really mean is that if all the above conjunctions are present, the man becomes an utter pauper. But if some of them are bad and some are good, he may be reduced to poverty, but may not become an actual beggar. 757.

There are some people, who lose wealth after marriage, but again get rich after some time. If Sukra and lord of the 7th join cruel Shastiamsas and have beneficial aspects or conjunctions, the person will first lose money after marriage, but will get wealth again after some time. If the beneficial aspects and conjunctions are absent, he will not get again money, but will continue to be poor. 758.

The subject is now shifted to marriages at great distances. Human mind is very peculiar and complex. Generally marriages in close places are beneficial. Because the expenses are small, conveniences are great, facilities for relations are obvious and the husband and wife can frequently meet their friends and relations. A man in America marries a girl in Australia. The difficulties of meeting often, the expenses, the dangers of travelling and other worries will be great. Suppose a man in Calcutta marries a lady in the same place, they will have all facilities for meeting and enjoyment. If the lord of the 7th combines with an evil planet and those two should be in a Thrikona or 5th or 9th, if Sukra or the second house is combined with a malefic, the marriage will be from a distant place. When these combinations have beneficial aspects or conjunctions, the evil will be considerably lessened.

If an evil planet occupies 10th, 2nd or 9th and 7th has a malefic, joining cruel Amsas or possessing evil aspects, the marriage will be at a distance. Amsas must be taken as 60th divisions   In the latter it is the malefic in the 7th that should be in evil Amsas or the 7th itself. We have it said in a general way in Astrology, that to produce evil results, the house, its lord, as well as the planet in it must be bad to produce complete evil results. The man may marry at 10,000 miles or 1,000 miles, or 100 miles. All these are distances, but there is much difference. If the occupant as well as the lord of the house and the house are in evil conjunctions, or aspects, the measure of evil will be full. It will decrease with the increase in these lords being associated or aspected by benefics. 760.

Stanzas 761 to 771 inclusive.

If the lord of the 7th is less powerful than the lord of Lagna and joins combustion, unfriendly or debilitated Navamsa or Rasi, he will be married in a family, which is lower in scale, and degraded in position. 761.

If the lord of the 7th is more powerful than the lord of the birth, and joins a beneficial Navamsa, or possesses beneficial aspect or conjunction, is in Vaiseshikamsa, or is in deep exaltation, he will get a wife from a family higher in caste, position and social status. 762.

If the lord of Lagna is less powerful than the lord of the 7th and combines with a malefic or a debilitated Navamsa or is in the 8th house, or is in the Avaroha Bhaga, he will be far inferior in caste and social position to his wife. 763.

If the lord of Lagna is more powerful than the lord of the 7th and is found in Aroha Bhaga or deep exaltation, or combines with a benefic and occupies Kendras or Thrikonas, he will be far superior in caste to his wife. 764.

If the lord of the 2nd, becomes more beneficial, than either of the lord of the 7th or the 7th house, he will get a wife from his equal caste, and she will have good temper and devotion to her husband. 765.

If the lord of birth, is a friend of the lord of the 7th, there will be love between the married couple, if they are enemies, the couple will be enemies, and if they are neutrals, the relationship will be ordinary. 766.

If the lord of the 7th joins unfriendly or debilitated houses, or is aspected by a malefic when in combustion, or combines with evil planets without beneficial aspects, the man will get sorrow through his wife. 767.

The wife's characteristics, color, beauty, etc., will have to be determined by the most powerful among the lord of the 7th, the 7th house and the lord of wife. 768.

If Guru occupies the 7th, or the 7th is beneficially aspected the wife will be fair and virtuous. If the 7th is occupied or aspected by evil planets the wife will be ugly and her character questionable. 769.

The house of the lord of the Navamsa occupied by the lord of the 7th is called Kalatra Rasi. The house of exaltation for the lord of the 7th is called Kalatra Rasi. The Navamsa of the 7th is also called Kalatra Rasi. 770.

The Janma Rasi of his wife will fall in any one of the above mentioned three houses, or in the Thrikonas of any one of them. If the wife's Rasi does not fall in any of them, then the man will be issueless, 771

NOTES.

Though the real object of marriage is the sexual happiness and reproduction of the human species, there are other external conditions which add to or take away from the happiness, which should attend all marriages. A man may marry a loving, good and attractive girl and so far as his sexuality and reproduction, are concerned, they may be happily situated. But suppose, the girl comes from a lower caste or a degraded or disgraced family, the couple will be subjected to social stigma or idle scandals, and their environments and social relations make them unhappy or take away much from their real happiness and mutual love. But when both the boy and girl come from the same community or caste and are well matched in other respects, there will be entire happiness and agreeable social relations. Social stigmas are galling sources of misery

Therefore there is much in marrying persons and the selection should always be carefully made, and calmly analysed. Marriages for money, for estates, for employments, or for simple brute passious stand self-condemned and should not be encouraged. Character, family traditions, and agreeable temper and polite behaviour should, as far as possible, be secured. Birth represents the persons own caste, creed, position and characteristics ; 7th represents that of the wife or the husband. The lord of the 7th should be weaker than the lord of birth, should occupy combustion, unfriendly or debilitated Navamsa or Rasi, to give a wife, who comes from a family lower in caste, disgraced or degraded in position, and then necessarily possess a questionable character. The sources of strength and weakness to planets have been well explained in the first portion of this work.

If the lord of the 7th does not possess the evil combinations stated above, then the wife comes from an equal position. Suppose both the lord of Lagna and that of the 7th are equally bad, then the man and his wife will be equally bad and no happiness in its real sense should be predicted when they are bad. 761.

For various reasons, sometimes a man gets a wife from a higher and nobler family, and in this case the conditions are reversed. The lord of the 7th should be stronger than the lord of birth, be beneficially aspected or conjoined, be deeply exalted and occupy a Vaiseshikamsa, to get a wife from a higher, richer and nobler family than his own   762.

It is one thing to be a poor and honorable man, and possess good caste, and another to be poor and also degraded and disgraced in society.

A wife may come from a richer family, but her husband though poor may be quite honorable, and dignified. But if the lord of the 7th is far superior to that of the birth and the latter is debilitated, aspected by evil planets or conjoined with them, the husband will be from a low and disreputable family, while his wife will come from a nobler family. These combinations seem to indicate, conditions before the marriage, and not what may happen to the couple after the union. His occupying the 8th is bad, as also Avaroha.

Aroha means the planet acquiring greater and greater strength while *Avaroha* means the planet in his fall or approaching his debilitation. Aroha means the ascending, while Avaroha means going down or descending.   763

The birthlord to be stronger than that of the 7th, or be in Aroha (ascending) or Paramochha (deep exaltation) or combine with good planets, and occupy quadrants or trimes then the man will be far superior to his wife in caste and creed. All over the world there are social distinctions, and history has never recorded of a country, where these social distinctions in some shape or other are not observed.   764.

If lord of the 2nd should be more beneficial than the lord of the 7th or the house itself, he will get a wife from his equal caste and she will be agreeable, devoted, and good-tempered towards her husband. When the 7th house is occupied or aspected by benefics, or possesses beneficial Vergas, or is hemmed in by benefics, or its lord is exalted or otherwise powerful, the house may be said to be beneficial. Equality in caste, creed and finances, will be more conducive to marital happiness and will generally throw the couple into greater love and sympathy. 765.

Here is a stanza which is difficult to reconcile with the general principles of Astrology. The lord of the 7th of any house or Lagna will never be a friend of him. Is it possible, therefore, to condemn Venkatasa on this ground, or are we to understand something different from what the sloka ordinarily means. Take Mesha, the 7th is Thula, Mars and Venus are enemies. Take Vrishabha and Vrischika, again Venus and Mars unfriendly. Mithuna and Dhanas or Buda and Guru are enemies, Kataka and Makara, or their lords, Moon and Saturn are not friends. Simha and Kumbha, or Ravi and Sani are bitter enemies. Kanya and Meena or Buda and Guru are enemies. Thula and Mesha or Sukra and Kuja are enemies. Vrischika and Vrishabha or Kuja and Sukra are enemies. Similarly for other signs. These are permanent friendships and enmities. There is also temporary friendship, and so, the author probably refers to this more than to the permanent. When the lord of the 1st and 7th are friends, the couple will be loving. When they are enemies, the husband and wife will be enemies, when they are neutral the pair will be indifferent. 766.

Some will have pain, some pleasure and some indifference through their wives and husbands. Venkatasa now gives an idea of such marriages. The 7th represents wife and its lord should be debilitated or in unfriendly houses, or aspected by malefics, when he is in combustion or in conjunction with evil planets, without beneficial aspects, wife will bring sorrow and misery. Beneficial conjunctions will improve the combination, combustion, unfriendly houses and debilitation are bad for any planet, and they produce miserable results. 767.

There are three, *viz.*, the lord of wife or Sukra, the lord of the 7th house, and 7th house itself. Whichever of these three, is most powerful, it would influence the color, beauty, character and physical composition of the wife. In the next he gives some more useful information which should be specially noted. For Mesha, the lord of the 7th is Sukra, the 7th is Thula, and the lord of wife is Sukra. For Mithuna, the lord of the 7th is Guru, the 7th is Dhanas and the lord of wife is Sukra. Her personal appearances, will have to be determined by the most powerful among these three. The power of a planet consists in its position, occupation, ownership, associations, aspects, and how it is situated in the Vergas. 768.

If Guru is in 7th, or it has good aspects, the wife will be fair and virtuous, Virtue and fairness are not always in union. A virtuous woman may or may not be fair, and so also, a fair woman may or may not be virtuous.

Evil planets in the 7th, make the wife ugly and bad or immoral. 769.

The lord of the 7th occupies some Navamsa. Its lord has some house, and that is called Kalatri Rasi. Take an illustration.

	Moon Rahu	Birth	Saturn		Lagna Guru	Rahu·	
Ravi Buda Guru	RASI				NAVAMSA		
Sukra		Kethu Mars		Buda	Kethu	Ravi Sani Kuja Sukra	Chandra

Here the lord of the 7th is Kuja. He occupies Thula Navamsa. Its lord is Sukra. His house is Vrishabha and Thula. One of them must be called the Kalatra Rasi. There are five planets who own two houses each and only two, the Sun and the Moon who own only one house. When there are two houses which house should be taken ? Venkatasa is unmercifully silent or vague on a most important point like this. We may or will have to take both the houses of a planet as *Kalatra Rasis*. The lord of the 7th must necessarily be exalted in some house. In the horoscope under notice, the lord of the 7th is Kuja and he is exalted in Makara. Hence for this horoscope Makara is a Kalatra Rasi. The Navamsa of the 7th here will be the 4th of Thula *viz.*, Makara, and it is already a Kalatra Rasi. The Navamsa of the 7th will always be that in the 7th which is represented by the Navamsa in Lagna. The Navamsa of Lagna is the 4th here and so the 4th Navamsa of the 7th is Makara. For Thula we count from Thula and for Vrishabha we count from Makara. 770.

Janma Rasi is the house in any horoscope where the Moon falls at the time of birth. The above stanza is given to find out, whether a girl will be married to a person or not and how to find out the Janma Rasi of the girl. This should fall in any one of the above three named Kalatra Rasis, *i. e.*, in Thula, Vrishabha or Makara. As a matter of fact, the Janma Rasi of the wife of this horoscope falls in Vrishabha as she has Rohini as her Star, or the Janma Rasi of the wife will fall in the Thrikonas of any one of them, or in the 5th and 9th houses, in the above named Kalatra Rasis. If it does not fall there, the man will have no issues. The author does not say, whether such a woman does or does not become the wife of the man. From the stanza it is implied that a girl's Janma Rasi may not even fall in the Thrikonas, and that when it does not fall, the person will have no issues. Probably by this be seems to hint that the potency of reproduction will be gone by the Janma Rasi of the girl not falling in any one of these abovenamed signs. This will specially be useful in venturing predictions about the probabilities of a certain couple getting married or not. When many horoscopes are submitted to Astrologers, for marriage consultations, by applying this rule he may eliminate such of the girl's horoscopes. whose Moon does not fall in any one of the houses named above. Even if such a marriage takes place, the union will be fruitless and the objects of marriage, namely, the proper begetting of legitimate children, will be thwarted, and the domestic happiness for want of children, will be greatly lessened. 771.

Stanza—The woman whose Rasi is Vrishabha, Simha, Kanya, or Vrischika will bear few children. But if these are occupied by benefics, she will have many sons adorned with noble qualities. 772.

NOTES.

In each horoscope, Moon falls in some sign and it is called *Janma Rasi.* The ascendant or *Birth* is different, but both may fall in one and the same sign. *Putra* is given in the original and it means a son. But I believe it is used by Venkatasa to denote children. The 5th, its lord and the lord of children Guru, determine the sex, number, fortune and qualities of children. Impotent signs and planets seem to produce few children. Vrishabha has Kanya as the 5th owned by the impotent planet Buda. If Vrishabha is occupied by Guru, then as lord of children he will powerfully aspect Kanya and give many excellent children. Simha has Dhanas as 5th, and though owned by a male planet Guru, who is also lord of children, there will be few children on account of its martial nature. Kanya has Makara as 5th, owned by the impotent Sani. Vrischika has Meena as 5th, but on account of its fishy nature, there will be few children. Benefics in Janma Rasi give many and excellent children. Out of 3 benefics, Guru is male, Sukra is female, and Buda is impotent. Full Moon is also classified as a benefic and he is a female. Females in Janma Rasi give feminine and males, there masculine issues. The extent of fortune and excellence of character will have to be determined by the sources of strength of the benefics. Evil planets in conjunction with benefics take away much of their merit. Evil conjunctions in Janma Rasi without benefics produce undesirable results. 772:

Stanzas 773 to 775 inclusive.

The Sun in the 7th gives connection with barren women. Moon in the 7th with servile women and Mars in the 7th with barren or menses women. 773.

Mercury in the 7th produces union with poor, dancing or mercantile women. Jupiter in the 7th with Brahmin and Venus in the 7th with pregnant women. 774.

Saturn, Rahu and Kethu in the 7th, give sexual connectiou with mean or menses women.   Rahu in the 7th, gives their connection with a pregnant woman.   Saturn in the 7th gives union with black and dwarfish woman.   775.

NOTES.

These three verses are plainly put in English and do not require long notes. The word used in 775 is *Pushpini* or a woman who has just matured. But it may also refer to menses women in general. Venkatasa does not particularly say what sort of female she will be when Kethu occupies the 7th. Even here the sources of strength and weakness must not be forgotten. Exalted Ruda will give a rich prostitute, while a debilitated Buda will give a woman of the lowest prostitute or mercantile caste. 773-74-75.

Stanza—Similar results will have to be predicted by the planets in the 4th house, and the places of sexual union have to be determined by the Sun, etc., in the 4th house. 776.

NOTES.

Fourth house represents morality, and when it is occupied by malefics, adulterous connection may be predicted and when benefics are there, connection with wife in such states, as have been represented above ought to be guessed. When Guru is in the 7th, pure and exalted, certainly it would be revolting against the principles of astrology to say that a man will commit a more horrible sin than when Ravi or Kuja occupies it. It may be questioned as to whether there could be any difference in adultery and immoral deeds. Vedas and Dharma Sastras, along with the moral codes and usages of various nations, declare certain connections as more immoral than others, although adultery can never be classified as a meritorious deed.

To commit adultery with his own mother will be more horrible than with his sister, or a distant relation or a female who lives in open prostitution. Like love or gratitude, there are degrees of merit and sin and these will have to be determined by the strength of planets. About these incestuous or highly immoral connection, refer to my Self Instructor on Astrology. 6th Ed.

Sexual union is not confined to bed room and declared night times. There are fellows who seek opportunities and women who gratify them in a variety of ways, means and places which are really startling and shocking to innocent people, but which are all the same committed in open violence of all sense of shame, civilisation, culture and religious injunctions. Some of the dirty women and men at the head of even religious movements, commit, and connive and recommend shocking forms of sexual gratification, and mankind blindly follow them in such nefarious deeds. Some commit adultery in regular bed rooms, some in cattle sheds, some in boats and carriages, some in temples and churches and mosques, while others take to closets, privy and slaughter houses, while yet others have minds to roll in streets, haystacks, and filthy sewers. There are some who have unnatural connections, and the " history of prostitution" published by the enlightened English and American Authors records many mischievous instances of immorality. Venkatasa gives a clue as to places where sexual union takes place, by the planets occupying the 4th house. 776.

Stanza—Sun in the 4th gives union in the jungles, Moon in houses, Mars close to walls, Mercury places of enjoyment, Jupiter godly places, Venus near watery places, Saturn in horse stables and monkey menagery, and Rahu in stables occupied by elephants, etc. 777.

NOTES.

The translation is easy. By this, one should not run away with the idea that the man or the woman will have sexual unions always in such places and nowhere else.

When it is said that a boy reads well in the school, it never means that he will not study or read outside school premises.

The man's inclinations are shown here. They seek pleasure in
gratifying their sexual passions in localities referred to when it is
possible or available. 777.

Stanza—When the four Kendras are occupied or aspected by
malefics, the person will commit sexual union like a quadruped.
778.

NOTES.

Eighty-four varieties of sexual union and methods are described in Kokkokam or Sanskrit sexual sciences and the curious
may refer to them for details. It seems that if all the quadrants
are occupied by pure malefics without any beneficial rays to
modify them, there may be greater guilt than the form of sexual-
union. Here it means that benefics in Kendras prevent such
unions. 778.

Stanzas 778 and 779 A.

If three Kendras are occupied by evil planets, the connection
will be like quadrupeds, or if the 4th house is occupied by Sani,
Ravi or Kuja, the operation will resemble that of a quadruped.
779.

If Rahu or Kuja occupy 7th or 4th, the union will be similar
to a quadruped. 779A.

NOTES.

Here the question arises as to what is meant by the expression "like a quadruped." It may refer to the way they
operate or the violence with which they approach their mates.
There seems to be repetition in the latter portion of the two
stanzas. 779—79A.

Stanza—If the lord of the 7th aspects the 4th, and joins Sukra
or his house, the person will kiss the sexual organ. If the lord of
Lagna joins debilitation or such a Navamsa, he will be guilty
of kissing sexual organs. 780.

NOTES.

From a scientific point of view, the subject is of the highest importance as showing the various noble and debasing mental currents which affect a man in his earthly career. There are some who think food and sexuality are simple necessities, about which much care and attention need not be bestowed and so simply take, in an indifferent way, what they get, and have union with wife or other women, as they do about calls of nature. On the other hand, there are many who live, to gratify these appetites and leave no stone unturned to satisfy their unholy passions. In the enjoyment they show all sorts of disgusting solicitude, and adopt methods which are quite undesirable and immoral. Some nasty practices are invented and practised, and the most enlightened nations are guilty of the greatest violations in such matters. There are some who kiss the sexual organs of females, while the women are equally guilty of such male practices. The aspecting of the 4th by the lord of the 7th with Sukra, or in the houses of Sukra, namely, Vrishabha or Thula, or if the lord of Lagna joins his debilitated Rasi or Navamsa, the man will kiss female organs. When there are beneficial conjunctions or aspects, no such practices should be predicted. 780.

Stanza—Kuja in the 7th gives the wife dried up breast, Sani, Rahu, etc., give loose or hanging breast, Ravi gives erect and hard breast, other planets give desirable and attractive breast. 781.

NOTES.

A woman becomes attractive by good teeth, good breast, and good eyes. A lady with a well-developed breast, and a good face, will be very attractive and pleasing. A dried-up breast shows hot temperament, and a loose or hanging breast, an unhealthy constitution. A female will be comely when she possesses a well-developed and attractive breast. Unfortunately many ladies pine for such breasts and many lovers go in search of them. A healthy and well-grown breast will give good and nourishing milk, and children who drink it will become robust and healthy. Sani, Rahu, Kethu, and waning Moon produce loose or hanging breast. Guru, Sukra, Buda and full Moon produce an attractive and healthy breast in the wife. 781.

Stanza—If an evil planet occupies the 7th, her breast will be unequal. The wife will have an unequal breast, when there is an evil planet in the 7th, whether its lord is a malefic or benefic. 782.

NOTES.

When the two breasts are unequal or of different dimensions, the appearance becomes repulsive. An evil planet in the 7th causes this unequality. 782.

Stanzas 783 and 784.

When there are two benefics in the 7th and its lord conjoins a benefic, the wife will have her breast equally developed, but when there is an evil planet in the 7th, the breast will become unequal. 783.

If the lord of the 7th joins a benefic, is a watery planet, conjoins a watery sign, and possesses the aspect of Guru, the wife's breast will be huge and highly developed. 784.

NOTES.

Watery planets are Moon and Venus. Watery signs are Kataka, Makara and Meena. Half watery signs are Kanya and Kumbha. A huge breast, beyond proportion, though pleasing to some, will be repulsive to many. To produce this growth in a round and compact manner, there must be beneficial conjunction to a watery planet in a watery sign and with the aspect of Guru, who is corpulent. Among these huge breasts there are some which are loose and hanging, and which produce quite a repulsive appearance, while compact and rounded large breasts are attractive and add beauty to the lady. 783—84.

Stanzas 785 to 794 inclusive.

If Ravi or Kuja joins Sani, Rahu or Mandi and the lord of 7th becomes a malefic, the wife's sexual organ will be large. 785.

If the lord of 7th is Guru or Sukra and joins a beneficial Navamsa, his wife's sexual organ will be moderate. But if he joins a malefic, the sexual organ, will be long. 786.

If the lord of the 7th is Sani, the sexual organ will be short or small, if Chandra, the organ will be moderate, and if Buda, the organ will be long and large. 787.

If the lord of 7th joins a watery sign, lord of wife is in a watery house, and the 7th happens to be a watery sign aspected by Purnachandra, the sexual organ of the wife will be secreting and agreeable. 788.

If the 7th is watery and joins Chandra and is aspected by Sukra and Buda in a watery sign, the wife's sexual organ will be secreting. 789.

If Purnachandra occupies **7th,** and is found in a watery Navamsa, and is aspected by Guru occupying a watery sign, the wife's sexual organ will be always secreting and pleasant. 790.

If Sukra in a watery sign, joins his deep exaltation Navamsa, and is combined with Ravi, the wife's organ will become secreting after sexual connection. 791.

If the lord of 7th joins a dry sign, or the 7th is a dry sign, or a dry planet is in 7th, the wife's sexual organ will not be secreting and will be dry and disagreeable. 792.

If the 7th or its lord has evil aspects, and is between two malefics, and has evil conjunction or aspect, the organ will be dry and non-secreting. 793.

If the 7th, being watery, is occupied by a malefic, and though possessed of the aspect of a watery planet, the wife will have a dry and unsympathetic sexual organ. 794.

NOTES.

Venkatasa now refers to the quality and quantity of the sexual organ of the wife.   That couple will be happy, whose sexual adaptation is well fitted or adjusted.   If a man has a long male organ, and the woman has a small sexual organ, or *vice versa*, there will be no happiness in passionate embraces, and the couple will begin to hate each other's company from the inequality of the sexual organs and the want of real enjoyment.   The private organs, when not properly fitted to each other, become repulsive, so also, when they are not sympathetic or attractive towards each other.   This most vital question of sexual adaptability, has been most shamefully neglected by the most cultured of the Western nations and hence the shocking number of divorces among them.   In the American States, there were as many as a million divorces in one year and it is not surprising to see a woman joining with half a dozen men in wedlock in the course of a year or two.   Among such nations, the high ideal of *Pativrata* or unshaken feminine chastity so dearly Cherished by the Hindus, will necessarily be rare.

There are some sexual organs, male or female, which are disagreeably short or unfortunately long and deep.   In such cases, *Yonikula* (see my Astrological Mirror) or sexual adaptability should be particularly noticed.   In the case of breasts, the matter is different, as suppose a woman has a loose and hanging breast of ununusual dimensions, that does not interfere with sexual union or reproduction of human species.   But it cannot be so with sexual organs.   Suppose the female has a deep organ and the male has a small one ; there can be no real happiness, and unless the two organs meet at a certain depth, and come in contact, there can be no reproduction.   Penetration, to a certain degree, is absolutely necessary for real sexual correspondence and the production of issues.   And the word *Ardra* is used with reference to Yoni or sexual organ of the wife.   In Sanskrit it means kind, or sympathetic.

There are some female organs which are attractive, moist, secreting certain fluids, which add happiness to sexual union, and attract the male organ by a natural sympathy. There are others which are dry, unattractive, and give no pleasure to the opposite organ when it is in union. All these details conduce to real happiness and hence the author elaborates on them in his book. Some organs, begin to be attractive after some operation and these are also named here for reference. The quality of the organ must be excellent, to invite the sexual operation, and produce also pleasure and love to the operator. Some female organs, are repulsive and after a single union the man begins to hate the work and seeks gratification from other sources. Like Saliva in the tongue, there is some fluid which should keep the female sexual organ, moist and attractive. A dry mouth will be a source of pain as also a dry *Yoni* (sexual organ) which gives no pleasure and no attraction.

The conjunctiou of Ravi or Kuja with Sani, Rahu, or Mandi, (*Son of Sani*) with the lord of 7th as a malefic, produces a huge sexual organ in the wife out of proportion to the body. 785.

A moderate sexual organ in a man or woman will be a blessing and it gives facility for enjoyment. When Guru or Sukra, becomes the lord of the 7th, and combines a good Navamsa, the wife's organ will be moderate and agreeable ; but if Guru or Sukra joins an evil planet, the organ will be long. Length refers both to external dimensions of the male and also to the depth of the organ in the female. 786.

The junction of Ravi and Sani produces a long organ, while, if Sani is the lord of the 7th, the organ will be short, Chandra as lord of the 7th produces a moderate organ, while Buda as lord of the 7th produces a long organ. 787.

Watery signs and watery planets seem to produce proper secretions in the wife's organ and make it agreeable and enjoyable.

Venkatesa is confusing to a degree. The lord of the 7th, and the lord of wife Sukra, must be in watery signs, as also the 7th house, and these must have the aspect of full Moon, to produce a sexual organ moist, agreeable and able to give real happiness. I am afraid the author gives many combinations for an ordinary result. Any one of the above conjunctions will be able to give such a result. 788.

The 7th being a watery sign, should combine and these must be aspected by Sukra or Buda, in a watery sign to make the wife's organ secreting. 789.

If 7th is occupied by full Moon, who must be in a watery Navamsa aspected by Guru in a watery sign, the organ will be moist and agreeable. Chandra must be in the 7th house, and occupy a Jala Navamsa. If such a Moon is aspected by Guru, who occupies also a Jala Rasi, then the organ will be agreeable. 790.

Sukra should be in a watery sign and in the Navamsa of deep exaltation, *viz.*, Meena and join Ravi, the organ will become moist and secreting after co-habitation. This means that it will not be agreeable before the union. Probably there are other organs which do not attain to such a state even after sexual correspondence. Dryness and disagreeableness in a female organ repel the man or give him unhappiness. Whether Ravi should join Sukra in the Rasi or Navamsa, the meaning is not clear. It may be presumed to be in the Rasi. 791.

Here the 7th may be a dry sign, its lord may be in a dry sign, or there may be a dry planet in the 7th house, to make the sexual organ, dry and disagreeable. Watery signs and planets have been explained in the 1st Chapter of this work. 792.

The 7th or its lord should have evil aspects, should be between two evil planets, and should have evil conjunctions or aspects to make the wife's organ dry and non-secreting. Here even after union there will be no secretion. 793.

If the 7th, being a watery sign, is occupied by a malefic, though it may possess the aspect of a watery planet, the organ will be dry and disagreeable. The 7th may be a watery sign, and may possess the aspect of a watery planet, but if a malefic occupies it, the wife's sexual organ will be dry and unsympathetic. Objection may be taken to the expressions, attractive inviting, etc., applied to secret organs, which are completely hidden from the public gaze by suitable clothing. The love of a man or woman for their mates does not always emanate from simple external appearance or organs which are publicly visible. There are also many other causes, such as human magnetism, ethereal currents, and an indescribable natural attraction. The external appearance sometimes is repulsive and we wonder how a fair man or a woman can love one of the opposite sex, when the person is quite ugly in external appearance. Here the ethereal and electrical currents emanating from all parts of the body may be the real causes for such irresistable attraction. 794.

Stanza—If the lord of the 7th has the aspect of Guru, occupies a good Shastiamsa and a beneficial Navamsa, having beneficial aspect, the person will have luxurious meals. 795.

NOTES.

Guru should aspect the lord of the 7th, who must also be in a beneficial Navamsa and Shastiamsa and must also possess beneficial aspect to give the man rich food. The original gives *Supa* or boiled dall, *Dadhi* or curds and *Ajya* or ghee. Among all nations richness in meals, varies according to tastes. The Hindu meal when served with the above three in plenty, will be a good one and this means the person must be in an affluent position to command good food. 795.

Stanza—If a powerful Jupiter aspects Mercury in the 7th and also by the lord of the 2nd, the person will have rich meals. 796.

NOTES.

Buda should be in the 7th and aspected by two planets, powerful Guru and the lord of the 2nd to give luxurious meals. *Supa*, *Dadhi* and *Ajya* are given with a view to denote good meals. 796.

Stanza—If Ravi or Kuja becomes the lord of 7th, aspected by a benefic or occupy the 5th house, the person will have occasional good food. 797.

NOTES.

If the lord of the 7th happens to be Kuja or Ravi, aspected by a benefic, or occupies the 5th, the person will have now and then good meals. There are many peculiarities in human nature and wonderful combinations occur. Rich meals, good clothing, fair female enjoyment, luxurious habitations and costly furniture, sometimes come to actual poor men or beggars, and it is very interesting to record certain experiences. Take a rich man who is a miser, who has a most beautiful but immoral wife. She will have a poor paramour who could hardly maintain himself. The miserly rich fellow, of course takes sorry meals and goes away on his work. The wife prepares grand meals or causes them to be cooked, gives them to her paramour, enjoys with him in her fine beds and soft sofas, while her miserable husband suffers pain and discomforts. The poor fellow has good combinations which give him fine meals, good female enjoyment and enjoys really the bed and furniture which the rich husband buys. Beyond the sentiment of being the proprietor of the house, wife and other furniture, the husband has no real enjoyment, while a poor beggar, who falls into the embraces of his unfaithful wife has all the real enjoyment, without the senti- ment of being called the proprietor by the public. Clothing, etc., are enjoyed in a similar way. Experiences of human life are strange and marvellous and these furnish rich food for Psychological studies. 797.

Stanza—If the lord of the 7th is a malefic, is located between two evil planets, and possesses the aspect of a malefic or occupies cruel Shastiamsas, the person will not taste rich meals, 798.

NOTES.

Poorer people form the overwhelming majority in the world and there are probably many who have no idea of rich meals. Such grovelling poverty exists in the world, that there are millions of persons who have had no real or substantial meal in their careers and who are foreign to luxurious meals, clothing and furniture. For this miserable combination, the 7th lord should be an evil planet, he must be between two evil planets, and must possess the aspect of an evil planet, or must join a cruel Shastiamsa. 798.

Stanza—If Guru or Chandra becomes the lord of 7th, occupying watery sign or Amsa, aspected by a watery planet, he will have milk and luxurious drinks. 799.

NOTES.

The lord of 7th must be Guru or Chandra, he must occupy a watery sign or Navamsa, and possess the aspect of a watery planet he will have rich drinks. The other watery planet is Sukra, and his aspect becomes necessary. There are some people who drink milk and other soft and nourishing drinks, but they never get intoxicated. There are some who roll under the weight of intoxicating drinks, and who do not care for milk, sherbet and other mild and useful drinks. 799.

Stanza—If the lord of the Navamsa occupies 7th, has the aspect or conjunction of a benefic, or occupies a beneficial Navamsa, the person will have mild and virtuous drinks, like milk, sherbet, lemon juice, etc. 800.

NOTES.

The 7th lord occupies some Navamsa and the lord of this Navamsa should have good Navamsas or beneficial conjunctions or aspects, to give good drinks and make him happy. Drinks in some shape or other, have been traced in all nations. There are some in India, who practice *yoga* or divine concentration of mind and who live entirely on milk or some herbs. They mix jaggery to milk and drink. There are also some, who drink jaggery sherbet or water filtered after being strongly mixed with jaggery called *Panaka*. 800.

Stanzas 801 and 802.

If there are many evil planets in the 7th, 6th or 8th and occupy cruel *shastiamsas*, the person will always eat poor and dry or withered articles. 801.

Belonging to Kasyapa Gotra, I, Venkatesa, the learned, have detailed the results of the Kalatra Bhava, after digesting the numerous Astrological works composed by the Maha Rishis. 802.

NOTES.

Evil planets in the 6th, 7th or 8th and occupyng cruel Shasti-amsas, like Pratapuri, Ghora, etc., will give the man dried or withered articles for food. This means, he will be poor, or, though rich, he will eat only dried up or sapless and dirty articles for his food and thus become a miserable man. Luxurious and nourishing food will be foreign to him. 801.

The learned Venkatesa, concludes the 7th Bhava by observing that he belongs to Kasyapa Gotra or genus of the Maha Rishi Kasyapa, that he is a learned man, and that he composed this Chapter for the benefit of the world by consulting the Astrological works of the Maha Rishis. None of these claim originality, a candour quite praiseworthy. 802.

NOTES.

As I have often remarked, the ways of Providence are inscruta-ble. I am a man of experience running over 50 years of intelligent life, much travelling, keen observation, wonderful recollection, and extraordinary powers of analyses. Added to these, I was practising law for ten years, and had ample opportunities of judging men and manners from my close intimacy and access with all classes of people, and a large number of nationalities. These enable me to write notes and pass remarks which are not superficial. They are the results of my long experience and special studies. It is not always the rich man that eats or enjoys well, nor the married husband who lives happily with his wife. We often see a handsome youth running after a dirty girl and a beautiful man eloping with a dirty looking beggar. The rich man often eats dry and stale food, while a poor beggar is fondled by the rich man's wife and given all the luxuries which he could not enjoy even in his dreams. Some men are strong, while big men are weak. There are some who earn, earn and earn, but never enjoy, while there are others who never earn, but always enjoy at the cost of others. The wonders of psycholo-gical world are themselves wonders for any analyses. 801 and 802.

END OF CHAPTER VI.

Ayur Bhava or Longevity

CHAPTER VII.

The most important question in Astrology concerning humanity refers to the term of life they enjoy during their present stay on the terrestrial plane. This is not only a very complicated, but also an extremely difficult matter to understand. Astrologers will have to exercise great discretion and prudence in judging of this Bhava, or signification and I shall try my level best to give the notes as full and comprehensive as possible. In my translation of Brihat Jataka of Varaha Mihira, I have given his system of calculations, for Ayurdaya (see Ch. VII) and here the author follows quite a different method, though the two converge towards the same point, *viz*, the determination of the length of life a man has in this world. First the reader should have a rough idea of the term of life and then determine which period and sub-period will be specially critical.

Stanza 803.

From the 8th house have to be learnt the length of life, death, secret organ, cause of death, happiness from food, the place of death, disgrace and degradation.

NOTES.

The span of life varies from being thrown out in a state of fœtus after conception to various terms of life extending over and above one hundred years. There are some who have lived to 2 or 3 hundred years and other unlimited terms of life are recorded in Puranas and religious works. See my notes on longevity in my " History of Vijayanagar or The Never-to-be Forgotten Empire" (P. 17 Ch. II). Ravana lived 50 lacs of years, Dasaratha 60 thousand years, Rama 11 thousand years, Suraswaracharya 800 years. The planets indicate the results of previous Karma and the man can augment or take away from his allotted term of life indicated by the planets, by his virtuous deeds. Tapas or

1

deep and undisturbed concentration on the Infinite or by his evil deeds and reckless and sinful behaviour. Ayurveda gives a clue to the methods by which life can be prolonged or shortened and Yoga gives a mental power which is able to defy the ordinary laws of nature and attain to terms of life which are practically unlimited or *aparamita*. From the 8th house, the happiness from food, disease and health of the secret or sexual organs, the manner and causes and place of death, and disgraces to which a man will be subjected, have to be ascertained and Venkatasa gives different combinations in this chapter to indicate the results in these phases of human life. 803.

Stanzas 804 to 810 Inclusive.

If the lord of the 8th joins the 12th with a malefic, there will be short life. If the lord of birth and the lord of the 8th join the 6th house, life will be short. 804.

If the lord of the 8th joins his own house, life will be long. If Sani is in his own house, friendly or exaltation sign, there will be long life. 805.

If the lords of birth and 8th combine in 6th or 12th houses, and the lord of 6th or the 12th occupy birth aspected by a benefic, there will be long life. 806.

If the lord of the 10th is in his own, friends or exaltation sign, there will be long life. If the lords of birth and 10th occupy Kendras, long life may be foretold. 807.

If the lords of 1st, 8th and 10th combine with Sani (*Bhanuja*) and occupy Kendras, there will be long life. If the same lords join their own houses or are in Konas (5th and 9th houses) life will be long. 808.

If the Kendras are occupied by benefics and the lord of Lagna combines with a benefic aspected by Guru, very long life may be predicted. 809.

If the lord of 8th occupies birth, aspected by Guru and Sukra and the lord of birth occupies a Kendra, there will be full life. 810.

NOTES.

Here the translation has been easy and does not require any further explanation. What has the lord of the 10th to do with life is not clear. The lord of birth influences the body. The lord of life is Sani and the house of longevity is the 8th, and also the 8th from the 8th or the 3rd from Lagna. Tenth represents means of life, command, reputation, etc , I suppose the lord of the 10th has also to be considered in predicting the term of life. Long life or *Purnayu*, means from 75 to 120 years. Terms of life above 120 years go under the name of Aparamita Ayardaya or unlimited term of life and these have very special conjunctions. The aspect of Guru minimises all evils and adds great vitality as also where Guru combines. Lagna is the basis for all predictions, and therefore its strength and the power of its lord are very essential in all calculations concerning human events whatever they may be. Where he is weak, or Lagna is ill-occupied, all superstructure will be shaky. 803 to 810.

Stanza 811.

If evil planets occupy 6th, 8th and 12th houses and the lord of Lagna is powerless, life will be short or there will be no issues. 811.

NOTES.

Dusthas or evil houses are 6th, 8th and 12th and when these are occupied by malefics, the person will have short life or will be issueless. If there are beneficial conjunctions or aspects or even if these evil planets occupy beneficial *amsas* or Vergas, the evil results will be considerably modified. This seems to be a special combination, which makes the man issueless in case he does not die early, although no reference is made to house, or lord of issues. 811.

Stanzas 812 to 817 Inclusive.

ff the 8th house occupies cruel Shastiamsas, and the lord of the 8th or Sani combines with or is aspected by malefics, there will be short life. 812.

There are three terms of life called Alpayu, Madhyayu and
Purnayu. Before 32 years it is called Alpayu, and after that
it is Madhyayu. 813.

It is Madhyayu, when the life is above 32 and below 70 years,
After 70 years it is Poornayu. If the lord of Lagna is an
enemy of the Sun, there will be short life. 814.

If the lord of Lagna is ordinary with the Sun, there will be
middle life and if the Sun is a friend of the lord of birth, there
will be long life. If the lord of Lagna is powerless and Guru
occupies Kendras or Thrikonas, and malefics occupy 6th, 8th and
12th, the person will have middle life.

If Sani is powerful, while the benefics occupy Kendras or
Thrikonas and if the 5th or 8th is occupied by a malefic, there
will be middle life and the same result happens if the evil planet
is in Lagna, or Kendra or Thrikona. 815, 816, 817.

NOTES.

Lagna should occupy a cruel Shastiamsa and lord of Lagna
or Sani should be in conjunction with or aspected by an evil
planet, to produce short life. Even in conjunction with a malefic
planet, some difference must be made as per his strength. Suppose Mars joins Sani in Makara or Sani joins the birth lord
Sukra in Thula, the evil certainly will be minimised. Those
who die before they complete 32 have Alpa or short life. Those
who die above 32 and before 70 have Madhya or middle life, and
those who live above 70 and die before 100, have Poorna or long
life. Above hundred years, the life is said to be Aparimita or
unlimited. Some authors classify life quite in a different way.
Those who die before they are 8 years have Balarishta. Those
who live above 8 and die before 20 have Madhyarista, and those
who live above 20 and die before they are 32 have Yogarista.
These are called Aristas or misfortunes. Those who live above
32 and die before 50 are said to have Alpayu or short life. Those
who live above 50 and die before 75 have Madhyayu or middle
life, and those who live above 75 and die before 120 have

Purnayu or long life   And those who live above 120 years have Aparimita or unlimited terms of life. The classsification is elastic and may be taken within some limits. In my Astrological Self Instructor, 6th Ed. many combinations are given to illustrate these various terms of life.

Venkatasa is caught several times in his own net. Either he gives combinations from a flow of his own ideas or he must have had good reasons and authority for such statements. He introduces the idea, that if the lord of the birth is an enemy of the Sun, the life will be short   Then all those who are born in Makara, Kumbha, Vrishabha and Thula, must have short life as Sani and Sukra, lords of those houses, are bitter enemies of Ravi. But facts don't agree with this statement, and I myself have lived over sixty-six, with my Lagna in Vrishabha, and my father lived 77 years, with his Lagna in Thula.   Here, the reader must not run away with the idea, that simply because the Sun is an enemy of the birth lord, the life will be cut short, or because he is born in a Lagna whose lord is a friend of Ravi, that he would live long.   There are hundreds of other circumstances, which go to determine longevity of a person, and what the reader will be advised to is to make some allowances, good or bad for such planetary influences.   Where the Sun is ordinary with the birth lord, he produces middle life and where he is a friend, long life. When the lord of Lagna. is powerless, Guru occupies a Kendra (1—4—7—10) or Thrikona (5—9) and evil planets are in 6th, 8th and 12th, there will be middle life.   Here there is a strange mixture of influences good and bad   Powerless birth lord produces short life and misfortune.   Guru in Kendra or Thrikonas gives long life and evil planets in *Dusthas* give mixed results. Evil planets in 6th give long life, they cut away life early when they are in 8th or 12th.   The lord of life is Sani and if he is powerless, and Kendras or Thrikonas are occupied by benefics, and if a malefic joins 6th or 8th, there will be middle life.   Evil planet in Lagna or Kendra or Thrikona will give middle life. But if Thula is Lagna and Sani is there, he will give long life. 814 to 817 inclusive.

Stanzas 818 and 819.

Those born in short life, the lord of the Vipat would inflict death, those born in the middle life, the period of the enemy of the birth lord would kill and those born in long life will have their death in the period of the 8th lord. The term of life should be determined as per combinations which follow in this and other chapters. 818—19.

NOTES.

Terms of life should not be hastily judged. Some combinations show Balarista, while Adliyoga, Kesariyoga, etc., point out long life. Dasas and Bhuktis may point to early death, while Gochara, and Pindayurdaya may show long life. What Venkatasa means is, that the student should note all the *pros* and *cons* for the term of life and then using his own clear judgment founded on actual study, instructions under an able preceptor, and his long experience, he must proceed to fix when death is likely to happen and when serious dangers attack but does not take away his life. (*See Chapter VIII of my Brihaljataka.*)

Those who have short life combinations will generally die in the 3rd Dasa. A man must be and is born in some constellation and a Dasa is ascribed to it. The second star from it will give the second Dasa and the 3rd will give the 3rd Dasa. The first or birth star is Janma, the second goes under the name of Sampat, and the 3rd star under the name of Vipat or danger. Say a man is born in Asvini. He gets Kethu Dasa. The second from it will be Bharani and ruled by Sukra Dasa. The 3rd is Krithika ruled by Ravi. If the man is specially lucky, and possesses long life combinations, then alright. But if there are Alpayuryoga combinations and the man is born in Aswini, he will generally die in the 3rd Dasa or Ravi Dasa.

The person who has Madhayuryoga, will be killed during the period of his enemy. Kuja governs Mesha, and he who is born in Mesha, can be killed by the periods of his enemies, *viz.*, Sukra, Buda or Sani.

Those who have long life combinations will be killed by the period which belongs to the lord of the 8th. Take Kataka. The person born in that Lagna, with long life will be killed by Sani, who is the lord of the 8th house Kumbha. 818—819.

Stanzas 820 to 828 A. Inclusive.

If the lords of Lagna and 8th with a malefic join powerfully the 6th house, the person will be killed either in battle or by instruments. 820.

If the lords of 6th and 8th join the 6th with Rahu, and Sani joins Kethu, the person will be killed by instruments or thieves, during their sub-periods or periods. 821.

If the lords of 6th and 8th join the lord of the 4th, the person will be killed by vahanas. If the lords of 6th and 8th join Guru, he will die by dispeptic diseases. If the lord of birth and Guru join the 6th, he will die by indigestion. 822.

If the lords of Lagna and 4th combine with Jupiter, the person dies by indigestion. If the lords of 8th, 4th and 2nd join together and occupy the 8th, the person will die by indigestion. 823.

The death of a person should be predicted during the period or sub-period of the lord of the 8th. The death of father, etc.. should be predicted when they combine or are aspected by him, 824.

The person dies by poison when the lords of the 2nd and 6th combine with Sani and occupy Dusthas. If these lords join Rahu or Kethu and occupy Dusthas, he will die by hanging. 825

If Sani becomes the lord of 6th and joins with Rahu or Kethu he will have danger from beasts. If he joins Guru, danger arises from elephants. If he combines with Chandra, there will be danger from horses. 826.

If such Sani joins Ravi, danger will arise from horned brutes. If he combines with Kuja, there will be danger from dogs. 826 A.

Excepting in exaltation, or in his own house, Sani in the 6th causes danger from dogs.

If the lords of birth, 4th and 9th combine Kendras or Thri-konas, there will be death to father with the mother.

If powerless Chandra occupying 8th with Rahu, joins another malefic, the person will die by Pisacha troubles.

If Sani occupies 8th with powerless Chandra, the person suffers from Pisachas aud he will have danger by drowning. 827-28-28A.

NOTES.

In these following stanzas the author tries to sketch the combinations for the various forms of death a man may meet, and hence these verses become very important as revealing to us, the various sources of danger to life, and how he should be prepared to meet them or try his best to overcome those evil influences by timely and well-directed *shanties* or remedies. It may be asked here whether such dangers could be averted, and whether there is any real possibility of success in such undertakings. I have elaborately discussed on these vital points of Karma Theory in my Introduction to the Astrological Self Instructor Part II 6th Edition, and also in many of my articles on the questions of remedies in the 17 volumes of my Astrological Magazine. I beg o refer my readers to them for fuller explanations.

All *Karma* produces results or a certain *momentum* in a certain direction. This *momentum* or *resultant* is not a destiny, nor is it unalterable. As Shakespere says " Man is thus or thus by himself." He has made his Karma and reaps its results, but these results can be modified, altered or neutralised by fresh Karma, and the success of such undertakings (remedies) depends upon an accurate knowledge of the intensity of the past Karma, and how to meet it by fresh Karma, which will overcome its effects. We throw a ball with a *momentum*, of course it goes at a certain rate and to a certain distance. But nobody would be justified in saying that counter currents cannot be set afloat to augment or retard this momentum by other agencies. When the Sun is very powerful, what is the remedy. To get an umbrella made of ice blocks and neutralise the effects of his heat and other burning agencies by such devices.

The highest value of Astrology, as a science, is to know the nature and full extent of the evils which are in store for man, and to seek and adopt remedies by which he can soften those evils and get over them. The value of medicine is not simply to know the nature of diseases but also to procure remedies for getting rid of those ailments.

There are persons who die by one thousand and one causes. Diseases and dangers are innumerable. Nobody can exactly name or classify all sources of death and danger, some die by weapons, some by accidents, some by over-eating, others by under-feeding, some by drowning, some by wild beasts of various denominations, some by slips and downfalls, others by human humbug and rascality, some by poisons, some by fires and burns, some by excessive sexual intercourse, some by vile reptiles, some by inexplicable internal diseases and some by sudden excitements, fears, joys, and intoxications. Here Venkatesa gives some of the sources of danger, a man will have, and how he can overcome those dangers, by timely remedies. 8th house represents danger and death. Lagna represents the general basis for physical constitution. 6th house represents, debts, diseases and enemies. Therefore all danger seem to arise from these houses and their lords and also the lords of life, disease and death. When the lords of 8th and 1st are with a malefic, occupy the 6th house powerfully, the person will be killed in a battle or by war instruments. When these planets are not powerful in the 8th and only occupy the 6th in a powerless manner, there will be a show of danger and he will escape. 820.

If the 6th house is occupied by its lord, lord of the 8th and by Rahu, while Sani oins Kethu, he will be killed by weapons or

2

by thieves, during their periods and sub-periods. This will be
a clue to get the correct time of death.

If the lords of 6th, 8th and Rahu are in 6th house, Sani with
Kethu must necessarily be in the 7th from 6th or 12th from birth
and this will be a bad combination as 3 evil planets are in the 6th
and two evil planets will be in the 12th and all aspecting each
other. The time of danger will be in any one of these five planetary sub-periods or periods, and there will be a great danger.

Take an example :—

Kethu Sani	Birth		Chandra
	RASI		
Guru			
		Ravi Sukra	Rahu Buda Kuja

Lord of 6th is Buda. Lord
of 8th is Kuja. They both are in
6th with Rahu. Sani and Kethu
are in the 7th from them or in
the 12th from Lagna. Ravi and
Sukra are unfavourable. Danger
may be predicted in the sub-
periods and periods of Buda,
Kuja, Rahu, Kethu or Sani.
Thieves give no small amount of trouble and adopt various methods to despatch their enemies. 821.

Where the lords of 6th and 8th should join the lord of 4th,
the author does not say. But it would be appropriate if all these
are in the 4th, the house of vehicles and conveyances. *Vahanas*
means in Sanskrit all kinds of conveyances made and used by the
ingenuity of man. A man is carried by another man, this
also falls under *Vahanu*. If planets are bad, then death results.
If they have beneficial combinations or aspects, then the fall
will not result in death. These sources of strength and weakness must be ascertained by the Astrologer and then the prediction should be made. Indigestion is a hideous form of disease
which breeds so many other forms of diseases, that it would take
a big volume to deal with them. In fact, in Sanskrit Ayurvedic
Science, all diseases, external or internal, take their final source
from dispepsia or indigestion and hence *Ajirna* is a dreadful one

which should be very carefully avoided by every sensible and prudent man. Guru with the lords of 6th and 8th, wherever they may be, produces death from indigestion. If the lord of birth and Guru join the 6th, there will be death from indigestion. 822.

The conjunction of the lord of birth and 4th with Guru produces a similar result. Here also due consideration must be given for planetary exaltations and beneficial aspects and conjunctions. There are some people who suffer from dispepsia in a mild form and live to a long age, others die by its violent attacks and serious complications. There will also be death from indigestion when the lords of the 2nd, 4th and 8th occupy the 8th. 823.

Generally the person dies during the period of the lord of 8th, or in such planetary sub-periods and periods who are in conjunction with or aspected by him. Here also the author gives another clue, viz., the times at which parents, brothers, children, etc., will die. If the period of the lord of the 9th comes, aspected by or is in conjunction with the lord of 8th, then danger to father must be predicted, if he aspects the lord of 5th, then death to children, if he combines with the lord of 4th, danger to mother, if he aspects or joins the lord of the 3rd, then danger to brothers and sisters, and if the lord of the 7th joins him or is aspected by the lord of the 8th, death must be predicted for wife and so forth. These different combinations must be very carefully examined and after ascertaining their various sources of strength and weakness, death or serious danger must be predicted for such as are indicated by the lords of the houses, and lords of the events. 824.

Dustas are 6th, 8th and 12th. The word is a contraction of Dusta (bad) and sthanas (houses or places).

If the lords of 2nd and 6th combine with Sani and occupy 6th, 8th or 12th, the person dies by poison. But if these two lords of 2nd and 6th join Rahu or Kethu and occupy 6th, 8th or 12th, the person dies by hanging. Here he may be hanged by others or he may hang himself as in suicides. People die by hundreds and thousands by actual poison and by deleterious drugs and foods

administered to them by their enemies and persons interested in their
death for selfish purposes. Some are poisoned for sexual purposes,
others for their wealth, some for the trouble they give to people,
and some for litigation. Human psychology is a curious study,
and it reveals inner currents, and cross currents which are difficult
to trace and analyse. People poison others sometimes from motives
of sheer revenge, while some are drugged to death for supposed
wrongs, which exist only in their imagination. Death by poisoning is more common among the royalties and aristocracy than
among the poorer classes. The reasons are obvious. 825.

If Sani owns the 6th and joins Rahu or Kethu, death will be
brought about by beasts. The author does not say where they
should be. Experience and general principles of Astrology should
guide us. We may understand the previous combination as necessary also here. Sani, as lord of the 6th I suppose, should be in
Dustas with Rahu or Kethu to produce this evil result. Wild
animals are dangerous and kill the people. But sometimes domestic animals also prove to be dangerous when they are excited,
or goaded to a dangerous degree or by their inherent wicked nature.
If Sani joins Guru, danger from elephants and Sani with Chandra
from horses should be predicted. Here also author does not say where
the planets should be. The danger will result in death when the
planets are bad and only in injury when they are good. Take
Kanya as Lagna, Sani becomes the lord of 6th Kumbha, and
suppose he occupies 12th Simha with Guru. Suppose Simha is
Lagna and Sani lord of Makara 6th, occupies Kataka with Guru.
In the former case the danger is greater because Sani occupies
Simha, an unfriendly sign, with Guru not so powerful. In the latter,
Sani is in Kataka not an unfriendly sign and with Guru in exaltation.
The danger will be light in the latter. Similarly for Chandra. 826.

These cases happen only for two Lagnas, *viz.* Simha and Kanya.
Here alone Sani becomes the lord of the 6th. People born in other
Lagnas may also die from these dangers, when Sani does not own
he 6th, but there will be other combinations to produce similar

results. In all these verses, there should never be made any presumption that where the specified combinations are not found, results indicated will not be present. The author could at best give only a few conjunctions of planets, out of the thousands which may have been enumerated in other works, Jyotisha comprises 400,000 Stanzas or Chaturlaksha, and it is not possible for any single author either to have read the whole, or to have made a summary of the whole science. If Sani joins Ravi, the danger will be from horned beasts, like bulls, cows, buffaloes, stags, and other animals with horns. If Sani combines with Kuja, death or danger should be predicted from dogs. 826A.

When Sani is in exaltation or in his own house, he will cause danger from dogs, when he occupies the 6th house. In the above verses his ownership of 6th produces bad results, and here his occupation is mentioned.

If the lords of 1st, 4th and 9th are in Kendras or Thrikonas, then father with mother will die during the periods and sub-periods of these planets. The stanza is vague and not to the point. What does Venkatasa mean by saying that father with mother will die in their periods and sub-periods? The lords of the 5th and 9th are good and they don't produce evil. 4th is a Kendra, and when owned by a malefic, he does not do evil. The lord of birth, when he occupies Kendras or Konas is considered as good. Why then should these three planets produce death to both parents when their Dasas and Bhukties come. Death of parents, both at a time, should be considered as a great misfortune, and specially this will be so where father is an earning and influential member of the family. The readers may bring in their own intelligence and experience and give any interpretation which may strike them. I am not one with the author in his views here.

If powerless Chandra, with Rahu combines with another evil planet and occupies the 8th, troubles and danger from Pisachas (*Devils and Ghosts*) must be predicted. A handful of experience is worth ten cartloads of theory and whatever many of the shallow.

brained modern scientists may say, the existence of Pisachas or Devils has been amply proved and thoroughly demonstrated. See to my notes in the earlier portions of this work Page 229. In the creation of God, there seem to be two sets of Pisachas, one set created by Him and occupying a separate Loka or plane of existence and with functions and forms peculiar to themselves and another set, who are called into existence by avarice, evil deeds, etc., by the liberated ghosts of dead persons in various walks of life. Great varieties are enumerated in Sastras among these two sets. *Bhotas, Pretas, Kamini, Mohini, Pisacha, Sakini, Karna Pisacha, Dhakini, Prarabdas, Jalini, Marani,* etc., are some of the varieties. The troubles from pisachas are very curious and are quite inexplicable on any other medical hypothesis. Women suffer from Pisachas more than men, and young women more than old women. The denomination *hysteric fits,* is not only stupid, but does not in the least explain the wonderful vagaries of Pisachas when they possess men and women, and it looks only a clumsy cloak to shield modern medical and scientific ignorance, when they are not able to explain Devilish Phenomena or find any means to exorcise them.

Powerless Chandra and Sani in the 8th, cause danger from Devils, and also from water. Danger from water includes both drowning and also from watery diseases, like dropsy, excessive urine, etc. 827—28—28A.

Stanzas 829, 830.

If weak moon joins Kuja, Rahu or Sani and occupies 8th, 6th or 12th, death will come by insanity, or by Pisacha troubles. 829.

If the 8th is occupied by Rahu or Kethu, he will get death from Chaturthika. If the lord of the 8th joins Rahu or Kethu, and the 8th falls in cruel Shastiamsas, he will certainly suffer from Chaturthika. 830.

NOTES.

Kshina Sasanka is the word used in the original and it means weak moon. From the 10th or Dasami of the dark half of a Lunar month to the 5th or Panchami of the bright half of the next Lunar month, Chandra is said to be Kshina or powerless. If such a weak moon joins Kuja, Rahu or Sani (and Kethu must also be included by the term Rahu) and occupies *Dustas*, he will die by madness or lunacy or by dangers from Pisachas. Devils sometimes kill suddenly persons, by fears, loss of blood or nervous exhaustion and sometimes by slow tortures of various kinds. Madness, insanity and lunacy take away the life in various ways. 829.

Chaturthika used in the original has various interpretations. It means intermittent fever coming every 4th day. It also means Sudra. as he belongs to the 4th caste in the Hindu social system. Some have intrepreted that the person will have danger or death from Sudras, but I am inclined to state that *Chaturthika* here means intermittent fever. This is a very persistent fever which reduces man to a low state of vitality and kills him by slow degrees. Complications of other diseases may also set in. If 8th house falls in cruel *Shastiamsas* and the lord of 8th combines with Rahu or Kethu, the person will have troubles or death from Chaturthika. This may also refer to troubles and dangers from Sudra classes. There are various forms of intermittent fevers *Dwayahika*, *Thrayahika*, *Chaturthika* and *Panchahika*. Serious danger should be predicted when the lord of the 8th is bad and combines with Rahu or Kethu and ordinary troubles when they are in exaltations or good associations and aspects. 830.

Stanzas 831 to 840 Inclusive.

If Ravi in debilitation occupies the 6th or 8th aspected by a malefic, the father will be killed by royal anger and will also lose money through kingly displeasure. 831.

If Kuja occupies the 5th or 10th aspected by an evil planet, maternal uncles will die. If such a Kuja has the conjunction of Sani, his son will die. If Chandra occupies the 5th with an evil planet, the mother will die. 832.

If Ravi occupies the 5th or 10th aspected by a malefic, the father will die. If birth and Chandra, have the conjunction of two evil planets, the person will die. 833.

If Chandra is eclipsed by Rahu or Kethu, having the lunar ring, and aspected by an evil planet, the child will die at once. If Chandra in Chitta, Pushyami, or Poorvashadha, occupies birth, he will kill mother, children and maternal uncles in the 1st, 2nd and 3rd quarters respectively. 834.

If Sani and Kuja with Rahu, combine in 11th or 9th, the father will die. If Chandra and Kuja, occupy the 8th, aspected by a malefic, the child will die early. 835.

If Kuja, with an evil planet, combines in the 3rd house, aspected by a malefic, there will be destruction to brothers. If Chandra joins 7th with an evil planet, aspected by another malefic, the mother will die. 836.

If Rahu with an evil planet, occupies 7th, aspected by a malefic, the father will die. If 7th is occupied by Sani, Kuja and Sukra, there will be death to his son. The occupation of the 3rd and 6th by evil planets and the 12th by benefics will cause death to the child. 837.

If Chandra conjoins with or is aspected by the evil planets in the 4th or 8th, the child will die. If Chandra and Ravi combine in Lagna, and all the evil planets occupy the 12th, without beneficial aspects, the child will die. 838.

If Ravi is in the 7th and Chandra is in birth and evil planets are in the 12th, the person will lose his children.

If the Sun and Moon are in the 12th, unaspected by benencs, the person will become dull. 839.

If Ravi or Chandra occupies the 12th, without beneficial aspect, the person will have sight in one eye. If the lord of the 3rd with Chandra occupies 6th, 8th or 12th, the child will be nursed by the milk of another woman. 840.

NOTES.

Ravi represents father and Chandra mother, debilitation and

occupation of 6th or 8th with evil aspects, causes the death of the father by royal anger, and also the confiscation or loss of his property. Beneficial aspects give considerable relief. If the aspect of a malefic produces evil results, much more his combination, This is but a fair scientific inference. When the father does some offence against the State, then he will be hanged or killed and his estate will be confiscated. 831.

Maternal uncles are represented by Buda. But here a special combination is given which causes death to maternal uncles. Among the Hindus attachment to maternal uncles is very great. The author says " *will die.*"

But when will they die, is not clear. From the previous stanzas, it must be inferred as occurring in the periods and sub-periods of planets who cause the Yoga. This may happen in Kuja's or the periods of the evil planet who aspects Kuja. Here also care must be taken. Meena is birth and Kuja is in the 5th or Kataka aspected by Sani in Vrishabha, the death of the maternal uncle will be early. Suppose, Kanya is Lagna and Kuja is in Makara with Sani, the death of the uncle will occur later on and the uncle will be rich and influential as Kuja is exalted and Sani has Swakshetra. These sources of strength and weakness should never be overlooked by the prudent astrologer in his predictions. If Sani joins such a Kuja, his son will die. This means that the person will have a promising son and his loss will be keenly felt by the parent. Chandra in the 5th with an evil planet will kill the mother early. Beneficial aspects and conjunctions will add vitality to the combination and the life of the mother will be prolonged. 832.

The death of the father must be predicted if the Sun occupies the 5th or 10th with an evil planet, or possesses malefic aspect.

Chandra should be in birth, with two evil planets to kill the child early. There are Lagna and Chandra Lagna. I believe that if there is one evil planet in Lagna and another malefic with Chandra

3

in a different sign, without beneficial aspect, the child will die early, or if Lagna has Chandra and two evil planets there will be early death. 833.

If in the eclipse of the Moon, by Rahu or Kethu, there is a lunar ring and an evil planet aspects him, the child will die at once. Eclipses are very unfavourable times and children born during such times will hardly live. But if they survive the danger, they become great persons. 834.

If Chandra is in the 1st Padam of Chitta, and occupies the birth, the mother will die.

If Chandra is in the second Padam of Pushyami and occupies the birth, his children will be killed, and if Chandra is in the 3rd Padam of Poorvashadha, maternal uncles will die. 834.

Sani, Kuja and Rahu in the 11th or 9th will kill the father. In the 11th evil planets are good, and why they should kill the father early is not clear. 9th of course represents father and evil planets there cause injury to him.

Chandra and Kuja in the 8th with evil aspects despatch the. child early from this world. 835.

Third house represents brothers. Kuja is the lord of brothers Kuja in the 3rd aspected by an evil planet causes destruction to his brothers. There are some unfortunate men, who are born with a lot of brothers and sisters, but who lose them all during their lives. Danger to mother is predicted by the occupation of 7th by Chandra with a malefic and aspected by another malefic. 836.

Sun in the 7th combined with a malefic and aspected by another evil planet, kills his father. Kuja, Sukra and Sani cause destruction to children. With evil planets in 3 and 6 and benefics in the 12th, the child will die. The general principle is that evil planets in 3rd, 6th and 11th, add vitality to life. But this may be a special combination, which neutralises the length of life. 837.

If Chandra joins or is aspected by the evil planets in the 4th or 8th house, the child will die. Ravi and Chandra in Lagna and evil planets in the 12th without beneficial aspects will kill the child, The conjunctions of Chandra and Ravi occurs on an Amavasya or new moon day. Children born on such days hardly sarvive early dangers. If benefics aspect or join either birth or the 12th, early death will be avoided. 838.

Sun in the 7th and Moon in birth with evil planets in the 12th, will destroy his children. There are some very unfortunate people, who get a large number of children and lose them all in their life time. Those who have no children, are not so unfortunate as those who get them and lose them. Beneficial aspects redeem the evil to some extent. When the Sun and Moon are in 12th without beneficial aspects, the person becomes dull. Want of comprehension and dullness of intellect are really misfortunes. Such men or women will always appear in false situations and their work suffers loss from want of intellect. It is a special gift of God to possess good memory, piercing intellect, and comprehensive foresight and judgment. In their absence the man will be a failure in worldly matters. 839.

If Ravi or Chandra occupies 12th without beneficial aspect, the person will have sight in one eye and the other will be defective. Ravi and Chandra represent eyes of the Energies and when they are defective the sight will not be good.

If the lord of the 3rd occupies *Dustas*, the child will be nursed by other women. That is he drinks the milk of other women and his mother will not have milk and the child will be taken care of by others for various reasons. To be nursed by one's own mother is a fortune. To be neglected by her is a misery. Now a days the glitter of false civilisation has made many mothers neglect their children with an erroneous idea that their health would suffer, forgetting that natur heas given them paps for this special purpose.

A great mistake could hardly be committed by mothers. The

affinity of the child, to its mother, in physical and mental
characteristics, cannot be questioned, and while this is so, there is
no logic or sense in their neglect of their own children, and subject-
ing them to get milk from other women whose characters, physical
and mental, are certainly quite alien to those of the children. Their
own nature, suffers considerably from the drying up of secretion of
milk, which nature has implanted in them, and through such
neglect, the health and mind of the mother must necessarily suffer
as also of the child. Such deleterious effects may be tangible or invisible, but that they affect the mothers and children, is an
indisputable fact. Those children who have been nursed carefully
by their own mothers are certainly strong and healthy, while the
mothers are not at all affected by tending their own darlings. But
the perversions of the age are often inexplicable and inexusable. 840.

Stanza 841.

If the lord of Lagna is powerful, and the lords of 4th and 9th
being powerless, join the 8th, the person will lose both his parents,
at the commencement of his life. 841.

NOTES.

The lord of 4th indicates mother, while the lord of 9th
represents father, and if both are in 8th, the house of death, parents
will die very early. The lord of birth, being powerful, protects the
child, while the powerless lords of 4th and 9th cause death to
mother and father early. Beneficial aspects give some protection. 841.

Stanzas 842 to 844 inclusive.

If the Sun and lord of 9th occupy Dustas or if the Sun and
lord of 9th occupy Kendras or Konas, the person will never see the
face of his children. 842.

If the lord of 9th Ravi and Sani occupy 6th, his father will
die during the night or if these three planets combine with the lord
of the 6th, the death of the father will occur during the night.
If those three planets do not combine with Chandra and the lord

of the 6th, the father will die during the day.   843.

If the lord of 4th, Chandra and Sukra powerfully occupy the 6th, the mother dies during the night.   If Sani and lord of 4th combine in the 6th, she dies during the night.   If lord of 4th and Sukra do not combine with Chandra and do not occupy the 6th or join the lord of the 6th, the mother will die during the day.   844.

NOTES.

To have the mother or father die in the night, specially for a religious man, will be a great misery and infliction.   Besides the whole inmates would be put to great inconvenience.   Death itself, whether during the day or during the night, is a source of trouble and anxiety, but in the nights the troubles are enhanced.   As the language is very simple, no notes seem to be necessary here. 842-3-4

Stanza 845.

If there are planets in the 4th house, the mother will die in that Ayana, which is indicated by the 4th house.   If there are no planets, then the Ayana is indicated by that Rasi which is occupied by the lord of the 4th.   845.

NOTES.

This Stanza requires some explanation.   Take an illustration.

The Sun in the signs of Makara, Kumbha, Meena, Mesha, Vrishabha, and Mithuna causes Ootharayana.   In the other signs he causes Dakshinayana.   In the horoscope there are no planets in the 4th house.   The lord of the 4th is in Kumbha and the death of the mother should occur at the

	Chandra Rahu	Lagna	Sani
Ravi Buda Guru			
	RASI		
Sukra		Kuja Kethu	

beginning of Ootharayana.   This itself should not be taken as the sole guide as there are other combinations which are more im-

portant and which influence the native more strongly than any
of the above ordinary observations.   845.

Stanza 846.

When there are two or more planets in the 4th, the Ayana
should be reversed.

If the lord of 9th occupies 8th or a movable sign, the father
dies at a distance.   846.

NOTES

When there are two or more planets then, the Ayanas should
be reversed and foretold.   If the 4th house is in Ootharayana,
then the death of the mother will be in Dakshinayana and *vice
versa.*

The death of a father is a great event in a Hindu family. In
the European life, where the laws are unjust on their faces—A
European dies and his estate devolves on his eldest son.   The
other children, sons and daughters born of him must shift for
themselves. Are they not born to him? have they not been reared
by him? Are they not of his blood and seed? In what way do
their affections and attachments differ from the eldest? Where
then is the logic and justice of turning them out penniless and
enriching only one son, because he comes out first into the family.
The Hindu idea seems to be more equitable   All the sons get
equal shares, and the eldest formerly used to get a special share
called Jaista Bhaga, now removed by the modern legislature?

When, therefore, the father dies at a distance, a great deal of
confusion ensues in the estate and its accounts and it will be a
great misfortune for the children to lose their father at a distance.
Chararasis are movable signs.   846.

Stanza 847.

If the lord of the 9th is in a fixed or double-bodied sign, the
person will be present when his father dies.

If the Sun and Moon occupy Kendras or movable signs, the person will not burn his father or mother at the place of their death. 847.

NOTES

Different nations have different methods of disposing off their dead. Some burn them. Some bury them. Some throw them away to beasts and birds and some hurl them down hills or elevations. Some throw them to rivers or oceans, and some embalm them and keep them for long ages. Thus in the latter part of the stanza, instead of burning the bodies where they die, the person may remove them to some distant places or cremation may be conducted at a considerable distance. 847.

Stanza 848.

If the Sun and Moon are in double-bodied signs, the person will not burn the parents in time.

If the lord of 9th is powerful, and the lords of Lagna, 4th and Chandra are powerless, there will be terrible misfortunes at the time of the death of his mother. 848.

NOTES.

Parents may die and the children may not be at hand. The dead bodies may be kept for some time for the return of sons, and then they may dispose of them as per their religious tenets. The death of a mother is a real misfortune, but it may be attended with other unbearable misfortunes, and this is what is indicated in the latter half of the stanza. 848.

Stanza 849.

If there are many malefics in the 8th, there will be severe complaints in the secret organs. If 8th is aspected by benefics, health must be predicted. If 8th is combined or aspected by benefics, great happiness must be predicted for sexual organs.   849.

NOTES.

In man the sex organs are the places of comfort, and   disease. Leaving aside diseases in the earlier periods, almost all complaints are to be traced to   sexual   irregularities   in   the   after   life.   Men and women seek and offer sexual pleasures which   prove   the   bane of society, the scourge of off-spring,   the   battering   ram   of   their physical health, and   the   wreck   of   their   moral   stamina.   The history of prostitution is a key to   all   the   hideous   transactions which civilised nations resort to and   which   under   the   cloak   of social gloss, eat into the very vitals of   healthy society.   But   facts are facts and there they are. 7 or 8 hundrèd thousand divorces in a year prove the low moral stamina of America.   The   gluttony   of France in sexual unions, has been the wreck of   the   French   nation in the powers of reproduction.   England combines drunkenness   to debauchery and Italy is famous for its delicate   vices.   The   brutal passions of Russia are matters   of   historical   evidence,   and   the Turkish baths and shampooning bodies are   notorious   memoranda of their morbid sexual appetites.   All such vagaries touch the sexual organs and produce a variety of diseases in those regions which are truly appalling.   Evil planets must not   be in   the 8th,   and   when they are there, there must   be   beneficial   aspects   or   conjunctions. When the sexual organs are healthy and are properly exercised, the pleasure they give to the couple is the   highest, but   when they   are diseased, the morbid minds take more   pride than   pleasure in such indulgences.   849.

Stanzas 849 A. & B.

If the 8th is combined by evil planets, the person takes   rough food.   If benefics, occupy the 8th,   he gets   delicate   food.   If the lord of the 8th combines with a malefic, or is aspected   by him,   or joins an evil Navamsa, the person will be disgraced.   If the 8th   is an evil sign, he will be disgraced.   But if   the 8th   has   beneficial conjunctions or aspects, there will be no disgrace.   849 A. 849 B.

NOTES

From the 8th house so many human events are sketched that a student will naturally get confused in their predictions. Suppose there are good planets in the 8th, the man gets delicate and luxurious food, his sexual organs will be healthy and he will not be disgraced. There are men who take very luxurious meals and who have most rotten sexual organs on account of their excessive indulgences. Evil planets give rough food and diseased sexual organs. Then all poor people eat rough food but all their sexual organs are not always rotten. Unless they are debauchees. Here, the author only refers to the house and planets in that house. There are the lords of events whose strength and weakness must specially be taken before correct predictions are ventured. Suppose 8th is occupied by Jupiter and Mercury two good benefics. Health must be predicted for sexual organs. But suppose in this horoscope, Venus and Mars and Saturn are in the 7th or 4th, then the person will have diseased sexual organs and his morals will be of the lowest type. Similarly, great care should be taken in venturing predictions on superficial observations. The mind of the Astrologer must take a comprehensive view of the whole and analyse facts well. As there are nine planets and twelve zodiacal signs, all human Phenomena, physical, mental and financial must be predicted from the permutations and combinations of these in various forms. We take the second. It denotes many events. Eyes are to be judged by the second house. The house must be strong. The lords of eyes are the Sun and the Moon and their strength should be taken. Planets in the second affect the sight, planets with the lord of the second will have influence and so forth. 849 A. 849 B.

Stanzas 849-C to 851 inclusive.

The person will die in a foreign country when the 8th is movable, when its lord combines in a movable sign, and when Sani occupies a movable sign or Navamsa. 849-C.

4

The person will die in his own house when the 8th falls in a fixed sign or Navamsa, when its lord does the same and when Sani also is similarly situated. 849-D.

When the 8th falls in double-bodied sign or *Vergas* (divisions). the person dies on the way. When the lord of the 8th occupies Kendras, the lord of birth becomes powerless, he will die above 30 and below 32 years. Those born in stars, similar to their fathers, will kill them. 850—851.

NOTES.

Sani is the lord of life and death, 8th is the house of longevity and its lord must be taken into consideration. To die in a foreign country, there are great hardships to be endured. Relations and early friends will not be at hand. The necessary care and nursing will be wanting. Surroundings will not be agreeable, sentiment of neglect will cause great worry, and the person feels that his death is miserable. When Sani, 8th house and its lord are *Charas* movable signs, the death occurs in a foreign place. But when all these fall in Dwiswabhava (double-bodied like *Mithuna, Kanya, Dhanus and Meena*) he dies on the way, a still more lamentable event, as conveniences would be at a low ebb, and neglect considerably enhanced. The burial or cremation will not be as desired and the man feels that he dies in neglect and misery. But when all these are in fixed or *Sthirarasis*, then the person will die at home and in his own house. Differences in distance, comforts, burial or cremation, etc., must be adjudged according to the strength of planets, houses and occupants. Though death separates soul from the body, and it is immaterial where this liberation takes place, the mind of humanity has been trained in such grooves as to attach great importance to the surroundings at death, and the disposal of the body after that event. Among the religious Hindus, the feeling is genuinely cherished that a death in his own house, surrounded by his early relations, friends and associations, and a religious cremation or burial as per their shastras are matters of real significance

and that neglect in these indicates misfortune of a serious kind.
For a sceptical mind it really looks absurd to attach any importance
to the disposition of the dead body after life leaves it—whether
beasts of prey devour it, whether it is hurled down a precipice, or
thrown into water, or buried or burned, in an honorable and religious way or disposed of by low caste men.   But the religiously inclined are of different opinion, and this feeling of an honorable
burial is so strongly felt among the soldiers, that the greatest risks
are sometimes run to rescue their fallen comrades in battle·
When the lord of birth is weak, and the lord of the 8th occupies
Kendras, death comes after 30 years and before 32 years. The most
unfavourable conjunction during those two years will cause his death·
The person endangers his father's life when his constellation is the
same as that of his father.   The text says it will kill him.   For
example—if the father's star is Bharani, and the son's also is
Bharani, there is death to father.   Here, the student must not run
away with the idea that death occurs to father as soon as the child
is born. What the author means is that when the two stars are one,
there is danger to father.   This may be enhanced by other evil
combinations or neutralised by good conjunctions. 849-D—850-851.
Stanza 852 to 856·

Those females who are born in the same stars as their mothers,
will kill them.   Those born in Chitta, in Kanya Lagna, in Pushyami
in Kataka Lagna and Poorvashadha in Dhanur Lagna or whether
the Lagna and Chandra are aspected or unaspected by by benefics,
will kill fathers, mothers, sons and maternal uncles.   The person
born in the 3rd Padam of Hasta and Makha will kill parents. The
person born in the 1st Padam of Poorvashadha and Pushyani will
kill his father. The person born in Chitta, Vishakha and Hasta, kills
mother.   The mother will die when the child is born in the middle
of Mrigasira. Four ghatis in the beginning of Moola, Makha and
Aswini and in the last of Raivathi and Ashlasha form *Ganda* (danger)
Kala (time). Out of these four ghatis forming *Ganda Kalas*, the
person born in the 1st ghati kills the mother, the father dies in the
second ghati, the 3rd proves dangerous to himself and the 4th ghati
will destroy brothers. 852 to 856.

NOTES.

A girl born in the same star as her mother kills her mother.
A child born in Kanya in Chitta, one born in Pushyani in Kataka
Lagna, one born in Poorvashada in Dhanur Lagna,—here moon will
be in Kataka and Dhanus respectively and Kanya will have Chandra
only when he is in the first two quarters of Chitta—will destroy
fathers, mothers, sons and maternal uncles. The author is wrong
in including sons (putras). Here can a child born kill a son. Sons
can only be born when the child lives to a certain age, gets married,
reproduces children and then if there are evil combinations, he can
kill his own children. Sometimes Venkatasa falls into unpardonable errors, and seems not to have realised his duty as a compiler.
His learning is unquestionable and his verses have a free flow, but
here and there he falls into such glaring errors that either he was
very careless or mistakes must have occurred in copying his manuscripts. Venkatasa says in the above cases the good aspects of
benefics will give no relief. I beg to differ from him entirely. Take
a concrete case. A child is born in Pushyani in Kataka. Chandra
and Lagna are there. It Guru is in Kataka he is exalted. His
combination with Chandra in his own house gives him long life and
prosperity and if he is aspected by Sukra in Makara certainly I would
not predict evil results to his parents or other relations at least
early in life as Venkatasa asserts. Experience must be our test. The
person born in the 3rd quarter of Makha or Hasta will destroy
parents. The child born in the 1st padam of Poorvashada and Pushyami kill his fathers. Here by using the plural fathers the author
probably refers to paternal uncles. The person born in Chitta,
Vishakha and Hasta destroys mother. When a child is born in the
middle of Mrigasira—middle refers to 25 to 35th ghatikas of that
constellation, the mother dies. Four ghatis in the commencement
of Moola, Makha and Aswini and the last of Raivathi and Auslasha
form Ganda (danger) Kalas (times) Nine constellations give
36 padams and four Rasis. With Auslasha end the first four rasis.
With Jaista end the second four signs and with Raivathi the last
four signs. The end of the last star of the first one-third and the

beginning of the second one-third of the Zodiac is called dangerous time. Similarly the end of the second one-third and the beginning of the third one-third form dangerous time and so also the end of the 3rd one-third and the beginning of the 1st one-third form Ganda Kala. Therefore the first four ghati s in Aswini, Makha and Moola are dangerous times. The last 4 ghatis of Raivathi and Auslasha are bad, but Venkatasa does not say about Jaista which is a real ommission. The last 4 ghatis of Jaista are also bad. These are *Sandhis* or junction times, and are productive of injurious results. The first ghati of these stars (*24 minutes*) kills mother, second the father, third dangerous to the child himself and the fourth destroys brothers. These refer to both the four ghatis in the end as well as in the beginning of the constellations named. 852 to 856.

Stanza 857.

The last ghati of Panchami, Dasami, Pournama and Amavasya in both halves of the Lunar month, is injurious. 857.

NOTES.

On reference to a correct almanack, the duration period of the lunar days can easily be ascertained. Then the last ghati of the 5th, 10th, 15th or Poornama and 30th or New moon day, produces evil effects. Those born on such occasions, will die as they form Sandhis or through junctional deleterious effects. 857.

Stanza 858.

The first Navamsa of Mesha, Simha and Dhanus, and the last Navamsa of Kataka, Vrischika and Meena constitute dangerous times. 858.

NOTES.

In treating of Balarista, Varaha Mihira, says that *sandhi* times cause death, and it is stated by another authority, that the last half ghati of Kataka, Vrischika and Meena and the first half ghati of Mesha, Simha and Dhanus are productive of death to children born.   858.

Stanza 859.

When a child is born in Thithi and Nakshatra Gandas, the parents will die.   When he is born in Lagna Ganda, he will himself be killed.   When a child is born when these *3 Gandas* are present it will die immediately and will cause destruction to the whole family.   But when such a child manages to live, he will be subjected to various menial services and miseries of an unexampled nature.   859.

NOTES.

Sandhi in Sanskrit means a junction. In such places the vitalising influences are neutralised and injuries are produced.   It is a remarkable fact in human domestic history that the birth of children, though hailed with satisfaction at the time, gives often cause for serious complaints.   If these children are unlucky, they cause destruction to themselves, to their parents, to their brothers and sisters, to their properties and to the whole family sometimes, so that the birth of a most unlucky child, is heralded by the destruction or extinction of the whole family and its properties.   859.

Stanzas 860 to 867 inclusive.

Draw up a *Narachakra* and place the constellations from Hasta, etc., in the Head, etc., as follow :—

In the Head—-Hasta, Chitta and Swathi

  ,,   Face—Visakha, Anuradha and Jaista

  ,,   Neck—-Moola and Poorvashadha

  ,,   Shoulders—Oothrashadha and Sravana

  ,,   Hands—Dhanista and Satabisha

  ,,   Heart—-Poorvabhadra, Oottarabhadra, Raivathi. Aswini and Bharani

  ,,   Belly—Krittika

In the Sexual organ—Rohini

,, Knees—Mrigasira, Auridra. Punarvasu, Pushyani and Auslasha

,, Feet—Poobba and Oottara. 860—861.

He will have short life whose birth star falls in the Feet, if it falls in Knees, he will be always fond of war or quarrels, when it falls in Sexual organ, he will commit adultery with others wives— If the Janma star falls in Belly, he will have ordinary wealth, if it falls in the Heart, the person will be exceedingly rich, if it falls in Hands, he will be immoral, if the star combines in Shoulders, the person will be sorrowful, if it joins Neck, he will be fond of enjoyment, if the star occupies Face, he will be fond of charities and wealthy, and if the star occupies the Head, he will be a King or Ruler. When the star falls in the Head, he will live hundred years, in the Face, he will have 80 years of life, in Neck it will give him 70 years, in the Shoulders, he will have 60 years of life, in the Hands, the life will be 30 years, in the Heart he will have 90 years, in the Belly 50 years of life is indicated, in the Secret organ forty-five years of life is granted, if born in the Knees, the life will be twenty years and if born in the Feet the life term will be closed after ten years or ten months. 860 to 867.

NOTES.

We have already seen that *Kalapurusha* or Time and space personified as representing the Infinite Vibrations needed for the work of Creation, Protection and Destruction represents the whole Bhachakra or the circle of Light and that those organs of Kalapurusha. which are occupied by benefics, will be sound and healthy while those which are occupied by malefics indicate disease and deformity. (See my English Translation of Brihat Jataka, Stanza 4, Chapter I.) The birth of any person must fall in some star and that has a definite place in the Narachakra or the Figure of a man. A boy is born in Aswini. This falls in the Heart of the Figure and represents great wealth. As the figure

is permanent in Aswini, these must always produce millionaires.
This will not be so.   The influences of the stars here given are,
one of the so many other sources, which have to be taken into
account, but which by themselves cannot and will not produce
all the results ascribed to them.   Hasta, Chitta and Swati fall in
the Head and are declared to give 100 years of life.   If this
simple fact of a man being born in Hasta, Chitta or Swati is
enough to give 100 years then all the complications, all the difficulties and doubts, and the five different systems of calculating
the length of life, the various sources of strength and weakness, of the week days, lunar days, months, years, planets, stars,
divisions of signs, and their relative positions at time of birth may
well be neglected, and the Astrologer, with one verse on the tip of
his tongue can proclaim himself sufficiently great to make predictions of human events.   Aswini, as any other constellation,
contributes its own mite in the moulding of human affairs
and the adept in astrology will have to read a lot, digest
his knowledge, analyse it carefully and with the experience
of a real business man, backed by true sincerity and honesty,
must proceed to make predictions. Like in the preparation
of medicines where many things enter into the composition of a *laham* or churnam (medical preparations) all things
have to be considered well in Astrology and there should be no
superficial generalisations and careless and off-hand predictions.
As the language of the verses is simple, no further notes have been
added Venkatasa only gives planetary combinations for longevity
but does not enter into the mathematical portions.   He seems
to have deviated a little in his information about the length of
life by introducing combinations which do not strictly belong to
terms of life, but as all other questions of humanity, depend upon
the life of the party, nothing can be irrelevant in this chapter of
Ayurdaya.   860 to 867.

End of Chapter VII.

CHAPTER VIII.

DHARMA BHAVA OR NINTH HOUSE.

Stanzas 868—869.

From the 9th house we have to examine—father, Guru or Preceptor, grand children, sympathy, law, reilgions, devotion, leadership, nature, fellow eaters or friends, charities, devatas, wealth, wife and maternal uncles. When the lord of the 9th house is a benefic, powerful, or is well conjoined or aspected, all these would prosper and give him happiness. The reverse would be the case when they are evil. 868—869.

NOTES.

All events in human life are capable of giving him pleasure or pain, but there are some which are more important than others Without a father, man can have no existence, and no humanity can therefore thrive without human seeds. Ninth is important and relates to father, more important in one sense will also be a man's Guru or Instructor. In Sanskrit though Guru is loosely app'ied to all instructors, the special reference will be to a religious preceptor. He moulds man's moral and spiritual character, and finally leads him to salvation if he is capable and wel -disciplined. If man's existence ends with his physical nature, then the father alone becomes the most important as giving existence to him, and none e'se need he mentioned. But father may become his Guru and give him also moral and spiritual training and enable him to achieve greatness. Some eminent men have made their sons more eminent than themselves, both by giving a good physique by their healthy seed and sowing it at an auspicious time and also by imparting to them the secrets of sound moral and literary education which enabled their progeny to become even greater men than themselves. It is a great pleasure to have grand children and Sastras bless him. Love and sympathy to mankind are high virtues which ennoble their possessers. Charity blesses a man. Company of good people at dinner is an indescribable source of pleasure and education, while

5

bad men make the dinner a veritable repulsion and source of inexplicable pain and nuisance. Religious devotion is a noble trait and when properly regulated it confers great advantages here and hereafter.

Men differ in tastes, physical, moral and religious. Different people follow different religions and in the history of world's nations, ancient or modern, no individual nation has ever followed one undisturbed religious system of thought. The greatest religious systems, viz., Brahminism, Christianity, Mahomedanism, Buddism, Zorastrinism, Confucianism, Jainism, etc., have given rise to various shades and differences in their conceptions of the principal deities connected with their objects of worship, and it may safely be affirmed that even in a large community or family, the members composing it hold often radically different religious views concerning their God or Gods. These peculiarities of conceptions of God are to be found out by an examination of the 9th Bhava. Maternal uncles give sometimes great help to their nephews, and bring them up with fraternal care and solicitude. Charities extol a man, and make him a real benefactor. Man often wants to be a leader and his capacity and chances to succeed well as a leader are to be judged by the 9th house. Good or bad nature is of great value and wealth is the great hinge on which the whole world literally turns. Devatas are Natural Forces or Energies embedded in the womb of the all-powerful Time, which are able to help or retard creative, protective and destructive phenomena. Sanskrit, a wonderfully constructed language possessing in each of its *Aksharas* a quantity of sound vibrative energy, enables a man by the proper initiation and repetition of a compound of these energies, and pronounced by an individual, authorised to do so by properly constituted and elevated Gurus, to attract any one or many of these Natural Forces called *Devatas* and with their help to perform sometimes prodigious acts. Their nature and the extent to which he will be able to command or invoke their help can be judged by the 9th Bhava. When the lord of the 9th is powerful, well situated in the Vergas and well combined or aspected by benefics, and when the 9th is conjoined by good planets, all these Bhavas or events ascribed to the 9th will flourish and prosper well. But when evil planets have the ascendancy, the results would be reversed, that is all these events will give him trouble, loss and misery. He now goes to explain the details at considerable length in this chapter.

Stanza 870.

If evil moon occupies the 9th as a weak or debilitated planet, or in Neechamsas or Sukra is bad and occupies evil conjunctions and Neechamsas, or if the lord of the 9th is debilitated or occupies a Neechamsa, the person will be guilty of intercourse with his Guru's wife. 870.

NOTES.

Adultery has never been sanctioned by any religion, but some religious systems sanction either a plurality of wives or husbands, the latter being rare. But there are some acts of adultery which are considered more heinous than those of others. Say a man has connection with his mother, mother-in-law, paternal or maternal aunts, sisters, and wives of brothers, and preceptors. Among the Hindus, Guru is held as a sacred personage and his wife necessarily holds a high moral rank. Any undue familiarity with her will be shocking to the feelings of a good Hindu. Ninth house represents religiousness and devotion. A debasing Moon or Sukra who also represents mother and the debilitation of its lord, will conduce to evil thoughts and if they are powerfully evil, they will lead him to commit these abominable sins. The planets may be debilitated in the Rasi or Navamsa. If there are beneficial conjunctions or aspects, the evil is mitigated and the astrologer should not blindly run with his evil predictions. 870.

Stanza 871.

If the lord of the 9th combines with an evil planet and has the aspect of a debilitated planet, the person will covet others wives.

If the lord of the Navamsa, occupied by the lord of the 9th combines with an evil planet and is aspected by a debilitated planet, similar results may be expected.   871.

NOTES.

Here the lord of the 9th or the lord of the Navamsa occupied by the lord of the 9th should have evil conjunctions and debilitated aspect to produce adultery in a man.   Coveting other unmarried or widowed women is quite different from committing adultery with the wives of others.   The latter seems to be more heinous than the former.   871.

Stanza 872.

If the weak Moon joins the 9th in debilitation or its Navamsa in debilitation and is combined with a malefic, the person will have connection with women older than himself.   If Sukra joins 9th with an evil planet, and joins the deep debilitation there or its Navamsa, he will commit adultery with his Guru's wife.   872.

NOTES.

The latter portion is almost a repetition of the 2nd half of Stanza 870.   The Moon must be a weak Moon or Kshinachandra, must have evil conjunction, and must join the debilitation Navamsa or Rasi of the 9th house.   Each sign has 9 Navamsas, one of which may happen to be the debilitated Navamsa of that sign.   Take Aries.   The Navamsas for this are 9 from Mesha to Dhanas including both, and the Kataka Navamsa may be said to be its *Neechamsa* as its lord Kuja gets his debilitation there.   872.

Stanza 873

If the lord of the 9th joins a debilitated Rasi and Navamsa and combines with Sukra, he will be guilty of sexual correspondence with the wife of his Guru.   If the lord of the 9th combining with a benefic joins a beneficial Navamsa or if the lord of Dharma—Jupiter—oins beneficial Navamsa or Rasi and does not occupy evil *Shastiamsas*, the person will be determined in doing good and will not yield to evil temptations. 873.

NOTES.

Dharma is the 9th, and the lord of Dharma is Guru, the greatest benefic among the planets. Venkatasa lays great prominence on the occupation of Shastiamsas and his readers therefore should have all the planets and the Lagna in degrees and minutes, so that the Amsas he refers to may easily be recognised and given effect to. 873.

Stanzas 874, 875.

If Jupiter or Venus joins the 9th and combines, exaltation, own or friendly Navamsas and conjoins with the lord of the 9th, the person will be well skilled in meritorious knowledge or Dharma Sastras

If the lord of the 9th joins the Navamsas of Guru, Sukra or Buda, aspected by benefics and is located betwixt two benefics, he will do meritorious deeds. 874—875.

NOTES.

The translation is easy. The junction of the lord of the 9th with benefics like Guru and Sukra, specially when they are powerful n their good Amsas, will produce a man of virtue and moral behaviour. The beneficial Navamsas of Guru, Sukra and Buda are, Meena and Dhanas, Vrishabha and Thula and Mithuna and Kanya respectively. Beneficial Navamsas produce good results and cruel Amsas produce evil results. The aspects or conjunctions of benefics, will always have a tendency to produce good and avert evil. 874—875.

Stanza 876.

If a benefic occupies the 9th and the Navamsa or other minute divisions of that house, falls in evil or cruel Shastiamsas, the person does charity for selfish purposes. 876.

NOTES.

There are many who proclaim charities or benevolent acts for serving secretly their selfish interests. An Aristocrat naturally stingy, subscribes liberally for a poor or orphan fund to get a title to please a ruler, or to have his name talked of and published in the Newspapers. Most of the modern charities are conducted on this hateful principle where sincerity and religious devotion are mostly absent. 876.

Stanza 877

If the 9th is occupied by malefics, and 9th falls in a malefic Amsa, and if the lord of the 9th joins cruel sub-divisions, evil planets or is placed between two malefics, the person will be fond of sinful deeds. 877.

NOTES.

The 9th should not have a malefic, it should not fall in an evil Navamsa, its lord should not be with evil planets, evil sub-divisions and should not be in the middle of two evil planets. Say there are 3 planets in a house. Here the lord of 9th is Guru and he is in conjunction with evil planets Sani and Kuja. But if he is not in their middle much evil is removed.

Guru is in the 1st degree of Virgo.

Sani in the 15th degree.

Kuja in the 29th degree.

So, though Guru is in the same sign as Sani and Kuja, the conjunction is not unfavourable as the distance is 15 degrees and above. Suppose Guru was in the 20th degree, then he would be between two evil planets, viz., Sani behind and Kuja before him. Suppose Sani was in Kanya, Guru in Thula, and Kuja in Vrischika. Then he will be between two evil planets. Even here some modifications are needed, say Sani is in the 1st degree of Kanya, Guru in the 15th degree of Thula, and Kuja in the 30th degree of Vrischika. Though between two evil planets Sani in the 12th and Kuja in the second, Guru is not so bad as he would be, when Sani is in the 30th degree and Kuja in the 1st degree of Kanya and Vrischika respectively.

In the first the distance between Sani and Guru will be 44 degrees, and Guru and Kuja will be 45 degrees. Therefore, as long distances prevail, the evil is not so great. But in the second case, the distance is only 15 degrees on either side and therefore the evil influences are strong and mischievous. 877.

Stanza 878.

If the lord of the 9th, lord of Dharma, *viz.*, Guru and the 9th house, occupy beneficial Navamsas and beneficial Shastiamsas and have beneficial aspects, the person will be a sincere and real devotee to acts of justice and merit and his thoughts will be pure and religious. 878.

NOTES.

The lord of the 9th must be pure, 9th must be pure, and Guru must be pure to make a man a real devotee. In this world, which is characterised by its wonderful and inexplicable variety and differences, the minds of men offer the greatest obstacles for solution. In fact, if a careful study of mental science is possible, man will be found most incor stent with himself at every phase of his existence. The seven stages of life, so beautifully described by Shakespeare, offer seven huge mountainous ranges of difficulties and it is scarcely possible to say when one stage changes into another and why and how it undergoes such constant changes. Many are putting on false appearances of what they really are not. This may be for good or evil. A real *Yogee* sometimes is found appearing as *Bala* childish, *Oonmatha* insane, and *Pisacha* or one possessed of an evil spirit. This is done with a view to drive off people, not to trouble him in his sublime contemplation. On the other hand there are dissimulators, who put on all holy appearances, to attract the unwary public, to enrich themselves at their cost and thus, under the guise of disinterestedness and saintly professions, serve their nefarious selfish purposes. The 9th house, its lord, and the lord of Dharma Guru, enable the Astrologer to say what sort of a man he really is. 878.

Stanza 879.

If Rahu and Sani occupy the 9th, combine in cruel Amsas, and aspected by Gulika and if the lord of the 9th occupies cruel Amsas, the person will be cold-hearted, engaged in inflicting miseries and injuries on mankind and quite unsympathetic. 879.

NOTES.

Some are extremely cruel, while others are extremely loving and innocent, yet others, the large majority in the world range in different shades between these two extremes. Rahu and Sani are the most cruel planets and *Sani vat Rahu* or Rahu is similar to Sani in Nature, is beautifully expressed. When these two planets occupy the 9th house, and possess the aspect of even a more worse planet than themselves, *viz.*, Gulika or the son of Sani, it can easily be seen that the last grain of mercy and love from the man will be sucked up by these planets, and the person will become the most cruel-hearted and the worst in sympathy. 879.

Stanzas 880-881.

If the lord of the 9th is a benefic, and the lord of father, *viz*, Sun joins a benefic or a benefic combines in the 9th, the person will have paternal happiness. If the lord of the 9th or the lord of father joins Paravatamsa exaltation, own or friendly Navamsas, paternal prosperity should be predicted. 880 - 881

NOTES.

In this world man derives the greatest benefit or the greatest injury from his parents, specially from the father for males and from the mother for females. If, at the time of birth, the father is engaged in cruel death-inflicting and destructive work, there is a great natural tendency for his sons to inherit his propensities and learn his brutal trade If, on the other hand, the father is engaged in loving and useful and benevolent work, children naturally inbibe these good characteristics and become good men. The butcher's son from the early childhood, will learn to lose sympathy for killing, whereas the son of a philanthropic man learns love, sympathy and self-sacrifice from the very start in his life. The 9th house represents father and the lord of father is the Sun. When the 9th, its lord and the Sun are well situated, the father will be prosperous and will thus give great advantages to the training of his boys.

Besides there is always dignity and self-respect in tracing an honorable pedigree and some families have noble traditions. There are others, who have a series of cruel deeds to relate in their families, and if the children of such families want to become good and benevolent men, they have much up-hill work, in society in as much as they have to unlearn a lot of unpalatable things, and learn many good virtues by great determination, if they want to become honorable and respectable people. A good man's son has a starting credit and a bad man son has an initial discredit. 880—881.

Stanza 882.

If the lord of the 9th is more powerful than the lord of the birth and the lord of father the Sun is aspected by benefics, the man will be obedient and filial to his father. 882.

NOTES.

It is a source of pleasure and honor to be an obedient and dutiful son. Sri Rama gained his immortal reputation by his

obedience to his father's commands although his personal interests were made to suffer in a most glaring manner for the
fulfillment of a previous promise made by his father to his step
mother.   World honors those who are filial and obedient to their
parents.   There are others who treat their parents in a most
shameful brutal and disgraceful manner.   Although the modern
highest enlightenment, wants to give man his perfect liberty
(rather *license*) it has not yet the audacity to proclaim anything
publicly against parental duties.   In this combination, the lord
of Lagna —representing the man, should be less powerful than
the lord of the father, the Sun, and the lord of the 9th house which
represents father.   882.

Stanza 883.

If the person is born in the 8th Lagna from that of his
father, or if the lord of the 8th in the horoscope of his father
occupies his Lagna, the person will take away the good Karma
from his father and will end his existence by performing his
death ceremonies.   883.

NOTES.

Here what the author seems to mean is that when the
man's birth takes place in the 8th Lagna (*house of death and
danger*) from that of his father, or the lord of the 8th in the
father, occupies his Lagna, the father has danger and death as
the result.   883.

Stanza 884.

The person will be equal to his father if he is born in the
10th Lagna from that of his father ; he will inherit his property
if his Lagna falls in the Lagna or the 3rd house from his father's
Lagna.   884.

NOTES.

The birth Lagna of the son should be in the 10th house
from the birth Lagna of his father, to make him equal his father
and his Lagna should fall in the same house as the Lagna of his

father or that of the 3rd from it to make him inherit his father's property. Venkatasa here gives a new combination for paternal inheritance which is not explained or even referred to by Varaha Mihira in his Karmajevadhaya, where he says the person will inherit his father's estate if the Sun occupies the 10th house from a man's birth Lagna (see p. 142 Ch. X of my English Translation of Brihat Jataka). 884.

Stanza 885.

If the person is born in the 6th or 8th house from the Lagna of his father, he will blame and criticise his father ; if the person's Lagna falls in the 2nd, 9th or 11th from the Lagna of his father, he will be obedient and dutiful to his parent. 885

NOTES.

The Lagna of the son should not fall in that of the 6th or 8th from his own Lagna. When it falls like that, the son will blame and disregard his father. But when the son's Lagna falls in the 2nd, 9th or 11th from his father, the son will become dutiful, obedient, and will always speak well of his father. There are various temperaments in this world. Some are given to devotion, respect and reverence. But there are others, who are always given to back-biting and blaming including even their own parents and Gods and Gurus. 885.

Stanza 886.

A person born in the 8th, 9th or 10th constellation from that of his father will do the work of his father with his sons and grandsons in a cheerful and willing manner. 886

NOTES.

The father is born necessarily in some constellation. or Nakshatra, if the son is born in the 8th, 9th or 10th from that star he will do the work of his father with his own children and grand children. Here it means that such a child will have his

father living for a long age, so that, he son) may be able to beget sons and grandsons himself and then help his father in his
works or perform the obsequies with his progeny. The person
therefore must have long life to see his great grandson and enjoy
their help and co-operation with the works he may be engaged
in   886.

Stanza 887.

If a child is born in the last star from that of his father, and
the next two, *i. e*, in his own star and the second from it, the
child will go to distant countries and cause his father sorrow and
misery. 887.

NOTES.

Say a person is born in Aswini. The Antya or last from it
will be Raivati. Ravati and the next two will be Aswini and
Bharani or the 27th, 1st and second stars from his fathers constellation. Such a person will travel to distant places and cause
sorrow and misery to his father. This sorrow may be from the
fact of his absence from the father, or from other open or secret
acts of hostility or disobedience, which may cause misery to his
father. 887.

Stanza 888.

If the lord of 9th occupies 1st, 3rd or 9th, or if he is powerful
and joins exaltation, the person will be dignified and good
natured. 888.

NOTES.

Human natures are as different as their physiques and as
complicated as the animals and vegetation. Good nature and
gentlemanly behaviour are ornaments on which a man may take
pride. Evil nature and envy are the greatest deformities for
human minds. 888.

Stanzas 889 and 890.

If the lord of the 9th joins Kendras, or Thrikonas, aspected by and combined with benefics, is powerful and conjoins beneficial Amsas like *Faravata*, etc., the person will be surrounded by wealth, and will have happiness through them. 889.

If the lord of Lagna joins 11th, the lord of the 11th joins the 9th, the lord of the 9th combines in the 2nd and is aspected by or combined with the lord of the 10th, the person will become extremely rich. 890.

NOTES.

Venkatasa now takes the reader to combinations to powerful wealth. Whatever the dry Vedanthists may say about wealth and worldly prosperity, mankind in general are after them and their accompaniments, power, influence and enjoyment. Even to do charitable acts, one must have abundant wealth. Without it he would be nowhere, and could do nothing valuable or beneficial to himself, to his relations, to his friends or to his community or to his nation. But there are good methods of acquiring it and spending on useful purposes. The second combination produces much wealth, great dignity and unbounded influence and power. There are three sources of power under the patronage and guidance of the Goddesses *Lukshmi, Parvathi* or *Durga* and Saraswathi, and beautifully classified by the ancient Maha Rishis. Lukshmi is the Goddess of wealth and commands unbounded power and influence. Saraswathi represents education and wisdom, and all other sources of power or influences must be subordinated to her power. Parvathi or Durga is the representation of political and kingly power, and this can do wonders, as you can all see what can be done by authority, and backed by it many things may be performed. 889—890.

Stanza 891.

If the lord of the 9th combines with the lord of the 3rd and joins beneficially or possesses such aspects, combining in beneficial

Navamsas and Shastiamses the person gets wealth through his brothers. 891.

NOTES

The combination of the lords of 9th and 3rd with beneficial conjunction or aspect, and joining good Navamsa and Shastiamsa, will give brothers wealth. Different people get wealth from different sources, and that which is acquired by the exertion of his own hand, being considered as the best among them. Some become wealthy by hateful and shocking means. Some condescend to prostitute their own mothers, sisters, wives and daughters and seem to take pride on the wealth thus acquired through these disgraceful means Some keep leather trade and become rich. Some get wealthy by shocking murders Some by the hateful methods of forgery and perjury. These cannot congratulate themselves on such wealth which is acquired by foul, and rascally means 891

Stanzas 892 and 893.

If the lord of the 5th joins the 9th and combines with or aspected by the lord of the 9th, or if the lord of children, *viz.,* Guru occupies 5th and has conjunction with or aspect by the lord of the 9th, the person will have much wealth through his children. 892.

If the lord of the *Gnathies* occupies the 9th and the lord of the 9th the *Gnathi Sthana* and combines with Gnathi Karaka, he will earn money through his cousins. 893.

NOTES.

Gnathi in Sanskrit refers only to cousins on the paternal side and never to first or remote cousins on the maternal side. According to the Hindu law, the cousins, on the father's side, however remote, have special claims on his inheritance, and therefore to get money through them would be a source of pleasure as per sentimentalism of a Hindu. The Gnathi Sthana is the

6th, the most hateful house for a man as it refers to debts, enemies—the Gnathies being generally put into this list and diseases The lord of cousins is Buda, or Mercury, and the readers should have all these facts before him when he ventures on his predictions. 893.

Stanzas 894 and 894 A.

If the lords of the 7th and 9th exchange their houses, and have conjunction with the lord of wife Sukra, he will get money through his wife.   The lord of 7th must be in the 9th and the lord of the 9th should be in the 7th with Sukra. Here Sukra can only be with one of them, probably the author wants him to be with the lord of the 9th.

NOTES.

This combination is given only in the first half of the Stanza. The second half refers to a matter altogether different in purport. 894 and 894 A.

Stanzas 895—896.

If the lord of the 6th is an enemy of the lord of the 9th, and occupies the 9th house, the person will get money from his enemies· If the lord of the 9th occupies the 8th aspected by unfriendly and debilitated planets, occupies cruel Amsa, and joins such unfavourable places, the person will become poor.   If the lord of the 9th joins the lord of the 6th, or 8th or 12th, his wealth will disappear. 895—896.

NOTES.

Some are born wealthy, but soon through their past and present bad Karma it dissolves, leaving them nothing.   Some are born very poor and never get rich.   Some suddenly get rich and poor and this is repeated many times.   Their lives are called chequered. Getting money from the enemies is considered generally a very delightful thing and many stake their whole fortunes to get rich at the cost of their enemies. Revenge and envy are natural to man and base natures revel in glory when these are satisfied.   Few men rise superior to these ignoble qualities, and fewer still to appreciate merit among their enemies and honor them as they deserve. All these characteristics are pointed out by Venkatasa in his own lucid style. 895—896.

Stanza 897.

If the lord of 9th or 9th is aspected by or combined with Jupiter and Venus, or if the lords of the 1st and 2nd join together and occupy the 3rd, the person will again get his wealth. 897.

NOTES.

This means that he will be wealthy first, then lose it, then gain it again.

These are common occurrences among mankind. Battles are won and lost, to be won again, crowns are lost and gained to be los again. Fortunes are made and unmade several times in the course of a short life. 897.

Stanza 898.

If the lord of 11th joins 9th, the lord of 9th joins Lagna, and the lord of the 9th joins 11th, he will regain his lost wealth. 898.

NOTES.

There is no consistency in this stanza. If the lord of the 11th joins 9th, the lord of the 9th joins Lagna, then again how can the lord of the 9th join the 11th. It looks absurd on comparing several printed and manuscript copies, one work gives an intelligent stanza. I wonder how some of the printers and commentators publish such absurd and irreconcilable conjunctions which are wrong on their faces. The verse runs thus—If the lord of Lagna occupies 9th and the lord the 9th is in Lagna, and if the lord of the 11th combines in the 9th, the person will regain his lost wealth. Here the meaning is that the lords of Lagna and 11th must be in the 9th while its lord should be in the birth. This is quite possible and sensible. 898

Stanzas 899 to 906 inclusive.

If the lord of the 9th is powerful and joins 5th or 9th, aspected by or conjoined with Guru and Sukra, the person will become a great devotee and attain elevation in Yoga practice. 899.

If the lord of the 10th or 9th joins Devalokamsa, and is aspected by Buda occupying Paravatamsa, the person becomes a real *Brahma Gnani* or one who knows about Para Brahma. 900.

If the lord of the 9th is exalted and aspected by benefics, and a benefic occupies the 9th, the person will do great and good charities. 901.

If the lord of 9th joins Paravatamsa aspected by Guru, and the lord of Lagna is also aspected by Guru, the person becomes a great benefactor. 902.

If Lagna or its lord is aspected by the lord of the 9th, and the lord of the 9th occupies a Kendra or Thrikona, the person will do great charities. 903.

If the lord of the 9th joins *Simhasanamsa*, and is aspected by the lords of the birth and 9th, the person becomes a great benefactor. Some of the verses have been very badly preserved. How can the lord of the 9th be aspected by the lord of Lagna and again by the lord of the 9th. Another manuscript says—If the lord of the 9th joins Simhasanamsa, aspected by the lord of Lagna or the lord of the 10th, the man becomes extremely liberal and does great charities. 904.

If these *Danayogas* or combinations for great charities, exist in horoscopes, which have combinations for wealth or combinations for Raja Yoga, then they help men to do charitable deeds on a large scale. But suppose these combinations for generosity or charity occur in horoscopes which have neither wealth nor polifical position or power, they will be useless and produce no good results. 905—906.

7

NOTES.

Well directed and timely charities are so many blessed deeds which add lustre and merit to the donor. They elevate his soul, remove all feelings of selfishness, add comforts to the needy and the deserving, and make the individual a gem to his family, community, society and to the nation. They are honored throughout the world, when they are genuine, and do their charitable work because they feel real sympathy for the distressed humanity. Pretenders are in the line and they are easily found out and given their due. He is right when he says that the combinations for charity may exist without money, influence or power, and when such men have them, the results are disappointing. What can a poor man do? He is a burden to himself, to his family, to his community, to his society, and to his nation. So far I agree with Venkatasa, but suppose the poor does charitable work by labour and brain, really such work must be appreciated and honored. There are so many petty acts which a poor man can do by way of charity that it would be a mistake to say that he cannot be charitable. 899—906.

Stanzas 907—914.

If the person born in Danayoga happens to be a Brahmin Purohit or priest, he will do the charities. If they happen to be other than Brahmins, then attribute to them such charities as are sanctioned by their caste and religions. 907.

If the lord of the 9th joins 4th, the lord of the 10th occupies a Kendra, and the lord of the 12th joins Guru, the person will become extremely liberal. 908.

If Buda is exalted and is aspected by the lorp of the 9th, and the lord of the 11th joins a Kendra, the man will be very charitable. 909.

If the lord of 11th occupies 11th, the lord of the 10th is powerful and is aspected by the lord of the 9th, the person will receive liberal charities or donations. 910.

If the lord of the 5th occupies the 9th, combined with the lords of 9th and 10th and aspected by the lord of Lagna, he will become undoubtedly very wealthy.   911.

If the lord of the Navamsa, occupied by the lord of the 9th, combines with or is aspected by Guru and Sukra, the person will have great respect and regard for Gurus or Preceptors.   912.

If a benefic occupies the 9th and has combination with Guru and the lord of the 9th occupies a Mrid Bhaga, the person will have great devotion to his preceptors.   913.

For the edification of the learned, the 8th and 9th Bhavas have been well explained by Venkatasa Daivagnya belonging to the felicitous Kasyapa Gotra.   914.

NOTES.

The stanzas are easy and do not require any special commentaries.   Reverence to Instructors in true Religion is an absolute necessity to give expansion to the soul of the disciple or chela and make him a Mahatma. Gratitude in men is a precious quality and the greater the gratitude, greater will be their nobility. Ingratitude is the blackest color in a man's character which cannot be erased, and which has been branded as a veritable sin by all classes.   Cases of extreme liberality and miserliness are worthy of deep attention. They touch two different poles, and are thoroughly antagonistic.   A truly liberal man is an ornament, while a truly miserly man is a deformity to his society.   In nature, all shades of liberality and miserliness exist and must be tolerated.   Doing charity is nobler in every way.   Receiving charity has various phases. Charities   or donations   may be   given   for   various purposes. Learned   men, holy   and   religious   men,   innocent and god-fearing men may receive charities and they deserve them. The   right   kind of charity will be   only   possible with deservin men. Giving money to poor but evilly inclined persons will be money ill-spent.   Food may and must be given to all classes of persons irrespective of caste, creed, age, sex or nationality, but ready money should be given only to deserving men. A holy man receives a charity and spends it for good purposes. If a thief, cut-throat or a debauchee receives ready money, off he goes to bad acts, such as drinking, whoring, thieving, and gambling. Much discretion should be used in giving such donations. When men are actually starving for want of food and water, as God's creatures, they must be lovingly and sympathetically fed as far as possible. 907 to 914.

End of Ninth Bhava and Chapter VIII.

———

CHAPTER IX.
DASAMA BHAVA.
Tenth House.

Stanza 915.

From the 10th must be ascertained, occupation, command, reputation, residence and travelling in foreign countries, respect, dignity, means of livelihood, actions, wisdom and religious knowledge, place, and servants, by the clever Astrologer. 915.

NOTES.

This is an important house, and men are naturally anxious to know how, where and by what means they earn their livelihood, and what professions and business would pay them best. This anxiety is common to mankind, and every one wants to know what his future will be, to what height of power and wealth and respect he would be raised and by what means or methods he could earn a decent and respectable living. No science in this world can throw real light on these matters as astrology can, and here is the nobility of the science to throw good light on the future and enable mankind to achieve success, distinction and affluence. Tenth house is very significant and it should be carefully studied. This house is called Karmasthana and all the actions man may do come under the influence of this Bhava. Man does good and evil for serving his interests. Whatever may be his aims, he must do some actions to accomplish them. Whatever he does comes under *karma* or that which is to be done or that which has been done. A man wants to commit a murder. He does many acts to finish his intention. He wants to build a charitable institution for the good of the people. Here too he has to do many things before he could complete this charity. All this is Karma and all his actions have to be found out with reference to the 10th house. Residence in foreign countries will be profitable or ruinous as he directs his mental battery in the right or wrong direction. Command over servants implies success or failure in agriculture, industry, enterprise, adventure or military operations or religious propoganda, as he knows how to advance his commands or how to mismanage them. 915.

Stanzas 916 and 917.

If the lord of the 10th is powerless and joins an evil planet, he will become irreligious or go against the principles of his religion. If the lord of 10th, Guru and Buda are powerful, the person will perform religious sacrifices. 916.

If the lord of the 10th is aspected by benefics, and Jupiter and Mercury are powerful, the person will perform many important religious sacrifices.

If Guru, Sukra and Buda occupy the *Dusthas* or 6th, 8th and 12th houses from Lagna and have evil aspects, they make the man give up all pretensions to good or religious acts. 917.

NOTES.

The question of religion is a complicated one and much more complicated will be the solution to give about the different religious systems as to which of them is the best. Bloody, cruel, barbarous and destructive wars and butcherries have been conducted in the name of religions and when dispassionately examined in the light of justice and fair play, many of these cannot be defended by any known principles of divinity. But good men have been seen in all nations and amongst all religious

systems, and this goodness is generally attributed to religiousness and fear of God as propounded by those religious doctrines.
Again various forms of religious sacrifices have been named
among the different religions, and many of them have the common object of removal of sin, purification of mind, elevation of
soul, and the production of a better state of future existence in
the order of evolution. Hindu religious observances and various
sacrifices, have two principal purposes One to give the performers, a better state of existence in the Cosmos, when the
performers will it so or make *saṇkalpa* like *jyotistomay swarga-
kamo yejata* and the other is to give them complete emancipation from the grosser environments and amalgamate their souls
with that of the **Supreme Soul** when the performers have no
special aim and do the religious rites for the sake of God and
humanity. Guru, Sukra and Buda, the three benefics must be
strong and also the lord of the 10th house, when religiousness is
to be produced. When they are not strong, and when they
occupy evil houses like the 6th, 8th and 12th and are subjected
to the combination or aspect of evil planets, irreligiousness in all
its branches will spring up and make the man hateful, reckless,
and sinful. 916—917.

Stanza 918.

If Buda, Guru and Sukra occupy the 8th house, or if the
lords of the Rasis occupied by the lords of the Navamsas occu-
pied by Buda, Guru and Sukra combine the 8th house from
Lagna, they cause destruction to all meritorious work. If Rahu,
Kethu or Ravi occupy the 10th, the person will bathe in the
Ganges. 918.

NOTES.

Buda, Guru and Sukra occupy some Navamsa. The lords
of these Navamsas occupy some Rasis and if the lords of these
signs or Rasis are found in the 8th from Lagna, they destroy the
germs of merit in a man and make him quite irreligious. Bathing
in the Ganges or the Ganga has been given special virtues in

purifying the mind, elevating the soul and giving salvation to the man. This is a knotty point and requires some explanation on the so-called scientific and logical basis. A clear exposition will not be unwelcome within the narrow space allowed in a note like this. The influence of the body and the mind on each other, has been recognised by all the civilised nations. The body is purified by the seed, soil, food, clothing, air, water and the surroundings of a man. When the blood is pure, invigorating and refreshing, it must elevate the mind and the nervous system which composes it. The water of the Ganges has been tested and found to be capable of destroying various forms of germs or bascille which corrupt the blood and injure thus the human system. Of the whole lot of rivers, known to the ancient or the modern world, the most remarkable is the Ganga. This is the finest and the best river in the world. Its water can be safely preserved for hundreds and thousands of years and has been so preserved in many religious families and Mutts in India. In my own house, the Ganga water brought by my grand-mother, long before I was born, and I am now 67 years old, is still preserved and it is as pure, as clear and as tasteful as the Ganga water brought by me from Haridwara some 20 years ago. I have seen water of the Ganges pure and fresh in ancient religious families and Mutts brought some 3 or 4 hundred years ago and I am assured by some that there are waters of the Ganga, which have been brought and preserved for over five or six hundred years. This long preservation is only possible with the Suddha Ganga or pure Ganges water before its junction with the Janma near Allahabad Afterwards, the water cannot be preserved so long and it gets corrupts very soon. This is a natural phenomenon which stands unrivalled in the history of rivers, and when it possesses such preservative and vitalising powers without putrefaction, certainly there must be some subtle electrical and ethereal currents which have the power of purifying the bodily organs and thus enable the mind of the man to be purified to a remarkable extent, and obtain merit and salvation from its purity, a fact indisputably recognised by all religious systems. Are not some of the poor Christian Missionaries to be pitied in their ignorance of physical and mental phenomena and the remarkable influences they exercise on each other. Is not the attraction of the people of the whole of India to its waters an undoubted proof of some irresistable power, which the Ganges exercises even over the greatest Indian minds like Vasista, Vyasa, Parasara, Sankaracharya and Vidyaranya. When a person exercises his influence over thousands and millions of people, surely there must be something in him which deserves recognition. When 3 to 4 hundred millions have been proclaiming about the efficacy of the water of the Ganges, over any other water in the world, and this reputation has been continuously felt for thousands of years, the opinions of a few insignificant people like some of the Christian preachers, may be entirely omitted as a non-existing and worthless fact, and their brains, if they have any may be pitied rather than be recognised as factors in pronouncing our judgment. Rahu, Kethu or the Sun in the 10th house will give the man the opportunity of a bath in the Ganges. 918.

Stanza 919.

If Meena becomes the 10th house and Buda or Kuja occupies it, the person will have *Mukti*. If full Moon and Jupiter occupy the 10th, when it falls in a watery sign, he will have the merit of bathing in the Ganges water. 919.

NOTES.

In the Sanskrit language in which Venkatasa has written Sarwartha Chintamani all the ideas given above are familiar to people and they do not require much explanation. But in a foreign Christian language like the English, these religious notions are quite foreign and they have to be explained at some length to enable the readers to understand what they signify. *Mukti* means final emancipation for the soul from births and rebirths and all grosser surroundings. The Christians look to the

Resurrection day When will that come and why does it come at all. Watery signs are Cancer, Pisces, Capricorn and Virgo Meena is the last sign and when that falls in the 10th, occupied by a benefic, there will be salvation. 919.

Stanza 920

If the lord of the 10th combined with Sukra, joins a Kendra in exaltation, he will bathe in holy waters like the Ganges and get purification.

If Buda is in the 12th or its lord occupies exaltation, the man will be purified by baths in holy waters like the Ganges 920.

NOTES.

The following rivers have been considered as very holy after the Ganges, viz., the Jamna, the Godavary, the Saraswathi, which can be seen near Kurukshetra running in a small channel, the Narmada, the Sindhu, and the Cauvery. These seven rivers are remarkable for their sanctity. Bathing in some ponds are also considered efficacious. The pond of Maha Magha at Kumbha-konam, Chakrapushkarani on the bank of the Ganges near Manikarnika ghat, at Benarese, or Kasi and some at Ramas-waram. and other holy places are considered as sacred 920.

Stanza 921.

If Buda occupies 10th with Guru or Soumya, he will cause temples, mantapas and other religious buildings to be con-structed. If Buda occupies the 10th with its lord, then he will be engaged in restoration and repair of old religious buildings. 921.

NOTES.

Buda is called Soumya as he is the son of Soma or the Moon. But since he is to be with another Soumya than Guru, it must mean Sukra who is a benefic. Here full moon, when powerful will be classed as a benefic. Some are fond of building temples, their Prakaras or compounds, Mantapas, Chatras, etc.,

8

while there are some, who rightly think that when we have any number of old and grand religious buildings, it would be sounder policy to repair and preserve them, than to build new ones with limited means and allow them soon to get out of repairs and decay.   Both probably are wanted as units of the world for new construction and old reparation.   921.

Stanza 922.

If the lord of the 10th, occupies 10th in Gopuramsa, joining Mridwamsa and aspected by a benefic or the lord of the 9th, the man will have wells, ponds, tanks and other such useful works constructed.   922

NOTES.

As the Devil can cite scripture for his own purposes, each charitable man quotes many authorities or arguments for the kind of work he will be engaged in and spends money and energy on them.   There may be temples but there must be water convenience for them when they are not close to perennial rivers. Tanks, wells, canals, ponds, lakes, etc., are highly useful and those who build them will be real benefactors to humanity. When a planet gets 4 good Vergas or sign divisions he is said to be in Gopuramsa.   Mridwamsa is one of the 60th divisions.   In India those who perform Yagnya or religious sacrifices are held in great esteem and really they have to lead a strictly moral, laborious and self-sacrificing lives.   Their religious duties are onerous and extremely taxing and almost everyday their religious observances hardly give them time to attend to any other work. They rich y deserve the honor that is shown to them.   922.

Stanza 923.

If the lord of Lagna joins 10th, and the lord of 10th joins 9th, without evil combinations, or being himself evil, and aspected by benefics and occupying beneficial Navamsa, the person will perform Yagnya or religious sacrifices   923.

NOTES.

There are many varieties of *Yagnyas* or religious sacrifices, some of which may be named here for ready reference. Adhana or commencement to keep a continuous fire ; Agnistoma or Somayagnya, when the performer becomes a Somayaji and then he will wear those peculiar earrings, after the fashion of crocodiles ; Chaturmasya, Atirathi, Vajapaya, Poundarika, etc. Aswamedha, Gomadha, Naramedha, Gajamedha, Pasumedha and other varieties are too numerous to be enumerated here. 923.

Stanza 924.

If the lord of the 9th joins 8th in exaltation combining with a malefic, occupying a debilitated Navamsa, and combines in cruel Shastiamsas, he will have the sacrificial rites disturbed and disappointed. 924.

NOTES.

The lord of the **9th** should be in exaltation and occupy the 8th with a malefic, join a Neecha Navamsa, and occupy a cruel Shastiamsa to break off the sacrifice when everything is ready and the man has spent his money and labour over its preparation. He will be disgraced in the public, and will suffer loss in various ways and the indignity will certainly be felt keenly by him. 924.

Stanza 925.

If Mercury is exalted, and the lord of the 10th is in exaltation and aspected by Buda or joins with exalted Mercury or joins Mercury and both are placed in the 7th, the person will perform religious sacrifices. 925.

NOTES.

Mercury is exalted in Kanya, and the lord of the 10th in exaltation should be aspected by Mercury. Buda aspects the 7th and Meena is the 7th from Kanya and Sukra is exalted here. Mercury and Venus could never be separated beyond 60 degrees and therefore the combination does not hold good. The lord of the 10th cannot be in exaltation and yet join Mercury in exaltation. No two planets can be found exalted in one and the same house. The lord of the 10th may be in conjunction with the exalted Buda. The lord of 10th may join Mercury and both may occupy the 7th as required. 925.

Stanzas 926 to 930 inclusive.

If the lord of the 10th is a benefic, combines with or aspected by a benefic and occupies a beneficial Navamsa, the person will be in a position to issue orders or commands. 926.

If the Sun or Mars occupies the 10th and the lord of the 10th occupies a Kendra, the orders will be strict and cruel. 927.

If the lord of the 10th combines with Sani and joins the lord of the 8th, and joins a Kendra or cruel Amsa, he will issue rigorous or cruel orders. 928.

If Rahu joins the 10th with Mandi or if Mandi joins 10th, with Rahu or Kethu in the 8th and the lord of the 9th occupies a debilitation, the commands will be cruel. 929.

If the lord of the 10th joins a Kendra, combined with or aspected by a benefic, and joins cruel Shastiamsas, the commands will be cruel. 930.

NOTES

Commands may be cruel, sympathetic, -tasteful, or loose. Discipline means very strict orders, obedience to which must be enforced with unsparing rigour. In military matters where the fate of Empires and Kingdoms will hang on the ready obedience and strict performance of the commands the necessity will be real. In matters civil of course, a little more latitude may be allowed or convived at. Sugreva, the Commander-in-chief of the Vanara army which followed Rama to conquer Lanka, has left a name for Agnya or command which is even feared to-day as strict. Strict orders are different from cruel and unsympathetic orders. Supplying the servants with all their wants and exacting the work may be strict but not cruel. But not attending to the comforts of the servants and still goading them to do hard work will be cruel. Suppose a servant's wife is on death bed, and he is ordered to leave her and go away, when another could be spared to do work is cruel. If the lord of the 10th occupies Kendras, he seems to exercise cruel influences though joined or aspected by benefics. Evil planets in the 10th generally make the person cruel. Good planets loving and sympathetic. The greatest generals while being strict, have been noted for their tact, sympathy and love for their servants or followers. Some have a supreme knack to manage their servants, while many have the greatest knack to quarrel and get into loggerheads with their subordinates. All these should be made out by the 10th house. Hannibal, the great Carthagenian general led his soldiers into the greatest dangers, but he was loving and sympathetic so much so, that not a single instance occurred when his soldiers complained of his harshness or rebelled against his orders. Alexander the Great had many mortifications of his soldiers rebelling against him. 926 to 930.

Stanzas 931 to 934 inclusive.

If Chandra occupies a Kendra aspected by Guru or Sukra, and occupies Paravatansa, etc., he will have pure reputation. 931.

If the lord of the 10th joins benefics or is between two benefics or combines beneficial Navamsas, his reputation will be pure. 932.

If the lord of the 10th is a benefic, occupying exaltation, own or friendly houses, and joins beneficial Shastiamsas, he will have unsullied reputation. 933.

If the lord of the 10th joins Devalokamsa or Simhasanamsa, and the lord of Lagna is very powerful, his reputation will be pure. 934

NOTES.

When five favourable Vergas or divisions or signs combine, they go under the name of *Simhasanamsa.* If seven favourable Vergas combine, they give rise to Devalokamsa. *(See p. 39 ch. I supra).*

These are all sources of strength and weakness for planets and the Astrologer should be careful in taking them into proper account before he ventures on his predictions. Reputation may be a bubble, not to be relied on, and not to be counted. But will there be any man who really does not care for it. The world may be unreal for a true Vedantist, but even he will be careful about his good name. Some are very particular about their reputation and ommit to do many sinful deeds for fear of jeopardising their reputation. Others are indifferent, but still do not willfully prejudice their good name. A pure reputation will be an ornament to a person that gives him a moral lustre before which the brightest of diamonds cannot hold their heads. Unless men are really good and god-fearing, and possess abundance of love and sympathy, they can never secure this precious commodity. 932—33—34.

Stanzas 938 to 937 inclusive.

If the powerless lord of the 10th joins malefics, and occupies cruel Shastiamsas, he will have evil reputation. 935.

If Saturn, combining with the Sun, joins the 10th, aspected by evil planets, or joining evil Navamsas, or is placed in the midst of two evil planets he will have bad reputation. 936.

If the lord of the 10th or the 10th is combined with benefics, or joins exaltation or own house, he will be respectful and determined. 937.

NOTES.

Notoriety or evil reputation should not be coveted. They come only as the resultants of bad actions. Man should avoid bad Karma and try to keep his heart and actions clean. **This** requires great determination and serious self-sacrifice. Moral **currents** must be strengthened and fortified. Immorality in any shape should be scrupulously avoided. These things can be accomplished by great determination and simple and innocent life. Dignified behaviour and solicitude to keep self-respect, are virtues which require constant practice, and good associations, godly thoughts, and love will bless the man with dignity and pure reputation. 936—937.

Stanzas 938 to 940 inclusive.

If Guru or some other benefic occupies the 10th and its lord joins a benefic or is placed between benefics he will command respect. 938.

If an evil planet joins the 10th, and is aspected by a malefic if the lord of the 10th is in debilitation, or joins evil Amsas, he will become shameless and disgraced. 939.

If the lord of the 10th occupies a movable Navamsa, he will be fond of travelling, if he is in a fixed Amsa, he will not be given to travelling, and if he occupies a common or Dwiswabhavas Amsa, he will travel sometimes and remain at home at other times. 940.

NOTES.

The translation of these stanzas is so easily and clearly given that it does not require many commentaries. Venkatasa refers to the nature of the Navamsa occupied by the lord of the 10th. There are others, who say that when there are a large number of planets in movable signs, the person will become a great or restless traveller, if the majority are in fixed signs, he will be averse to travelling and if they are in common signs, he will travel and take rest alternately 939 940.

Stanza 941.

If the lord of the 6th joins 10th and the lord of the 10th is with Sani, and has connection with the lord of the 6th, the person will command many servants. 941.

NOTES.

How can the lord of the 10th have *Sambandu* the original word used in the stanza with the lord of the 6th unless he also joins the 10th where Venkatasa has located the lord of the 6th, but he may have his aspect, comparing with other versions, one copy says that the lord of the 10th with Sani should be in any of the Kendras The latter is more suitable and to the point. Sani represents servant classes and his elevation and favourable influence give the man many servants. 941.

Stanza 942.

If the lord of the Navamsa occupied by the lord of the 10th, combines with Sani or occupies any of the Kendras, he will have control over many male and maid servants. 942.

NOTES.

The lord of the 10th must be in some Navamsa. If the lord of this Navamsa combines with Sani or in any of the Kendras, he will have male and female servants in large numbers. 942.

Stanza 943.

If the 10th, or its lord joins benefics or Sani, the question (Prasna) will be completely successful. 943.

NOTES.

From horoscopy Venkatasa takes the reader to a little bit. to horory or *Prasna*. I have already referred to this branch in the earlier portion of this work and here the author says that if the 10th house or its lord combines with a benefic or Saturn, the object of the question will be completely successful. This seems to be out of the way and does not fit in here, as Venkatasa has never in the treatment of *Bhavas* referred to Prasna ; whereas Varaha Mihira in his Brihat Jataka refers to horory. Another version is that the above combination produces many male and female servants. 943.

It is a blessing to have good and faithful maid servants. They are generally more faithful.

Stanza 944.

From the lord of the 10th the success of the object of question may be determined. If the 10th is occupied by evil planets there will be weakness in the knees. 944.

NOTES.

Weakness in the knees will be a serious defect for working men and men engaged in military operations, 10th represents success and from it the success or failure of the question may be determined. 944.

Stanza 945.

If the lord of the 10th joins fourplanets in the Thrikonas or Kendras, the person will become a *Jevanmukta.* If there are four or more planets in the 10th, they make the person *a sanyasi.* 945.

NOTES.

In Brihat Jataka *(see my English Trans. p. 182 Ch. XV)* four planets in any house, are able to produce Pravarajja or Sanyasa Yogas. Here Venkatasa observes that there must be four planets in the 10th house. Jevanmukta is the highest and purest development of mind by severe and devoted yoga practice which enables a person to become one with the *Supreme Being* at any time he likes. This will be obtaining a sort of passport which allows him to become one with Para Brahma. The object of the Sanyasi is to attain Moksha on emancipation from births and rebirths. Vasista and other Maha Rishis, Ravi and other important planets and many Maha Munis are Jivan Muktas or beings who have raised themselves to this sublime height by unrivalled Thapas or devotion and contemplation of God, and who can go to the Supreme Being as they are in their present shapes if they so pleased. Under the orders of the Almighty, they are doing certain duties and they can go away

9

to him whenever they please. For Jevanmukta Yoga, the lord of the 10th must join four planets in one house in Kendra or Kona and thus literally there must be five planets in a Kendra or Kona, including the lord of the 10th to produce this grand mental state and power. 945.

Stanza 946.

If the lord of the Lagna, unaspected himself by any other planets, aspects Sani, or Sani unaspected by any other planets aspects the lord of Lagna, the person will become a Sanyasi. 946.

NOTES.

The lord of Lagna and Sani, being pure and unaspected by any other planets and unaspected may be made to include uncombined—aspect each other, then there will be Sanyasa Yoga. In these aspects the peculiar houses of aspect for Sani should also be included. If it is only the 7th aspect, then the moment Sani aspects the lord of Lagna, the latter must aspect also Sani in the 7th. But sometimes Sani, unaspected himself by others, may aspect the lord of birth in the 3rd or 10th. 946.

If Chandra occupies a Drekkana of Sani and is aspected by Sani, the person becomes a Sanyasi.

Stanzas 947—948.

If Chandra occupies the Navamsa of Sani or Kuja and 'is aspected by Sani, there will be Sanyasa Yoga. 947.

If the planet who causes *Sanyasa Yoga* combines with Rahu and occupies cruel Amsa, or joins with Gulika, there will be no Sanyasa, so say the learned in Astrology. 948.

NOTES.

It must be confessed that Venkatasa who sins on the ide of verbosity and minutie in some Bhavas, say the 7th, where he gives details of even sexual organs of man and woman, is unpardonably brief in his treatment of this most important Bhava, the means of livelihood and how to get money. Besides giving a few combination for sacrificial rites, possession of servants and becoming Sanyasis or *Muktas*, he has not a single word to say about Karma-Jeeva, or by what kind of work a man lives and earns money and power. The whole chapter is most shabbily treated by this learned Daivagnya and I refrain from saying anything more. I don't think my readers would be satisfied with these few combinations in the 10th house, and those which have been given do not generally concern the overwhelming majority of mankind. About Mukti and other sublime things, the ordinary run of mankind are not in sympathy. About the performance of religious sacrifices, certainly very few souls are concerned. Why then is it that Venkatasa, the learned Astrologer, has been so unmercifully short in the treatment of this Bhava. In fact I can find no reason why he should have been so careless in the treatment of a Bhava, which concerns every man in the world, and about which there seems to be a universal craving for greater information. I shall however give here a few hints which may be remembered by my readers. *(See pp 143, 44, 45 of my English Trans. of Brihat Jataka Chapter X.)*

"From the Sun, etc., the acquisition of wealth must be predicted, through father, mother, enemy, friend, brother, woman and servant respectively, when he occupies the 10th house from birth or Moon or through the lord of the Navamsa occupied by the lord of the 10th from birth, Moon or the Sun." St. 1 of Chapter X.

If the Sun is in the 10th paternal property, Moon in the 10th maternal property, Mars in the 10th through enemies, Mercury in the 10th through friends, Jupiter in the 10th through brothers, Venus in the 10th through women, Saturn in the 10th through servants. This applies to planets when they are in the 10th. But suppose there are no planets in the 10th, then take the lord of the Navamsa, occupied by the lord of the 10th from Lagna, or Moon or the Sun. If that lord is the Sun—wealth or money through scents, gold, wool, medicines, etc,

If he is Moon—agriculture, watery products, dependence upon women, etc.

If Mars—minerals, fire, weapons, adventures, physical strength, etc.

If Mercury—writing, mathematics, poetry and fine arts.

If Jupiter—Brahmins, Priests, Gods, mines, manufactures and charities.

If Venus—gems, silver, cows, buffaloes, etc.

If Saturn—labour, execution, carrying and by low artisanship.

For more detailed information I refer the readers to my English Translation of Brihat Jataka and Astrological Self-Instructor, 6th edition, 948.

End of Dasama Bhava,

LABHA OR ELEVENTH HOUSE.

Stanza 949.

Means of gains, elder brother, ears, ear ornaments, should be ascertained by the learned. 949.

NOTES.

Eleventh house signifies a great number of events in human life, but Venkatasa has enumerated only a few relating to this house. A man gains or earns money and other articles by various means and these are detailed here, elder brothers, and their prosperity, ears and their ornaments will have to be ascertained with reference to the 11th house. 949.

Stanzas 950 to 955 inclusive.

If the lord of 11th is in exaltation, Kendra or Thrikona, and if the 11th is between two benefics, there will be much wealth. 950.

If the lord of the 11th is aspected by or in conjunction with the beneficial Iord of the 10th, and occupies exaltation, own or friendly signs and Vergas or divisions there will be much money.   951.

If the lord of the Navamsa occupied by the lord of the 11th is a benefic and occupies a sign between two benefics, there will be great gains.   952.

If the lord of the Drekkana, occupied by the lord of the 11th is a benefic and is aspected by the lord of the 10th, there will be much money.   953.

If the lord of the 11th is aspected by the lords of the 2nd and 4th, and combines with the lord of the 9th, there will be great wealth.   954.

The wealth comes from that direction which is ascribed to the lord of the 11th at the time of birth and the wealth may also come from the direction indicated by the lord of the second house.   955.

NOTES.

This is called *Labha* Bhava or house signifying gains in general. Between the second house and the 11th, some distinction may be made though not so well defined by the astrological writers.   The second is called Dhana Bhava or house of money while the 11th is called Labha or house of gains.   The distinction seems to me to be between money, *i.e.*, in cash, and coin, therefore metallic, in which paper currency must be included under the orders of the Government and gains in general by which we may include all sorts of articles which go to make a man comfortable but which are not hard cash.   A man gets a thousand silver or gold coins.   This is Dhana   He gets grains, clothes, cattle, horses, carriages, houses, etc., and this is Labha   Of course one can easily be converted into the other, and *vice versa* but still there is some difference between a man who gets a suit of clothes as a present, and a person who gets a bag of coins.   The lord of the 11th must be in exaltation, his own or friendly house, or beneficial Navamsas or other divisions,

and must be aspected by benefics or be placed between auspicious
planets.   I have already explained what is meant exactly by position between benefics in my notes above.   The planets have directions and they have been given in p. 34 (st. 5 of ch. 2 of *my Eng.
Tr. of Br. Jataka*).   If the lord of the 11th governs east, the wealth
comes from that direction.   The direction of the wealth must also
be indicated with reference to the lord of the 2nd.   But these two
are not enough.   The lords of the Dasas and Bhuktis or periods
and sub-periods, and the planetary movements, as per *Gochara*,
will also influence the directions from which money or other articles
flow.   949 to 955.

Stanza 956.

If there are evil planets in the 11th or the 11th if owned by
evil planets, destruction to wealth must be predicted.   And also
when the lord of the 11th joins evil planets, there will be loss of
wealth.   956.

NOTES.

Venkatasa has committed a glaring error which is unpardonable in the light of extensive knowledge which he possessed as an
author and a scholar in Astrology.   Vedas have laid down the
blessing.   " Sarevagrahaha Shubha Ekadasasthana Phalada Bha-
vantu."   All the planets *good and evil* are productive of the highest
good when they are in the 11th or Ekadasa.   The great astrological
principle is that evil planets, *viz.*, Sani, Kuja, Ravi, Rahu, Kethu,
badly associated Buda and new Moon or Kshinachandra, are good
and produce prosperous results when they are in the 3rd, 6th and
11th houses from Lagna.   Referring to the recognised and authoritative works in Astrology, we find that only good results are ascribed
to planets in the 11th and never any evil.   Ravi in the 11th is a
powerful factor in a horoscope and he will be able to ward off all
dangers from whatever sources they may come like his own rising
rays destroying the darkness in any place where he makes his
glorious appearance.   How then can Venkatasa say that evil planets
in the 11th produce poverty and loss of money? Benefics in
Kendras and Thrikonas are productive of favourable results.   The

Sun and Mars are powerful and valiant when they occupy the 10th Kendra. Of course, if the lord of the 11th is in combination with evil planets or evil Vergas, his power to do good may be diminished, but evil planets as well as good planets are all-powerful in the 11th house and Venkatasa is completely wrong in the first half of stanza 957. *(See p. 211. Eng. Tr. of Br. J. by me).* 956.

Stanza 957.

If the lord of the 11th is a benefic and has beneficial aspects, or is powerful, the person will have good ear ornaments. 957.

NOTES.

Different nations have different forms of ornamentation, as different nations have different varieties of food and clothing. Some nations have nothing like ear ornaments, in which case the greatest ornament for them would be a good and strong ear. Among the Hindus diamond and pearl ear ornaments even among the males may be often seen as ornamentation and fashion. 957.

Stanzas 958 to 961 both inclusive.

If the lord of the 11th joins evil Amsas, or has evil conjunctions or aspects, destruction or loss to ornaments may be predicted. 958.

The healthy or diseased condition of the ears may be predicted by the lord of the 11th or 3rd. 959.

The prosperity or misery of the elder brothers must be predicted by the beneficial conjunctions and occupation of Vergas by the lord of the 11th, and their misery by his weakness and malefic conjunctions. 960—961.

NOTES.

A good ear is a source of blessing and deafness and disease in the ears will be a great misfortune. People with deafness are averse to meet their friends and relations and are unwilling to

attend public functions.   *Sans* any sense will be a disqualification
for public purposes.   The longevity and prosperity of elder
brothers will have to be ascertained by the strength of the 11th
house, and its lord, and also by Mars.   It will be a source of
advantage to have a good and earning elder brother.   The prosperity of younger brothers will have to be judged by the lord of the
3rd house.   Here brothers include sisters also.   If the lord of the
11th is a female, feminine planets combine in the 11th, and its
lord joins with powerful females, prosperity to sisters must be
predicted.

Venkatasa has not done justice to this important Bhava.
Influential friends and the large gains from their kind offices have
not been detailed here, and he also says very little about the other
events, signified by this house.   Sometimes he is unpardonably
long and sometimes unpardonably short.   This probably depended
upon his extensive studies of some Bhavas, and cursory perusal of
it others, or may be due to his own indifference or other circumstances which prevented him from elaborating some Bhavas, and
profusely writing upon others in a jolly or good mood.   958—961.

(*End of Labha Bhava*)

VYAYA BHAVA
OR THE
Twelfth House.

Stanza 962.

All sorts of expenditure, falling into hell, deformity in the
limbs, left eye, the two feet and bed room, should be ascertained
from the 12th house.   962.

NOTES.

This is an important house, as important as any in Astrology.
The prudence of a man, and his moral stamina, general respect,
family traditions and prosperity and peace in life depend upon how
he behaves in his expenditure.   If he spends on good and useful
purposes, he will be a happy man and will be helpful to others, and

also to himself ; but if he misspends on immoral or irreligious ways he will be ruined in every way and he will be unhappy and wretched. Hell or Heaven will be the result of bad or good expenditure respectively. Deformity in the limbs will be a misfortune, and when this is serious he will be useless. Eyes are the most precious gems for a human being. If they are lost or defective, world and its grandeur cannot be appreciated by him.

Feet are important limbs. All his locomotion and usefulness depends upon their strength. Their defect will uufit him for many useful occupations. Bed rooms, though not so important, on the surface of the question, have really great sexual significance, whose far-reaching effects can hardly be appreciated by the ordinary readers. In the production of happy, healthy, long-lived, prosperous or miserable, ugly, short-lived, or criminal children, bed rooms have the most potent influence and they should be particularly clean, attractive, sweet scented, and agreeable for sexual operations· When a man and woman join sexually, their moods, health, pleasurable or painful sensations, thoughts agreeable or otherwise, and passions to meet vigorously at the sexual operations, affect directly their future-off spring, and this is completely borne out by religious, medical, hygenic, moral and practical experience. Therefore, there are three places, which should be as clean, as attractive, as richly furnished, and as comfortable as possible. (1) Rooms where men take their meals. (2) Rooms where they sexually join and enjoy and (3) Rooms or places where they discharge their foecal and urinary matters.

When the surroundings, where men take their food, are dirty, unwholesome, and repulsive, the food gets into the stomach with disagreeable, and injurious ethereal and electrical currents, generates there all sorts of distempers, and dangerous gases, corrupts the blood circulation, weakens the nervous system, disturbs the magnetic fluids, and impairs the general health, upsets the brain cells, and makes it quite insufficient. Temperament of a man greatly will be moulded by the conditions of his life and where these are desirable and attractive, his temper will improve in the right direction. People may laugh at the idea of a closet or privy being clean. Great intellects have realised the fact that at these places, where they discharge their dirt, when they are clean and attractive, some of their finest flashes of brain occur and hence they sought lovely and lonely places to " *ease*" themselves and get finer ideas after they have eased themselves. An easy motion is an index to good health. All medical theories are agreed in saying, that so long as a man has clean motions his health will be good, his system vigorous, and his brain bright and efficacious. Physical or mental filth, should never be allowed to accumulate, and should be removed as early as possible and as cleanly as could be. Bed rooms therefore are specially decorated on nuptial days, and all attractive furniture is kept there, and all possible luxuries are provided to make the couple enjoy life and act agreeably in sexual connections. 962.

Stanzas 963

If the 12th is occupied by a malefic, its lord is an evil planet, and aspected by a malefic, money will be spent on sinful purposes. 963.

NOTES.

People spend money. The greatest rake, drunkard, and gambler, are spending their monies as liberally if not more liberally than the greatest charitable and philanthropic men. Why should then there be any difference in honoring them. We shall drop the misers here. Those who follow sinful ways, ruin their good family reputations, their own name, their health and their intellect by their expenditure of wealth, while the good and the charitable man, by spending money on meritorious deeds, adds value to his good reputation, enriches his pure family traditions, adds good health by pure mental currents and commands the real admiration of the public. Evil planets in the 12th, evil aspects to it and to its lord, will make the man waste money on sinful deeds. 963.

Stanza 964.

If the lord of the Navamsa, occupied by the lord of the 12th is a benefic, occupies a beneficial Navamsa, and is aspected by benefics, the person will spend money on real charitable works. 964.

NOTES.

Money spent on building places of worship, digging canals, tanks and wells for public uses, planting plantations, and other fruit-bearing trees for charitable purposes, feeding the poor and the needy, the old and the decrepid, orphans, and distressed and good women and infants, helping education and so forth are considered as good and real charitable acts. 96-;.

Stanzas 965 to 978 inclusive.

If Sani, Rahu or Mandi join the 12th or combine with its lord, occupying cruel Navamsas, money will be sinfully spent. 965.

If Guru and Sukra occupy the 12th aspected by Buda or Chandra, joining Paravatamsa, etc. Money will be spent on moral and meritorious purposes. 966.

If the lord of the 12th is in Thrikona or Kendra aspected by a malefic and occupying a cruel Shastiamsa, money will be wasted on immoral purposes. 967.

If the lord of the 10th is evil and aspects or combines with the lord of the 12th, who occupies an unfriendly or evil Amsa, the money will be wasted. 968.

If the lord of 12th is aspected by or combined with the beneficial lord of the 10th and occupies exalted, own or friendly Vergas, the money will be spent on moral purposes. 969.

If the powerless lord of 12th is joined or aspected by the lord of the 6th and combines with Gulika or Rahu, the person will lose money through enemies. 970

If the lord of the 12th is aspected or combined with the powerless lord of the 7th and occupies cruel Amsa, the man will lose money through females. 971.

If the lord of the 12th is combined or aspected by the powerless Kuja, and joins cruel Amsa, there will be losses through brothers. 972.

If the lord of the 12th is combined or aspected by the powerless lord of the 4th, and joins malefics and cruel Amsas, the person will waste money on mother. 973.

It the lord of the 12th is combined or aspected by the powerless lord of the 5th and joins cruel Amsa, the person will have to waste money on children 974.

If the lord of the 12th is combined with or aspected by the lord of the 9th or the lord of father Ravi, money will be spent on father. 975.

If the powerless lord ot the 12th, occupies cruel, or debilitated Amsa, the person will have deformed limbs. 976.

If the 12th occupies various evil or cruel Vergas, and its lord combines with Sani, Mandi or Rahu, there will be deformity in the body. 977.

If the lord of the 12th joins malefic Amsa, cruel Amsa, or evil planet, and is aspected by evil planet, the person will go to hell. 978.

NOTES.

The verses are easily translated and do not call for many notes. A man may spend money, profitably or unprofitably on one thousand and one ways. As man's temperaments are peculiar, so also actions proceeding from his idyosyncrasies. There are people who spend any amount of money on wives, on mothers, on uncles, on horses, on carriages, on lands, on industries, on speculations, on cousins, on brothers, on fathers, and on so many other directions. Some of these are indicated here by planetary combinations. Junctions with malefics, occupation of cruel Amsas and Vergas and evil aspects, make the man spend in evil ways, while beneficial conjunctions, aspects and Vergas give expenditure in the right direction. 965 to 978.

Stanza 979.

If Rahu and Mandi combine in the 12th, and aspected by the lord of the 6th, or combined with the lord of the 8th, the man will fall into Hell. 979,

NOTES.

What is Heaven and what is Hell, are questions which are explained by various religious systems in many ways.

Some say these are concrete and substantial places like the countries of the earth and others say they are imaginary and will be variations of mind. Where the mind feels miserable it is Hell and where it feels well it is Heaven We are not here to discuss on the merits of the various doctrines regarding the conceptions of Hell and Heaven. Good work takes a man to Heaven whatever and wherever it may be Evil work lodges him in Hell. 979.

Stanza 980.

If the lord of the 12th occupies a cruel Shastiamsa and is aspected by malefics, the person will have Hell. 980.

Stanzas 981 to 983 inclusive.

If the lord of the Drekkana, occupied by the most powerful among the two planets, the Sun and the Moon, happens to be Guru, the person gets into Devaloka, if he happens to be the Moon or Venus, the person goes into Pitruloka, if he happens to be in the Sun, or Mars, or Mercury, he goes to Hell. If that lord of the Drekkana possesses beneficial aspect, the person occupies some high position in the Loka, he ascends.

If the lord of the Drekkana who causes the above combinations is exalted, the person will have exalted Loka, if he is debilitated, he will go to Narakaloka, and if he is ordinary, he will occupy ordinary Loka, 981 to 983.

NOTES.

I have already referred to the question of the existence of Heaven and Hell. Now another knotty point is introduced by Venkatasa which requires some explanation from the so-called scientific light of to-day. Sciences are ever changing, both their bases on which they are supposed to be based, and the theories and practices dependent on such conceptions are also changing. Therefore to say that any event or fact can be based on the adamantine foundation of science is a mere verbosity which means nothing permanently in Nature I call attention to the rapid advancement and progress of physical sciences during the last one hundred years in the most enlightened countries of Europe and America, and request the readers to consider dispassionately whether there is anything like permanent bases for their scientific theories. They are sitting their grounds almost every year, and what were found to be based on the adamantine basis of science, some years ago have been now changed, and another foundation has been substituted. This is but natural since they did not hit at the Truth.

Mental development is the forerunner of physical experiments and discoveries. The present enlightened nations have never given instances, where their greatest men, have spent years after years, in long contemplation on the Sublime and the Universal Intelligence Neither have they ever sat in that deep renunciation of worldly pleasures and objects, in serious penance and austere life to know more about the Invisible Forms of Energies, which are often producing what they are pleased to call abnormal Phenomena and Freaks of Nature. Even for ordinary physical development in the several lines, deep concentration and constant exercise of mind are needed. How then can they ever expect advancement in mental power, when its currents are scattered on the numberless wants which the want of the present enlightened nations, has created for them, and without which they think they could not exist conveniently. These mental distractions take away from the capacity and efficacy of the brain, make it shallow with reference to depth of thought and quite unfit it to grasp the higher Invisible Agencies which deep contemplation alone can give them. How then are they qualified to judge of the existence and non-existence of Lokas or worlds other than our own, when the greatest psychic development is needed to locate and find them.

Judging by the laws of continuity, as some of the advanced European scholars have done, the existence of higher developed souls, must be admitted as a matter of proved science, and when these are existing they must be located in some planes or spheres, where they take their abodes, clothed in bodies peculiar to their developed state, and live under laws, which are suitable to them. The possibility of the existence of the plurality of worlds has been admitted by the greatest men of the day, and this admission, great as it may be, after deep thinking and various Astronomico Physical experiments, is a common doctrine enunciated by all the 18 *Puranas* (old writings and truths) written by Veda Vyasa and he says he has collected the information from still older works. Whence their name *Purana (old)* as opposed to Navina, new. Men of different temperaments die. One, a really charitable man, a second, very avaricious, a third a god-fearing and saintly sort of man, a fourth, a strong-minded moral hero, a fifth a cowardly beggar, a sixth, a pronounced liar, a seventh a notorious brigand, an eighth, a callous debauchee, a ninth, a smooth-faced villain and a tenth, a national patriot. All these die. It would certainly be absurd to say that all the souls or lives, after their separation from the body, will have the same plane, or sphere of existence, and will be surrounded by the same physical or mental conditions in their altered states. By the laws of continuity all these will have to serve their rounds of existence in the *Comos* and in certainly different planes and forms   These planes of existence may conveniently be called Lokas or worlds which have their own Phenomena suitable to their composition. Pitruloka, Patalaloka, Swargaloka, Indraloka, Suryaloka, Chandraloka, Angarakaloka, Brahmaloka Gandharvakola, Kinnaraloka, Kimpurushaloka, Nagaloka, Bhuvarloka,Suvarloka, Mahaloka, Janoloka, Tapoloka, Satyaloka, Vitalaloka, Sutala-Loka, Rasatalaloka, Mahatalaloka, Talatalaloka, Pisachaloko, Siddhaloka, Sadhyaloka, Yakshaloka, Rakshasaloka and so forth are named by our works and no one has any authority to say that all these are fictions of priestly craft, unless he has himself produced his credentials for his expanded   soul.

It would be mean and degrading to consider that a European savant is the dictator to the world. A great debauchee may observe judging by his own nature, deeds and experience that it is impossible for man to remain unattracted when he is in the vicinity of women. On the other hand, a platonic hero will rightly observe, that he has never been subjected to carnal passions and has always looked upon other women when in their company in the light of his own mother and sisters. The greatest dacoit will observe, from his own experience and nature, that it is nonsense to say that a man can ever remain unattracted by the properties of others, while the greatest philanthropic would declare, that it is not human nature to covet others properties and remain unmoved, when others are in distress and trouble. The scientific men of to-day need not arrogate to themselves, the powers of judgment over all Phenomena in the Universe, and if they are fair-minded, they would at once see the force of Newton's remark that his own knowledge, was like a grain of sand in the mighty ocean and like Socrate's saying that the sum total of his knowledge was that he did not know anything.

When a man goes to a town he falls into his own level in society. When a person dies, the acts he has done in this life with the results of those which he has to his credit from his

former states of existenee or past Karma will determine in what
plane of existence or Loka, he should be placed in and there he
will he lodged, till he is transferred from there again, either
promoted or degraded, as per his own Karma and that of the
Karma which his children, relations and friends do for him. A
man dies and finds level in a certain Loka as per his deposit of
past Karma. This he obtained, we shall say, by constructing a
reservoir for public and charitable purposes. So long as that
Dharma goes on, his deposit in that Loka will remain unim-
paired and he will be there in a certain rank or station. Suppose
now his children, out of disregard for their father, cut off the
reservoir, defeat his object and sell away the materials and lead
a life of prostitution. His deposit suffers, he will be degraded
and transferred to some inferior plane of existence or Loka.
Suppose instead his children spend another large sum, build
other charitable institutions and dedicate their merit to him.
He gets fresh additions to his deposit of good Karma which after
a certain standard or extent, gives him a higher plane of existence
and a better Loka. An ordinary example will make the meaning
very clear.

A is the father of ten sons, and possesses a lac of rupees.
He does some charities and occupies after death a certain Loka
as the result of his good Karma. Suppose he spent Rs. 50,000 on
these charities and left the other half to his sons. If the sons
are mean-minded and undutiful they resume the properties
devoted to charities, and spend the amount on immoral purposes
His deposit of Rs. 50,000 by doing good deeds, must go away and
he will be degraded say into a pauper plane. But if, instead,
his sons out of noble spirit dedicate the other half of a lac also
for charitable purposes, certainly his own deposit of half a lac,
now gets expanded by the charitable act of his sons and becomes one lac and takes him into a higher plane where he will
hold a higher rank and status so instead of, like fools, pooh-
poohing these ideas of Lokas, Swarga Naraka, etc, the wise

11

readers would do well to carefully consider over these arguments and satisfy themselves by extensive reading and real Yoga practice that these are real Phenomena in the world which have substantial and tangible existence in planes which may be lower or higher in the scale of creation and which may give greater pleasure and peace or greater pain and disturbance. Here Venkatasa observes that if the lord of the 12th is in exaltation beneficially aspected or combined, the person even after death will occupy a higher position. By such observations like these, it looks that even in these Lokas and other regions where men may go after death, distinctions of rank seem to be observed according to the good or bad Karma which he will have to his credit, and his elevation or depression there is shown by the exaltation or debilitation of the lord of the 12th and his associations. 981 to 983.

Stanzas 984 to 986 inclusive·

If a benefic is exalted or occupies the 12th, aspected by a benefic and occupying good Amsas like Devaloka, etc, he will have Heaven. 984.

If the lord of the 10th joins Devamsa, or the 12th house is aspected by a benefic, he will have Heaven. 985.

If the lord of the 12th joins benefics, occupies a beneficial Navamsa, and has conjunction with beneficial planets, his eyes will be good. 986.

NOTES.

From Heaven and Hell the change comes to eyes. The two houses representing the two eyes are the 2nd and the 12th, and when these are powerful and their lords are well situated, combined and aspected by benefics, the eyes will be good and attractive· Some have attractive eyes while others have quite repulsive eyes· 984 to 986.

Stanza 987.

If the lord of the 12th is otherwise, the eyes will not be good and so also feet have to be found out by the 12th Bhava. Most of the combinations by which eyes, etc., can be found out have been given in the Dhana Bhava or treatment of the 2nd house. 987.

NOTES.

When the lord of the 12th is evil, has evil conjunctions and aspects, and occupies debilitation, unfriendly or cruel Amsas or Vergas, disease should be predicted for the left eye and also for the feet. The right eye should be judged from the 2nd house. When good planets are there, and have beneficial aspects, the sight will be powerful and attractive. 987.

Stanza 988.

If the 12th is occupied by Guru, Sukra and Buda, the person will have good conveyances or carriages, horses, etc. The house of conveyances is the 4th and whatever combinations hold good, these will also have to be considered here. 988.

NOTES.

Here Venkatasa suggests that with reference to 12th, conveyances, horses, etc., may be determined as they have been stated in the 4th Bhava. Very few writers have offered such suggestions. But this may be included on the principle of expenditure and hence waste of money. 988.

Stanza 989.

If the 12th house or its lord has beneficial conjunctions and occupy beneficial Vergas, the person will have luxurious cots as also swinging cots. 989.

Stanza 990.

If the lord of the 12th is in exaltation, aspected by or in conjunction with benefics and occupies beneficial Vergas, he will sleep on rich and luxurious cots. 990.

NOTES.

Sleeping on the ground floor has been condemned both by medical theories and also by the long experience of the various nations. There seems to be a sort of poisonous gas—vayoo or air—which spreads itself at about four o'clock in the morning at a height of one or 2 feet from the ground and its inhalations will prove injurious to the brain as well as to the general health Hence he will be a happy and energetic man who daily passes his night on an elevated plane and cots serve also various other scientific purposes. 990.

Stanza 991.

If the lord of the 12th is in deep exaltation and is aspected by the lord of the 9th, the person will possess cots of great value, of various fashions and decked with valuable gems and precious stones 991.

NOTES.

Downy beds cost a great deal of money, are soft, excite sexual passions and afford great pleasure. In the production of children though sexual union will be the same on the part of the poorest as well as the richest, the manner, the environments, the cleanliness and the artistic nature of the furniture and paintings in the bed rooms have a great and striking effect upon the fortune, health, morality, education and wealth of the offspring. Therefore, furniture in the bed rooms and the manner of sexual intercourses have great significance and ought to have much weight in the determination of future offspring. 991.

Stanza 992.

If the 12th or its lord combines with a malefic, occupies cruel Amsas, and gets the aspects of malefic planets, and joins bad Vergas, there will be no happiness in the bed rooms. 992.

NOTES.

A good sleep for a man is a real tonic for his health and mind. A disturbed or uncomfortable sleep will be an indescribable misery, sleeplessness is a real misfortune and they are unhappy mortals who are devoid of this precious gift from Heaven. 992.

Stanza 993.

If the lord of Lagna is debilitated or joins the 12th aspected by the lord of the 6th and combines with Sani, Mandi or Rahu, there will be no happiness in the bed rooms. 993.

NOTES.

Sani, Mandi and Rahu are evil planets and whenever they join any good lords, they produce miserable results. 993.

Stanza 994.

If Sukra and Chandra occupy the 5th, or the 5th is aspected by them, the person will worship Goddesses. 994.

Stanza 995.

If the 5th is occupied by evil planets, the man will worship Kavi or Govinda. If Chandra is found in the 5th, the person will worship the Goddess Yakshini. 995.

NOTES.

Among the Hindus, as well as among other nations, there is a great variety in the conception, liking, worship and selection of objects of worship. All worship in any form is good, but some are more favourable and profitable than others from a spiritual point of view. Sun worship is almost universal as no other Deity could be conceived as more efficacious in giving life, prosperity and final destruction. All the Vedas are devoted to the interpretation of his glory Yakshini, Sakeni, Dhakini, Bhetala, etc., are forms of Energies which possess certain supernatural powers and which are exhibited undoubtedly by some men in India. The psychic development here in India remains unparallelled. 995.

Stanzas 996 to 1002 inclusive.

If the 5th is occupied with or aspected by Kuja, he will be devoted to Subramhanya or Bhairava. If Buda joins or aspects the 5th, he will be devoted to Saraswathi. If the 5th is combined or aspected by Guru, he will be devoted to the God Vishnu If Sukra joins or aspects the 5th there will be devotion to Chamundi. If Sani occupies or aspects the 5th, he will worship the God presiding over Smasanas or burial grounds. If Rahu or Kethu is in the 5th, or aspects it, he will be devoted to Goddesses. If the lords who cause these various forms of devotion are exalted, or in friendly Amsas, the devotion will be for self-protection and elevation, but if they are in different Amsas or Vergas, the devotion will be for serving other people. If such a lord be aspected by benefics or occupies beneficial Vergas, the devotee will have peaceful Gods or Goddesses, and if such a lord is aspected by evil planets or occupies cruel and evil Amsas and Vergas, he will have cruel Deities. If two or more planets occupy the 5th and have mixed aspects and join mixed Vergas, the person will devote himself to many Gods and Goddesses. If the lord of the birth becomes a friend of the lord of the 5th, the God will be a friend, if there is enmity between the two, the God will become unfriendly and if they are neutral, the God also will be indifferent. I have detailed the various combinations for the 12 Bhavas in a useful manner, and all these particulars I have related in these are selected from ancient authors, and they are found in their learned works. 996 to 1002.

NOTES.

Venkatasa says that he has selected all the particulars mentioned in his treatment of the 12 Bhavas or significations from the works of the ancient Maha Rishis for the edification of the public and if anybody wants to know whether all these particulars are in the ancient works, he assures us that they are found there. This is a master stroke of frankness, and confession and he very cleverly shifts away all burden of responsibility from his own shoulders and rightly places the same on the shoulders of Maha Rishis, who alone were in a position to give us Astrological results from the cultivation of their Divya Dristi, aad seeing those results with their expanded visions. He has now finished the 12 Bhavas and will enlarge upon Rajayogas, results of Dasas and Bhuktis in the next chapters. In scme Bhavas he is more elaborate than their importance demanded and in others he is hort beyond reason or rhyme. We cannot quarrel with him. He has written what all he could write and what all he though, proper and our simple duty lies in thanking sincerely an author who has taken so much trouble in selection and so much labour in their clear exposition and explanation. 996 to 1002.

End of Dwadasa Bhava.

CHAPTER X.

RAJAYOGAS

OR

Combinations for Political Success.

If six planets are in exaltation, the person will become King of Kings or a Powerful Emperor. If five planets are in exaltation and Guru is powerfully occupying the Lagna, the person will become a mighty Sovereign. 1003.

NOTES.

In the first part of the stanza, there should be six planets in exaltation to produce a great Emperor. From time immemorial there have been various grades of rulers and their histories and biographies are very interesting and instructive study. Whether we call a person Ruler or President or Chairman or Secretary, the analogy of power and influence determine what he is and what Rajayoga applies to him. Prince Bismarck and Gladstone, of recent years, were great Statesmen and exercised tremendous influences greater than their Princes, but still they were not actual rulers. Rajayoga, I believe, applies only to those who wield executive functions and not to ministerial lines unless so named. Six planets cannot be exalted, unless it be in the Solar month Aries or Mesha. For when Mercury is exalted in Virgo, the Sun and Venus cannot have exaltations. But when the Sun is exalted, Venus can be exalted, though not Mercury, but all the other planets can be in exaltation. In the second part of the stanza, if five planets are in exaltation, with Guru in Lagna occupying beneficial Vergas, the person becomes a great Sovereign. 1003.

Stanza 1004

If Kumbha becomes Lagna with Sukra in it, and four other planets become exalted without occupying evil *Navamsas* or cruel *Shastiamsas*, the person becomes a King, 1004.

NOTES.

Six planets in exaltation will make a man a great Emperor or King of Kings. Five planets will also make him a King of Kings provided powerful Guru occupies the birth. Four planets in exaltation, without malefic Navamsas and cruel Shastiamsas with Kumbha as Lagna conjoined by Sukra will give royal power But if these exalted planets are in evil Navamsas and Shastiamsas, they may spoil the royal power and degrade him or make him an ordinary Sovereign. 1004.

Stanza 1005.

If Vrishabha is Lagna with Chandra in it and 6 planets are in exaltation, the person becomes a King. If Vrishabha becomes Lagna with Chandra in it and 6 other planets are found occupying their own houses, the person becomes equal to a Monarch. 1005.

NOTES.

The first part can never happen and Venkatasa here again falls into an absurd position. I cannot say that he was ignorant of mathematics. One who did not know mathematics, could never have written such an able exposition of the Astrological Science. In Vrishabha, Chandra is exalted. How can then 6 other planets, *viz*, Ravi, Kuja, Buda, Guru, Sukra, and Sani become exalted at the same time. This is absurd. I give below the exaltation of all the planets.

12

Here all the planets are in exaltation and this is an absurdity and a gross miscalculation. When Buda is exalted, Ravi and Sukra can never be in exaltation. And when Ravi and Sukra are exalted, Buda can never be in exaltation. If Ven-

Sukra	Ravi	Chandra	
	Rasi		Guru
Kuja			
		Sani	Buda

katasa simply repeated the idea from the ancient authors, then he ought to have told us so, as did Varaha Mihira, in his combinations of Vajra, etc., Yogas. The second portion is feasible. *(See p. 161 of my Eng. Tr. of Br. Jataka.)* 1005.

Stanza 1006.

If Vrishabha is Lagna and all the planets are exalted and do not occupy debilitated Navamsas, the person will become equal to a King. When Vrishabha becomes Lagna, and all the planets are in their Mulathrikonas or own houses, the person will become equal to a King. 1006.

NOTES.

Again Venkatasa repeats a great blunder. When all the planets are in exaltation, Chandra must be in Vrishabha and he is unpardonably stupid, in not only committing a mistake he has already made, but in ascribing less power than a King to a person born, when the seven planets are in exaltation. When 6 planets make a man King of Kings or a great Emperor, how can 7 planets in exaltation make him a King's equal ? 1006.

Stanza 1007.

If there is one exalted planet, aspected by a friendly planet, the person will become a lord, and if such an exalted planet is in conjunction with a friendly planet, he will have influence, authority, wealth and good reputation. If there is a planet in Neecha, or unfriendly, or cruel Amsa, the person will have no wealth; if there are two such planets he will be miserable; if there are three such planets, he will be a fool and stubborn; if four, he will suffer from diseases; if five, he will suffer imprisonment; if six he will be a murderer or butcher and if seven planets are so. he will be a horrible sinner. 1007.

NOTES.

Venkatasa sometimes runs too fast and forgets what he has to say and what he should not. When seven planets cannot be exalted, these seven planets again can never be debilitated at one and the same time. This is a natural corollory. Of course planets in debilitation, in malefic Amsas and evil Shadvergas, in evil conjunctions and malefic aspects and in evil or cruel Shastiamsas, must produce bad results, and the intensity of the evil increases as one, or two or more planets are so situated. Good or evil planets, must be in beneficial signs, Amsas, Vergas, combinations or aspects, or exaltations to produce auspicious results. 1007.

Stanza 1008.

Those who are born in Vargottama Lagna, those who have planets in the Vesisthana, those who have planets in the Kendras and those who have Karaka planets will be lucky and influential. 1008.

NOTES.

Vargottama refers to the first Navamsa of the movable, the 5th Navamsa of the fixed and the 9th Navamsa of the double-bodied signs, or in other words when analysed it means that if the Navamsa of any sign falls in the same sign, it becomes Vargottama. Thus Mesha Navamsa in Mesha Rasi,

Vrishabha Navamsa in Vrishabha Rasi, Mithuna Navamsa in Mithuna Rasi, and so on become Vargottamas. When a man has his Navamsa falling in Vargottama, without reference to other combinations of planets, he becomes one of note; *(see p. 22 and 147—My Eng. Tr. of Br. Jataka)*. Vesisthana is the second from the Sun, and whoever has planets in the 2nd house from the Sun, will become fortunate, those who have planets in the four Kendras become lucky and those who have Karakas will also be lucky. *(see Notes on st 133 and 34 P. 118 supra)*. Planets with reference to each other at the time of birth occupying certain houses become Karakas. Thus—if Gurn occupies the 9th house from the Sun at birth, he becomes a Karaka. Sani in the 11th from Chandra at birth becomes a Karaka Sani becomes Karaka to Kuja when he occupies the 11th from him at birth. These have been detailed by me carefully in my previous notes. There is another method mentioned in other works about finding out Karakas. A planet in exaltation, Mulathrikona or own house at the time of birth occupying a Kendra from birth becomes Karaka to another planet who joins another Kendra from birth and occupies exaltation, Mulathrikona or own house. Similarly other planets become Karakas. Such positions are favourable. 1008.

Stanza 1009.

If birth is occupied by Chandra, 4th by Guru, 10th by Sukra and Sani joins exaltation or his own house, the man becomes equal to a King. 1009.

NOTES.

There are some persons who are called uncrowned Kings, who wield great influence with the masses, who command great respect and who can accomplish great deeds by their personal exertions. 1009.

Stanza 1010

If Buda and Guru join together or aspect each other the person will command great respect from Kings.   1010

NOTES.

The junction of Guru and Buda or their mutual aspect signifies great influence and power. Their junction in various Rasis will of course produce different results. Suppose they join in Makara where Guru is debilitated, or in Meena where Buda is debilitated or in Kataka where Guru is exalted, or Kanya where Buda is exalted, it cannot and will not produce the same results. A learned man resides at the court of a petty ruler, and commands great respect. The same man may honor the court of an emperor and he commands great respect there also. Here in these two courts though the love and respect of the rulers may be the same, the results must certainly differ in quality and quantity. The best remuneration a petty ruler may give, may extend to a thousand or two thousand rupees, while the emperor may give him one or two lacs of that precious metal. These differences in their relative sources of strength and weakness, should not be forgotten.

There is a special merit in the conjunction of Guru, lord of education and Buda lord of intelligence. When education and intelligence happily combine, it would be next to impossible, not to command influence and power from the higher circles. However much a ruler may be worthy himself, he cannot pull on the car of his administration all alone. He must seek the help of educated and intelligent people, and where these two are happily blended, surely the person cannot remain unnoticed by the ruling authorities, unless and until the man himself renounces the world, retires to a forest, and spends a life of deep contemplation and Yoga practice. Even then he will not be let alone. Sovereigns sought the help of the great Maha Rishis and honored them as they deserved.   1010.

Stanza 1011.

If the lord of the house occupied by a debilitated planet, or the planet who would be exalted in that house occupies a Kendra from Chandra, there will be Neecha Bhanga Rajayoga, and the person will be charitable and command the respect of rulers. 1011.

NOTES.

There are Neecha Bhanga Rajayogas, and Raja Bhanga Neechayogas. These Yogas must be clearly understood. Some people who are born on the lap of misery and wretchedness, will merge into prosperity and greatness and attain to eminent distinction. Example—Napoleon, a poor soldier's son became an Emperor. Hyder a poor Naick's son and a cattle grazer and gardener became a great Sovereign. Sivaji born of a commander himself of 5 000 horse or *Panchhazari* became a great monarch. The combinations in their horoscopes indicated poverty and low position at birth and greatness and prosperity later on in life. Say there is a debilitated planet at the time of birth. Then his tendency will be to send the man to a low level or low position in society. But, if he, or the lord of that debilitated house, or the planet who would be in exaltation there, occupy a Kendra from the Chandra Lagna or from the position of the Moon, the misery will disappear and prosperity will dawn. 1011.

Stanza 1012.

If Chandra occupies any other than the Lagna Kendra, or any Thrikona, and is aspected by Guru, and is otherwise powerful, the person will be equal to a King in wealth, power and influence. 1012.

NOTES.

Chandra will be powerful when he is full, when he occupies beneficial house or Amsa, and has no evil aspects or conjunctions and when he is in exaltation. The other Kendras and Thrikonas are 4th, 7th and 10th, or 5th and 9th. 1012.

Stanza 1013.

If planets in debilitated Rasis, occupy exalted Navamsas, they produce wealth equal to a king. If they are in exalted Rasis and occupy debilitated Navamsas, they will not produce good. 1013.

NOTES.

As per Venkatasa's explanation it is better to have a debilitated planet in the Rasi and occupying an exalted Navamsa, than to have a planet in exalted Rasi and occupying a debilitated Navamsa. This is but right. Planets in Rasis are indicators of rough results. Planets in Amsas are more powerful so much so that powerful planets in Shastiamsas produce great Rajayogas 1013.

Stanza 1014.

If there are exalted and powerful planets in the Eastern half of the Zodiac, the person will have kingly power and wealth in the first half of his life, and if there are exalted and powerful planets in the Western half of the Zodiac, he will have power and success in the latter half of his life. If there are exalted and powerful planets both in the Eastern and the Western halves of the Zodiac he will have power and prosperity all through his life. 1014.

NOTES.

The Eastern half of the Zodiac means the first six houses from the Lagna. The Western half of the Zodiac signifies the next six houses or from the 7th to the 12th houses inclusive. 1014.

Stanzas 1015 to 1017 inclusive.

If benefics occupy the first, or the second, or the 3rd Khandas, they produce good results in that Khanda. If malefics join the Khandas, they give similarly misery, sorrow and pecuniary losses. 1015—16—17.

NOTES

Take the term of life and divide it into 3 equal divisions.
Each is called a Khanda or division. Take the 12 signs from the
12th house from Lagna and divide the whole Zodiac into 3
Khandas or equal divisions. Each will be called a Khanda. Thus
the first Khanda contains the 12th, 1st, 2nd and 3rd Bhavas completely. The second Khanda will include the 4th, 5th, 6th and
7th Bhavas from Lagna. The third Khanda will comprise the
8th, 9th, 10th and 11th Bhavas completely. If there are more
benefics in the 1st Khanda, he will be more successful and happy
in the first one-third of his life career. If there are more benefics
in the second Khanda he will be happy and prosperous in the
second one-third of his life. If there are more good planets in the
3rd Khanda, the man will be happy and successful in the last one-
third part of his life. Suppose the man's life comes out as 60
years after calculation. This divided into 3 equal parts will
give 20 years to each division. But if benefics are scattered
over the three Khandas, the success will be uniform throughout
life. The evil planets in excess in any of these Khandas, will
produce misery, poverty, sorrow and death to close relations. Some
say the Khandas should be taken from Lagna.   1015—16—17

Stanzas 1018 to 1020 inclusive.

If Guru joins Lagna, Buda is in one of the Kendras, and if
these two are aspected by the lords of 9th and 11th, the man will
be equal to a king.   1018.

If Guru joins 7th, with the lord of the Thrikona, aspected by
the lord of Lagna, he will be equal to a king.   1019.

If Sani in exaltation or Mulathrikona joins a Kendra or Kona
aspected by the lord of the 10th, the person becomes equal to a
king.   1020.

NOTES.

Thrikona includes the 5th and 9th houses. Sani has his exaltation in Thula and Mulathrikona in Kumbha. A person may not be an actual king or ruler. But he may be a merchant prince, a great statesman, a highly learned and influential Zemindar, or one who commands much wealth and many men. In all these cases the king will be forced to give him respectful treatment and consider him as almost his equal. People honor some men as they do their rulers, and often in history such influential men have deposed kings and set up others on the thrones by their influence. 1018—19—20.

Stanzas 1021 and 1022.

If the lord of the 10th joins exalted or friendly Navamsa and joins the 9th house, occupying Paravatamsa, the person will become a leader among rulers. 1021.

If Guru joins 5th and Chandra occupies a Kendra from him, if the Lagna falls in a fixed sign and its lord occupies the 10th house, the person will become a king. 1022.

NOTES.

Kings are melting away like ice before the heat of public pride, like mushrooms and Democrats are springing up. But whether there is aristocracy or democracy, the power and influence of wealth and position are there and the Rajayogas should be applied to them who are leaders. Marriage for example is celebrated and cemented in different regions in various ways and under various and curious customs and rituals. But the result is the same, *viz.*, the sexual junction of the man and the woman for procreation and gratification. Similarly Rajayoga means power, influence and financial strength and whoever will have them, he will be a ruler or commander of many men and he has Rajayoga. 1021—22.

13

Stanzas 1023 to 1028 inclusive.

If Guru is in 12th, and Sani, Ravi or the lord of 3rd occupies
the 11th and the lord of Lagna joins the 12th house from Guru, he
becomes a king of kings. 1023.

If all the planets are in Poorva shatka, and Chandra is aspected
by the lord of the 9th, he will become a ruler. 1024.

If the lord of the Navamsa occupied by Chandra joins a Kendra or Kona from Lagna, or occupies a Kendra from Buda, he will
be honored by Kings and will become their equal. 1025.

If Chandra in conjunction with Kuja occupies the 2nd or 3rd
house from Lagna, and Rahu occupies the 5th, he will become equal
to a King. 1026.

If the lord of the Navamsa occupied by the lord of the 9th,
joins the 4th or 5th house from Lagna, he will become a superior
King. 1027.

If all the planets occupy the first 6 houses from the lord of the
10th, and these fall in the Poorva shatka, he becomes a King of
Kings. 1028.

NOTES.

The translation is easy and does not require many notes.
Poorva shatka refers to the first 6 houses from Lagna and Apara
shatka or Uttara shatka refers to the next 6 houses. Some take the
first Shatka from the 12th house, and count it from the 12th to 5th
house, and the other 6 houses from the 6th to the 11th houses inclusive. When doctors differ, who should decide? Guru must be
in the 12th house, and the 12th from him would be the 11th from
Lagna, and here Sani or Ravi or the lord of 3rd must be with the
lord of Lagna. If all the above planets are there, the Yoga must
be intensified, since one planet alone is able to cause the Rajayoga.
Chandra must also be in the Poorva shatka, and must possess th.

aspect of the lord of the 9th.   This aspect can only be special, and not the aspect in the 180th° apart, as the author wants all the planets in the first 6 houses. Chandra joins some Navamsa. The lord of that Navamsa must be found in a Kendra or Kona from Lagna or be in a Kendra from Buda wherever he may be.   This seems to have special efficacy in the production of Rajayoga.   If Kuja and Chandra are in conjunction and occupy the 2nd or 3rd while Rahu occupies the 5th house from Lagna, this gives rise to Rajayoga. The exaltations and debilitations of these planets certainly affect the Rajayoga considerably.   The lord of the 10th will be found located in some house and all the planets must be located in the first 6 houses from him, but this combination should occur only in the Poorva shatka and thus it practically means that the lord of the 10th must be in the Lagna to produce this Rajayoga. 1023 to 1028.

Stanza 1029.

If Lagna falls in Chara, its lord falls in a movable sign and Navamsa, and the lord of the 9th also falls in a movable sign, he will live in a foreign country with his father.   1029.

NOTES.

Living in a foreign country with father, and other relations is passable to some extent. But living in a foreign country alone would make a man home-sick although his prospects may be very cheering.   Wealth and happiness enjoyed without friends and relations will not give that intense pleasure and satisfaction which it would give when we are surrounded by early friends and close relations. 1029.

Stanzas 1030 to 1033 inclusive.

When there is full combination of Rajayoga, the good results must be predicted.   Otherwise Rajayoga should not be predicted. When Chandra joins Oottamamsa, Guru is not found in Neechamsa, and Ravi is located in Shubhashastiamsa, position equal to a King, must be foretold. 1030.

If two, or three, or four planets are in debilitation while joining Shubhashastiamsas and if Ravi is found in his exaltation Navamsa, the person will be equal to a King   1031.

If the lord of the Navamsa occupied by any lord of debilitation, occupies a Kendra or Kona from birth and this falls in a movable sign, and its lord also is in a movable sign, the person becomes a King.   1032.

If Rahu and Sani occupy the 10th aspected by the lord of the 9th, and the lord of birth joins a debilitated planet, the person will become equal to a King.   1033.

NOTES.

Actual Rajayoga occurs only when planets are powerful. They can give political power and much more valuable, the title. Philosophers may dream that *Titles* are no more than empty bubbles, which may burst at any moment; religionists may sigh at the vanity of people coveting titles; wise men may shake their heads at the emptiness of such distinctions; but humanity is humanity, and will remain as humanity and most of them are running in the same grooves of thought. Very few can resist the temptation of accepting a Title, and many are willing to pay very heavily for such high sounding names and empty titles. A rose may smell as sweet by any other name, but the name itself would be endearing, and if a rose had the intelligence and consciousness, it would certainly refuse, any other name than that by which it would be honored. Some Statesmen are *defacto* rulers, but they have not the title of a Sovereign. They covet it and pay for it very heavily too sometimes. Statesmen may command often more authority than their rulers, but they cannot be called Kings though wielding royal power, People may run away with the idea that if there are planets in debilitation, they will become very low class men. The above combinations have shown the falsity of these ideas. Even when there are four debilitation planets they will produce Rajayoga if they occupy good Amsas and if the Sun is in an exalted Amsa. Amsas seem to exercise very powerful influences and these should be taken note of particularly. Movable signs and Navamsas seem to wield great potency in causing Rajayogas. 1030 to 1033.

Stanza 1034.

Rajayogas have been detailed in the above Stanzas both by Bhavas, Amsas and also by exaltation and Mulathrikonas. If in a horoscope more than one Rajayoga exists, then the political success must be predicted in a more intensified form. 1034.

NOTES.

Various combinations have been enumerated causing Rajayogas. The last term applies from the greatest emperor to the meanest political power holder, but special combinations indicate only rulers or their equals in power and wealth. Suppose there are four or five Rajayoga combinations in one horoscope. One of them will give him Rajayoga. But when several of them are present, he will become a King of Kings or a Ruler of Rulers, or a Statesman among Statesmen. There are many grades of Kings or Presidents, and all of them cannot be compared as equal in power, wealth, or the extent or influence they are able to wield. In the following Stanzas, the author begins to give those combinations which cross and neutralise the Rajayogas and prove prejudicial to the interests of the persons concerned. These may be called *Raja Bhanga Nichayogas*. Some Sovereigns achieve success and power, rule for some time and then lose power or are dethroned or ousted from their political significance by their subordinates. Instances in history of such Potentates are many and sometimes very harrowing, but there they are and they suffer all the indignities of poverty and loss of political status. Often they are prisoners, sometimes they are shot like public felons, sometimes they are banished and sometimes they commit suicide. Witness the fates of Napoleon, Tippu, Humayun, the late Czar of Russia, Kaiser, and other powerful Potentates. They once wielded great power and then were turned out or killed. 1034.

RAJAYOGA BHANGAS.

(Degradation from Position.)

Stanza 1035.

If Jupiter is combined with Rahu or Kethu and is aspected by an evil planet, the person will become a Pariah or a low caste. If Jupiter joins debilitation or combines with another planet in debilitation, though a Brahmin, he will pursue the career of a low caste man. 1035.

NOTES.

For a full discussion and reason for castes, please refer to my notes on *P. 35, V. 7, Ch. II of Eng. Tr. of Brihat Jataka. See also Bh. Gita, Ch. XIV and XVII.* Castes are made by professions and mental status. An evil-minded Brahmin degrades himself into a Pariah by his mean Karma, and an exalted minded Pariah raises himself to the level of a noble caste. The avocations and the power to follow them originally gave rise to castes. Those who prayed constantly to God, who renounced worldly pleasures, and spent austere lives and those who spent their whole lives in religion, education and services became Brahmins. Rahu and Kethu have been classified as Chandala grahas or Pariahs. Guru and Sukra as Vipras or pure in mind and body. Though Guru and Sukra are classed as Brahmins, the purest Brahmin is represented by Guru, and Sukra represents a more diplomatic Brahmin as he is the Guru or Preceptor of the Rakshasas who were Brahmins by birth, but followed Chandala Karmas. When Guru is spoiled, the purity of man's Karma becomes questionable and he resorts to evil deeds, 1035.

Stanza 1036.

Even though Guru joins Rahu, Kethu or Sani, if he is aspected by Sukra or Buda, the person though born as a Sudra, will be blessed with noble qualities, learning, wisdom and conduct similar to a holy Brahmin. 1036.

NOTES.

Caste gives a person a birth advantage like birth in a royal, aristocratic or rich family.   These birth advantages may be turned to profit, comfort and influence by clever individuals, or they may be lost and brought to disgrace by pride, self-interest, sin and immoral tendencies by ignorant men.   1036.

Stanzas 1037 & 1038.

If Chandra with Kuja occupies Mesha, possessing the aspect of Sani, the person will live by mendicancy.   If birth is occupied by debilitated Chandra, and aspected by Sani, the person will be a miser.   If debilitated Chandra, unaspected by benefics, occupying cruel Shastiamsas or Navamsas, occupies Lagna, the person lives by mendicancy.   1037—1038.

NOTES.

The word used in the original is *Bhikshatana*, which means making livelihood by begging.   There are varieties of begging, a few of them have been considered by mankind to be honorable. The great Shankaracharya lived under trees and begged for his meal every day.   But this was done for the benefit of the world and he was honored.   He entirely divested his extraordinary mental energies for the elevation of the ignorant and the wicked and never begged a meal more than he actually wanted to satisfy his hunger. But there are professional beggars, who follow this line, because it entails no troublesome work, and possesses no risks.   They have all to gain and nothing to lose.   Specially now-a-days, with the disregard for honor and truth, mendicancy has become a roaring trade, and some of these so-called beggars are much better off than the average citizen to whom they go to beg.   The mendicancy proceeds from a debasement of the mind, and as Chandra represents mind, and Ravi soul, their debilitations cause meanness and enable the man to set at nought the sentiments of honor and self-respect. 1037—1038.

Stanzas 1039 to 1050 inclusive.

If Chandra combines with Sani, and occupies the 7th betwixt evil planets, the person will suffer from Asthma, Consumption, Jaundice, etc. 1039.

If Sani joins 4th, Kuja 7th and Chandra 10th, there will be deformity or loss of limbs. If Ravi and Chandra exchange their houses or Navamsas, leanness of body should be predicted. 1040.

If the Sun, Moon, Mars and Saturn occupy the 8th, 6th, 2nd and 12th houses respectively, the person will lose his sight by that disease which is attributed to those planets, or will have his eyes pulled out by the rulers. 1041.

If Lagna has Guru and 7th is occupied by Kuja, he becomes an *Oonmada*. If Sani is in Lagna and Kuja joins 7th or 5th, the person will be insane or erratic. 1042.

If the Sun occupies 3rd, 6th or 12th and if Kuja or Chandra occupies 5th or 9th, he will become insane, stupid or unsettled in mind. 1043.

If Ravi and Chandra occupy Lagna or 5th or 9th, Guru joins 3rd or any Kendra, and Sani becomes the most powerful at the time of birth, the person will become mad. 1044·

If Buda and Chandra are in Kendras, the person will be unhappy and deranged. If Sani, Chandra and Ravi are in Kendras, the person becomes dull and will live on others property. If the lord of 10th occupies 12th, the lord of 12th joins 2nd and evil planets conjoin the 3rd house, the person will be dull, and will live at the cost of others. 1045.

If the lord of Lagna is in debilitation in Rasi or Amsa, and evil planets are in the 6th and 8th houses and Kemadruma obtains at birth, the person will do mean acts, spoil others wives, and will eat worthless food. 1046.

If Sani occupies Lagna, the person will destroy his family and will have short life, when he is not aspected by benefics. When he occupies debilitated or unfriendly Navamsa and when the other planets are located in other than the 10th house, it will make him live by beggary. 1047.

If the lord of Lagna joins 12th, 10th is occupied by an evil planet, and Chandra combines with Kuja, the person will become an *Abhisasta*, resident in a foreign country, live by beggary, and possess a sorrowful body. 1048.

If all the evil planets occupy the 8th, and Chandra and Kuja join Kendras, they produce Gadayoga, and make the man mad or deranged. 1049.

If Buda, Chandra and Sukra combine with Guru and occupy Kendras, and Rahu joins Lagna, the person will be bereft of his own religious deeds and take to those of a low caste. 1050.

NOTES.

The author here gives some combinations for poverty and beggarly life. Kemadruma is formed by Moon, when there are no planets on either side of him in a horoscope. *(See P. 172 of my Eng. Tr. of Brihat Jataka.) (For Gada see P. 161.)* The combination for Gada given here does not correspond with what has been stated by Varah Mihira, and both of these differ from that given in Satayoga Manjari and Jataka Parijata. We have only to lay our hands and select those which tally well with our personal experiences. *Abhisasta* is one who is devoid of all honor, and who commits heinous sins like *Brahmahatya, Strihatya*, etc., a pronounced sinner. When Chandra, Sukra, Buda and Guru are in Kendras, the author gives unfavourable results and I beg to differ from him as my humble experience in the examination of more than 20,000 horoscopes has never shown me a mendicant, or a sinner, or a dullard when all these planets are in Kendras. Their conjunction

14

is good and occupation of Kendras has been admitted to be favourable.   On what authority Venkatasa places his experience I cannot say.   *Oonmada* means one who is intoxicated by pride and whose head is turned away from sanity.   Mendicancy cannot be defended as an honorable means on any reasonable ground.   There are certain creeds and sects whose profession is beggary, but who work for it in their own way and who cannot be called vagabonds and idlers. *Yogas* means conjunctions of planets, and these may be either Suyogas or good combinations and Duryogas or evil combinations. When two chemical substances meet, they produce a conjunction and the resultant will be a third one.   The different positions of the planets from each other, from the Lagna, from the Navamsa and other Amsas create so many cross electrical and ethereal currents, that by their combinations or expulsions, the various states named above will be produced.   1039 to 1050.

Stanzas 1051 to 1054 inclusive.

If Sani with Kuja occupies 6th or 8th from Lagna, the person will be deranged.   1051.

If evil planets occupy 6th, 8th and 12th houses, Guru joins Paridhi and does not occupy Kendras, the person will become insane.   If evil planets are not combined or aspected by benefics and join 10th or 2nd when Guru is powerless, the person will become deranged.   1052.

If the lord of 9th joins 12th, and the lord's of Lagna and Chandra Rasi occupy the birth, uncombined or unaspected by benefics, the person will lose property, wife and children.   1053.

If Chandra joins a Sani Navamsa, or Sani aspected by benefics and benefics in Kendras and also by the lord of Lagna, the person will destroy his family and will be a hard-hearted man.   1054.

NOTES.

The translations are given in simple language and no notes seem to be necessary. 1501 to 1054.

Stanzas 1055 to 1060 inclusive.

If the lord of Lagna is in the 5th or 12th from Chandra, and is aspected by evil planets occupying 8th, or if Chandra occupies 10th and is aspected by evil planets in 8th, the person will live by very mean occupation. 1055.

If Sani joins Guru in the same Navamsa, when he is in the Navamsa of debilitation or unfriendly sign, the person will have much sorrow, be devoid of wife, children and wealth, and will eke out a miserable existence. 1056.

If Simha becomes Lagna with Sani in exaltation, occupying a debilitated Navamsa or has evil aspects, the person though born in a royal family, will fall to a very low social position. 1057.

When the Sun occupies the 10th degree in Libra *(his greatest fall)* he will destroy even one thousand Rajayogas, which may have been caused by other planetary conjunctions. 1058.

If Sukra falls in debilitation, he will similarly destroy many Rajayogas. So also dark planets, comets, meteors and other unfavourable phenomena destroy Rajayogas. 1059.

If Sukra occupies the 12th in debilitation, or occupies the Navamsa of Sani, and the Sun and the Moon in the 7th are aspected by Sani, the person will become a slave to all conceivable miseries and wretchedness. 1060.

NOTES.

I refer my readers for an explanation of Aprakasagrahas or dark planets, meteors, comets, etc., to Brihat Samhita by Varaha Mihira. The European system of Astronomy has recognised the great intensity of heat in the dark end of the spectrum, showing thereby that dark planets like Rahu, Kethu, Mandi, Ardhaprahara, Gulika, Yamakantaka and other Upagrahas have got great powers of absorption of light and hence vitalising agencies, and that those who are born under such influences will suffer miseries more than others. A man may be born in a respectable, influential or royal family, but if his previous Karma is bad, he will suffer all sorts of miseries and troubles, and perhaps may be thrown into the folds of abject poverty and disgraceful occupations. Such instances are many. 1055 to 1060.

Stanzas 1061 to 1068 inclusive.

When Chandra is in debilitation, Kuja in the 7th and Sani in Lagna, there will be brain disorder. If Sani occupies Lagna, Chandra in the 7th is aspected by Sukra, the person will suffer imprisonment. 1061.

If Chandra or Ravi fall sin the 12th, Sani occupies the 5th or 9th, and Ravi occupies debilitation in Rasi or Navamsa or falls in an unfriendly Amsa and joins 7th or 8th house, the person suffers from tooth ache and eye troubles. 1062.

If evil planets occupy 4th and 5th houses and Chandra is found in 6th, 8th or 12th, the person will have blindness. If those planets who contribute to blindness are beneficially combined or aspected, there will be no loss of sight. If they have no beneficial aspects, but are subjected to evil aspects, there will be blindness certain. 1063.

If Chandra is in 10th, Buda in 7th and Sani in 2nd, the person will have defective limbs. When the planets causing this Yoga are defeated in planetary fight, are in debilitation, unfriendly or cruel Amsas, he will surely suffer in loss of bodily organs. 1064.

If Chandra occupies Simha, Makara, Kataka or Meena Navamsas and has the conjunction or aspect of Sani and Kuja. the person will suffer from leprosy. 1065.

If Chandra joins Kataka, Vrischika or Kumbha Navamsa and combines with Sani, the person will have diseases in the sexual organs. 1066.

If Chandra with malefics combines with Rahu and joins 12th, 9th or 8th, he will be highly irritated, revengeful and always engaged in quarrels with others. 1067.

I, the learned Venkatasa, have thus summarised the combinations for Rajayoga and also the combinations which would destroy such Yogas and make the man miserable. 1068.

NOTES.

Where should Chandra have conjunction with Sani and Kuja ? is a question which is not clear. Chandra is made to occupy certain Navamsas, and then he is made to have the conjunction or aspect of Sani or Kuja. When he is in the Navamsa, the aspect must naturally refer to Navamsa. But in the jumbling up of combinations and aspects, sometimes both may be guessed or both may be included. Since the aspect and conjunction are not specified, we think they must be in the Rasi more than in the Navamsa. Diseases in the sexual organs are of various and very painful nature and are generally the results of excessive sexual indulgence. But there are also certain cases where the husband and wife may be virtuous people, but still they may get venereal complaints of a serious nature on account of the want of agreement in the physical and mental compositions and characteristics. The presence of venereal complaints are not always the forerunners of immoral habits in this Janma or birth Care should be taken by the Astrologer in attributing virtues and vices to the horoscopes ; and combinations of planets should be examined in all their aspects and bearings. Venkatasa uses *Dhimata* or highly intelligent to himself. This is but right. Apart from what others may have to say about authors, they must also have great confidence in themselves and in their learning before they can write boldly and authoritatively. A quarrelsome man makes a bad citizen in every way. He quarrels with his own people, relations, wife and children, with neighbours, with officials and with all those who come in contact with him in any capacity. It is not necessary he should have a cause for quarrel ; he is gifted by nature to do so on every occasion and even on the slightest provocation. He quarrels for its own sake and for the love he has for quarrels. He is an evil that society can hardly tolerate, but he will be inflicting pain on all alike by his innate love for quarrels and uncontrollable temper. 1061 to 1068.

CHAPTER XI.

ARISTADHYAYOGA.
(Misfortunes.)

Stanzas 1069 to 1071 inclusive.

Some make predictions by planetary combinations, and some give out results by periods and sub-periods. The learned find it difficult to determine the longevity of a person without these two systems. 1069.

There are three divisions of longevity, the Alpayu, Madhyamayu and Oottamayu. Before 32 years, it is Alpayu ; from 32 to 70 it is Madhyamayu and after 70 years it is called Dirghayu. Some say after one hundred years it is called Oottamayu. 1070—1071.

NOTES.

The life of a person is the basis on which the whole fabric of human career has to be founded. If the longevity is wanting, what can the combinations of Rajayogas do to a person. The main divisions are :—

1 Alpayu or short life—up to 32 years.
2 Madhyayu or middle life—32 to 70 years.
3 Dirghayu or long life—70 to 100 years.
4 Oottamayu or excellent longevity—Above one 100 years.
5 Aparimitayurdaya or unlimited terms of life.

There are some persons who are alleged to have lived more than 150 years, and puranic personages are said to have lived for thousands of years. I have carefully discussed this important question of longevity in my notes in the History of Vijayanagar, and I would refer my readers to them for a full discussion of this most important subject *(See p. 17—18 ch. III Never-to-be Forgotten Empire.)* The question is very interesting and has been ably handled by me in my History (See also p. 17 of Chronology appended in my History.) Long terms of ages mentioned in the Puranas by the Christian Bible, by the Era makers like Vikramaditya and modern example; recorded in the histories of several nations, prove that longevity may be both constitutional, hereditary and acquired by good Karma, like active habits, noble thinking and deep and divine concentration. Venkatasa has omitted three other terms of longevity, *viz* :—

1 Balarista—life up to 8 years.
2 Madhyarista—from 8 to 20 years.
3 Yogarista—from 20 to 32 years.

The question of longevity must be determined both by the combination of planets and also by the Dasas and Bhukties of planets. This is not all. Kalachakra determines the life ; planets grant certain periods to the fœtus, soon after its entry into the mother's womb, called the *Graha Datta Pindayurdaya*, and also by the planets specially in Kendras and Thrikonas and also by the Kalas or lustre and brilliancy which planets indicate in the Navamsa and styled Amsayurdaya. *(See ch. VII p. 98 to 108 of my Eng. Tr. of Brihat Jataka.)* 1069 to 1071.

Stanza 1072.

It is not possible to determine the length of life for children below 12 years of their age and therefore they must be protected in their dangers to life by Japas, Homas and worship of Devatas and Brahmins. 1072.

NOTES.

Balarista up to 8 and Madhyarista up to 12 years, possess special dangers to children, and Venkatasa recommends, that as the determination of longevity before 12 years becomes extremely uncertain, it would be safer for parents, guardians and those interested in the preservation of the lives of their children from early graves, to adopt special remedies to avert the evil influences and safeguard their lives. Various energies will be found in Nature, some of them being creative, some protective and some destructive. The skill of the Astrologer must enable him to foresee from what dangers the lives of the children are threatened, and prescribe suitable santhies to overcome the evils indicated by the planets. I have very lucidly explained these remedial matters in my " Astrological Magazine," and also in my Introduction to the study of Astrology, 6th Ed. to which I would refer my readers for fuller details. 1072.

Stanza 1073.

Some children die before they are 12 years by the faults or sinful deeds of parents, some die by Balagrahas, and some are killed by evil conjunctions of planets in their horoscopes. 1073.

NOTES.

What are the Sins, what are the Balagrahas, and what are the evil combinations which kill children before they complete their 12 years have to be well understood A man commits a certain sin There will be some visible or invisible result. Visible is demonstrable and therefore can easily be grasped, but there are some invisible acts or thoughts which cannot be seen, but which all the same produce direct and tangible results. Say a person, out of envy and meanness, poisons a child. If he is detected, he receives some punishment, and that settles the dues to be given to his sinful act, but suppose he is not detected, could he escape from all moral responsibility and be treated by God and His Agent as they would do a horoughly innocent man? It would be absurd to think so on its face. Suppose he even does not poison the child, but feels envy and jealousy at him and thinks ill of him and wishes constantly his misery and death. Can it be said that he is not a moral delinquent, that he can escape God's punishment and live and be rewarded as an innocent man can do? Certainly not? He has committed sins for which he should receive punishment. These sins of parents will be visited upon their progeny and therefore it is very highly essential that parents should behave well both in their own interests and in those of their dear children, whose safety and prosperity have been entrusted to them by Providence and their own previous Karma. *Balagrahas* are those energies in Nature which have great potency to attack specially children under 12 years of age, and of special temperaments and characteristics, and who inflict serious danger and cause even death to them, unless the children are specially protected by Pujas, Charms and Mantras from competent and holy Brahmins and other saintly sort of people. There are certain evil combinations causing Balarista and children easily succumb to such deleterious influences. All these sources of dangers must be considered. 1073.

Stanza 1074.

Strength and vitality to the children must be predicted by the potency of the lord of birth, and their debilities by the lords of the 12th, etc. 1074.

NOTES.

Lord of birth must always be powerful, must occupy a good place, must be in good Vergas, must have beneficial combinations and aspects and must not have evil conjunctions or aspects, must not occupy evil Vergas, to make the person, happy, strong, peaceful and progressive. The birth is the basis on which the whole career of man depends, and when it is not good, though he may be successful, he will not be happy. 1074.

Stanzas 1075—1076.

Longevity has three divisions, short, middle and long, and each
of these again has 3 divisions, short, middle and long, 1075—1076.

NOTES.

Alpayu extends up to 32 years. This has 3 divisions. There
are children who die for example say, when 2 or 3 years. There
are boys who die at 18 or 20 and there are young men who die in
their 31st or 32nd year. All these have Alpayu, but a child that
dies at one or two, a boy that dies at 16 and a youth who dies at
32, cannot be classified as having enjoyed the same term of life or
done the same amount of work. There is a world of diffrrence
between a baby that dies in a few months and a man who dies when
he is 32 years of age. Therefore in the Alpayu itself there are 3
divisions, Alpa Alpa, or short short, Alpa Madhya or short middle,
and Alpa Purna or short long. The child at 2 or 3 has short short
life. The boy at 15 has short middle, and the youth of 31 has
short long term of life. Take for middle life. Those who die at
33, who die at 50 and who die at 70 are not and cannot be the
same. In fact, those who live up to 70 years now-a-days may be,
said to have had long life. I don't know if 10 per cent live to more
than this age. Those who die at 33 or 34 though they fall in the
division Madhyayu, are still not far away from those who die at 32.
Therefore they fall in middle short, those who die in 50 fall in
middle middle, and those who die at 70 fall in middle long. Then
we have persons dying in 70 or 72, in 90, and after a hundred.
Here the man who dies in Madhyapurna or middle long in 69 is not
far away from him who dies in 72. But the latter falls in long
short, one who dies at 85 in long middle, and one who dies at 99 in
long long periods of life. Thus longevity is divided into 9 terms
and care should be taken to note the various distinctions. 1075—76.

Stanza 1077.

When Kuja Dasa falls as the 5th, or Guru Dasa when it becomes 6th, or Sani Dasa when it happens to be the 4th. or when
Rahu Dasa falls as the 7th, the person will be killed. 1077.

NOTES.

Say a man is born in Bharani. The Dasa will be Sukra's at
birth. To this person Guru Dasa becomes the 6th in order, *viz..*
Sukra (1), Ravi (2), Chandra (3), Kuja (4), Rahu (5) and Guru (6)
Guru therefore possesses special Maraka or killing powers, and it
must be cleverly escaped by suitable remedies taken in due time-
Suppose a man is born in Aswini. He gets Kethu Dasa at birth.
Then comes Sukra (2), then Ravi (3), then Chandra (4), and Kuja
comes as the 5th and therefore will be specially powerful as a death
inflicting Dasa. 1077.

Stanza 1078.

The Dasa of the lords of 3td, 6th and 8th are difficult ones and
when these are aspected by evil planets, they kill the person positively. 1078.

NOTES.

The term used in Sanskrit is Vipat, Pratyak and Vadabhesa—
or counting according to Taras, they mean 3rd, 5th and 7th, but the
several commentators have taken these terms to be 3rd, 6th and 8th
and they seem to be right. When the Dasas of the lords of these
houses occur, they hardly allow the man to survive, specially so
when they have evil aspects or conjunctions. 1078.

Stanza 1079,

The Dasas of the lords of 3rd, 6th and 8th specially when they
are in debilitation, combustion and unfriendly houses, having evil
aspects, will inflict death. 1079.

NOTES.

Planets in debilitation, in defeat in planetary fight, in unfriendly signs and combustion are evil and much more so when they also
own 3rd, 6th and 8th houses. When such evil planets have cruel
aspects, they kill the man in their Dasas. 1079.

Stanza 1080.

Those born in Rasi Sandhies, die early. This will be certain
when evil planets aspect them. 1080.

NOTES.

A Rasi or house of the Zodiac extends over 30 degrees and the
a st 3 degrees of the one and the first 3 degrees of the next will form
the Sandhi or junction where the vitalising forces are neutralised.
These last Navamsas and the first Amsas are causative of death
and danger and this will be certain when evil planets aspect or conjoin them. 1080.

Stanza 1081.

If such children born in the junctions of signs, manage to live
through the good Karma or actions of their parents, then the persons will become Kings and will command horses, elephants and
wealth. 1081.

NOTES.

Children born in the junction of Rasis rarely escape death, but
if the parents are clever, consult a competent Astrologer and adopt
the necessary remedies and prevent early death, the child becomes
a grand personage and will reach a high political stage. Therefore
there is a very serious responsibility on the parents of such children
to take every possible care, get the necessary advice, and have the
remedies performed. 1081.

Stanza 1082

If Ravi and Chandra occupy the 3rd, or occupy evil signs possessing evil aspects, the child will be sickly and will hardly survive 3 years. 1082.

NOTES.

The conjunction of Ravi and Chandra can only occur on Amavasya or New moon day when Chandra will be lifeless and lustreless. Third house represents longevity and when they are there or when they join evil signs, like Makara, Kumbha, Vrischika, etc., and have evil aspects, the child will not live more than 3 years, and will also be sickly. 1082.

COMBINATIONS FOR IMMEDIATE DEATH.

Stanzas 1083 to 1085 inclusive.

If weak Moon joins Lagna and cruel planets, occupy the 1st Drikkana of the 7th house, the child dies at once. 1083.

If all the planets occupy Aupoklimas in a powerless state, the child will live 2 or 6 months. 1084.

If the lord of Lagna with Ravi joins debilitation or combines in the 8th, the person dies early, or though living will be a dead one. 1085.

NOTES.

Anpoklimas are 3rd, 6th, 9th and 12th houses. Whateversl may be the theories connected with the possession of children, it must be admitted, that when born, they should live to give joy and comfort to their parents. Child bearing is no joke, and whatever may be the tenderness of the father, there can be no question as regards the endearments of the mother. Man only

procreates, but the woman has to carry the seed for nine months
in her body, nourish it with her own food, bring it up as a part
of her own body, and then nurse it with the greatest tenderness
when the babe is unable to attend to its own wants.   Therefore
the death of children soon after their birth is a real misfortune
and hence all the Astrological writers have agreed in saying so.
In the last stanza the author says that the child will die, but if
does not, it will live as a dead man· Here he means that his
condition will be miserable and he will feel every second that he
is a dead fellow and ought not to live. 1083, 1084 & 1085.

Stanzas 1086 to 1090 inclusive.

If Rahu, except in the signs of Mesha and Vrishabha, occupies the Lagna, the child will die—or if evil planets occupy the
2nd and 12th houses from Lagna or they occupy 7th, 8th and
12th houses, there will be immediate death. 1086.

If Chandra is powerless and evil planets are in the 8th, the
child will live up to 8 years. If Chandra joins Lagna while evil
planets occupy Kendras without beneficial conjunctions, the child
will live up to one year. 1087.

If lord of Lagna occupies Lagna with evil planets, and is
aspected by Sani and Guru and does not occupy the. 8th and the
birth falls in Rasi Sandhies, the child will die in his 6th. 8th or
12th year. 1088·

If weak Moon joins 6th, 8th or 12th houses, or if he is not
weak, but joins cruel planets and has beneficial aspect, the child
will live up to 8th year, or if aspected also by evil planets, it will
die straight after birth. If there are malefic and beneficial aspects, the child may live for 4 years. 1089.

If Guru occupies Lagna, Sukra in Mithuna, aud Buda in
Thula, and is aspected by evil planets in the 8th, the child lives
up to 1 or 8 years. 1090.

NOTES.

Great care should be taken in determining the term of life. The strength of the evil and good planets must be well calculated and analysed, the strength of the Moon and Lagna and its lord should be noted and special combinations which confer longevity should be taken into consideration, and then the Gochara movements should also be amalgamated into the system, the Dasas and Bhukties should be incorporated and in the light of all these combinations the term of life should be determined. When Sukra is in Mithuna, Buda cannot be in Thula and *vice versa.* Therefore the stanza has to be interpreted thus :—If Buda and Sukra are in Mithuna or Thula,-the meaning becomes sensible. Rasi Sandhies or junctions of Rasis have been explained in the Balarista chapter in Brihat Jataka. The last quarter of the constellations forming the sign and the first quarter of the constellation commencing the next sign will be Rasi junctions. Birth should not fall in the last four degrees or the first four degrees of any sign. 1086 to 1090.

Stanza 1091

If Guru occupies 8th house, a sign of Kuja and is aspected by Ravi, Chandra, Kuja, Sani and not aspected by Sukra, the child will die within 3 years. 1091.

NOTES.

Kuja's houses are Mesha and Vrischika. One of these should fall in the 8th with Guru there, and this Guru should have the aspect of all the other planets excepting Sukra. This can only happen when these are in the second from Lagna, or some of them like Kuja and Sani may aspect in special ways from other houses. 1091.

Stanzas 1092 & 1093.

If the lords of 6th and 8th join Kendras, and Retrograde Sani occupies Kuja's house and is aspected by the powerful Kuja, he will die within 2 years. 1092.

If Sani joins Lagna or 7th from it, or occupies with Chandra, Kataka or Vrischika. and benefics join Kendras or 11th, the child dies very early observes Yavana· 1093.

NOTES.

When benefics are found in Kendras, they protect the child against all Balarista.   Benefics in the 11th house certainly add to the term of life and never take it away.   Sani in Lagna or with Chandra is bad and evil planets take away the term of life when in Lagna.   How benefics in Kendras, or 11th, can make the child die very early, I cannot understand and I beg to differ from Venkatasa in the interpretation of this stanza.   If such a combination exists, I should certainly venture my opinion in favour of the longevity of the person though Sani may be in the Lagna or 7th, or with Chandra in Kataka or Vrischika·   In the latter, Chandra is debilitated and in conjunction with Sani, the life may be cut short, but suppose Guru is in Kumbha, Sukra and Buda are in Simha, or all these benefics in the 11th house or Kanya.   I should certainly predict no Balarista, although the child will pass through dangers early in life.   Readers may take their own view in these matters· In this particular case Venkatasa quotes Yavana as authority for this combination· The original contains *Yavanopadista* or stated so by Yavana. Varaha Mihira mentions two Yavanas—1 Yavanacharya and 2 Yavanaswara, and Bhatotpala hints that the latter was a ruler of Cabul. Yavanacharya seems to have been a very learned and voluminous author. 1093.

Stanza 1094.

If Guru is in debilitation or occupies one of Kuja's houses and the child is born in *Sandhi Thraya* he will die within a month. 1094.

NOTES.

The three Sandhies are (1) **Lagna Sandhi,** (2) **Nakshatra Sandhi** and (3) **Dasa Sandhi.** The last portions of any is gnerally bad ; and destuction to life and property, or the three Sandhies or junctions as dangerous to life may be the last half ghati of Kataka and the first half ghati of Simha the last half ghati of Vrinschicka and the first half ghati of Dhanas and the last and first half ghati of Meena and Mesha respectively. Apparently Guru's position in Mesha and Vrischika do not produce long life. As has been remarked by me in my previous writings, the grandest Chemical Science is Astrology and particular, houses, planets, constelltions, and angles, produce such poisonous maters that those who are born under the influences die straight or manage to live only for a short time. 1094.

Stanza 1095.

If powerful Sun or Moon joins Lagna, and evil planets occupy Kendras or Konas or 8th, and if Sukra, Ravi and Chandra join one Rasi, the child dies before one year. 1095.

NOTES.

The first part refers to Lagna being occupied by powerful Ravi or Chandra, and evil planets in Kendras, Konas and the 8th and the second means, Ravi, Chandra, and Sukra must be in Lagna, and evil planets in Kendras, Konas or 8th house to kill the infant within a year. 1095.

Stanza 1096.

If Chandra occupies the 20th Bhaga in Kumbha or the 21st Bhaga in Vrishabha or Simha the child will die early. 1096.

NOTES.

A Rasi or Sign is divided into 30 Bhagas and each Bhaga

denotes a degree. The 20th degree in Kumbha and 21st degree
in Vrishabha and Simha occupied by Chandra will kill the
child. 1096.

Stanzas 1097 to 1099 inclusive.

If Chandra occupies the 23rd degree of Mesha, when it
falls in the 8th, the 22nd degree of Kataka and the 4th degree
in Thula, the child dies soon. 1097.

If Chandra joins the 20th degree in Makara, the 1st
degree of Kanya, the 18th degree in Dhanas and the 10th degree
in Meena he will cause death to the Child· 1098.

If Chandra occupies the 22nd in Mithuna he will cause
destruction to the Child.

The degrees indicate the years when death may be predicted to the Child. 1099.

NOTES.

Certain degrees occupied by Chandra in the 12 Signs have
been indicated as causing death. This may require a little
more explanation though the language is not ambiguous ; only
eleven out of 12 Rasis have been named and Vrischika has
been ommitted altogether. Why I cannot easily understand.
A child is born in the 21st Bhaga occupied by Chandra in Vrishabha or Simha, he will die in his 21st year, or before that
age. Suppose Chandra occupies the 4th degre in Thula, then,
Venkatasa means that the child cannot live for more than 4
years The number of the dgrees occupied by Chandra indicate probably the atmost limits of the age to which such a child
can live· In these degrees 23 seems to be the highest figure
reached, and Chandra seems to exercise the greatest influence
on the life of young childrn without reference to periods and
sub periods. The strength of Chandra forms a very important
item of life in early days. 1098. 1099,

Stanza 1100.

If an unfriendly evil planet to the lord of Lagna or
Chandra occupies the Lagna, he will cause destruction to child.
But if the evil planet in Lagna is a friend of the lord of Lagna
or Chandra, he will not cause death 1100.

NOTES.

The lord of Lagna is styled Lagnadhipathi and the lord
of the house occupied by Chandra is called Janma Rasayadhi-
pathi. The evil planet in the Lagna must not be an enemy of
the lords of the house of birth and Chandra Lagna If the evil
planet in Lagna is a friend of the lords of Lagna and Chandra,
he will not kill. 1100.

Stanza 1101.

If there is enmity between the lord of birth and the lord of
the house joined by Chandra, there will be danger. If beneficial
planet occupies the Lagna, there will be no danger. If there are
Kuja, Ravi and Sani in the 8th, there will be danger within a
month, and Kethu occupying Lagna will send the child to the
grave in two months. 1101.

Stanza 1102.

Yavanas aud others have predicted many Rajayogas, which
lead to kingly power and position. This will only happen to persons born in royal families, but if such Rajayogas caused by evil
planets occur to persons born in other than royal families, they
kill the children. 1102.

NOTES.

Venkatasa makes a sweeping observation that those born
with combinations indicating royalty in royal families are said, by
Yavanas, to become Kings and others born in non-royal families

with such combinations are killed at once by the unfavourable conjuntions. This means that combination for royal family members produce Kings and for members of other families, these very same combinations cause immediate death. I humbly beg to differ from him and also from those Yavanas, who assert such a statement. Cases like Napoleon, Hyder, Sivaji, Nizam-ul-Mulk ₫nd hundreds of others, born in the midst of great poverty and adverse conditions, have achieved thrones and more than thrones by their personal exertions. They must have possessed combinations for royalty certainly to raise them far above the rank of ordinary princes and rulers, and they did not die at once. Here what he probably means is, that royal power does not easily come to persons born in non-royal families and we can quite understand these conditions. But the lowest have become the greatest and the greatest have been reduced to the lowest pitch by planetary com. binations indicative of their tremendous previous good or bad Karmas. When a higher tank-bund breaches, the damage will certainly be greater than when a small bund breaks. The birth advantage goes a great way to political power and success. None can deny this proposition. Akbar, Alexander and other rulers who have the *Great* affixed to their names would probably have not become great if they had to fight their way from the lowest rungs of the social life. A man born with a large financial credit at birth with ordinary prudence and foresight, can, not only keep it, but can also increase it. But a person born in abject poverty hus to fight tremendous battles in his life to get to the lap of the social life and then to sustain it. When a very lucky combination obtains in a horoscope, unless he has a large fund of previous good Karma, to enjoy the sweets of life, he will not live, long. 1102.

Stanza 1003.

If Ravi occupies 10th, being a house of Kuja or Chandra aspected by evil planets and not conjoined or aspected by benefics, he will die very soon. 1103.

NOTES.

This combination can only obtain for 3 houses, *viz.*, Mesha, Kataka or Vrischika. Ravi must be in one of these houses, and this must become the 10th from Lagna, he must have evil but no beneficial aspects. 1103.

Stanza 1104.

If birth falls in Nigala, Pakshi, Pasa or Sarpa Drekkanas, conjoined by evil planets and not aspected by benefics or by the lod of Lagna, the child dies early. 1104.

NOTES.

For description and details of Drekkanas or one-third divisions of a Rasi, please refer to my notes on Brihat Jatuka Ch. 27 p 260—65. The second Drekkana of Mithuna is a Pakshi Drekana. The 3rd Drekkana of Kataka is a Sarpa or Serpent. The irst of Makara is a Nigala (chain) Drekkana. 1104.

Stanza 1105.

If Ravi, Chandra, Kuja and Guru, or Kuja, Guru, Sani and Chandra, or Ravi, Sani, Kuja and Chandra, are found combined in one house at birth, the child dies in 5 years. 1105.

NOTES.

Three combinations are given, two of which occur only on a New Moon or Amavasya day, for it is then only Ravi and Chandra can combine in one and the same house. The other has no reference to Ravi, and it may occur on any day. It is generally stated that those born on Amavasya days hardly live, but when they survive the early danger they become clever, great and reputed persons. 1105

Stanza 1106.

If Ravi and Buda are combined and have no beneficial aspects, the child will die even if it stays with the Devas within 11 years. 1106.

NOTES.

Devas are Celestials who have great mental energies. What the author means is that if Ravi and Buda are in one house, and possess no beneficial aspects, the child will die certainly before it is 11 years. 1106.

Stanza 1107

If Ravi, Kuja and Sani are combined in Lagna, and weak Moon joins any one of the houses of Sukra, unaspected by Guu, the child dies before 7 years. 1107.

Stanza 1108.

If Kuja joins a Kendra in combustion, combining with o is aspected by Sani, the boy dies before 4 years. and no mathe matical calculations are needed. 1108.

NOTES.

The author observes, the Astrologer may save his calcula-tion if he finds in a horoscope, that Kuja is in combustion, joins a Kendra, and combines with or is aspected by Sani, the child dies positively within 4 years. 1108.

Stanza 1109.

If weak Chandra, aspected by all evil planets, occupies the 8th house from the lord of the birth, the child dies before 9 years. 1109.

Stanza 1110.

If the lord of birth is evil and joins the 12th house fror

Chandra, aspected by another evii planet, or accupies the Navamsa of Chandra, the child dies before 9 years. 1110.

NOTES.

Here Venkatasa has selected combinations of planets for determining the particular periods before which the children are expected to die. The combinations are clearly given, but the exaltations and other sources of good power should not be over. looked in the determination of these ages. Sun and Moon, Mars and Jupiter may be in Aries, and I shonld certainly not predict an early death for various reasons. Their simple combination is not enough to kill. Take Kataka as Lagna and place these four in the 10th or Mesha. Sun is exalted, Kuja is in Moolathrikona, Guru is in friendly house as also Chandra. There may be danger, but there will be no death. 1110.

Stanzas 1111 & 1112.

If Rahu occupies Lagna, combined with or aspected by an evil planet, and all the benefics in Drisyachakra and all the evil planets in Adrisyachakra, the child dies in the 5th year. 1111.

Stanza 1112.

If Rahu occupies the 7th aspected by Ravi and Chandra and not aspected by benefics, the person dies in the 10th or 12th year. 1112.

Stanzas 1113to 1120 inclusive.

If Lagna falls in Kumbha, Vrischika or Simha, combined with Rahu, and not conjoined with or aspected by Guru, the peron dies in his 17th year. 1113.

If weak Moon is aspected by evil planets, and also by Rahu the infant dies in a few days. 1114.

If the lords of Lagna, and Chandra Lagna, occupy 6th, 8th or 12th houses from birth, combined with Ravi having no beneficial conjunctions or aspects, the person will die in his 12th year. 1115.

If the lord of Lagna occupies 7th and combines with a malefic or Rahu in Kendras aspected by evil planets, will kill the child. 1116.

In the above stanza, some say the child will die in the 10th or 46th year. The Rasi should be multiplied by 3 and year and month should be ascertained. 1117.

If Ravi, Chandra and Kuja join the 5th, not combined by benefics, the child will die in the 9th year. 1118.

If lord of Chandra Lagna is Ravi, and if that Ravi combines with Sani and joins the 8th house with a beneficial aspect, the boy dies in his 12th year. 1119.

If Kuja happens to be the lord of Lagna and occupies it, aspected by all the evil planets, the child dies in the 4th month. 1120.

If 6th and 8th houses are occupied by evil planets without beneficial aspects and the lord of Lagna joins Aupoktuna, the child dies. 1121.

If the lords of Lagna and 8th, without beneficial combinations, occupy each others houses, or join the 12th or 6th houses without the combination of Guru, the person will die in his 18th year. 1122.

If the evil planets in the Kendras are not aspected by Chandra or other benefics, and if Chandra joins 6th, 8th or 12th, the person dies in his 20th year. 1123.

If Ravi and Guru occupy (Kitarasi) Vrischika which should be Lagna, and if the lord of the 8th joins a Kendra, the person dies in his 22nd year—1124.

If Chandra, in conjunction with Rahu, occupies 7th or 8th, and Guru combines in Lagna, the person dies in his 22nd year—1125.

If Ravi occupies the 8th house while Chandra joins Sani, the person dies in his 19th year—1126.

If Sani joins a Lagna, which is unfriendly to him and benefics combine in Aupoklimas, the person will certainly die in his 26th or 27th year—1127.

NOTES.

I have explained clearly what is meant by Drisya (visible) and Adrisya (invisible) Chakras or globes in my notes on Bri-Jataka. I refer my readers to them.

When Rahu occupies the 7th and aspects Ravi and Chandra certainly Kethu must be with them as the distance between Rahu and Kethu is exactly 180 degrees—1111-1112.

When the Lagna is combined with Rahu, Kethu necessarily falls in the 7th and these two evil planets take away the vitality of life—1113.

When weak moon is aspected by Rahu he must be in conjunction with Kethu. Rahu and Kethu have only aspects in the 7th house—1114.

When Kataka falls as Lagna, and Chandra is there, then the lord of Lagna and Chandra Lagna will be himself. 6th, 8th and 12th houses are called *Dusthanas* or evil ones, planets in them generally cause Balarista or early death—1115.

The Stanza in the latter half is vague and does not clearly say what has to be done. The Rasi is generally the house occupied by Chandra. This house, has to be multiplied by 3 for what purposes, and what is the future procedure is not clear—1117.

Malefics in Thrikonas are always bad, and when Ravi and Chandra join together it will be a new moon day and non conducive to longevity—1118.

This can happen only when Chandra occupies Simha. Then the lord of that Lagna will be Ravi, he should join with Sani and occupy the 8th from Lagna, and possess a beneficial aspect to give a life for 12 years. In all these cases named by Venkatasa the meaning is that the child will have death or danger in that particular year. These combinations indicating death at particular periods, may be greatly modified by beneficial conjunctions and aspects, and even here there are differences as when benefics are in exaltation, they give greater good than when they are in deep debilitation—1119.

Take Mesha as Lagna, with Kuja there, aspected by Ravi, Sani, Buda, and Chandra in Thula. Will the child die in the 4th month. The lord of Lagna is Kuja and he is in his own house and Moolathrikona, Sani the lord of life and death is in exaltation, combined with Ravi, Buda and Chandra. Suppose Guru aspects the Lagna from Dhanas. I should certainly give the child a longer life than 4 months—1120.

Aupoklimas are, 3rd, 6th, 9th and 12th houses, 9th becomes a Thrikona and is beneficial in its results. Lord of Lagna in an Oopachaya must be good and conducive to long life—1121.

The lords of Lagna and 8th (*the house of longevity*) must be strong and well associated to give long life. Their unfavourable positions will kill the child earlier—1122.

Chandra plays a very prominent part in giving or taking away longevity. His power, associations and aspects should be particularly noted in the Dusthanas. He produces early death—1123.

Kita means Vrischika. This as Lagna with Ravi and Guru in it and the lord of the 8th from Lagna in a Kendra will kill the child in his 22nd year. The combination requires a little better explanation. Vrischika as Lagna with Ravi lord of 10th in it as also Guru lord of 2nd and 5th houses. For Vrischika the lord of the 8th is Buda, and how can Buda be in any Kendra from]Ravi, when the longest elongation of him fro.n his master never exceeds 23 or 24 degrees. Therefore it is out of question to find Buda for Vrischika Lagna when Ravi is there to be iocated in the 4th, 7th or 10th Kendras. Generally by kendras these 3 houses are meant. We have of course, one possible combination viz , Buda may be in Lagna Kendra along with Ravi and Guru. But when Buda and Guru combine specially in Lagna they get directional strength and also peculiar energy to give good and I humbly beg to differ from Venkatasa in his statement here. He sometimes commits glaring mistakes—1124.

If Chandra with Rahu occupies 7th, then Guru with Kethu will be in Lagna, Guru and Chandra in Kendras produce Gajakesariyoga which gives long and glorious life. Did Venkatasa remember all these in writing such stranzas -1125.

Here Chandra may be in any house with Sani. Beneficial conjunctions and aspects will avert or modify much of the evil in these combinations—1126.

Kuja and Ravi, are bitter enemies of Sani, Chandra and Guru are not such enemios. Vrischika, Mesha and Simha Lagnas are very unfriendly to Sani—1127.

Stanzas 1128 to 1146 both inclusive.

If the lord of Lagna, not in conjunction with a benefic, is between two evil planets and if the Lagna happens to be the same as his father's, the person dies—1128.

If evil planets occupy 1st, 2nd and 8th, and benefics join in Panaparas and Aupoklimas, the person dies in his 28th year—1129.

If Chandra is between the lords of Lagna and 8th and Guru occupies the 12th from Lagna, death comes between 22nd and 32nd year—1130.

If the lord of 8th is evil, and is aspected by Guru and another evil planet or if the lord of Lagna is in 8th he will die in the 28th year—1131.

If the lord of 8th joins a Kendra, and the lord of Lagna is powerless, the man dies in his 30th or 32nd year—1132.

If one of the lords of the Lagna and 8th, joins 8th and the other is powerless, he will die between 30 and 32 years—1133.

If Sani occupies the Navamsa of the 8th and a powerful malefic joins Lagna and benefics occupy Panaparas and Aupoklimas the man dies between 30 and 32 years—1134.

If malefics join each other, the lord of Lagna has evil aspects and weak moon joins the 12th house, death comes between 30 and 32 years—1135.

If lords of Lagna and 8th occupy Kendras and some planet is found in the 8th and benefics are not in Kendras the person dies in his 32 year—1136.

If Chandra in combination with Ravi, occupies a Kendra, the lord of 8th in a Kendra, a malefic joins 8th and no planet occupies the birth death comes in the 32nd year—1137.

If the lords of Lagna and 8th occupy the 8th with malefics and uncombined with benefics death comes in the 27th year—1138

If Chandra occupies the 9th house from Lagna in the reverse order, the lord of the 8th in Kendra, aspected by powerless benefics death comes in the 30th year—1139.

If the lord of the 8th joins with lords of the 2nd and 9th, and lord of birth occupies 8th in conjunction with or aspected by malefics, and unaspected by benefics death comes in the 24th year—1140.

If the lord of 8th joins Lagna, and the lord of birth is powerless death comes at the 32nd year—1141.

If Chandra and the lord of Lagna occupy Aupoklimas and the lord of 8th has malefic aspects and is powerless, death happens between 30 and 32 years—1142.

If Guru and Sukra are in Kendras, and the lord of Lagna with a malefic joins Aupoklimas and the birth falls in Sandhyakala, the person lives up to 36 years —1143.

If powerless Ravi, in the midst of two malefics, joins an unfriendly sign which falls as birth, and is not aspected by benefics death comes before 36 years—1144.

If Chandra and Kuja are in Lagna, Kendra and the 8th are not occupied by benefics, and Mandi joins birth he will have 36 years of life—1145.

I the learned Venkatasa, have summarised the combinations for longevity by my good selection for the pleasure and profit of the educated men—1146.

NOTES.

Stanxas 1120 to 1146. The verses have been very carefully and clearly translated and they do not require any special notes, as the readers can easily keep horoscopes, apply the principles and see what terms of life each horoscope gets, as the result of special combinations named in the above paras. In all these cases, care must be taken to analyse the sources of strength and weakness, and any astrologer who foregets to remember this salutary advice will cut a sorry figure in his future predictions. For the various terms of life and the methods I would refer my readers to my notes on Chapter VII. Brihatjataka and Self Instructor.

End of Chapter XI Aristadhyaya.

CHAPTER XII.

ARISTA BHANGA OR

ANTIDOTES FOR MISFORTUNES.

Stanzas 1147 to 1164 both inclusive.

As a sincere offering of prayer to Vishnu destroys all sins, so also does Guru avert all misfortunes when he powerfully joins the birth—1147.

If the lord of Lagna is very powerful, and is combined with or aspected by benefics, occupies Kendras, and is unaspected by malefics, the person will have long life and great wealth—1148.

If full moon or the moon who occupies beneficial signs and Amsas, has the aspect of a powerful Jupiter, he will avert all dangers and give him long life and happiness—1150.

If Buda, Guru or Sukra, is powerful and occupies a Kendra without malefic associations or aspects, the person will have all his misfortunes removed—1151.

Even when Chandra occupies an unfriendly sign, if he combines with Guru, Sukra or Buda, and joins beneficial Drekkanas he will avert all dangers as does the Great Vishnu, all the sins of a man when he prays devoutly—1152.

Though Chandra may join 6th or 8th, if the child is born during the night in the bright half of the lunar month, and Chandra has beneficial aspects, or if the child is born during the day time, in the dark half of the lunar month, and Chandra has not the aspect of evil planets the child will be protected from all dangers—1153.

If Chandra joins beneficial Rasi or Navamsa, commands beneficial aspects and is full, he will protect the child from all evils as Garuthman protects from all serpents—1154.

If Guru shines brilliantly and joins a Kendra he will protect the child from all misfortunes. Also if Guru, Buda, Sukra and Chandra join beneficial Navamsas, the child will be well protected—1155.

If the lord of Chandra Lagna is a benefic joins a Kendra and has beneficial aspects, he will protect the child. If evil planets are aspected by benefics occupying beneficial vergas, the child will be protected—1156.

Rahu occupying 3, 6. or 11, without malefic conjunctions or aspects, and possessing beneficial influences will protect the child from all evils as the wind can blow way threads of cotton opposed to its fury—1157.

If full moon combines with or is aspected by benefics, and possesses no malefic associations, he will protect the child from all misfortunes. If full moon has the aspect of all planets he will protect the child—1158.

If benefics are powerful, malefics are powerless, and the birth falls in a beneficial sign combined with or aspected by a benefic, the child will be completely protected—1159.

Rahu in Aries, Taurus, or Cancer protects the child from all evils, as does a generous hearted Monarch, the faults of a servant to whom he has extended his gracious full pardon—1160.

Even weak Chandra, when he joins beneficial Vergas and has beneficial aspects, will protect the child as does the juice of the bark of the half burnt pomegranate fruit, the persom suffering from loose motions or diaharria.

If the lord of Chandra Lagna joins birth and has beneficial aspects, and Chandra is in exaltation and aspected by Sukra, the child will be protected from all misfortunes—1162.

If Chandra is in exaltation, or friendly Rasis or Amsas, or his own Navamsa, or Vergas, or beneficial divisions combines with or is aspected by benefics, is powerful, and has no malefic associations or aspects, he will melt away misfortunes of intensity like the rays of the sun, melting away the dews—1163.

I, Venkataswara, Brahmin of the Velnadu community, have made a selection of all the Aristabhanga combinations in my present work named Sarwartha Chintamani—1164.

NOTES.

Stanzas 1147 to 1164.   The principal factors in averting dangers and deaths enumerated in this Chapter may be summarised as follows ; the moon seems to play the most important part, both in the infliction of early death and also in its aversion.   Jupiter plays no less a part in the preservation of the life of children, both by his combination and also by his aspects. Planets in evil Rasis, Navamsas, Drekkanas, and other Vergas have a tendency to inflict evil, and unless they are powerfully neutralised by beneficial aspects and combinations, the flow of misfortunes will be easy and rapid. Planets, benefics or malefics, occupying beneficial Rasis, Amsas and Vergas, have a strong tendency to give long life, to avert all evils and to add prosperity and happiness to persons   Chandra must be full, powerful, in exaltation or good Rasis and Amsas, and must have beneficial conjunctions and aspects to do good.   Guru shines most brilliently, when he is in exaltation, when he is in good conjunction, when he is not combust, or in evil associations or aspects Guru is able to avert evils of the greatest magnitude.

Provided he is free, powerful and has brilliant rays.   All these various sources of strength and weakness must be well balanced, they should be carefully analysed and compared, and the delicate differences should be well noted by the experts in Astrology, before future predictions are ventured.   By careful mathematical calculations, the Bhavas should be ascertained, the combinations should be determined, the aspects should be fixed, and the degrees of power and weakness should be scrupulously noted, so that when judgment as to the longevity or happiness of a child is expected or given, every care should be taken to see no errors creep into the records and no prejudices should be allowed to play their mischief.   All these are scientific and deducible from premises.   But a higher. order of judgment power should be cultivated with a view to make the deduction certain.   It is the will power of concentration and contemplation on God in the right methods.

People think when they pray to God, he does not appear or

grant them their requests. For the water to boil, there is a certain quantity of heat needed. Will it boil and bubble before that degree is reached or created? Similarly each event is dependent upon certain preliminaries before it can assume the form of success. Mental composition, strength, currents, and combination present a very wexed question for solution and if some complain that their prayers are not attended to even by the all impartial, and gracious God, the only answer that could be returned, will be to say that the intensity of the mind is not enough and it must be strengthened. Water to be frozen requires a certain degree of cold. If it has not frozen by an experiment or by the application of cold, the reason. able answer will be to have the cold increased to the necessary degree. When a real devout mind offers its prayers to Vishnu, all his sins will be effaced and he will be purified. Similarly when Guru is glorious, powerful and situated in the birth the child will be completely protected—1147.

In all horoscopic combinations, birth and the power of its lord, Chandra and the lord of the house occupied by him should be taken particular note of. If the lords of Lagna and Chandra Lagna are powerful and well situated dangers will be averted—1148.

Lord of the 8th denotes the length of life and Chandra represents mental thread. These two in beneficial Drekkanas, will protect the child. Dregkana is ⅓rd of a sign and gets 10 degrees for its extent—1149.

Full moon, or moon in powerful beneficial divisions aspected by or combined with Jupiter gives protection—1150.

The three benefics are Guru, Sukra and Buda, Guru is the most powerful and next in efficiency comes Sukra. Buda is good or bad according to association. If any one of these, in full power, occupies a Kendra, there will be protection. If all of these are in Kendras, the longevity will be largely increased—1151.

Though Chandra may be in an unfriendly sign, when he occupies beneficial Drekkana and has the combination of a powerful beneficial, Guru, or Sukra or Buda, the child will be protected. As holy and religious Brahmin Venkatasa takes his similes and metaphors naturally from his religious love and devotion. Praying to Vishnu devoutly takes aways all sins, and so also good combinations destroy all dangers by their beneficial rays—1152.

A difference is made between children born during the day and night and also during bright and dark half of a lunar month. Moon is powerful in the waxing half of the month and then during the nights. He is powerless during the waning half and is said to be powerful then during the day time. The exact logic of this is not plain, but when Sastras pronounce a judgment I have no voice to say anything against it, and we must expand our mental vision and understand the underlying principles, before we have any voice to oppose such principles—1153.

Garuthman is the white necked kite, considered to be a sacred bird, from the peculiar cry it makes, resembling the name of Krishna. In Bhagavadgitha, Krishna says that it is most sacred among the birds. This bird carries aways serpents and eats them. No other kites are observed to do this. The comparison is made to Garuda. As he is able to suck all poison from snakes Chandra in beneficial, Rasis will avert or suck away all evil influences from other combinations—1154.

Guru is said to shine brilliantly when his rays are pure, large and appear like crystal, and when he does not suffer by combustion (contact with the sun) by defeat (contact with powerful Mars) and with evil planets like Saturn, Rahu or Kethu—1155.

Beneficial planets, in beneficial amsas should aspect evil planets to give protection. This may also mean, evil planets should be in beneficial amsas and should be aspected by benefics to afford protection—1156.

Rahu in 3-6-11 affords good protection and gives wealth, without malefic conjunctions and possessing beneficial associations. I am extremely doubtful about the principles laid down here by

Venkatasa. Kuju, Sani, Kethu, Rahu, weak Chandra and badly associated Buda are evil planets. The general principle is that evil planets in 3—6—11 and benefics in 5, 4, 7, 9 and 10 and birth are conducive to longevity and prosperity. If one evil planet Rahu is able to extend protection to life by his position in 3 or 6 or 11, why should the conjunction of another evil planet take away life, against the approved principle laid down above. Readers may carefully study this point from the various approved works on astrology—1157.

Of course full moon, possessing beneficial aspects, and conjnnc-tions affords protection. When all the planets, good and bad aspect Chandra, protection also is extended—1158.

Powerful benefics add vitality, powerless evil planets cannot do much damage. Birth in a beneficial sign, with the combination of a benefic will do good—1159.

Rahu is considered to be specially powerful in Mesha, Vrish-abha where he is exalted, and Kataka and he affords protection—1160.

When the bark of the Pomegranate fruit is half burnt, and the juice is extracted and administered to cases of loose motions it will bind the bowels and afford protection. This is a medical receipr Though moon may be weak or powerless, if he joins beneficial Vergas, hora, Drekkana, Navamsa, Dwadasamsa and Thrimsamsa, he will become good and give protection—1161.

Sukra's aspect to Chandra, when he is in exaltation or benefi-cial Rasis will give special power for protection—1162.

This verse is a recapitulation of the whole of the previous stanzas and the principle is to give good protection to child Chandra must be powerful—1163.

Venkatasa, by calling himself Sarma indicates his Brahmin origin and also observes that he belongs to the Velanudu community or section of the Andra or Telugu Brahmins—1164.

Stanzas 1165 to 1189 both inclusive.

Persons who live about 32 and die before 70 years, are said to have middle life—1165.

If Kuja's house falls as birth with Chandra in it and malefics and benefics are outside Kendras he will die in his 33rd year—1166.

If Chandra, and the evil lord of the 8th join Kendra or Kona, and are aspected by the evil planets in the 10th house he will die in his 33rd year—1167.

If Sani and Chandra join birth and Kuja is located in Kumbha, he dies in his 33rd year—1167A.

If the Sun joins birth and is placed betwixt two malefics, and Jupiter is found in Gemine, which should be the 8th from birth the person will die in his 37th year—1168.

If the lord of the 8th joins birth, and Kuja also in birth or joins fixed signs which should fall in 8th or 12th he will live up to 42 years—1169.

If Guru is in a Kendra, Sani in the 10th and birth falls in a movable sign the person lives up to 44 years—1170.

If Makara becomes Lagna with Kuja there and Sani and Guru are in the 10th Thula, he will be wealthy, learned in many sciences and will die in his 48th year—1171.

If the lord of Chandra Lagna joins 8th with an evil planet from birth, and the lord of lirth with a malefic combines in 6th, and if both these are powerful, and have no beneficial aspects the person dies in his 45th year—1172.

If Mesha falls as Lagna with full moon aspected by a benefic the person becomes a lord or Prince. If such a moon is aspected by a malefic he dies in his 48th year —1173.

If Sani joins birth, and combines with other planets, and Chandra joins 12th or 3th from Lagna, he will become a Vedanthee or wise and pious man and will die in his 52nd year—1174.

If birth falls in Dhanas combined with Guru, and the 8th is combined by Rahu and Kuju he will live up to 57 years.

If the lord of 8th jotns 7th and Chandra joins malefics he will live up to 58 years-- 1175.

If the lord of the 8th with Guru joins birth and Kumbha becomes one of the Kendras with malefics in it, the person will be a Brahmaguani or yogee, happy and will live up to 60 years—1176.

If the 8th is occupied by a malefic, the lord of birth in the 12th and the lord of 8th joins birth, he will be mean, living in disgrace on his family, and will die in his 60th year—1177.

If Sani is in birth, Chandra in the 4th, Kuja in the 7th and Rani in the 10th and Sukra, Guru or Buda joins any one of these Kendras, the person will become a prince cr lord and will live to 60 years—1178.

If Sukra joins 10th, and is aspected by Buda, Guru and Chandra and Guru occupies 5th he will be wealthy and become a prince and live up to 60 years—1179.

If Sukra occupies birth, Buda and Sani in Kendras, and all the rest of the planets in the 3rd and 11th houses he will become a lord and live to 60 years—1180.

If the lords of Lagna and Chandra Lagna are in the 8th and the lord of the 8th in a Kendra he will become leader of men, and blessed with good reputation and wealth. He will live to 66 years—1181.

If there is a planet in the 4th from Lagna, Guru and Sukra join Kendras, or occupy birth he will be good natured, and will go to heaven in his 60th year—1182.

If Guru joins Lagna, and combines with Ravi and Buda, Sani n Meena, and Chandra in the 12th he will be wealthy, learned in all shastras, and live up to 66 years—1183.

If Chandra, in exaltation, occupies birth, Sani in debilitation, and Ravi in the 7th, he will be wealthy and will live up to 66th year—1184.

If Sani, in debilitations, joins a Kendra or Kona, benefics join Kendras, or Ravi in conjunction with a benefic occupies a Kendra, he will be a wise leader, and die in his 65th year—1185.

If Ravi, Kuja, Sani and the lord of the 6th join Kendras, and Guru and Chandra are not in 8th or 12th houses, he will be very very learned, charitable, well knowing (*Gnani*) man of capacity and knack, and will live up to 70 years—1186.

If a very powerful benefic joins a Kendra, no benefic in the 8th and he possesses the aspects, of birth lord, he will live up to 70 years -1187.

If Kuja occupies 5th, Sani in debilitarion, and Ravi joins 7th, he will live up to 70 years—1188.

Yavanas and other Munis have given numberless combinations for middle life. I have only made a careful selection of only a few. Those who read these Yogas sketched by me, understand them properly and apply them carefully to horoscopes, will be sure to command respect and reputation. These combinations may be applied to questions, birth times and also for marriages 1189.

NOTES.

Stanzas 1165 to 1189. For classification of these different terms of life see notes on 1070.

He gives combinations for death from 32 to 70 years and classifies these combinations under Madhyayuryoga or terms of middle life. The stanzas are easy and do not require any notes·

Stanza 1190.

If all the planets occupy the first 6 houses from birth or the next 6 houses, the person will have long life —1190·

NOTES.

The word all does not include Rahu and Kethu, for if we include them, both of them can never be in the first 6 houses. The first 6 houses are birth, 2nd, 3rd, 4th, 5th and 6th, and these houses should be occupied by benefics and malifics. This is one combination which gives long life. The next is that all these planets are to occupy the 7th, 8th, 9th, 10th, 11th and 12th houses. This will also give long life—1190.

Stanzas 1191 to 1233 both inclusive.

If all the benefics powerfully occupy the first 6 houses from birth and all the malefics powerfully join the other 6 houses, the person will be good natured, agreeable, full of enjoyment, prosperous and will live up to 80 years—1191.

If Buda joins Lagna, Chandra in the Kona and Sani in the 9th, he will live up to 87 years—1192.

If all planets occupy odd signs, and the birth falls in an odd sign with the full moon there, the person will have great wealth and long life—1193.

If all planets join even signs and combine with the waning moon, and birth falls in an even sign, the person will have great wealth through females—1194.

Yavanas and others of that school give great wealth to all long lived persons. Varahamihira and others separate longevity from wealth—1195.

Wherever differences in combinations and results are predicted by Yavana and Varahamihira, I have expressed my own opinion. Those differences rise occasionally—1196.

If Chandra combined with Guru, occupies a Kendra, aspected by a benefic, and other planets occupy other than their own houses, the person lives up to 80 years—1197.

When benefics occupy Kendras, malefics are not in 8th and 6th, and Chandra occupies the 6th, the person will have 86 years of life—1198.

When malefics join 3-6 and 11 and Chandra occupies 6th or 8th and Guru joins a Kendra, the person will become lord of towns and also live long—1199.

If there are 3 planets, in the 5th, 9th, Kendras or 8th or if 5 planets are found in Kendras he will be wealthy, moral, and live more than 100 years—1200.

If Guru occupies a Kendra from the lord of the birth, and evil planets are not in Kendras or Konas, he will be happy and live to 100 years—1201.

If Chandra occupies birth or is in his own Amsa, or joins Meena or Kataka, the 8th house is unoccupied, and Guru occupies a Kendra he will live to more than 70 years—1202.

If Guru is in Kendra, and Ravi and Kuja are in birth, or in the 8th, he will be wealthy, lord of men, and live up to 100 years—1203.

If the last Navamsa of Meena falls as birth and 4 planets are in Kendras or if birth falls in Simha, and four planets are found in the 5th and 9th houses, the person lives up to 108 years—1204.

When 3 planets are in exaltation, Vrishabha falls as Lagna and Guru is in Kataka, or when Kuja joins Makara, Guru in Kataka, and all the other planets are in Kendras, the person will live up to 108 years -1205.

If Guru is in Lagna, Sukra in the 4th and Chandra with Sani, without malefic associations combines in the 10th, he will live long, will have excellent reputation for his vast and profound learning.—1206.

If birth falls in the latter half of Makara, with Chandra in it

Kuja is in the previous half, and Guru joins a Kendra, he will have long life—1207.

If Guru occupies the first half of Dhanas, and birth falls in the second half, and Chandra and Sukra occupy a Kendra from Sani, he will have very long life—1208.

If Buda occupies the first half of Kanya and birth falls in the second half, and if 3 or 4 planets are in exaltation he will have a long life—1209.

If malefics join 3-6 and 11, Buda occupies the last Amsa of birth Lagna, Sani in Lagna and Guru or Sukra in a Kendra, he will have long life—1210.

I Kuja occupies the first half of Mithuna and it becomes the Lagna, and the other half of Lagna is conjoined by Guru, Buda and Sukra occupy Kendras, he will live to more than 100 years and will be a happy and wealthy man—1211.

If Lagna falls in Kumbha with Ravi in it and Guru is in the 2nd or 12th from it, he will live up to 1000 years by chemical and Yoga means and will be a Yogee of a high order—1212.

It Simha becomes Lagna with Guru in it, and Sukra in the 8th or Kataka and Buda in the 2nd or Kanya, and malefics are in 3-6 and 11 the person lives up to 1000 years—1213.

If Kuja and Ravi are in the 4th, Sani is in Lagna, Rahu in the 12th, and the rest of the planets are in the 2nd, he will live up to 2000 years—1214.

If Mesha becomes Lagna with Ravi in it with a benefic, Guru in the 10th, and Kuja in the 7th with full moon in the 12th he will live up to 2000 years by the help of Rasayana Sastras—1215.

If Vrishabha is Lagna with Chandra in it, combined with Buda, Guru and Sukra or if the other planets are in the 2nd, the person will go to Devandra Loka—1216.

If jupiter occupies one of his own houses as Lagna, no planet is in Mithuna, and Sukra is located in a Kendra, he will live for many years by the help of Rasayana and join Indra Loka—1217.

If all planets, benefics and malefics, join in one house, which should be a Kendra or Kona, he will die at once, and if he does not so die he will live by Mantra Siddhi, to many Yugas—1218.

If there are no malefics in 5 and 9, and no benefics in Kendras, and the 8th is free from malefics, he will become equal to a Deva—1219.

If birth falls in Vrishabha with Sukra in it, Guru in Kendras, and other planets are in 3-6 and 11, he will obtain Indra Padavi by Rasayana and Mantra—1220.

If birth falls in Kataka, Sani in Thula, Guru in Makara and Chandra in Vrishabha, he will he happy, and will attain to Brahmaloka by Rasayana and Mantra—1221.

If Kataka falls in Vargottama, Guru in a Kendra, Kuja in the 7th Sukra in Simha Navamsa, he will have unlimited longevity by Rasayana etc—1222.

If Buda joins the last of Kanya which falls as birth, Guru occupies Gopuramsa in the 7th or Sani in Mridwamsa, he will have unlimited tern of life—1223.

If Sukra joins Devalokamsa, Kuja in a Kendra, Guru occupies Simhasanamsa, he will become equal to a Deva—1224.

If Sukra in Oottamamsa occupies a Kendra, Sani in Paravatamsa, and Guru in Swargalokamsa joins a Kendra, he will extend his term of life by various medicines—1125.

If Guru in a Kendra joins Gopuramsa and Sukra in a Kona occupies Paravatamsa, and birth falls in Kataka, he will live to Yugas—1226.

If birth falls in Kataka in the Navamsa of Dhanas, Guru

is in Kataka, 3 or 4 planets join Kendras, he will have Brahma-pada—1227.

If birth falls in Vargottama in Vrishabha, Sukra is in 3rd or 11th and joins Gopuramsa he will have Brahma Pada—1228.

If birth falls in Dhanas in the Navamsa of Mesha, Sukra in Lagna and Guru in the 7th and Chandra in Kanya he will have Paramapada—1229.

If Kumba becomes birth with Guru in it, Buda joins 5th in Gopuramsa etc., he will have Brahmapada—1230.

Guru in a Kendra, Sani in the 11th, Ravi in the 2nd, Chandra in the 7th and Kuja in the 9th, he will live to many Yugas by Mantras —1231.

If Guru and Buda join Konas, Kuja occupies Vrishabha as Lagna, and Chandra joins Gopuramsa etc., he will live up to 2000 years— 1232.

If birth falls in day time, in the bright half of the lunar month, Guru in a Kendra, Kataka falls as birth in the day time of Sukla Paksha, Kuja in the 7th and Sani in the 4th, he will live up to 10,000 years—1233.

NOTES.

STANZAS—1191 to 1233.

As almost all the technicalities have been explained in the earlier parts of this work, very few notes are needed. The language has been simplied to a degree that a little attention to its exposition will make the meaning clear.

Buda in Lagna gets directional strength, Chandra and San may be in the 9th or Chandra in the 5th and Sani in the 9th— 1192.

Birth as well as all planets should be in odd signs, and full
moon should be in birth to give wealth and longevity. If any
of the planets are in even signs, this combination is spoiled—
1193.

Here all planets, including new moon should be in even
signs and also birth should fall there. The person will get wealth
through females. Here the person may have wealth through
his wife's immoral conduct, or he may fall in with a widow or
other woman who is rich, or he may trade in females, act as a
pimp or broker among prostitutes and earn money or he may get
good wealth from legistimate means from his wife, mother,
sisters or other female agencies—1194.

There are two sets of Yavanas, Purana and Navina. Bhatotpala observes that he saw some quotations from Purana
Yavanas. These Yavanas may have been Javanese, Ivans, or
Yavanas coming from distant N. W. parts of Asia (see my
history of Vijayanagar). These maintain, very erroneously that
long lived persons will always be wealthy or holding political
power. This can never be correct. There are very oldmen
within my own experience, and in my own village and as my
own servants, men of 90 and 95 and they are extremely poor.
Long evity and wealth are two different things. Both may go
hand in hand or one may forsake the other altogether. Wealthy men die at very early ages. Varaha Mihira and others of
his school are perpectly right and in his Ch. on Ayurdaya he
plainly says that longevity has nothing to do with wealth or *vice
versa*—1195.

Venkatasa seems to have read both these systems and
whereever there are differences, he expresses his own opinion,
a very right procedure on the part of a compiler—1196.

The combination of Chandra with Guru and another benefic
will certainly be a good one. Why should the other planets be

in other than their own houses ? When they are in their own houses they are strong. Why should they be not so ?—1197.

Benefics in Kendras produce good, malefics should not be in 6th or 8th, as they produce danger in the 8th. They are good in the 6th and Chandra is bad in the 6th. Probably each combination generates a series of electrical currents which produce definite results. Therefore, we cannot find fault with a chemical formula based on experience—1198.

Malefics in 3-6-11 are powerful. Chandra in the 6th or 8th is evil, Guru in a Kendra is good. How in this case Chandra becomes beneficial, and conduces to wealth and longevity is difficult to conjecture, but remembering plametary bodies are chemical store houses, peculiar conjunctions, like peculiar compounds of medical drugs, produce good although individuals composing the compound may be injurious. Poison is deleterious and causes death and danger to life, but in combination with another drug or metal it may become perfectly beneficial—1199.

Five planets in Kendras are a good conjunction. 5th and 9th are good· 8th again is bad but we have discussed a combination from Kalidasa's Oottara Kalamrita, that when the lords of the 6th, 9th, 11th and 12th are in each others houses, or are in conjunction they produce a splendid political position—1200.

Evil planets in Kendras and Konas are bad, but Kuja and Ravi in the 10th, and Sani in the 7th are good and produce Rajayoga and the greatest known monarchs like Rama, Ravana, Harischandra, etc , had Ravi in the 10th· The lord of birth is as significant in power as the birth house itself, and therefore benefics, specially Guru in a Kendra from the lord of birth or even from the lord of Chandra Lagna must produce good—1201.

The potency of moon in giving or cutting short longevity has been already dwelt at considerable length in the previous paras. Gurus beneficiency cannot be underrated—1202.

Ravi and Kuja here in the 8th have also been given good results, but by themselves without the special combination named here, they will produce death and danger—1203.

The last Navamsa of Meena signifies great power to give emancipation from worldly sins and also wealth. Chandra there or Guru indicates good. Four planets in Kendras with birth in Meena, produces longevity. Simha as Lagna, with four planets in Konas, produces a good longevity of 108 years—1204.

Three planets in exaltation will give long life, (see my notes on Chapter VII, St. 6 p, 104-5, Br. J.) Guru and Kuja are exalted in Kataka and Makara respectively—1205.

Guru in Lagna, Sukra in 4 and Sani and Chandra in 10 without malefic associations, produce a splendid conjunction for vaster udition and good reputation founded on his depth of scholarship—1206.

The rasi, is divided into two equal halves each called a hora. Birth and Chandra must be in the second hora of Makara. Kuja in the 1st hora, will be in ordinary exaltation as his deep exaltation will fall in the 28 degree of Makara and Guru must be in a Kendra, in Mesha, Kataka, or Thula. This gives long life—1207.

Guru must be in the 1st hora of Dhanas his own house and Moola Thrikona, birth should fall in the 2nd hora, Chandra and Sukra must be in a Kendra from Sani whereever he may be, longevity is produced—1208.

Buda is in deep exaltation in the 15th degree of Kanya. He must be in the first hora, birth should be in the 2nd hora and 3 or 4 planets must be in exaltation. Here Buda may or may not be in exaltation. When Buda is in Kanya, Sukra and Ravi can never be in exaltation, and therefore the other four planets will be Sani, Guru, Kuja and Chandra—1209.

Malefics here, will be Ravi, weak Chandra, Kuja and Rahu and Kethu. Buda and Sani to be in Lagna but Sani in the earlier degrees and Buda in the last Amsa. Guru or Sukra should be in a Kendra. Long life means more than 70 years or Poornayu—1210.

This combination indicates long life and also great wealth. Birth should be in the first hora of Mithuna with Kuja in it, Guru in the 2nd hora of Lagna with Buda and Sukra should be in Kendras. This means that Kuja, Guru, Buda and Sukra should be in Kendras to give 100 years of life and happiness and wealth —1211.

Kumbha as birth with Ravi in it, Guru to be in Meena or Makara, the person is given 1000 years of life to be obtained by Rasayana Sastra. This and other subsequent verses require a full explanation for they introduce subjects which are utterly foreign to English readers and readers among the Natives of India, whose minds are saturated with modern scientific jingle and who are not willing to grant any theory or fact, which their sciences do not understand. A few arguments will clearly show the utter futility of their conceptions and the wrong premises on which they base their arguments.

1. As candid men endowed with a grain of honesty in their brains, they must admit that they do not represent the sum total of wisdom in the world or proclaim that there can be no facts which they have not understood.

2. They have not understood the principle of life and their perfections in chemistry and physics, are, at most, only superficial experiments from which no sound inferences can be drawn.

3. They have no means now at their command to refute logically any statement of facts which have been recorded in the ancient histories, and their simple observation that such and such facts cannot be true, or cock and bull stories, is not enough to convince any reasonable man of the soundness of their own argument.

4. Every decade, nay every year, their old theories are being replaced by newer discoveries so much so that atoms, elements, ether, magnetism and electricity, are undergoing remarkable changes, that they cannot affirm about the statubility of any modern theory.

5. Judging by the laws of continuity, of whose value in the scientific speculations they are giving its weight, other worlds, other creatures, and other spheres of existence have been declared to be possible, and not having understood correctly the principles of evolution they cannot now safely affirm as to how these states can be achieved and the principles involved in these rapid changes.

6. If chemistry has worked wonders on a small scale, has diminished sickness and improved health and term of life, will, it then be unreasonable to say that further deep knowledge in advanced chemical sciences, will not reveal to man, principles on which he can prolong his life, expand his intellect, improve his physique, minimise ailments, and live to terms of life which may look extraordinary to ordinary men and ordinary to extraordinary intellects.

7. The most advanced of modern scientists are thoroughly ignorant of the elementary principles of Yoga, how nervous energies can be strengthened by withdrawing mind from external sense engagements, and how the advanced vision (Yoga or Gnana Dristi) can be secured and utilised for experimenting with the higher principles of nature, and by what methods such expanded souls can comprehend events in the higher realms of natural phenomena which are far beyond even the conceptions of the greatest scientific intellects.

8. The limits of mental development, the wonderful work it can do when elevated and the possibilities of travelling to other worlds than ours, are still matters of hidden knowledge to the modern savant and he has to work assiduously and for many

centuries before he could compel Nature to reveal her hidden intellectual treasures.

9. Life therefor can be expanded both by chemical combinations, called Siddha ghutikas, and also by certain combinations which are the result of Yobgic development after severes penance, practice and patience.

10. Mantras are mental currents of a subtle nature which, taught by Sadgurus or properly constituted authorities, can be imparted with great force and potency from one individual to the other. The latter, after receiving it like a prudent son who inherits a certain amount of property from his father, may, by careful practice, hard labour, and much mental concentration, expand it store it. and use it for various purposes, which may relate to worldly prosperity, or which may take him to higher states of celestial existence. There is nothing absurd in this, and it is possible to augment and strengthen the ethereal currents of planets, increase life immeasurably beyond its normal term and rise to positions in mental world where the laws applicable will be quite different. My notes in my History of Vijayanagar on longevity may be read with great advantage (Chapter II, p. 17, Geneology p. 17). Yoga is the combination of nervous energy and a strong cohesive bond, which when, properly developed, raises the man above the terms of ordinary life, gives him command over the elemental forces and makes him fix his own end whenever he finds it convenient. Therefore one or two thousand years is nothing for a developed Yogi and it is recorded that by very high Yoga development the Maha Rishis prolong their lives. Anjaneya, Aswathama, Bali, Vyasa, Vibhishana, Kripacharya and Parasurama are still living. They are Chiranjeevies and will die when the present Kalpa concludes. Such a huge and interesting subject, cannot be put into a small space in a foot note, and those who desire greater information will be referred to Yoga principles and Brahma Sutras.

11.   Brahmapada—Yoga is directed by various individuals in various ways as wealth is used by the people to serve many objects. When Yoga strength is developed to a certain extent, it will enable a man to so as to a certain elevation.   Lokas or worlds are planes of existence, which require a certain amount of power, and which may be good or bad.   Tthere are millions of Lokas, each one having a specified object in creation and performing certain functions. Naraka Loka requires a man to be sinful, deproved and avaricious. Swarga Loka requires a certain quantity of merit.   The planetary Lokas have their reepective states of preparation and spirituality.   Indra Loka is reached by a person who practices some special forms of spiritual development.

12.   Brahmapadu denotes that a man by practising special virtues attains to Brahma Loka, and to spend his time blissfully at the feet of Brahma.   Vishnapadu, Kailasavasa, and Devalokas, require each in its turn special spiritual developments and conduct while the man tenants this earth in his grosser surroundings.

Pitruloka, Gandharvaloka, Nagaloka, Siddaloka, Pisachaloka, Kinnaraloka, Kimpirushaloka, Yekshaloka, Sadhyaloka, Charanuloka and so forth are attained by special mental currants.

Mirtyaloka, inhabited by us, human beings possesses the special capacity to training up its tenants, to reach any Loka, and even to attain the real Brahmapadam or union with the real cause of the unknowable universe.   There are 27 important Naraka Loka, or *Chells* which are reached by sinners of various grades, and for performance of various sins.

13   Rasa Vada may be taken as chemistry in a broader and more comprehensive sense.   The ancient Rasavada or the knowledge of mixing various juices of vegetables, minerals and animals, combined all the causes which produced an effect or effects.   The modern chemistry has to widen its conception and take in moral, religious and spiritual forces in the combination of any object. Myalaria produces fever, but why does Myalaria develop and pro-

duce such fevers. Man commits sin. Why does he do so? He is generous and charitable? Why is he so. Healthy men die suddenly while most sickly men live long. Why? some do not prosper through highly educated and capable. Why? From a careful knowledge of Rasuvadum life may be greatly prolonged—2112.

This seems to be a good combination, Sinha as Lagna with Guru in it, Sukra in the 12th or Kataka and Buda in the 2nd evil planets in 3-6-11 will give him a 1000 years—1213.

Sani in Lagna generally gives Balarista but when the child escapes it he will make him live long, Ravi and Kuja in the 4th, a Kendra add power to longevity, Rahu in the 12th and the rest of the planets *viz.* Chandra, Guru, Buda, Sukra and Kethu should be in the 2nd. When Rahu is in the 12th, Kethu can never be in the 2nd and he can only be in the 6th. When Ravi is in the 4th Buda cannot be in the 2nd. He can only be in the 3rd or 5th or 4th. Thus this is one of those unpardonable errors into which Venkatasa falls in the enthusiasm of his scientific treatment or it may be he has recorded these combinations from ancient Maha Rishis, who have given some combinations which are not possible now, under the present planetary movements, but which might have been quite possible many centuries ago, (see p. 161, Chapter XII, St. 6, notes on Br. J)—1214.

Mesha falls as Lagna with Ravi in it in exaltation, combined with a benefic, Guru in the 10th Makara debililated, Kuja in Thula 7th, and full moon in Meena, which is the 12th, 2000 years of life may be acquired by the help of chemical sciences. The Rasayanasastra of the Hindus is a far more advanced science than the experimental chemistry of the western nations—1215.

Going to Devaloka by the help of knowledge obtained by practising Yoga, and Rasayana, has been admitted to be a fact by the Hindu Puranas and Sastras. There is Videha Mukti and Swadeha Mukti. By the former is meant going to celestial spheres without the physical environments. By the latter is meant the going to those Lokas in this physical body. Inter communications between different worlds have been recognised as facts and as late as the 1st century before Christ, the famous Vikramaditya the founder of the Era Samvat, is said to have ascended to Indraloka, seen him there and returned in Indra's Vimana or aeroplane. A dispute arose between Rambha and Oorvasi, the graceful celestial dancers. as to whose music and danc· ing the palm should be given. Indra invited Vikramaditya as the most accomplished and mightiest monarch to decide this compli- cated question and he decided it in a most satisfactory way to both. Indra rewarded this blessed emperor with a Divine Throne, which he ascended by 32 flights of sseps adorned by double that numher of statutes, which were able to relate stories and prevent unworthy monarchs from ascending it. This throne was last seen in Vijiana- gar, during the time of Krishna Deva Rayalu. This is described as the grandest ever seen by the famous Mahomedan Historian and ambassador at the court of Devaraya II. in 1425 A. P. and measured 90 feet in square decked with the costliest gems and bordered by brilliant pearls.

The two Rasis of jupiter are Dhanas and Meena. He must be in one of them and Sukra must be in a Kendra which means he must be in Mithuna or Dhanas or Kanya or Meena. Kanya will be his house of debilitation and we may fix him in Meena in exaltation with Guru in it. There should be no planet in Mithu- na. Here the author observes that by the help of Rasayana Sastra he will go to Indraloka—1217.

When all the planets are in one house, the child will die at once, if not he will live to a long age· In last Vikari we had 7 planets almost within 30 degrees of each other, and this conjun- ction can last only for 2¼ days as then Chandra will move away —1218.

Here a combination is given by which the person becomes equal to a Deva. What is a Deva? The western scholars, have now opened their eyes to the exitsence of other worlds than ours and peoples inhabiting them. They are still hazy about such matters which are not and which cannot be revealed to them by their microscopes and telescopes. There are 33 crores of energies or forces, headed by Brahma creative, Vishnu protective and Iswara, destructive lords. These forces or energies have subtle forms of their own and though invisible to the flesh eye, can be seen with Divya Dristi or advanced mental vision. The cultivation of the mind in certain groves attains a specific form of condensation which can assume the shape of a particular Deva and this knowledge is concealed in Mantras, Tantras, Yogas, and Siddha Yantras. The mental power is the grandest, and its cultivation, by proper methods, will give a power, a capacity and an elevation, which have not been yet realised by western savants –1219.

Different Mantras and Tantras develop different capacities and this will enable men to go to different lokas and obtain, after death, different states—1220.

Kataka as birth, Sani exalted in Thula, or 4th house, Guru in Makara 7th in debilitation, and Chandra in exaltation in Vrishabha 11th, will give him by Mantra and Rasayana Siddhi or knowledge a person happiness and Brahma Loka—1221.

Kataka as birth with Guru in a Kendra, Kuja in the 7th Makara in exaltation, and Sukra in the Navamsa of Simha and birth also in Vargottama or Kataka Navamsa will give him unlimited term of life—1222.

When last Navamsa of Kanya falls as birth with Buda there with Guru in Meena or 7th in Gopuramsa or Sani in 7th in Mridwamsa will give unlimited life. When a planet joins 4 good Vergas it is called Gopura. The 19th of Shastiamsa is called Mridvamsa, (see notes on S. chin., pp. 34—39),—1223.

He attains a higher step in the order of evolution. When

properly controlled and directed, human energeis can take him even in his own purified body to different lokas and also to different states of mental development—1224.

Swargaloka is Devalokamsa. As deleterious medicines have the power to injure and kill a man so also have certain drugs the power of prolonging it. Rêthus is sperm, when it is well regulated concentrated and conserved, and lodged or incorporated in the brain life may be lengthened to any extent. Hence Iswara is called Oordhwa Reta and this incorporated in his head, has given him the tremendous fire in his 3rd eye, the power he possesses to burn and distroy. Medicine in Sanskrit is called Ayurveda or the science, which analyses the life principles and enables man to prolong it—1225.

Yuga means a huge division of time, *viz.* 43,20,000. Solar years, one thousand such years, makes a day for Brahma, one year of men, makes one day for the Devatas. There are Navamanas or nine measurements and all these are explained in Suryasiddhanta. By proper physical and psychic development, a man can manage to live for even many Yugas. Thapas and Yoga give great advantages—1226.

Brahma Pada is the junction of the jeeva with Brahma. Para Brahma is the highest and that which enables one to achieve it is called Moksha or final emancipation—1227—28.

Paramapada is final emancipation or Moksha, when man loses all grosser environments and joins finally the great source of power which is Infirnite Intelligence and is called PARA BRAHMA.

Birth in Dhanas in the first Navamsa Mesha, Sukra in birth Guru in Mithuna, in the 7th and Chandra in the 10th in Kanya, will give Paramapada—1229.

Guru in Kumbha as Lagna is good and Varaha Mihira says, that Guru in Kumbha is as good as he is in Kataka, (see p. 194,

Eng. Tr. of Br. J) and Buda in Mithuna is good. This combination fetches him Brahmaloka—1230.

Guru in a Kendra, Ravi in the 2nd, Sani in the 11th,
Chandra in the 7th and Kuja in the 9th will make him live
for many Yugas—1231.

Guru and Buda in the 5th or 9th are good. Vrishabha as
birth with Kuja and Chandra in four good Vergas gives a longevity of 2,000 years—1232.

The jump is to 10,000 years. Dasarata is said to have
lived 60,000 years. Rama 11,000 years. Ravana 50 lacs of
years. During recent times several have lived to hundreds.
Sureswaracharya lived to 800 years. (See my notes on long life
in His. of Vij. Never to be Forgotten Empire p. 17).

Birth should fall in Kataka in the bright half of lunar month
in day time and Guru should be in a Kendra, Kuja in the 7th and
Sani in the 4th, the person will live to 10,000 years—1233.
Stanza 1234.—

When Guru, Sani, Kuja and Sukra are in Konas or Kendras
from each other they give 10,000 years of life—1234.

NOTES.

Guru, Sani, Kuja and Sukra must be in Kendras from each
other, and they may also be from Lagna or Chandra if any one
of them falls there. Then the rest must be in Kendras. All
these may be in one Kendra or two or three or even four Kendras.
This is one combination, if these planets are in, Thrikonas, from
each other they will form another combination—1234.

Stanza 1235.—

If birth falls in Simha, and all the four quadrants are occupied
by benefics, and malefics join 3-6 and 12 the person lives up to
60,000 years—1235.

NOTES.

Probably Dasaratha, father of Rama, had this combination—
1235.

Stanza 1236.—

If Guru, Chandra, etc. ending in Sani join their deep exalla-
tions the person will possess knowledge which will make him
equl to Munis or he will be respected by them for his learning—
1236.

NOTES.

He uses etc. and concludes with Sani. All can become
exalted, but not Buda when Ravi and Sukra are in exaltation, or
Sukra and Ravi cannot become exalted when Buda becomes so
—1236.

Stanza 1237.—

If Sani, Ravi, Chandra and Kuja occupy regularly 4 houses
from Lagna, and all of them join Viseshikamsa, the person will
become equal to a Deva—1237.

NOTES.

Amaras are those who have no Marana or death. Indra
governs 33 crores of energies called Amaras or Devatas and
these forces never die. They take many formes and they can
never be destroyed—1237.

Stanza 1238.—

If Makara falls as Lagna with Kuja to Ravi regularly, Chandra joins Guru and birth takes place during day time, the person
will live to a Kalpa—1238.

NOTES.

I have explained what is meant by a Kalpa in my Astrological Magazine. The meaning in this stanza is vague and errone-

ous. He wants Kujadi to join Makara, etc. Kuja in **Makara** as birth in day time, Buda in Kumbha, Guru in Meena, **Sukra** in Mesha, Sani in Vrishabha, and Ravi in Mithuna. **Whe-** Ravi is in Mithuna, Makara can never fall as birth in day time Besides when Buda is in Kumbha, Ravi cannot be in **Mithuna** The stanza is vague and erroneous—1238.

Stanza 1239.—

If Guru or Sukra joins the last of Mesha as birth, **Chandra** in the first half of Vrishabha or Dhanas, and Kuja joins **Simha** Navamsa he will live for countless years—1239

NOTES.

If Kuja is in Thula, Mithuna or Kumbha he never gets Simha Navamsa. The chemical combinations formed by the particular positions of planets in Rasis and Amsas, are numerous and may become extremely powerful in extending longevity— 1239.

Stanza 1240.—

If Buda and Ravi are in Simha, Chandra in **Vrishabha**, Sukra in Mithuna, Sani in Thula and Kataka as **Lagna with** Guru in it, will make him a Rishi or his equal—1240.

NOTES.

Guru, Sani and Chandra are in exaltation, Ravi is in his own house, Sukra in a friendly house and Buda in a neutral's house. The combination is good. Kataka as Lagna with Guru in it is very good—1240.

Stanza 1241.—

Sani in Devalokamsa, Kuja in Paravatamsa and Ravi in birth joins Simhasanamsa, make a man equal to a Muni—1241.

NOTES.

All these Amsas have been well explained in Sarvartha-chintamani in the earlier parts. Here he has named the 3 evil planets—1241.

Stanza 1242.—

If Mesha falls as birth, Ravi in Makara or 10th, Guru in Kataka 4th and malefics in 3-6 and 11, the person becomes a great Muni—1242.

NOTES.

For classification and characteristics of Muni, Rishis, Maharishis, etc. reference should be made to Vedas and Puranas—1242.

Stanza 1243.—

I have now given combinations for longevity and unlimited terms of life from a careful selection made by reading works on astrology by the Ancient Maha Rishis—1243.

NOTES.

How, it will be seen that, Venkatesa takes no credit for any originality, but simply says that he has made selections from ancient Maha Rishis and has given out combinations for long life and also for unlimited terms of life. The question of living for over hundred years, ought to engage greater attention from the educated classes than it has been done. This attention will be to their own advantage and tbe world's progress. Great intellects, men of genius and talents in many shapes, grace the earth and suddenly disappear. These can be neutralised and long terms of life may be secured by a study of the rules of life, the secrets of Mantras, the practice of Yoga, good moral life and always keeping up a jolly and good natured life—1243.

End of Chapter XII.

CHAPTER XIII.

DEEPTADI BHEDAS

DIFFERENCES IN PLANETARY STATES.

Stanzas 1244 to 1248 inclusive.

Munishane treated at length the differences in Dasas, I shall make a summary of them here for readers—1244.

Grahas have 9 states 1 Deeptha, 2 Swastha, 3 Munditha, 4 Santha, 5 Hinsa, 6 Dukha, 7 Vikala, 8 Khala, 9 Kopa—1245.

That which occupies deep exaltation is Deeptha, in his own house Swastha, in 'a very friendly house Muditha, Santha, in a neutral's house Hinsa, in an unfriendly house Dukha, with a malefic Vikala, a defeated planet Khala, in combustion, with the Sun Kopa—1246.1247.

Authors have given results in accordance with the names given —1248.

NOTES.

In all sciences there are differences in system and explanation of facts. I have been taught the following as the Avastas and they seem to be more reasonable :—

1. Deeptha—in exaltation.
2. Swastha—in his own house.
3. Santhoshi or Muditha—in a friendly house.
4. Santha—in beneficial Vergas or divisions
5. Bala—retrograde
6. Peeda—end of Rasi or sign.
7. Dina—unfriendly sign.
8. Vikala—in combustion.
9. Khala—in debilitation
10. Bheetha—acceleration.

Differences in these can only be pointed out, but I cannot say why these differences are created, and on what observations these are based—1245, 46, 47 48.

Stanzas 1249 to 1257 inclusive.

In the Dasa of a Deeptha planet, the person will have, lordship of earth, enthusiasm, courage, wealth, conveyances, happiness, female children, respect of relations, rulers and friends—1249.

In the Dasa of a swastha planet—he will get wealth and power from a peaceful ruler, happiness, education, reputation, respect, wife and children, and charity—1250.

In the period of Muditha—good clothes, lands, scents, children, wealth, courage, many Puranas, music. charities, carriages, orna. ments—1251.

In the Dasa of Santha—happiness, courage, wife, issues. landed property, conveyance, learning, enjoyment, great wealth, respect from rulers, moral instructions—1262.

In the Dasa of Hina—he will have changes in residence, hatred of relations, will lead a despicable and mean life, worthless profession, and trouble by various complaints of body and mind—1253.

In the Dukha period—many sorrows on all sides, will have foreign residence and neglected by relations, and suffer from thieves, fires, and displeasure of rulers--1254.

In the Dasa of Vikala planet—derangement, sorrows, death of parents, and losses from children, females, carriages, clothes—1255.

In the Dasa of Khala planet—quarrels with wife and children and separation from them, loss of lands and money from enemies, blame from his own community, and always misery—1256.

In the Dasa of a Kopa planet—he will do many sinful acts, losses in education, reputation, lands, money, females. fines and confiscations and bodily ailments—1257.

NOTES.

The language is plain and does not reuuire any notes. He now proceeds to give the results of planetary periods in different states

Stanza 1258.

When the sun is in deep exaltation he gives money wife, children, lands, courage, reputation, political power, good and agreeable company, respect from rulers, travelling and success —1258.

NOTES.

The sun is in deep exaltation when he occupies the 10th degree in Aries. In other degrees there he will be exaltation· Even here there is some difference. From the 1st degree to the 9th he will be ascendant and good, from the 11th to the 30th degrees he will be descending, and will gradually lose his power for good— 1258.

Stanzas 1259 and 1260 inclusive.

In the period of Ravi in exaltation the person will have, increase in cattle and wealth, and grains, travelling, quarrels among relations and consequent travelling and residence in foreign countries, excessive adultery among dancing women, money from rulers, music and sense pleasures, enjoyment from carriages, horses, drums, and other parapharnalia, and mutual enmity—1259-60.

Stanza 1261.

In the ascendant Ravi Dasa—respect, happiness, charitable, wife, children and lands, horses, cows, elephants, cultivation— 1261.

Stanza 1262.

In the descending Dasa of Ravi—he will have loss in houses, money cultivation, and objects of love and taste, worry from fires and thieves, quarrels, anger of the Kings travels to foreign counttries—1262.

NOTES.

The Sun is in deep exaltation in the 10 degree of Aries and deep debilitation in the 10th degree of Libera. From the highest exaltation he will be descending till he has the greateat fall in

Libera, and he will be ascending from the 11th degree of Libera to the 10th degree of Aries. In the intervals of these falls and ascents, his results will have to be gauged by the rule of three. This is well explained in the Ayurdaya chapter in Brihat Jutaka to which I refer my readers for greater information—1261-62.

Stanzas 1263 to 1276 inclusive.

When the Sun is in debilitation he gives displeasure of Kings, and loss of reputation and money from such sources, loss of near relations and sorrow from wife, children, friends, disgrace and misery—1263.

When the sun is in greatest fall, he will give death and dangers, loss of houses, travel to foreign countries, death of parents, and loss to wife, issues, cattle, lands, and house property—1264.

In the Dassa of Ravi in Mulathrikona happiness from lands, wife, children, relations, respect and attraction from Kings, gains in cows, money, lands and conveyances and political success and acquisition of power—1265.

In the Dasa of Ravi in his own house—he gives happiness from relations, cultivation, money, reputation, respect by great education, and political respect, gains from lands, improvement in learning—1266.

In the Dasa of Ravi in a very unfriendly house loss of children, wife and wealth, troubles from children, cows and friends, misunderstandings among members of his own community—1267.

Ravi Dasa in an unfriendly house gives sorrow, loss of children, wife, money, dangers from rulers, fires, thieves, litigation, and quarrels with wife—1268.

Dasa of Ravi in a friendly house—respect by own community, children, servants, friends, rulers, residence in his own house, friendly relations with his own people, gains in carriages, lands, ornaments, and clothing—1269.

Dasa of Ravi in an intimate friend's house—great happiness, mental pleasure, enjoyment with wife, children and money, tanks and wells, conveyances, clothes, ornaments—1270,

Dasa of Ravi in a neutral's house —indifference among people, good crops, lands, gains, cows, horses, clothes, female issues and pleasure through them, and worries from debts —1271,

Dasa of Ravi in Debilitation—doing mean and despicable work and suffering from decease in the nails, mean temper, worries and troubles from families, children, grains, cultivation merchandise; and degradation—1272.

The Dasa of Ravi in conjunction with an exalted planet— great pleasure from gains, visits to holy and sacred shrines and rivers, worship of Vishnu, building compounds, tanks and wells, discussions on holy literation, and virtuous acquisitions—1273.

The Dasa of Ravi in conjunction with a malefic —sorrows and miseries from performing objectionable deeds, dirty and poor meals, rags and worthless clothing, earning livelihood by mean acts and emaciation from want of good food—1274.

The Dasa of Ravi in combination with a benefic—gains from lands, money, clothing, enjoyment with friends, agreement with relations, marriages and other festivities and pleasant conversation from such sources—1275.

The Dasa of Ravi aspected by malefics great sorrow, danger to father and mother, troubles to children and wife, emaciation from the losses caused by fires, thieves, and fines and penalties by princes—1276.

Dasa of Ravi aspected by benefics—reputation from great learning, pleasant conversations with children, wife and other females, comeliness, courage sexual happiness, happiness to parents, and respect and recognitions from rulers —1277.

Dasa of Ravi in a Kendra—misery resulting from happiness going out of native country, separation from relations, disturbances, to cultivation and fickleness or derangement of mind—1278.

Dasa of Ravi in a Kona—instability or insanity of mind, disgrace from ruler, unhappiness, death of father, neglect towards good and virtuous deeds — 1279.

Dasa of Ravi in an exalted Navamsa increase, acquisition of wealth by courageous and warlike deeds, enjoyment from various sources, sexual happiness, gains in females and clothing, and constant losses among paternal relations –1280.

Dasa of Ravi in a debiliated Navamsa travels resulting in losses to wife, children, money and lands, neglected by people and rejected by relations, mental troubles, and sufferings from fevers, and venereal complaints––1281

In the commencement of Ravi, Dasa—sorrow, sickness to father consumption and mental worry. In the middle, loss of cattle, and in the end advance and respect from education—1282.

The Dasa of Ravi in the 6th house—money losses, great sorrows, diseases from Gulma, and Kshaya, and panitra, difficulties in passing urine, and various venereal complaints—1283.

The Dasa of Ravi in the 8th—great bodily unhappiness or pains, poverty, intermittent fevers, disease in the eyes, fever and diahorrea, and travel to foreign places—1284.

The Dasa of Ravi in the 12th house—sorrow, loss of money, children, females, lands, parents, sin, travelling from place to place, fears and dangers from poisons, rulers, disease in the feet, quarrels from learning, conversation, friendship enjoyment, and company, and losses to horses—1285.

The Dasa of Ravi combining in the second house—sorrow and danger from begetting chil dren, from relations misery, harsh words and quarrels, revenge and loss of wife, and wealth, fear from rulers, loss of issues, lands, clothes and conveyances. If Ravi is in com. bination with a benefic, the evil results should not be predicted — 1286.

The Dasa of Ravi in the 3rd—great happiness and courage, respect of rulers, money gains, hatred of brothers and danger— 1287.

The Dasa of Ravi in the 4th house—danger to body, issues, wife, friends, lands, houses, forsaking his own country, losses in carriages and horses, and fear from thieves, poison, fires and weapons—1288.

The Dasa of Ravi in the 7th house—death or disease to wife, dirty and untimely meals, not properly cooked, and wanting in milk, curds, ghee and other palatable accessories—1289.

The Dasa of Ravi in the 10th house—acquisition of political power, wealth, friendship of princes, courage, success in undertakings, high reputation, success in all discussions, recognition of merits by rulers —1290.

The Dasa of Ravi in the 11th house—acquisitian of wealth, good and virtuous deeds, gain of power, happiness from wife, children, conveyances, ornaments, clothes, and physical enjoyments — 1291.

The results in planetary periods will be determined by the details given to planets in the chapter on tectraricalities, their charasteristics, means of livelihood ascribed to them, their combinations, aspects, their significances, lordships, and other particulars, which must be well studied—1292.

The Dasa of Ravi endowed with Sthanabala—gains from cultivation, cows, lands, conveyances, clothes, happiness, respect of Princes, wealth from others, attractiveness of body or appearance, doing good to all classes, high reputation, ornaments, engagements with relations and friends, and meritorious work, and pilgrimages to holy places—1293.

(See ch. II Notes on Br. Ja. p. 49.)

The Dasa of Ravi without Sthanabala—weakness, loss of money, foreign travel, hatred of relations, sorrow and foreign residence—1294.

The Dasa of Ravi with Digbala—he will earn money, reputation and respect from many directions and will enjoy them with happiness, power, ornaments and lands. If Ravi has no Digbala then these results will be negatived—1295.

The Dasa of Ravi with Kalabala—success in lands, cultivation, money power, respect among rulers. When Ravi has no Kala Bala, the results will be nullified—1296.

The Dasa of Ravi in Nisargikabala—he will get all sorts of pleasures and enjoyments unsolicited and without any efforts, wealth, ornaments, lands, articles of comfort, and clothes. But when Ravi has no Nisargikabala he will lose them—1297.

The Dasa of Ravi with Chestabala—self acquired wealth and reputation, great happiness and respect from Kings, wife, children, cultivation conveyances, and gems. When he does not possess Chestabala, he will suffer losses from these sources—1298.

The Dasa of Ravi when powerfuly aspected by planets—unexpected and large gains, all sorts of happiness. When not powerfully aspected these will not flourish—1229.

The Dasa of Ravi in junction in cruel shastiamsas—expelled from country, fear and trouble from anger of rulers, irritable and peevish, head-ache or giddiness, danger and death to father and his side relations—1300.

The Dasa of Ravi occupying Paravatamsa etc.,—good intelligence, reputation, much wealth, royal favours, good wife, issues, friends, and relations—1301.

The results of exaltation etc., will come first, then comes the results of places, third the results of aspects, similarly for evil planets—1302.

In the Dasa of Ravi occupying swrpa or pasa Drekkanna etc., —fear from serpents, poisons, fires, tanks, wells, and also many sources of sorrow and misery—1303.

In the Dasa of Ravi in exaltation, but occupying debilitated Navamsa—death of wife, death and danger to his near relations, troubles to children and dangers, so say the learned Munis—1304.

If Ravi occupies a debilitated Rasi and an exalted Navamsa— much happiness, and achievement of political power, in the com- mencement and loss of power and emaciation in the end—1305.

NOTES.

Stanzas 1258 to 1305 inclusive.

The results have been plainly stated by Venkataswara from the different points of solar positions, and he could not have done better. Even as he has done the work has bulged out into more than a thousand and eight hundred stanzas, and the readers have seen, that in spite of my scholarship, and the knack and capacity I possess for translating in brief and clear language, it has come up to more than a thousand printed pages.   Probably I could have omitted a few more explanations or shortened a few more illustrations but I think I have not been verbose, and the reader will see that it cannot be fur- ther abbreviated without loss of efficiency and lucidity.   Almost all the positions which Ravi could assume in a horoscope have been des- cribed. Take for example. Ravi is good in 10 and 11. But here he will give different results as he is exalted or debilitated or is in a friendly or unfriendly sign. Take Kataka as Lagna, with Ravi in 10 or Mesha. Ravi is exalted and also is in 10 and therefore good and powerful.   But suppose there is Sani also there. The results both of exaltation and Digbala should considerably be modified, but suppose there is also Kuja there. Then Ravi and Kuja become more powerful than Sani and the Phalam is good, and mixed with evil Saturn in results.   But if Rahu joins them, complications ensue, and no one writer however voluminous he may be, can give all possible combinations, which are endless and infinite in their adjustments, Ravi is the lord of some events in life, he becomes the lord of some Bhava or signification, and his different states also give him power to alter articles and objects which he governs. All these have to be taken into consideration, and in Dasa and Vidasa, and other sub and minor divisions, such as results must be selected as would suit Ravi's capacity, his power, and his various surroundings and sources of strength and weakness. The balancing of evidence is a great power and judgment must be strong in an astrologer before he can ever predict correctly events in the future. Suppose Makara is Lagna and Ravi is in Thula in his fall. He has digbala, but his debilitation has taken away much of his value. Put Sani in Thula. Then we have Sani in exaltation and Ravi in Neecha.

In the prediction of results of Ravi Dasa, for Kataka Lagna, when Ravi and Sani are in the 10th, and for Makara Lagna when the same Ravi and Sani are in the 10th, great gulf lies and if the astrologer is not careful, he will fall into hopeless confusions and errors. For Kataka Ravi is good as lord of 2nd and friend of its lord Chandra. For Makara Ravi is bad as the lord of the 8th and also as a bitter enemy of its lord Sani. Besides, results of exaltations among planets are different, and all these, though not enumerated in this work, the author presumes in the reader a clear knowledge of these technicalities and subject to their lordships, conjunctions, aspects and other sources of strength, and he expects the student to weigh the evidence well before any inferences could be drawn. Astrology is a noble, difficult, divine, and complicated. science and the reader should be careful and painstaking.

Chandra Dasa in Paramacha—flowers, clothes, respect, pleasure from wife, issues, wealth, and their associations and agreeable company—1306.

Chandra in exaltation—enjoyment from wife and children, milk, food, clothes, jewels, travels in foreign countries and quarrels among his own relations—1307.

Chandra in Aroha (*ascent*)—attraction, comeliness, wife, money, children, clothes, worship of God, Kingdom, good food, charitable feeding of holy Bramins—1308.

Chandra in Avaroha (*descent*)—losses and troubles to wife, children, clothes, happiness, mental worry and derangement, displeasure of his own kinsmen, fear from fire, rulers and thieves, and falls in wells and tanks—1309.

Chandra in a Neecha Navamsa—losses and troubles from various articles and sources, service under a mean ruler, unhappy meals, and mental worry—1310.

Chandra in Moolathrikona—great respect among sovereigns, money gains, acquisition of lands, children, wife, clothes, and jewels, happiness through mother, happiness and great sexual enjoyments —1311.

Chandra in his own house—large gains from cultivations, happiness, happiness from connection with beautiful and good dancing women, respect among official circles, female children and agreeableness among relations—1312.

Chandra in a bitter enemy's house—heavy losses from quarrels and litigation, dirty clothing and unwholesome food, and gains from lands, money, wife, children, water, conveyances—1313.

NOTES.

The latter part is against recognised principles of astrology and the language used signifies also their losses. (*See p. 126 Br. Jr :*) This view is corroborated by the next stanza. Some of the commentators have made a mess of this stanza. A negative added will set matters right—1313.

Chandra in an unfriendly Rasi—destitution in clothing and ornaments, travels in foreign lands, mean degrading service or engagements as mean servants, wandering in different countries neglected by friends and relations misery and unhappiness—1314.

Chandra in a friendly house—friendship with rulers, gain of wealth, and employment, and watery substances or products, clothing of various colors and descriptions, excellent and praiseworthy conversations and speeches—1315.

Chandra in a very intimate friend's house—great reputation from authorship and scholarship, and attraction through such a reputation to the rulers, and happiness, success and pleasure, through wife, children, lands, relations and friends—1316.

Chandra in a neutral's house—gains in gold and lands, small happiness, sickness among relations and travelling in foreign regions —1317.

Chandra in debilitation—accidents, danger, great sorrow, residence in forests and unhealthy places, pining and sorrow through imprisonment and confinement and chains in jails, want of food, displeasure of Kings, troubles ftom fires and thieves and danger to wife and children—1318.

Chandra when weak—losses among issues, wife, friends, Kingdom, money, power, lands, hatred of relations, mental trouble and derangement, mean profession, and heavy debts—1319.

Chandra when full—success in all attempts and from all sources. getting fame by publishing books and then attracting public attention and commanding respect from rulers, enjoyment and mental pleasure, from wife, children, money power, and doing good and charitable work—1320.

Chandra in conjunction with an exalted planet—mental elation, pleasure from sexual correspondence, wife, friends, and children— 1821.

Chandra with an evil planet—unhappiness from fire thieves, and rulers, loss of wife, children and relations, foreign travels, and doing sinful deeds--1322.

Chandra with a benefic—good deeds, gains in cows, lands,

clothes, jewels, gold, baths in holy rivers and ponds, and happiness from sexual enjoyment with other women—1323.

Chandra aspected by a malefic—doing unprofitable work, great anger, dirty meals, death of mother, or maternal relations—1324.

Chandra aspected by a benefic—extending help to others, great reputation, gaining desired objects, respect of rulers, and pleasure from getting watery products –1325.

Chandra in Mulathrikona—great wealth, many children, renunciation of worldly pleasures, after quarrels with relations, he will become their leader—1326.

Chandra in 4—death of mother, happiness, carriages, lands, success from cultivation, new houses, reputation, and publishing works of various descriptions under his name—1327.

Chandra in 7—getting wife, female children, good beds, clothes, mental worry and emaciation from excessive venereal complaints—1328.

Chandra in 10—reputation, good education, performing religious sacrifices, great happiness, lands, children, vehicles, clothes and enjoyment—1329.

Chandra in debililated Navamsa—great sorrow, disease in feet and eyes, quarrels, and defeats, and mental pleasure—1330.

Chandra in exalted Navamsa—great happiness, many sources of gain, respect of kings, good bodily development,—1331.

In the beginning of his Dasa Chandra will give respect reputation and happiness, in the middle loss of female children, and in the end gain of wealth, clothes and pleasures—1332.

Chandra in the 6th—sorrow, quarrels, hatred, fear from fires, thieves and rulers, danger from water, misery from diabettes and acquisition of riches—1333.

Chandra in the 8th—leanness of body, danger from water, misery, travels to foreign places, hatred of all classes, bad food, danger and death to mother and motherly relations —1334.

Chandra in the 12th—loss of lands, confiscation of grains and money, ejection from native place, and incalculable sorrow—1335.

Chandra in the 2nd—wife, sons, lands cows money, happiness, good milk and rich food, sexual happiness and boths in suered waters—1336.

Chandra in the 3rd—great happiness, many kinds of profits, determination, happiness to brothers, successful cultivation, good food, ornaments, milk and its products —1337.

Chandra in the 11th—acquisition of various kinds of articles, rich food, milk, clothes, sexual enjoyment, female children, mental elations,—1338.

Chandra in combustion—sorrow, hatred of relations, loss of wealth, fears from fires and rulers, death of mother, and losses in cultivations and grains,—1339.

Chandra in Sthanabala—riches, ruputation, education, feeding of Brahmins and worship of Gods, Pertaining to royal family, acquisition of kingdom, or lands, females, cloths ornaments, money from cultivation, earning profits by selling cows, good milk, and food, of a luxurious nature, ghee, curds, garlands and other enjoyments.—1340.

Chandra without Sthanabala—loss of house, and residence elsewhere, distruction of relations, and losses in cultivation of —1341.

Chandra with Digbala—getting various useful articles from many places, progress in education, friendship with rulers, respect among his own community, horses and elephants,—1342.

Chandra with Kalabala—lordship over men and horses, cows lands and cultivation, surrounded by educated men, and he will have conveyances ornamented by nails, hairs, tusks, skins and clothes 1343.

Chandra with Nisargikabala—gain of money without effort, lands and conveyances, respect of kings and many conveyances —1344.

Chandra in Drigbala—favours and wealth from mighty monarchs, helping poor, and gaining his desires, —1345.

Chandra in cruel Shastiamsas —great misery, danger to wife and children, displeasure of kings, haughty discussion, quarrels, —1346.

Chandra in beneficial shastiamsas—many children, servants and wealth, success, happiness and reputation, high education-1347.

Chandra in Paravatamsa—great renown, educational progress and pleasure, worship and happiness, baths in sacred waters —1348.

Chandra in cruel Drekkanas —disease, sinful deeds, causing troubles to cows and Brahmins,—1349.

In this Chandra Dasa the first results will be due to his positions in the Rasi, second the results will be due to Amsas he occupies and third the results will flow from conjunction and aspects,—1350,

KUJA DASA.

Kuja in deep exaltation—gains, success in battles or fights, respect and favour of kings, pleasure from brothers, females children and sweet conversations—1351.

Kuja in deep exaltation—lands, friendship with rulers, enjoyment of lands, riches, wife, children, friends and relations, horses and conveyances, and worthy residence in foreign countries—1352.

Kuja in Ascent—happiness, respect of rulers, minister, courage, pleasure, wealth in after life and happiness from cows, horses and elephants,—1353.

Kuja in Descent—loss of place and wealth, sin, anger and terror, and worry through them, residency in a foreign place, hatred of relations, fear and misery through fires, rulers.

Kuja in debilitation—protecting relations by mean profession, dirty and unwholesome food, destruction to cows, horses and elephants, own people, and troubles and fear from rulers, thieves and fires,—1355.

Kuja in Moolathrikona—good milk, food, drink clothes and ornaments, reading and hearing of puranas and stories of righteousness, elevation and purity of mind, prosperity to brothers and good cultivaticn—1356.

Kuja in his own house—wealth, lands, power, happiness and conveyances, two names and prosperity to brothers,—1357.

Kuja in a bitter enemy's house—quarrels, and sorrows, misunderstandings with rulers and members of royal family, sickness and loss to wife, children, friends, money, lands, and relations—1358.

Kuja in an unfriendly house—quarrels, troubles from enemies, sorrow, from thieves, fire, kings and poisons, disease in the anus genetal organs, urinal discharges and eyes and other difficulties —1359.

Kuja in a friendly house—reconiliation and friendship with enemies, fear from thieves and fires, quarrels with drunkards and gamblers, land litigation, destruction to cultivation, sin, sorrow and anger—1360.

Kuja in intimate friend's house—gains in lands and wealth from Princes, good food and clothing, sacrifices, marriages, acquisitton of wealth from foreign lands,—1361.

Kuja in a neutral's house—miscellaneous constructions and works in house, meals from difficult and dangerous sources, enmity from females, children brothers, enemies, kings and fires—1362.

Kuja in conjunction with a debililated planet—mental torture and derangement, servive work, eating at others places, destruction to wife and children also from rulers, fires and thieves,—1363.

Kuja in conjunction with an exalted planet—little happiness, food, drink, and clothes, leaving on hard labour, respect of rulers, and trouble to wife and children—1364.

Kuja in conjunction with a malefic—doing always sinful work, prejudicial to brothers, relations, Brahmins, Gods and religious —1365.

Kuja with a benefic—little happiness, emaciation of the body, disease in the bodily limbs, litigation about lands, and success in it, discussions in learning and foreign travels,—1366.

Kuja aspected by a benefic—loss of wealth and lands. If such a Kuja joins an exalted planet etc.,—he will give very good results, —1367.

Kuja aspected by a malefic—great sorrow and trouble, expulsion from the country from the anger of rulers, and thus misery from the separation of wife and children,—1368.

Kuja in a Kendra—sorrow from thieves and poisons, fatigue, quarrels and enmity and foreign residence,—1369.

Kuja in the 4th—removal from own country, hatred of relations, trouble from fires and thieves, respected by kings, travelling in deep and impenetrable jungles,—1370.

Kuja in the 7th—death to wife, disease in the anus and sexual organs. These will happen when Kuja is not in evaltation or combined with exalted planets—1371.

Kuja in the 10th—doing irreligeous and impious deeds sorrow, disturbance to power and influence, disgrace and education, and loss to wife and children,—1372,

Kuja with Ravi—sorrow, hatred and enmity with wife, quarrels in hiso wnlands and seeking shelter in other lands,—1373.

Kuja in the 2nd—good cultivation, growing wealthy among his own relations, paying penalties to rulers, and disease in the face and eyes,—1374.

Kuja in the 3rd—gives happiness, power, influence, respect among rulers, courage, wealth, wife, brothers,—1875.

Kuja in the 5th—death of children, derangement of mind, sickness, and if the 5th is an unfriendly sign sorrow from brothers and great sickness—1876.

Kuja in the 5th—gives great intelligence, reputation, tact and skill and disease in the eyes—1376a.

Kuja in the 8th—great sorrow and fear, small pox, enmity from food, and change of place—1377.

Kuja in the 9th—change of place, death of father and mother, trouble, disturbance to prayers, and great fear—1378.

Kuja in the 11th—success, power and Kingdom, wealth and happiness, determination, royal patronage, supporting others by recommendations, and personal attraction—1379.

Kuja in the 12th—fines and penalties, fear from rulers, destruction to place, children, wife, and foreign residence to brothers—1380.

Kuja in an exalted Navamsa—mental elation and pleasure, happiness from success, great sexual connections with dancing women, respect of kings—1381.

Kuja in a debilitated Navamsa—will become mean, mental worry and derangement, loss of wealth by fines from rulers, will be always fond of eating and sexual pleasures—1382.

In the period of Kuja in the beginning there will be losses from various sources and articles, in the middle fear and troubles from rulers and thieves and fires,--1383.

In the end destruction to brothers, wife, children and wealth, and fear from fire, urinal diseases and enlargement of spleen. These must be predicted only when Kuja is not in exaltation 1384.

Kuja in Sthanabala—happiness from wealth and wife, convenient places reputation, and happiness, and official worry 1385.

Kuja without sthanabala—changr of place, earning by mean and despicable profession—1386.

Kuja with Digbala—gains from kings, success in wars, cows conveyances, clothes, wealth, cultivation, fame in all directions and praised for brave and warlike deeds 1387.

Kuja with Kalabala—attaining corrected objects, great happiness, gains from silks ornaments, clothes and gems, umbrellas, cows, elephants and lands 1388.

Kuja with Nisurgikabala—getting all desirable objects from influence wtth kings, friends children, relations, cows, jewels, clothes, and bodily happiness—1389.

Kuja without this bala or power—loss of place, wealthy, eyes, dirty meals, dirty wife, rotten nails, danger to father, and sickness to brothers—1390.

Kuja in retrograde—great fear, troubles from thieves, fires, serpents, shelter in forests, repulsion—1391.

Knja in Drigbala—gains from all sources from the patronage of royalty, and happiness from children, friends, cows, lands ornaments, cloths, and good health—1392.

Knja in cruel shastiamsas—troubles from enemies, imprisonment and loss of wealth from all undertakings—1393.

Kuja in beneficial shastiamsas - good results must be predicted, marriage, religious sacrifices and help to fellow creatures—1394.

Kuja in Paravata etc.,—great pleasure, lands, wealth, enjoyment, wife. conveyances, good food and pleasure 1395,

Kuja in cruel Drekanna—mental worry, imprisonment fear from poison, and confinement in chains—1396.

Exalted Kuja in debilitated Navamsa—fears from fire rajas, poison, death of brothers, 1397.

Debilitated Kuja in exalted Navamsa —happiness from lands, wife, children, friends, and wealth—1398.

NOTES.

The Periods of Ravi Chandra, and Kuja have been elaborately sketched and the differences in results from the various states of planets, in their positions, combinations, aspects and other sources of strength and weakness have been given. Death may be caused by any planet and so also danger, mental worry, sorrow losses of children, wife, friends, relations, lands and conveyances But each planet has a way of doing an event and the details as to how that will be produced have been sketclud in the above stanzas. Full information has been thrown on this subject by Venkatasa and notes are hardly called for as the translation has been made so very lucid and plain. The principal sources of happiness or misery to an individual would be generally from want of money, increase of enemies, death and danger to wife, children, friends and relations, and troubles from loss of lands, conveyances, bad food, neglect of his own community, hatred of rulers, litigation, brothers, cousins, venereal complaints, bad company, thieves and fires unsuccessful cultivation, expulsion from ones own country and house, foreign residence and public disgrace, and bodily weakness, sickness, and losethsomness. Bad planets, or good planets in bad Amsas or Virgas, produce physical and mental trouble. Benefics produce good, planets in exaltation, in their own houses, Mulathrikonas, and beneficial conjunctions and aspects, produce good results. These various sources should be carefully remembered and analysed before predictions are ventured by the astrologer.

RESULTS OF BUDA DASA.

Buda in deep exaltation—great wealth and reputation from it, and happiness, lordship over men, sacrificial performances and good name thereby, female children, lands, riches and great enjoyment— 139?.

Buda in exaltation—respect and wealth, good wealth, enjoyment, children and possession of cows, horses, elephants, and their enjoyment—1400.

Buda in ascending—cows, cattle, horses, sacrifices, delicious food, ornaments, clothes, conveyances, gains from merchandise, lands, and satisfaction from giving health to others—1401.

Buda in descent—great sorrow and trouble, senselessness adultary and fears from rajas, fires and thieves—1402.

Buda in debilitation—senselessness, hatred of his community, loss of place and relations, foreign travel and residence in forest— 1403.

Buda in Mulathrikona—great happiness, education, reputation enquiry after Truth (God) hearing and reading of sacred religious books, and philosophic discussions—1464.

Buda in his own house—wealth in money, and grains, good merchandise, cows, children, money, and enjoyment, rich food, milk, clothes, ornaments, wife—1405.

Buda in a bitter enemy's house—great unhappiness, loss of money and appointment, hatred of relations, disappointments in good and religious work, sinful deeds—1046.

Buda in an unfriendly house—fear from enemies, and rulers, disturbance to education, degradation, bad food and loss of money, wife and children—1407.

Buda in a friendly house—gains, happiness, spread of his name and works, poetry and prose published under his name—1401.

Buda in an intimate friendly sign—great gain and happiness, respect and royal friendship, wife and children, and respect of relations—1409.

Buda in a neutral house—grains, clothes and children, loss of power, untimely meals, and fasting, senselessness, and cutaneous diseases—1410.

Buda in conjunction with a debilitated planet—great trouble, change of place, destruction to relations, irreligiousness, mental worry—1411.

Buda with an exalted planet—great happiness, wealth and good education, merchandise, cattle rearing and cultivation—1412.

Buda with a malefic—sinful work, loss to lands. money, wife, chiidren, cultivation, cows and lands—1413.

Buda with a benefic—great happiness enjoyment of power, pleasure and reputation, and delight from wife and children—1414.

Buda aspected by a benefic—great reputation, pleasure from learned discussions, sacred lore, attraction and elevation—1415.

Buda aspected by a malefic—loss of grains, destruction of relations, travels to foreign countries, change of own place, servile work and quarrels there—1416.

Buda in a Kendra—friendship with rulers, wealth, grains, children, wife, sacred sacrifices and other meritorious acts, respect of kings, reputation, sweet food, good beds clothes, ornaments—1417.

Buda in birth—lordship over people, protection of cows, cultivation, renown, parapharnalia of royalty like drums, music etc., luxurious conveyances, baths in sacred ponds and rivers, world ruputation—1418.

Buda in the 2nd—good education, respect and reputation, royalty or statesmanship—1419.

Buda in the 3rd—laziness, dispepia, enlargement of spleen or liver vomiting, loss of brothers, respect of rulers—1420.

Buda in the 4th—destruction of houses and grains, unhappiness, death of maternal relations, loss of service, and change of place—1421.

Buda in the 5th—cruel mind, great misery, mean acts, difficulties in public service and gain of wealth with great difficulty—1422.

Buda in the 6th, 8th or 12th—many complicated diseases in the body by the mixture of *Vata* (wind), *Pitha* (bile) and *Sleshma* (phlegm), iches, jaundice, bile, danger from rulers, fires, thieves, and emaciation—1423.

Buda in the 12th—loss or injury to limbs, hatred of wife and relations, fear from the anger of Raja, sudden danger to life by accident, forgetfulness and disappointments—1424

Buda in the 7th—children, wife and wealth, pleasure from education, pure and rich clothes, praise for his courageous deeds and friendship of many rajas—1425.

Buda in the 9th—gain of wealth, wife. children and enjoyment. baths in holy and sacred ponds and rivers, doing meditation, sacrificial fires and charities and religious ceremonies—1426.

Buda in the 10th—good work, elevated political position, enjoyment, authorship, renown for his deeds, gain of wife, children and riches—1427.

Worship of holy Brahmins, acquisition of kingdom or lands, lordship over men, development of poetical faculties, sacrifices, friendliness with relations—1428.

Buda in the 11th—acquisition of wealth by various means, by gifts, cultivation, patronage and merchandise—1429.

Buda in exalted Navamsa—gain of children, jewels and wealth, mental pleasure, sexual pleasures, hopefulness and courage and baths in sacred rivers and ponds—1430.

Buda in debilitated Navamsa—earning livelihood by mean callings, dependency, service—1431.

In the commencement Buda will give wealth and grains, in the middle, respect and gains from royal personages, and in the end hatred of his own people—1432.

Buda with Ravi — many kinds of mishaps, mental worry, hatred of relations and rulers, calumny and eye disease—1433.

Buda with Sthanabala—reputation, possession of royal power, mental courage, great enjoyment and performance of sacrificial rites—1434.

Buda without Sthanabala—destruction of place, fear for wife and children, residence in foreign territory, misery and many disgraceful acts—1435.

Buda with Digbala—becoming rich by getting money from various places, happiness, friendship of foreign princes, sweet scents and flowers—1436.

Buda with Kalabala—good health, peaceful life, respect from wife, children and rulers, baths in the Ganges and purification thereby—1437.

Buda with Nisargikabala—success and meritorious enjoyment without any attempts, learned discussions, hatred of relations death of mother, or maternal relations—1438.

Buda in retrograde — wife, children and wealth, Puranas, sacrifices and charities, baths in the sea—1439.

Buda with Drigbala—equanimity and love for all creatures, sexual happiness, and possessed of kingly power—1440.

Buda in cruel shastiamsas—great fear, worry from fires, thieves and rajas, these will happen when Buda is devoid of beneficial conjunctions or aspects—1441.

Buda in Mridwamsa etc,—gain of lands and great happiness, sympathetic heart, love for all creatures, cultivation, enjoyment, wealth and children—1442,

Buda in Vaiseshikamsa—great respect from rulers, sweet scents, flowers, and clothes, meditative happiness, pleasure from philosophic discussion—1443.

Buda in cruel Drikkanas—fear from authorities, thieves and fires, change and loss of place, great fear—1444.

Exalted Buda in debilitated Navamsa—power, wealth, reputation and happiness will suddenly disappear—1445.

Debilitated Buda in exalted .Navamsa—the man will have evil results in the beginning and happiness and peace afterwards—1446.

NOTES.

The stanzas are so clearly put, so simple and so explanatory that no notes are really needed. As regards Sthanabala, Drigbala etc. *(see my notes on Br. Jataka St.* 19 *p. 45)*

RESULTS OF GURU DASA.

Guru in Paramocha—kingdom, great mental pleasure, happiness, reputation, large numbers of horses and elephants, coronations and leadership of own people—1447.

Guru in Kataka—wealth in the latter half, respect of kings, travels in foreign countries, great political appointment, and a body emaciated by great sorrows—1448.

Guru in ascent—respect, gain of lands and wealth, musical enjoyments happiness from wife, sons, and rajas, great reputation by scholarship—1449.

The period of Guru gives—lordship or magistracy over villages and towns, or countries, wealth gained from Brahmin kings or high caste rulers, high intelligence, attractive personality and philosophic and philanthropic wisdom—1450.

Guru in descent—occasional happiness and subsequent misery, reputation and immediate disgrace, personal attractiveness, and political power and their loss again—1451

Guru in deep debilitation—destruction of houses. mutual misunderstandings, loss in cultivation and service under others—1452.

Guru in Mulathrikona—great happiness from kingdom, children, wealth, wife, lands, good conveyances, wealth, gained by self exertions, religious performances and sacrifices, and worshipped by people—1453.

Guru in his own house—gains from kingdom, lands, grains, happiness, clothes, good food and milk, p easure from cows, elephants and horses. poetical composition, meritorious deeds, and deep knowledge in Vedas and Agamas—1454.

Guru in bitter enemy's house—sorrow and mental distraction, land litigation, loss of wife, wealth and children, fear from thieves, rulers and fires, eye disease—1455.

Guru in an unfriendly sign—increase in land, wealth, beds, clothes, happiness, respect of kings, there will be sorrow always from wife, children, servants, brothers—1456,

Guru in Adhimitra sign—respect of sovereigns, noise of war drums, and arms, indicative of eminent rank, and acquisition of various articles from many distant quarters—1457.

Guru in a friendly house—friendship with royal personage, gains and reputations, success in literary discussions, rich food, sweet scents, soft meals, charities—1458.

Guru in neutral house—ordinary wealth given by Kings, cultivation, coins, lands, wealth, and pleasure through these and ornaments, decorated by varied colored clothes 1459.

Guru with a debilitated planet—mental worry, mean service, false blame, fear, disagreement between wife children and relations—1460.

Guru with an exalted planet—great happiness, constructing tanks, wells, temples and other meritorious buildings and respect of kings—1461.

Guru with a malific—evil thoughts and heart, outside meritorious pretensions, happiness from lands, money, wife and children—1462.

Guru with a benefic—travelling with kings, happiness from the gains of fine and delicate clothes, money from gifts or from kings and sacrificial rites—1463.

Guru aspected by a malefic—happiness, some courage, occasional reputation. occasional gains and losses from thieves—1464.

Guru aspected by a benefic—gains from kings, worship, feeding of large number of Brahmins, baths in holy waters and worship of Gurus—1465.

Guru in a kendra—lands, kingdom. and happiness from them and also from the wife, enjoyment from various articles of luxury and happiness, and leader among those who protect many people—1466.

Guru in birth—happiness, neat and fine clothing and

jewels, carried by men with drums of various descriptions, elephants, horses and conveyances—1467.

Guru in the 4th—three conveyances, new friends, if born in a Raja Yoga, kingly power, if not power and influence—1468.

Guru in the 7th—happiness from wife and children, travelling to foreign countries, success in quarrels, meditating on Parabrahma and doing virtuous deeds—1469.

Guru in the 10th—gains of kingdom and wealth, if born in a Raja Yoga he will get a kingdom, if not he will get wealth, wife, children and do virtuous deeds. He will enjoy all these as does a king and his commands will be obeyed and he will be like a lord—1470.

Guru in a thrikona—he will have women, children, riches, grains, wisdom, nice food and milk, clothes and silks, and conveyances, happiness and profits from these sources also—1471.

Guru in the 5th—will get initiation in Mantras, male children, great happiness, respect of Kings, Vedantic studies, progress in such lore—1472.

Guru in exaltation Navamsa—wealth and enjoyment like a king, gems, coralbeads, pearls, respect and friendship of all and great happiness—1473.

Guru in Neecha Navamsa—fear from the king, enlargement of spleen, cutaneous eruptions, change of place, hatred of relations, fear from rajas, thieves and fires, and from his own castemen—1474.

Guru with Ravi—troubled by fevers, lean, troubled by diseases in the upper body, cruel mind and disturbed family—1475.

Guru in the beginning gives great happiness and respect, in the middle wife and children, and troubles in the last portion—1476.

Guru in the 2nd—wealth, royal patronage, and learned discussions before princely assemblies, helpful to others and happy and successful—1477.

Wealth given by rulers, lands given by brothers or other females, scents,flowers, sandal,fine and costly clothes, ornaments, helpful to others, wisdom and courage—1478.

Guru in the 3rd—happiness from brothers, wealth, royal patronage, clothes and ornaments, scents and flowers—1479.

Guru in the 6th—health, gain of wife and children. These results will happen in the beginning but in the end, fear from wife, money and thieves and disease—1480.

Guru in the 8th—happiness, loss of his relations, change of place, and foreign travel in the commencement. In the end enjoyment from wife, children and royal patronage—1481.

Guru in the 11th—gain of kingdom, much trouble with rulers for the sake of wife, children, females and hatred of his own relations—1482.

Guru in the 12th—gain of conveyances, travels in foreign countries,many miseries from various sources—1483

Guru with Sthanabala—increase in lands, wife, children, clothes, horses. elephants, gold, clothes of varied colors. When Guru has *Digbala* he will be renowned in the world, Guru with *Kalabala* will enable a man to get wealth and respect from royal females—1484.

Guru with Nisargikabala — happiness. enjoyment,

pleasure from reading, sexual happiness, baths, in sacred river—1485.

Guru in retrograde—great wealth, children, wife, conquest and success, royal friendship, sweet scents, Chinese clothes—1486.

Guru in Drigbala—all sorts of enjoyment and wealth through the favour of Kings. travelling always in foreign countries--1487.

Guru in cruel Shastiamsas—great misery, disgrace from royal displeasure—1488.

Guru in beneficial Shastiamsas—great enjoyment, conveyances, respect from relations, sacrificial performances, marriage festivities—1489.

Guru in Paravatamsa—great happiness, fine meals, silks, gold, jewels, coralbeads—1490.

Guru in malefic Drikkana—imprisonment, confinement chains, quarrels with wife—1491.

Guru exalted in a debilitated Navamsa—acquiring great wealth which suddenly melts away—1492.

Debilitated Guru in an exalted Navamsa—though wealth melts away he will acquire fresh wealth—1493.

RESULTS OF SUKRA DASA.

Sukra in deep exaltation—pleasure from women, enjoyment of wife and wealth, wearing good clothes, food, sleep, wife and children, precious stones—1494.

Sukra in exaltation—losses from female connections, doing acts against world's opinion, danger to parents, misery, headache, respect of sovereigns—1495.

Sukra in Ascent—grains, clothes attraction, respect,

hatred of relations for doing good, loss of mother, sexual intercourse with other women—1496.

Sukra in descent—adultery with vigorous dancing girls, wealth, sorrow to females, relations and children, mental destruction, heart pain, venereal sorrows—1497.

Sukra in deep debilitation—He will be troubled by shooting pains, fear from frequent disappointments, suffering mental worry without courage, on account of the troubles of wife and children—1498.

Sukra in Mula Thrikona—great political appointment, mercantile success, wealth from female sources, renowned, learned in sciences—1499.

Sukra in his own house—females, children, wealthy, courage, always jolly, without hatred, doing good to others, greatness—1500.

Sukra in Adhisatrusthana—danger to wealth, wife and children, emaciated body from the occurrence of family troubles, enlargement of spleen, eye disease, glandular diseases—1501.

Sukra in an unfriendly house—death to children and wife, loss of money, fear from royal anger, doing all sorts of things for several purposes—1502.

Sukra in a friendly house—helping others, well read in sciences constructor of wells, tanks and gardens, punisher of criminals, possessing excellent qualities worthy of imitation—1503.

Sukra in an intimate friend's house—royal patronage, respect, happiness, cows. wealth, horses, elephants and collection of servants, aristocractic paraphernalia—1504.

Sukra in a Neutral house—venereal complaints, enlargement of spleen, disease in the anus and eyes, meagre happiness, fear from rajas, thieves and fires, publishing works under his name—1505.

Sukra with a debilitated planet—great fear, calumny against his name, sinful deeds—1506.

Sukra with an exalted planet—pain of kingdom, greatness, commander of armies, gold, jewels, flowers, clothes, soft beds, ornaments, and conveyances carried by men, paraphernalia of various drums and other royal music—1507.

Sukra with a malefic—loss of residence, quarrels with relations, doing sinful acts against his own religion, picking quarrels—1508.

Sukra with a benefic—desirable enjoyment, wife and children, grains, royal respect, horses and elephants in large numbers, corals, pearls, and precious stones, and carried by men—1509.

Sukra with evil aspect—destruction to respect and wealth, quarrels with females, sorrow, change of place, residence in foreign countries, and doing work degrading to his religion and community—1510.

Sukra with a beneficial aspect—acquisition of wealth, honored by his own sovereign, extending his authority over all people, handsome bodily complexion, pleasure from friends and children—1511.

Sukra in Kendras—carried on men's shoulders, rich clothes, females, flowers, scents, nine varieties of gems and ornaments, attractive body, doing pleasing work to people, wealth, good and profitable cultivation, enjoyment with wife in water and possession of valuable and costly selection of articles—1512.

Sukra in birth—gains from royal personages, successful cultivation, helping people, grea⁺ elevation of mind and happiness therefrom—1513.

Sukra in the 4th—kingdom, great happiness, conveyances carried by men, increase in cultivation, crops, wealth, in cattle, family, friends and relations, spread of reputation by his own exertions and determination—1514.

Sukra in the 7th—death to wife or travel to foreign place, great venereal complaints, enlarged spleen, great loss to relations, children and wealth—1515.

Sukra in the 10th—performing meritorious acts and sacrifices, wealth, lands from kings, acquiring fresh wealths good care of body and its glossy attraction, renown in various directions, great power or kingdom, and lands—1516.

Sukra in the 5th—begetting children, reputation, royal respect, many dependents and help to them—1517.

Sukra in the 9th—royal respect and gains, sacrificial work, happiness to Gurus and parents, reputation—1518.

Sukra in the 2nd—lord of wealth, and wealthy, luxurious food, good speech, helpful, respect and patronage from local sovereigns—1519.

Sukra in the 3rd—courage, and hopefulness, independent, clothes of variegated colors, conveyances and happiness through the prosperity of brothers—1520.

Sukra in the 6th—losses to grains, relations, wealth, children, brothers, female diseases, disappointments, fears from enemies, rulers, fires and thieves—1521.

Sukra in the 8th—wounds or injuries from fires, weapons, thieves, untimely or disturbed meals, occasional happiness, gains and respect from rulers, and reputation—1522.

Sukra in the 11th—respect of kings, scents, garlands, ornaments, clothes, money and children, gains from mercantile speculations, charities and works published under his name, good cultivation—1523.

Sukra in the 12th—respect of kings, wealth, grains and happiness through them, and their enjoyment, loss of place, death of mother, travelling and mental distractions—1524.

Sukra in the Navamsa of Guru—destruction to wife and children, disappointments in all his efforts, doing work against religious and moral principles, loss of mother and mental worry—1525.

Sukra in Simha—dangers of all descriptions and consequent mental sorrow, upward shooting pains in the body and diseases, poor inclination to be engaged in paying work or in religious devotion—1526.

Sukra with Ravi—tenanting an old and dilapidated house, quarreling with people, loss of wife, death of brothers and quarrels with all—1527.

Sukra with Sthanabala—respect and gains from rulers, ornaments, always engaged in learned discussions, Government honors and titles.

Sukra with Digbala—gives, great reputation, happiness from clothes, children, wife, and wealth.

Sukra with Kalabala produces—happiness, wealth, reputation, Government titles and pleasure—1528.

Sukra with Nisargikabala—great pleasure and happiness, he will get pleasure and enjoyment from cows, lands, wealth, brothers, mothers and grains and these in turn also will have prosperity—1529.

Sukra in retrograde—great respect and gains from rulers, aristocratic or royal power, accompanied by drums, conveyances of the paraphernalia of rank and position, clothes of various colors, territories, ornaments, political power and influence—1530.

Sukra with Drigbala—performing religious and sacrificial rites, pleasure from education, happiness from fine beds, cots, clothes, coronation, quarrels, and hatred of relations and friends—1531.

Sukra in cruel Shastiamsas—fear from dangers and accidents, rulers, fires and robbers, destruction to cultivation, cattle, grains and lands—1532.

Sukra in beneficial Shastiamsas—great happiness, construction of tanks, wells and gardens and worship of Gods—1533.

Sukra in Vaiseshikamsa—great enjoyment, conveyances, respect and pleasure from presents from rulers, wealth from brothers, sisters and own wife—1534.

Debilitated Sukra in exalted Navamsa—gain from cultivation, cows, lands, merchandise wealth, grains—1535.

Exalted Sukra in Neecha Navamsa—great misery, loss of lands and power, and place of residence—1536.

Sukra in cruel Drekkana—fear from enemies, imprisonment and great misery, chains and troubles from robbers—1537.

NOTES.

All planets, it will be seen, in exaltation produce good but this good will vary with the nature of the planets and the position they may have taken at the birth time. Ravi or any planet in exaltation will give good, but the positions they take make a great deal of change in giving the results. Take Kataka as Lagna and Vrishabha as Lagna, with the sun in deep exaltation. For Kataka, sun becomes the lord of the 2nd and occupies the 10th house in deep

exaltation. 10th house indicates Karma or means of livelihood, and command, power, political significance and so on.
Here the sun is not only very powerful in his exaltation
but also by his ownership and occupation of 10th house
which is specially good for him and Mars as giving Dig
or Directional strength. He will give unbounded power,
courage, success and wealth. Take now birth as Vrishabha. The sun owns the 4th house and occupies the 12th
house in deep exaltation. 12th is not a good house and the
results therefore will not be as bright as they would be
for Kataka. Take Kanya as Lagna and Ravi owns the
12th house, occupies the 8th or house of danger and therefore will not give good results. Sani in the 2nd gives
certain results, but for Kanya he will be in the 2nd Thula
in an exaltation and therefore good and for Meena, he
will be in the second Mesha, but in debilitation. Venkatesa gives some unfavourable results for Guru in the 11th
house, whereas other astrological writers are all agreed in
giving good results, not only for Guru in the 11th but also
for all the planets. Where and whence he got his authority to do so, I am not in a position to say, but he must
have had some authority for such a statement. All these
and many more points, to be gathered from long study
careful analyses and much devotion cannot be given, even
in brief in one single work and therefore those who wish
to be benefitted by such works are expected to be in touch
with the principles of astrology and to such learned
authors can give some help. To actual blockheads or to
utterly indifferent students they cannot do much. Brilliant as the authors may be the students must be more
brilliant than they are to understand them fully and utilise
their services to the fullest extent. Fair intelligence,
devotion and careful study will be passes which will take
the readers to the doors of zenith.

RESULTS OF SANI DASA.

Sani in deep exaltation—lordship of villages, countries and assemblies, great pleasures and enjoyment, death to father and hatred of relations—1538.

Sani in exaltation—change of country, fear from mental worries, sorrows, loss of cultivation, merchandise, and means of livelihood, quarrels with local rulers—1539.

Sani in ascent—acquisition of money from kings, gains from mercantile transactions, cultivation, lands, cows, horses, wife and children—1540.

NOTES.

There is clearly some mistake both in print and in manuscripts about stanza 1539. How can an exalted planet give unfavourable results, on the other hand the results sketched for Sani Dasa when he is in oocha or exaltation in Dasa Bhukti Chandrika is quite contrary to what Venkatasa says here. In Parasara it is stated that Sani in exaltation will give money, good reputation, love of relations and friends, pleasure and elevation of mind and lordship or high political power. There must be some mistake.

Sani in Avaroha—loss of power, wife, money and children, anger of kings and consequent losses, dependency, disease in anus and eyes—1541.

Sani in debilitation—loss of children, wife and brothers, great danger, and loss of cultivation and wife with mean service—1542.

Sani in Mulathrikona—residence in foreign countries, two names or titles, lordship over town and hatred of wife, children and public—1543.

Sani in his own house—hatred, strength, courage,

reputation, patronage of king, gold, ornaments and servants and confidence generated by his position and surroundings—1544.

Sani in bitter enemy's house—change of place, hatred of relations, fear from fires and robbers, disturbed food, and anger of servants, wife and children—1545.

Sani in an unfriendly sign—getting wealth from Vysyas and loss of lands, cultivation and place, and hatred of thieves and rajas—1546.

Sani in a friendly house—skilful in medical and miscellaneous work, wisdom, strength, courage and great sorrow—1547.

Sani in an intimate friend's house—happiness, respect of kings, increase of cattle, cultivation, merchandise—1548.

Sani in a Neutral house—ordinary intelligence, friendship of children, friends and wife, servants, hatred of relations, emaciation, consumption and billiousness and windy complaints—1549.

Sani with a debilitated planet—great fear, hatred of learned men, residence in a foreign country and following a despicable livelihood—1550.

Sani with an exalted planet—great happiness, some country, some cultivation and destruction to menials—1551

Sani with a malefic—secret sins, sexual intercourse with worthless women and quarrels and troubles with mean fellows and thieves—1552.

Sani with a benefic—great wisdom, help to others, gain of wealth, good cultivation and black seed crops, blackgrain etc., like gingelly seeds—1553.

Sani with a malefic aspect—loss of servants, children, brothers, wealth, wife, blame from others, dirty and untimely meals, scents and flowers—1554,

Sani with a beneficial aspect—he will have wife, children, servants, money—In the end there will be losses to cows, lands, merchandise, cultivation—1555.

Sani in Kendras—quarrels, fatigue trouble, and many deaths to children, wife, wealth, friends—1556.

Sani in Lagna—venereal complaints, change of place foreign residence and destruction of mother and maternal relations—1557.

Sani in the 4th—headache, anger of kings, burning of house, travelling and loss of power and troubles from rajas, fires and thieves—1558.

Sani in the 7th—great suffering, several diseases, great hatred, and death through female anger—1559.

Sani in the 10th—loss of religious Karma, loss of power and traveling in foreign countries, imprisonment and worry from rulers—1560.

Sani in the 2nd—loss of money, disease in the anus and eyes, anger of king and misunderstanding, disgust of food and mental distraction—1561.

Sani in the 5th—loss of children, mental worry, anger of kings and loss of servants, and hatred of relations, wife, and sinner—1562.

Sani in the 6th—trouble from enemies, diseases and thieves, poison and destruction to lands, houses—1563.

Sani in the 3rd—gains from cows, money and enjoyment, courage and great mental elevation and putting down the Arishadvargas and great happiness—1564.

Sani in the 8th—constant destruction to money, children, power, lands, servants, cows, and buffaloes and wife—1565.

Sani in the 9th—loss of father and Guru, foreign travel and loss of many relation—1536.

Sani in the 11th—great many and unsolicited gains in money, happiness, wife, children and servants and happiness, elation of mind and money acquired by good cultivation—1567.

Sani in the 12th—fear from and loss through robbers, rulers and fire, many misfortunes, change of residence, many dangers, sorrows and loss of relations—1568.

Sani with Ravi—hatred of caste people, adultery with other women, hatred of servants and children and attempts to do great acts which involve the commission of various sins—1569.

Sani in Neechamsa—living by mean and disgraceful work, dependency on many and sorrow to and from wife, children, money—1570.

Sani in Oochamsa—many happy and enjoyable comforts, foreign travel and lordship over villages, towns and assemblies or associations—1571.

Sani in the commencement—great sorrow, death of brothers, in the middle foreign travel and in the end residence in other's houses and food served out by them—1572.

Sani with Sthanabala—happiness from wife, issues, money, fear from fire, thieves and rulers, relations, diseases to eyes and in the arms—1573.

Sani with Digbala—spreading reputation and happiness, loss of lands, servants, wife, children and brothers and hatred of relations—1574.

Sani with Kalabala—fear from poisons and drugs, fear from wife, children, rulers; thieves, and gain of lands cultivation and grains—1575.

Sani in retrograde—disappointments and failures in work, loss of power, sorrow and brothers and money—1576.

Sani in cruel Shastiamsas—great fear, anger of kings. loss of place and confinement or jail—1577.

Sani in beneficial Shasti amsas—great happiness, wife. children, and money and respect of relation—1578.

Sani in Vaiseshikamsa—happiness, great respect of kings and gain of varied colored clothing—1579.

Sani in cruel Drekkana—great fear, gallows, loss or fear from fire, poison, kings—1580.

Sani in debilitation joining exalted Navamsa—misery and sorrow in the beginning and great happiness in the end—1581.

Exalted Sani in a debilitated Navamsa—great happiness in the beginning and sorrow and trouble in the end—1582.

CHAPTER XV.

RESULTS OF RAHU DASA.

Rahu in exalted in Vrishabha and Kethu in Vrischika, Rahu has Mulathrikona in Kataka, and Mesha as his friendly sign—1583.

The 7th from Rahu is the Mulathrikona and friendly house of Kethu respectively, the Dasa of Rahu in the 6th and 8th produces misery—1584.

Rahu in exaltation—happiness, political power and children, wealth and grains—1585.

Rahu in Neecha—fear from kings, fires and thieves, gallows, poison— 1586.

NOTES.

Rahu is Neecha in Vrischika and Kethu is Neecha in Vrishabha. The seventl. house is the setting signs for all planets— 1586.

Rahu's period gives troubles from fires, thieves and rulers, foreign residence, sorrow, forest residence and danger—1587.

Rahu in birth—derangement of brain, poison, fire, weapons, destruction of relations, sorrow and trouble and defeat in the battles—1588.

Rahu in the second—loss of money and power, bad food dirty and unsympathetic master, mental distraction, falsehood, and anger—1589.

Rahu in the 3rd - gain of children, money, wife, brothers, happiness, good cultivation, power, travelling and respect of kings—1590.

Rahu in the 4th—death of mother or his own death, loss of lands and wealth, anger of kings, falls from conveyances and many other sorrows—1591.

Rahu in the 4th—troubles from thieves, fires and relations, mental worry, disease to wife and children, and loss of wife's and children's relations—1592.

Rahu in the 5th—derangement, troubles in food, great litigation, quarrels, sorrow, anger of rulers, loss of issues —1593.

Rahu in the 6th—fear from thieves, fires and rulers, loss of friends, several diseases, enlarged spleen, billiousness, consumption, cutaneous eruptions or death—1594.

Rahu in the 7th—death of wife, foreign travel, loss of cultivation and money, fear from serpants, and loss of servants, wealth and children—1595.

Rahu in the 8th—death, loss of children, wife, fear from thieves, rulers, own people and fires, residence in forests and danger from wild beasts—1596.

Rahu in the 9th—death of father, foreign travel, loss of relations and Guru, sea baths, loss of money and children—1597.

Rahu in the 10th—hearing and reading of Puranas and sacred literature and baths in the Ganges—1598.

Rahu in the 10th is a beneficial sign will give good results as above stated and in a malefic sign, he will reverse the results or give misery, foreign residence—1599.

Rahu in a malefic sign with a malefic in the 10th will give—adulterous intercourse, Brahmahatya or killing or injuring good and holy Brahmins, bad accusations, and fear from fires to children and wife—1600.

Rahu in the 11th—respect of rulers, gain of money, grains, houses, lands and other comforts—1601.

Rahu in the 12th—travelling in different countries, mental disease, destruction to wife and children, loss to cultivation, to cattle, grains, lands, cattle, wealth—1602.

Rahu in Kataka, Vrishabha or Mesha will give money, education and pleasure and recognition from kings and pleasure from wife, servants and happiness to his soul—1603.

Rahu in Kanya, Meena and Dhanas—children, wife, lordship over the country, human conveyances, and in the end loss of all—1604.

Rahu in a malefic sign—bodily leanness, destruction to relations, fear from kings, deception by thieves, venereal complaints, asthma, consumption and urinal troubles—1605.

Rahu aspected by a malefic—irreligious, loss of service, sickness and troubles from thieves, rulers and fires—1606.

Rahu aspected by a benefic—wealth from kings, death to relations—1607.

Rahu with an exalted planet—gain of kingdom, wife, children and wealth, clothes, ornaments, sweet scents—1608

Rahu with debilitated planets—livelihood by despicable means, bad food and wife and worthless children—1609.

Rahu in the commencement gives sorrow, in the middle, reputation and happiness and change of place in the end and loss of Gurus, parents, etc.—1610.

RESULTS OF KETHU DASA.

Kethu gives in his Dasa—loss of wife and children, fear from kings, great trouble, education and loss of wealth relations, friends, fear from friends, thieves, fires, falls from conveyances and troubles from poisons or poisonous waters, weapons, foreign residence, sinful diseases, and such general troubles will come—1611.

Kethu Dasa gives—death to wife, children, anger of rajas, misunderstandings with thieves, loss from fires and cultivation—1612.

Kethu in a Kendra—disappointments, failures, loss or destruction to power wealth, children and wife—1613.

Kethu in birth—great fear, fever, dysentry, gonorrhea, small-pox and plague—1614.

Kethu in 2—loss of riches. rough speech, mental sorrow worthless food, headache—1615.

Kethu in 3—great happiness, hatred in mind, and with brothers—1616.

Kethu in 4—unhappiness, danger to wife and children and gain of houses, grains and lands—1617.

Kethu in 5—loss of children, derangement, loss of money through kingly displeasure—1618.

Kethu in 6—great dangers. fear from thieves, fires poison and running into debts—1619.

Kethu in 7—danger, losses of wife, children, mental worry and urinal diseases--1620.

Kethu in 8—great danger, change of place, loss of father, hardbreathing, asthma and consumption--1621.

Kethu in 9—dangers, death of Gurus, bad Karma—1622.

Kethu in 10—sorrow, mental disease, loss of credit, evil reputation and mental worry—1623.

Kethu in 11--happiness, prosperity to brothers, sacrifices and charities—1624.

Kethu in 12—misery, change of place, foreign residence, loss of sight and troubles from rulers—1625.

Kethu gives sorrow in the beginning, in the middle great fear, and fear or death in the end—1626.

Kethu aspected by a benefic—gems, happiness, wealth, territory, houses and personal attraction and determination and respect of kings—1627.

Kethu with a malefic aspect—death of father, fever,

dysentry, venereal complaints, cutaneous diseases and troubles from enemies—1628.

NOTES.

Rahu and Kethu it will be seen have not much to give in the shape of good but they have powerful resources of evil. Bodily diseases, mental troubles, sorrows from fires thieves, poisons, rulers and enemies and even from friends have been attributed to these dark planets. We are not in the slightest degree affected by the presumption of the Western Astrologers. Rahu and Kethu are planets, which are dark in Nature, which have great powers of absorbing all vitality from other planets and specially from the sun and moon and thus neutralise their good influences and improve their own bad rays which expand their wings, spread undesirable conditions and introduce, sorrow, loss, sickness, death and dangers into families where prosperity once reigned. Generally Rahu is better than Kethu, but, the latter has the capacity to free the man from his grosser surroundings, and give him final emancipation and eternal bliss. Rahu and Kethu have no independent houses called their own. They have three sets of influences and these should not be forgotten. In the whole of Brihatjataka, nothing is said about these darksome planets excepting in one place, where only the name of Rahu is mentioned in connection with the rulers of the 8 directions viz. Ravi, Sukra, Kuja, Rahu, Sani, Chandra, Buda and Guru as governing the 8 directions viz., East, South-east, South, South-west, West, North-west, North and North-east respectively. The name of Kethu is not mentioned at all. In the Parasara Dasa Bhukti Chandrika we have Rahu and Kethu Dasas given in full details. Other works also mention them. The house they occupy, the signification, the conjunction and the aspect, give them capacity to give different results. These differences may be studied with advantage in other works.

RESULTS OF ANTHAR DASAS OR SUB-PERIODS.

When the Sub-Period of a planet comes, who occupies his own Navamsa—personal attraction, great happiness, fixed wealth, acquisition of wealth from rajas, reputation —1629.

When the sub-lord is aspected by a benefic—good health, rich, well-known, personal attraction and comeliness, leader of people, meritorious and philosophic—1630.

When the major and the minor lords of planets are in, 6th and 8th—fear from kings, hatred of the enemies female quarrels, loss of wife and children, sorrow from thieves, fires and relations, mental disturbances—1631.

When the sub-lord is in the 12th from the major lord— loss of place, hatred of relations, foreign journey, quarrels with his own people, disease in the feet, eyes and heart— 1632.

When the sub-lord combines with the Dasanatha— loss to females, children, servants, money, cultivation, loss of service, troubles to his own people, sudden blames—1633

Sub-lord in the 2nd from the Major-lord—milk and food, valuable clothes, sweet scents, garlands, helping others, prosperity to his own relations and mental pleasure and enjoyment to his females, children and friends and relations—1634.

Sub-lord in the 3rd from the Major lord—wealth from rajas, happiness, sweet scents and articles, flower garlands, valuable clothes, ornaments, new friends, good and luxurious food, good health—1635.

Sub-lord in the 4th from the Major—gain of wife children, wealth, houses, relations, conveyances, milk and rich food, valuable clothing, ornaments, if sub-lord is a benefic he will get all these, but when he is a malefic, the reverse will be the case—1636.

If the sub-lord in the 4th from the Major—though a malefic, happens to be in his own house, exaltation powerful and well situated, he will give good results. But if this sub-lord, though a benefic, is not in his own house, or exaltation or powerful or well situated, he will not give good results—1637.

The sub-lord in the 5th from the Major—gain of children, if a malefic, loss of children must be predicted—1638.

The sub-lord in the 6th from the Major—if a malefic, fear from thieves or wounds, change of place—1639.

If a benefic, combined in exaltation or his own house or Mulathrikona, increase in happiness, gain of children and friends—1640.

If the sub-lord in the 7th from the Major is a malefic—death or danger to wife, children, relations, wealth and friends, fear from local rulers—1641.

If he is a benefic—and does not occupy an unfriendly or debilitated sign, luxurious meals, valuable clothes, ornaments—1642.

If the sub-lord is a malefic and is in the 8th from the Major—fears and danger of death, bad food, troubles from thieves, rajas and fires—1643.

If he is a benefic—happiness, and good results must be predicted in the early part of this sub-period and misery and trouble in the end—1644.

The sublord in the 9th from the Major is a malefic—irreligious or sinful work, change of place, mental disease—1645.

If he is a benefic—marriage, sacrificial works, receiving gifts—1646.

If the malefic sublord occupies the 10th from the Major—doing unholy work, disgrace, many dangers—1647.

If he is a benefic—enjoyment, constructing tanks, gopuras and such charitable buildings—1648.

If the sublord is a malefic in the 11th from the Major—acquisition of wealth, friends, children, permanent residence—1649.

If he is a benefic—good wealth and comforts, patronage with rulers, increase of prosperity to wife and children—1650.

If the malefic sublord is in the 12th from the Major—loss of wealth, anger of rajas, getting dirty residence, fixture in a place—1651.

If he is a benefic—carriages, enjoyments and wealth, fine clothes, ornaments, jewels—1652.

These results must be applied or indicated in all the Dasas and Vidasas, except when the planets are in exaltation Mulathrikona or in their own houses, when the sublords are in unfavourable positions both for the Dasa nath and also in their occupations, the results should be predicted, but when the sublords are in exaltation or beneficial Navamsas or Vergas, though they may be in the 6th or 8th or 12th from the Major lord, they give good results—1653.

If the malefic sub-lord combines with the Major or

occupies the 2nd or 3rd from him he will have sorrow and trouble, if he becomes a benefic, he will have prosperity and happiness—1654.

If the Major and minor lords of periods are malefics, there will be great fear, and loss of place, eyes, relations children, wealth and wife, fear from rulers—1655.

If the Major and minor lords happen to be benefics, he will gain places, ornaments, carriages ;

If the Major lord is a malefic and the sub-lord is a benefic, he will have happiness in the commencement, and in the end fear and sorrow—1656.

When the sub-lord is malefic and the Major is a benefic, sorrow and misery will come in the beginning and happiness and enjoyment in the end.

Periods of planets occupying Sirshodayas produce happiness in the beginning and periods of planets occupying Prustodayas and Oobhayodayas, in the end—1657.

Results of planetary periods, have to be determined, and explained after comparing all their sources of power and events indicated by them. This means a careful summary should be made—1658.

NOTES.

Planets occupy and must occupy some signs. These signs of the zodiac must have necessarily various forms, characteristics and peculiarities. Planets therefore occupying them must be differently influenced.

The zodiacal signs are marked out in Bhuchakra, which means a circle of light of the greatest brilliancy, and most wonderful potency. *Bha* in Sanskrit means that

which shines with great light, hence the sun is called
Bhanu. In that grand and wonderful circle of lights
twelve different signs of various forms comprise sub-
sides, or moulds which intercept that light and produce
shapes by which they have been specially named from the
resemblances, which they bear to natural Phenomena and
in fact which they have produced by their inherent capacity. We have electrical currents, and from this source
of light we want to give certain formations, like floral
lives, welcomes and other designs. What is the process.
When the light is continuous, we make designs of figures
whose outlines should be distinguished by electric light
but whose bodies should be able to shutout the unnecessary brilliancy and when these are brought and applied to
the fountain source of light it filters through the outlines
giving shapes of animals, or letters or other flowers or
fruits which we have in view for exhibition and which will
be exhibited in the glorious light. Suppose we have a black
surface and we cut certain figures in a white paper and stick
it to the former the result will be the production of the
outlines of figures in black on a white surface. Similarly
with reference to Bhuchakra and the process under the
guidance and discipline of God which has been going on
there from time eternal. In the twelve houses we see
within 30 degrees a formation resembling a ram, a bull,
a sexual couple in the act of embracing a crab, a lion, a
virgin, a balance, a scorpion, a centaur, a crocodile, a water-
bearer, and a pair of fish, with the head of one turned towards the tail of the other. Hence they produce Phenomena suitable to their forms, and natures and which they
are said to govern and rule. A lion has his home naturally in the forest and mountains, and such phenomena, are
produced by the sign Leo or simha and it is said to govern
them and to take to its production in that shape. Now

planets come next with their Mandalas or globes composed of chemical substances. Light acts upon all substances
produces chemical changes and peculiarities and different
results must naturally be expected from their action and
reaction. When these planetary globes are passing under
these electric lights contained in the houses called zodiacal
signs, the action of light and all its concomittant substances, like heat, sound, magnetism, electricity and ether,
work in their own mysterious ways produce immediate
and perceptible chemical changes in the objects subjected
to their powerful action and make them potent or impotent
to achieve certain results. The sun passes through the
360 degrees of the zodiac once in a year composed of 365¼
days roughly. The electric light in all of them, has not
been equally intercepted on account of the various substances which are exposed to its influence and therefore
any globes of chemical substances which pass under them
cannot and will not be affected uniformly from these
variations. The sun, therefore, when he passes in his
celestial revolutions under the zodiac, attains the highest
power to do good to men and human events when he is in
the 10th degree of Aries or Mesha and becomes the weakest to do good when he is in the 180th degree from it or
when he is in the 190th degree from the 1st degree of
Aries. The moon attains his highest activity and potency
to produce beneficial results, in the 33rd degree from the
1st degree of the zodiac in Mesha, and in the 180th degree
from it has his greatest fall Parama Neecha. Mars
attains his highest exaltation in the 298th degree of the
zodiac and his greatest fall in the 180th degree from there
or in the 118th degree in the zodiac. In the intermediate
degrees or spaces they go on losing or gaining potency as
they discend or ascend from their highest elevation or
greatest fall respectively. Even here they have some ex-

ceptions on account of the various degrees of zodiacal light to which they would be exposed and by which they would be affected. A land may be a vast surface of sand called a desert, but here and there may be oasis, which would present a fertile appearance and relieve the monotony of the dreary desert. The sun has his greatest elevation for doing good in the 10th degree of Mesha, called Paramochu and in his discent to his greatest fall in the 10th degree of Thula, he is said to lose his good potency in the proportion of the rule of three. Thus in Vrishabha Mithuna and Kataka this may hold good, but in Simha which is called his own house, he will gain power, and yield almost as bright results as he does in Mesha the sign of exaltation. Hence Venkatasa observes that in giving results of Dasas and Vidasas periods and sub-periods the greatest care should be taken to summarise the sources of evil and good influences mentioned in the different parts of this work and then predict the balance of good or evil as the case may be to the persons concerned. For Prustodayas, Sirshodayas and Oobhayodayas, see my notes on *St. 10 of Brihadjataka, Ch. I, p. 10.*

Astrology is a huge chemical science. Its principles apply to chemistry on a minor scale. If the composition of the different planitary globes, were carefully analysed and explained, then the principles of astrology will be thoroughly understood and the heavy gloom that envelops the horizon of human knowledge and prejudice in this department will be removed by the sunshine of real truth. The sun acts on the same principles on which he himself is acted upon by the great zodiocal light or Bhuchakra and himself undergoes all those chemical changes in nature which he produces on the objects which are called into existence by so many visible and invisible chemical agencies. These beautiful ideas have been partly explain-

ed by me in my notes under stanzas 7 and 8 of this work
in Chap. I—1658.

CAAPTER XVI.

RESULTS OF PLANITARY PERIODS AND SUB-PERIODS IN THE DIFFERENT BHAVAS OR HOUSES.

In the period of the sun in birth, the Sub-Periods of
Kuja, Chandra and Sani 'and Rahu produce sorrow, loss of
power and kingdom, money and houses—1659.

When the above named sub-lords are in Agochara
places, they produce the miseries mentioned above but
when they are in Gochara they produce beneficial results
and increase in these departments of human comforts—
1660.

Planets are said to be in Gochara, when they occupy
their own houses exaltation, Mulathrikonas and in intimate friendly signs and when they are not in combustion,
in 6th, 8th and 12th houses—1661.

Planets are said to be in Agochara, when they are in
combustion, debilitation, in the 6th, 8th and 12th houses and
when they are not in exaltation mulathrikona, etc.—1662.

NOTES.

This Gochara and Agochara should not be confounded
with the Gochara or the incessant planetary movements.
The last term applies always to their movements whether
they are in exaltations or debilitations and in fact there
can be no planet without its incessant revolutions and
movements. Here the distinction made is technical and
conventional. Gochara means that which can be seen
with the eye and Agochara means that which is invisible
or cannot be seen by the eye. These differences should be
particularly remembered by the readers—1662.

In the sub-periods of Guru, Sukra, Buda and Chandra in the period of the Sun in birth—there will be enjoyment from lands, cattle, cultivation, wife and children. 1663.

In the sub-periods of malefics in the Dasa of the Sun combined in the second house—harsh language, mental sorrow, eye disease and great danger and loss of wealth. 1664.

In the sub-periods of benefics in Ravi Dasa when he occupies the second house—great happiness, progress in education, favour of Kings, gain of clothes, ornaments and conveyances. 1665.

In the sub-periods of malefics when they have *Gochara* in the period of the Sun in the 3rd house—there will be good results. When they are in *Agochara* they produce injurious results. 1666.

When the Sun is in the 3rd beneficial sub periods produce, great happiness, courage, money, children and victory in battles. 1667.

Malefic sub-periods in the Ravi Dasa. in the 4th—death of mother, mental worry, and troubles from thieves, fires and rulers. 1668.

Beneficial sub-periods in the Ravi Dasa in the 4th—great happiness, gain of kingdom, money, children, wife, clothes and flowers and sweet scents. 1669.

The sub-periods of Sani, Kuja, Kethu and Rahu in Ravi Dasa in the 5th—troubles from thieves, fires, rulers, children and money. 1670.

The sub-periods of benefics in the Ravi Dasa in the 5th—happiness, carriages, ornaments and power. 1671.

The sub-periods of malefics in the Dasa of Ravi in the 6th—troubles from debts, thieves. fires and rulers. 1762.

The sub-periods of benefics in Ravi Dasa in the 6th—beneficial results and happiness in the beginning and unpleasantness in the end. 1673.

The sub-periods of Sukra, Guru, Chandra and Buda, in the period of Ravi in the 7th house—gain of wife, mental elations, conveyances, clothes and ornaments. 1674.

In the sub-periods of malefics in Ravi Dasa in the 7th— fever, dysentry, biliousness, troubles from enemies and diseases in the several organs. 1675.

Benefic sub-periods in Ravi Dasa in the 8th some sorrow, good beds, ornaments and clothes. 1676.

Malefic sub-periods in Ravi Dasa in the 8th—great fear, death, disease and dependency on others. 1677.

Benefic sub-periods in Ravi Dasa in the 9th—charity, sacrifices, great enjoyment and festivities. 1678.

Malefic sub-periods in Ravi Dasa in the 9th—destruction to Gurus and father and elders. 1679.

Malefic sub-periods in Ravi Dasa in the 10th—destructions to good Karma, fear from thieves, fires and rulers. 1680.

Benefic sub-periods in Ravi Dasa in the 10th house—pain of many lands, and lasting reputations. 1681.

Malefic sub-periods in Ravi Dasa in the 11th—great misery and sorrow in the beginning and happiness and enjoyment in the end. 1682.

Benefic sub-periods in Dasa in the 11th—gain of wealth, respect of kings, wife, children and favour of rulers. 1683.

Malefic sub-periods in Ravi Dasa in the 12th—loss and change of place, foreign residence, anger of king and disgrace. 1684.

Benefic sub-periods in Ravi Dasa in the 12th—gain of cattle, lands, clothes, grains, precious stones, corals and ornaments. 1685.

The sub-periods of Buda, Guru and Sukra in Chandra Dasa in birth—good health, favour of kings, carriages, clothes and ornaments. 1686.

The sub-periods of malefics in Chandra Dasa in birth—loss of cultivations, cattle and lands. 1687.

Malefic sub-periods in Chandra Dasa in the 2nd—fear from wife, relations, children and rulers. 1688.

Benefic sub-periods in Chandra Dasa in the 2nd—good food, clothing, drinks, mental pleasure, and hopefulness. 1689.

Benefic sub-periods in Chandra Dasa in the 3rd house—respect of kings and happiness. 1690.

Malefic sub-periods in Chandra Dasa in the 3rd—mental derangement, loss of brothers and courage. 1691.

Benefic sub-periods in Chandra Dasa in the 4th—great happiness and various comforts and enjoyments through kingly favour. 1692.

Malefic sub-periods in Chandra Dasa in the 4th—loss of houses, money, wife, fear from thieves, fires and rulers. 1693.

Benefic sub-periods in Chandra Dasa in the 5th house—great happiness, gain of wife, money, children, funds and clothes. 1694.

Malefic sub-periods in Chandra Dasa in the 5th—mental worry, misunderstandings, and fear from wife, children and rulers. 1695.

Malefic sub-periods in the Chandra Dasa in the 6th—loss of cultivation, indebtedness, venereal complaints, jaundice, consumption. 1696.

Benefic sub-periods in Chandra Dasa in the 7th—general friendship and the destruction of fears caused by thieves and fires. 1697.

Benefic sub-periods in Chandra Dasa in the 7th house—gain of wife, children, carriages, clothes, ornaments and enjoyment. 1698.

Malefic sub-periods in the Chandra Dasa in the 7th house—foreign travel, loss of children, wealth, wife and relations. 1699.

Malefic sub-periods in Chandra Dasa in the 8th house—defeat, death to children and wife, bad food. 1700.

Benefic sub-periods in Chandra Dasa in the 8th—great happiness, reputation, courage and carriages, ornaments. 1701.

Benefic sub-periods in the Chandra Dasa in the 9th—happiness to father, virtuous and sacrificial deeds, marriage, good women, wealth and enjoyment. 1702.

Malefic sub-periods in Chandra Dasa in the 9th—loss of merit, mental sorrow, loss of houses, kingdom and wealth. 1703.

Benefic sub-periods in Chandra Dasa in the 10th house—doing his own religious work, improvement in sciences, doing charity and good work. 1704.

Malefic sub-periods in the Chandra Dasa in 10th—irreligiousness, great fear, disgrace. 1705.

Benefic sub-periods in the Dasa of Chandra in 11th—gain of wealth, clothes, grains, carriages, territory and much happiness. 1706.

Malefic sub-periods in the Chandra Dasa in the 11th house—loss of wealth, cultivation, grains, disease in body and eyes, and troubles from rulers and thieves. 1707.

Malefic sub-periods in Chandra Dasa in the 12th— great trouble, enmity all round, loss of wealth. 1708.

Benefic sub-periods in Chandra Dasa in the 12th house—pains of clothes, flowers, wife, children, ornaments, and increase of carriages and happiness. 1709.

Malefic sub-periods in Kuja Dasa in the birth—cuts and wounds, great trouble, dyspepsia and great fear. 1710.

Benefic sub-periods in Kuja Dasa in birth—favour of kings, happiness and increase of brothers, lands and carriages. 1711.

Benefic sub-periods in the Kuja Dasa in 2nd—happiness to brothers, courage and hopefulness, educational progress, pains of ornaments, carriages and pleasure from prosperity. 1712.

Malefic sub-periods in Kuja Dasa in 2nd—loss of previous wealth, troubles from fevers,· displeasure of rulers and other sources. 1713.

Malefic sub-periods in Kuja Dasa in the 3rd—mental trouble and sorrow and destruction to brothers. 1714.

Benefic sub-periods in Kuja Dasa in the 3rd—happiness from food, clothes, jewels, cultivation, carriages and lands. 1715.

Malefic sub-periods in Kuja Dasa in 4th—great fear, destruction of houses and lands, and troubles from rulers, thieves and fires. 1716.

Benefic sub-periods in Kuja Dasa in 4th—prosperity to lands, cultivation, clothes, ornaments, happiness, cattle and conveyances. 1717.

Malefic sub-periods in Kuja Dasa in the 5th—destruction to cultivation, cows, grains, wealth, children and wife. 1718.

Benefic sub-periods in Kuja Dasa in 5th—comfort and enjoyment, children, respect of rulers, and acquisition of Mantras and their development by practice and concentration. 1719.

Malefic sub-periods in Kuja Dasa in 6th—troubles, miseries from thieves, fires and kings, small-pox, consumption and venereal diseases. 1720.

Benefic sub-periods in Kuja Dasa in 6th—friendship with kings, destruction to relations, mental sorrow in the commencement and happiness afterwards. 1721.

Malefic sub-periods in Kuja Dasa in 7th—troubles and sorrows from loss of wife, children and political power and in beneficial sub-periods great happiness, respect and patronage of kings, pleasure from carriages, ornaments. 1722.

Malefic sub-periods in Kuja Dasa in 8th—causing death and in benefic sub-periods great happiness, cultivation, cows and respect of kings. 1723.

Malefic sub-periods in Kuja Dasa in 9th—death of Guru and father, mental disease and sinful deeds. 1724.

Benefic sub-periods give cows, wealth, enjoyment, marriage, sacrifices and worship of Brahmins and Gods. 1725.

Malefic sub-periods in Kuja Dasa in 10th—great sorrow, Foreign journeys, pain and defeat. 1726.

Malefic sub-periods in Kuja Dasa in 11th—many territories, sweet scents, flowers, ornaments, conveyances. 1727.

The sub-periods of Sukra, Buda, Guru and Chandra give immense happiness, pleasure from charities and righteous deeds. 1728.

Malefic sub-periods in Kuja Dasa in 12th—many sorrows and imprisonment. 1729.

Benefic sub-periods in Kuja Dasa in 12th—happiness, convenyance, ornaments, in the end, change and loss of place, anger of kings and mental sorrow. 1730.

NOTES.

The various copies I have of Sarwarthachintamani do not give the results of benefic sub-periods in the Kuja Dasa when he is in the 10th house. Kuja in the 10th house becomes powerful by being possessed of Digbala and the results are favourable. When therefore, Venkatasa omits this important portion there must have been some reason probably in the course of copying. One stanza seems to have been omitted, otherwise we cannot account for such an omission. Kuja in *Parasara* when possessed of Digbala has been declared to give —pains from rulers, great success in battles, gain of lands, cows, conveyances, cultivation, clothes, courage, great reputation in all countries and success. Sometimes Venkatasa has the knack of directly contradicting himself as he does about Kuja in the 10th. Kuja and Ravi get Digbala or directional strength in the 10th house, and Venkatasa gives unfavourable results to Kuja in the 10th house *(see St. 1372)*. Then again under Kuja in Digbala Venkatasa gives favourable results and Kuja can get Digbala only in the 10th house. *(See St. 1387)*. *See also Notes on p. p. 45 and 49 Eng. Tr. of Bri. Jataka)*. From my own humble experience and the extensive reading I have in the Astrological literature, I may here give my view of the position of Kuja in the 10th as favourable, though the man will be unsympathetic to some extent. Judging by the above quotations and references, Beneficial sub-periods in Kuja Dasa when he occupies the 10th house from Lagna, must be good and profitable and produce happiness pleasure, success and wealth.

Malefic sub-periods in Buda Dasa in Kendras—disturbance to virtuous deeds, great sorrow, unstability or fickleness of mind, disappointments, loss of cows, gold, lands, clothes, change of place, great hatred, and breaks in educational careers. 1731— 1732.

Benefic sub-periods in Buda Dasa in Kendras—marriage, performance of religious and sacrificial work, charity, religiousness, increase in intelligence, favour of royalties, gains from cows, cultivation, lands, pearls, precious stones, conveyances, clothes, ornaments and happiness through these. 1733—1734.

Malefic sub-periods in Buda Dasa in Thrikonas—loss of wife, children and riches, disturbance to good deeds, mental disease, losses from merchandise, cultivation, relations, loss of power, great hatred of people and relations. 1735—1736.

Benefic sub-periods in Buda Dasa in Thrikonas—favour of kings, health, great happiness, *somapana*, works published in his name, getting titles or two names, good food, ornaments and lordship over men. 1737—1738.

Malefic sub-periods in Buda Dasa in 6 and 8—trouble from thieves, fever, dysentry, destruction of his relations, servants, wife, children, litigation, in many quarters and quarrels with relations. 1739—1740.

Benefic sub-periods in Buda Dasa in 6 and 8—great reputation, wealth, attractiveness and worship of Brahmins and Gods good results in the commencement and loss of happiness in the end, loss of cows, buffaloes, harsh words and fear from kings. 1741—1742.

Benefic sub-periods in Buda Dasa in the 3rd—good, courage and elation, enjoyment. and acquisition of wealth from various countries. 1743.

Success in education, favour of Kings, good food, and health, sacrifices and godly worship, marriage and reading of scriptures. 1744.

Malefic sub-periods in Buda Dasa in the 3rd—mental terror, destruction of brothers, derangement, and troubles from rulers, fear from thieves, fires, bad wife or woman and dirty houses, sinful, loss of cultivation, and troubles to horses, elephants, etc. 1745—46.

Malefic sub-periods in Buda Dasa in the 2nd house—fines and penalties, imprisonment, confinement and chains, poison, hatred of relations, loss from lands and cultivation, enmity with all, and doing irreligious deeds. 1747—48.

Benefic sub-periods in the above—gain of wealth, great love, worship of Gods and Brahmins, sacrifices, virtuous and charitable, Homas and japam or Godly contemplation, respect of relations, great exhiliration, progress in education and reputation. 1749—50.

Malefic sub-periods in Guru Dasa in Kendras—sickness, sorrow, loss of money from the anger of Rulers, lands, cows, cultivation, hatred of relations, disappointments, mental trouble, all these in the beginning, and happiness and enjoyment in the end 1751—52.

Benefic sub-periods in Guru Dasa in Kendras—territorial gain, mental pleasure, clothes, ornaments and carriages, charities, Homas, Japas and virtuous deeds, and respect of kings, help to many, festivities, gold and ornaments, clothing of various colors, 1753—54.

Benefic sub-periods in the Guru Dasa in Thrikona—great happiness, construction of temples, towers, worships of Gods, great love and wealth, prosperity to wife, issues and money, acquisition of wealth from various countries, reputation, success, and enjoyment. 1755—56.

Malefic sub-periods in the above—anger of wife, children and kings, death of relations, derangement, change of place, disappointments, disease, thieves irreligeous, adultery, fickleness, disgrace, and loss of corals and precious stones. 1757—58—59.

Malefic sub-periods in Guru Dasa in 6 and 8—doing irreligeous acts, loss of territory and money, death of relations, fear from Rulers in foreign countries, litigation of landed property, fear of disease. 1760—61.

Benefic sub-periods in the Dasa of Guru in the 8th—gives great happiness, lordship of villages and towns and countries and great renown, sound health, horses, elephants, clothes, food, enjoyment, and sugar, milk and curds. 1762—63.

Benefic sub-periods in Guru Dasa in 3—gain of carriages, clothes and ornaments, jewels, precious stones, gold, valuable clothes, lordship of country, ministership. Malefic sub-periods in the above—great fear, irreligiousness, destruction of his own family, foreign residence, great misery, and sorrows of many kinds, constant travelling, all these come in the beginning, and in the end happiness, carriages and good food. 1764—65.

Benefic sub-periods in Guru Dasa in 2—happiness, wealth, education, success, wife, children and enjoyment from kings, extended sympathy, great wealth, love, luxurious food, bodily health, sacrifices, charities and philanthropy. 1766—67.

Malefic sub-periods in the above—great sorrow, fines and penalties from rulers, hatred of relations, mental trouble, harsh words, dirty food, and acts, mean dependency. 1768—69.

Benefic sub-periods in Sukra Dasa in Kendras—gain of territory, respect of Rulers, gain of vehicles, ornaments, clothes, courage and hopefulness, reputations, politeness, wife, wealth and issues, mental courage and great wealth, power from rulers. 1770—71.

Malefic sub-periods in the above—loss of wealth, bad food, clothes, disturbance to good work, these will be enjoyed in the commencement, and happiness and comfort in the end. Gain of cows, lands, wealth and riches from distant places. 1772—73.

Benefic sub-periods in Sukra Dasa in Thrikonas—worship of Gods and Brahmins, and prosperity to children, wife, sacrifices, ornaments and success, health and attraction, getting all desires 1774—75.

Malefic sub-periods Sukra Dasa in Thrikonas—mental disease, and sorrow, bad health, disgrace, and troubles from fires Rulers and thieves, caught in the clutches of evil women, foul language, hatred of relations, mental disorder, bad dreams, fall of lizards. 1776—77.

NOTES.

Bad dreams are of various kinds and in fact dreams have a great classification and my reader may with advantage refer to my articles on *Dreams* in my Astrological Magazine Vols. 15 and 16. Nervous, and those magnetic currents which control nervous circulation have much to do in producing dreams. Three states are mentioned by Sanskrit Psychologists. First the wakeful state when the nervous currents are able to record the objective phenomena, and then transmit them to the subjective states of consciousness. Then we have the demarkation for dreams. When consciousness passes this stage into the *sushumna* Nadi or nervous junction, a curtain is drawn over the other two states and man apparently forgets, the external impressions and the objective Phenomena.

Dreams sometimes are mild, attractive and hopeful. At other times, they are indifferent. In the 3rd stage they are horrible and sometimes send the dreamer to paroxyms of grief and terror Dreams have great significations and often coming events can be read in their light with as much certainty as events in the future

can be read by the astrological principles. Fall of lizards on the
various parts of the man and the woman have been interpreted in
in that branch of science, and the brief outlines are generally given
in the Hindu Almanacs. The construction of male and female
bodies are differently arranged and hence, many of the omens, will
be auspicious to one sex while they are the reverse to the other.
The shaking of the right eyebrow indicates fortune to man, while
it forebodes evil to woman·   The shaking of left eyebrow for the
woman is good while it is bad for the man.   Objective phenomena
do not work in vain, and he will be a vain man, who vainly tries
to belittle events which have been worked out with relative usefulness.

Benefic sub-periods in Sukra Dasa in 6th, 8th and 12th—
great reputation, gain of wealth from royal patronage, comforts,
wife and children, clothes, carriages, ornaments, these will be in
the beginning, in the end mental sorrows, loss of Guru, hatred of
relations, destruction to family. Beneficial sub-periods give good
health, and enjoyment, luxurious invitations, silks, scents, flowers,
jewels.   In the beginning there will be all these good results, in
the end trouble and sorrow, from enemies, diseases, and thieves.
1778 to 1781.

NOTES.

Venkatasa has again omitted to mention what would
be the results, when malefic sub-periods intervene, when Sukra
Dasa comes, when he is occupying 6th, 8th or 12th houses. These
three houses are called Dusthas or evil houses·

Judging from the principles enunciated in the a ov e pages, it
looks that the results of malefic sub-periods when Sukra is in Dusthas, must be bad and undesirable and the native   should not expect any good from those sub-periods. In all these cases other
sources of strength and weakness must be carefully noted and remembered in venturing on future predictions.

Malefic sub-periods in the Sukra Dasa in 3—sorrow, and loss of riches, grain. loss of power, fear and trouble from thieves, fires and Rajas. land litigation among relations, loss of place.

Benefic sub-periods in the above—great comforts, respect of Rulers, courage, lordship over lands, villages and towns, carriages, ornaments, children, wife, servants, construction of wells, gardens, cultivation and tanks, virtuous deeds, success in education, elevation of mind and pleasure, worship of Gods and Brahmins, sacrifices, and good work and acquisition of two names or Government title. 1782 to 1785.

Benefic sub- periods in Sukra Dasa in 2—great love gain of wife, children and wealth, and protection of relations. 1786.

Malefic sub-periods in the above—fines and penalties from Government, mental sorrow. heart disease, eye complaint, unpleasant discussions, loss of cultivation, disappointments, loss of power and place, fear from fires, thieves and Rajas. 1787—88.

RESULTS OF PERIODS AND SUB-PERIODS
IN SANI (Saturn).

Malefic sub-periods in Sani Dasa in Kendras—loss of residence, foreign travel, troubles from Rajas, fires and thieves, death to wife, children, and relations, and money, disturbance to religious ceremonies, dependency, mental sorrow, enlarged spleen, and shooting pains. 1789—1790.

Benefic sub-periods in the above—great pleasure, coronation or respect and patronage from kings and lordship over towns and countries. These results will be enjoyed in the beginning and in the end suffering from diseases, blames, loss of relations, and money. 1791—1792.

Malefic sub-periods in Sani Dasa in Thrikonas—great troubles, death of father and children, disturbance to religious work,

windy complaints, eye disease, piles, quarrels with his own relations, worry in service and loss, sorrow, change of place and distruction of grain.   1793—1794.

Benefic sub-periods in the above—happiness, respect of Rulers.
gains from cultivation, extension of buildings, grains, health to
wife, children, relations, ornaments, friends and servants and performance of religious devotions.   1795—96.

Malefic sub-periods in Sani Dasa in 6—8 and 12—mental sorrow,
great trouble, loss of place and wealth, disease in sexual organs,
fear from poisons, fevers, fires and Rulers, death of intimate or
close relations, and loss of service.   1797—98.

Benefic sub-periods in the above—happiness, gains, healt
ornaments, personal attraction, lordship over lands, towns ar.
villages, mental pleasure, destruction to enemies, and increast
in grains and wealth   1799—1800.

Malefic sub-periods in Sani Dasa in 3 and 11—gain of wealth,
sorrow, and destruction to brothers, foreign travel, quarrels,
derangement, loss of servants, bad food, dependency, and sexual
connection with dirty and crooked women.   1801—02.

NOTES.

Here again Venkatasa has omitted as to what would be the
results in the benefic sub-periods when Sani is in 3rd or 11th. But
in another manuscript I have, the following results have been stated
—favourable results, enjoyment, and gains from the patronage of
sovereigns.

Malefic sub periods in Sani Dasa in 2—fines and penalties, great
disappointments. and imprisonment ; mental depression, bodily
disease, fever, dysentry, loss of territory, death of horses and elephants and danger from falls from conveyances.   1803—1804.

Benefic sub-periods in the above—determination, rendering help to others, pleasure from gambling, enjoyment of music, sexu. al pleasures, good food, ornaments, gain of service and promotion precious stones, corals and jewels. 1805—1806.

RESULTS OF SUB-PERIODS IN RAHU DASA.

Malefic sub-periods in Rahu Dasa in 1—many sorrows, troubles from fires, rulers and thieves, 1807.

Benefic sub-periods in the above—good enjoyment, increase in houses, lands, food, clothes, and ornaments—1808.

Malefic sub-periods in Rahu Dasa in 6—12—8—fear from thieves, Rulers, fires and bulls. Venereal complaints, asthma or hard breathing, consumption, bad food and clothing, loss of place and danger from kings. 1809—1810.

Benefic sub-periods in the above—in the beginning good results, great enjoyment, patronage and gains from rulers, gain of wealth. In the end loss of place and trouble from kings, mental worry, and loss of lands, wealth, clothes, children and relations. 1811—1812.

Malefic sub-periods in Rahu Dasa in Kendras—destruction of of houses by fire, eye disease, great danger to wife and children, mental worry, change of place, irreligious deeds and rejection by relations, sudden quarrels, and troubles from fires, thieves and Rulers. 1813—1814.

Benefic sub-periods in the above—occasional gains of grains, happiness, wealth and reputation, these will come by fits and starts in the beginning. and in the end loss of money by the anger of Rulers, defeat in battles, and literary discussions, and great fear 1815—16.

Malefic sub-periods in Rahu Dasa in Thrikonas—emacia-tion, trouble, doing sinful work, disgrace, bad food, loss of cultiva-vation, cattle and lands, breaches of promises and fighting thereby, courage, and fall of lizards.   17—1818.

Malefic sub-periods in the above—good deeds, gain of wife, children and money in the end, in the commencement some occa-sional gains, foreign travel, devotion to Mantras, great pleasure, wife, children and ornamen s.   1819—1820.

Malefic sub-periods in Rahu Dasa in 3-11—great happiness, favour of kings, in the end sorrow and trouble, fever from thieves, fires and rulers, mental sorrow and hatred of relations, and death of brothers.   1821—1822.

NOTES.

Again Venkatasa does not say what will be the results in the beneficial sub-periods in the above case. Different versions I have, are silent on this point. From a general knowledge of the astro-logical principles we have to presume, good results. Rahu in the 3rd and 11th is good, and all the planets are production of favourable results in the 11th.

Malefic sub-periods in Rahu Dasa in 2—mental sorrow and loss of wealth, wife and children.   1823.

Benefic sub-periods in the above—gains from mercantile tran-sactions, good speeches, and eloquence, good food, gain of orna-ments, clothes, carriages, loss of service and bodily disease and commission of secret sins.   1824—1825.

RESULTS OF SUB-PERIODS IN KETHU DASA.

Malefic sub-periods in Kethu Dasa in Kendras—disgrace, mental hatred, troubles from fires, thieves and rulers, loss of mother, wife, and destruction to good karma, constant travels, and sudden quarrels.   1826—1827.

Benefic sub-periods in the above—good health, happiness, advent of relations and their friendship, good food, ornaments, clothes, these will happen in the beginning, in the end loss of appointment, sexual sorrows, and destruction to family. 1828—1829

Malefic sub-periods in Kethu Dasa in Thrikonas—sorrow in the heart, many dangers, death of wife and sons and father, quarrels for place and with friends. 1830—1831.

Benefic sub-periods in the above—increase of lands, cattle cultivation, advent of relations and progress in education, good, meals, clothes, these will be in the commencement, in the end loss of place, and sudden quarrels and sorrows. 1832—1833.

Malefic sub-periods in Kethu Dasa in 6-8-12—death travelling to foreign places, nasty venereal complaints, enlargement of spleen, of urinal disorders, troubles from Rajas and thieves, all these will be in the beginning and in the end there may be some little happiness. 1834—1835.

Benefic sub-periods in the above—happiness and prosperity to wife and sons, gold, gems, ornaments, grains and clothes, enmity of his relations, headache, eye disease, complaint in the anus, courage in fighting out for his cases and fall of lizards. 1836—1837.

Benefic sub-periods in the Kethu Dasa in 3-11—favour of kings, various clothes and ornaments, carriages, flowers, garlands sweet scents, gain of gold from distant places and respect of relations. 1838—1839.

Malefic sub-periods in the above—doing bad acts, disturbing the work of others and living dependent on relations; abject dependency, dirty clothes in the beginning these results will happen; in the end happiness and prosperity to wife and children. 1840—1841.

Malefic sub-periods in the Dasa of Kethu in 2—many sources of sorrows, food from medicancy and mental trouble, loss to wife and children, great troubles and dangers, loss of money from Rajas and thieves and destruction to relations. 1842—43.

Benefic sub-periods in the above case—discussions, success, helping all people, rich food and ornaments, this will happen in the commencement, in the end occasional gain, harsh language, mental depressions and disappointments in his efforts. 1844—45.

NOTES.

Sarwartha Chintamani extends over 1845 Slokas or Stanzas, and as I have given some Sub-Divisions like A. B. C., to certain Stanzas, the total number may be put up at 1960. Though short and sweet in the original Sanskrit, the English translation could not be given so easily and so clearly. I don't want to blow my own trumpet about my qualifications and capacity to translate Sanskrit works into English, but I may here state without fear of contradiction that I stand second to none in point of this capacity. (See P. IX to *the Introduction to this work*). Venkatasa has done his best to take the reader through an extensive field of Astrological literature in the predictive portion and no reader should approach the work without a fair know-ledge of elementary principles in Astronomy or Siddhartha. In the last 3 or 4 hundred stanzas I have given very few notes simply because no necessity exists for notes and illustra-tions as my learned translation comprises in clear and unmistak-able language the principal information which Venkatasa wants to put forth in his immortal work. A few so-called commentators in the vernaculars have tried to fix him as a resident of Voragallu or Warangal in the Nizam's Dominions and his sect as that of a Brahmin belonging to the Velanadu community. In the body of the work, no reference has been made to either of these two facts

and we may therefore reject both of them as clumsy forgeries introduced at the end by Velanadu Brahmins to serve their vanity and
pride. He was called simply Venkatasa and he calls himself in
many places in the body of the work as the learned Venkatasa
which he was u ndoubtedly.

In his Dasas and Bhuktas or periods and sub-periods, he
largely makes quotations from Dasa Bhukti Chandrika of Parasara
and in some places they are imported wholesale. He succeeded
Varaha Mihira, and probably lived a few centuries before. It will
be seen from the results of sub-periods, that evil planets give more
evil, when they are bad, than benefics under similar conditions.
The lordships of planets and houses have not been explained in
the body of the book in detail. A very short summary is given of
the details to be indicated in the headings of the twelve Bhavas,
of course there is a necessity for the readers to know clearly the
different significations of the houses and also the lordships of the
planets. I have collected much useful information on this subject
and have given it here for ready reference. A man's difficulties
multiply in various directions as do his comforts from various
sources. To have disease bodily and mental, to have bad and
treacherous friends and relations, to possess troublesome wife,
children and servants, to be in the disfavour of rulers, kings and
influential aristocrats, to have cruel-minded tenants and cultiva-
tors, to own troublesome and ungrateful relations and dependents,
to lose money, lands, name, houses, conveyances, grain, ornaments,
clothing, comfortable place and residence, to constantly travel
in foreign and unsympathetic lands, in connection with business
which does not pay but which brings disgrace and loss, to live in
forests and caves and places of concealment, to get confinement,
bondages and imprisonment, to be disgraced in public assemblies
for various reasons or faults, to undergo mean and degrading
service under quite unsympathetic masters, to perform sinful deeds,

which are prohibited by his own religion and community, to get into drinking and whoring habits and the company of dark-hearted men, to join in unrighteous expeditions and be instrumental in causing misery and loss to innocent and harmless men, to fall into the company of dirty women and pander to third tastes and deeds, to acquire dirty and condemnable habits, to commit secret sins, and neglect his legitimate work and loyal duties, to be a cruel and unsympathetic parent, brother, or relation, to have nasty falls often from his carriages and conveyances, to get the curses of good and holy men, to have poverty and mendicancy, to be a dependent upon others for means of livelihood, to have deformity in person and mind, to be ignorant and dull, to get whorish wife, daughters and sisters, to be born in houses of ill fame and gambling, to possess tendencies to commit sinful deeds and to be rejected by his people, by his country and by his own nation and Government, are matters which may clearly be classified as misfortunes or bad luck.

To get a good wife, children, brothers, parents, relations friends and companions, to get money, promotions, respect, education, good and moral habits, to have strong, healthy, and vigorous constitutions, to possess active habits and energy for work to possess fertile lands, good tenants, faithful friends, relations and servants, to be free from personal pride and arrogance, to possess the favour of kings, rulers, and aristocrats, to have competency and affluence, to possess cattle, cows, horses, conveyances, grain, cultivations and money, to possess a vigorous and clear understanding, to get high and sound education, to claim sympathetic and helpful, masters, friends, and relations, to command good and loyal servants and subordinates, to have moral and religious devotions, to be pure and simple in life, to follow strictly virtuous principles, to have the capabilities of doing any work which may be delegated to him by government or master, to have a strong body and good digestive organs, to get luxurious food, fine clothing, fine bedding and rich furniture, to possess a good and wealthy and jovial sort of temperament, and to serve public purposes.

These are events of human life, which constitute what may be called human fortune. All these are the results of good planetary conjunctions indicative of good and meritorious karma in the past states of human existence. These fortunes and misfortunes have been explained by Venkatasa in his book and I have tried to make them as clear and as convincing as possible to my readers, and I cannot conclude my book without offering my humble and devoted prayers to that Almighty Power, from whom flow all sources of energy and who has enabled me, to complete this huge task, after a large number of years, spent in translating this work and without Whose help I could never have appeared before the public as a writer of note. I most devoutly dedicate this work to the supreme Intelligence from whom my Inspirations have come.

THE END.

This translation by me has been completed at 2 o'clock p. m. on the afternoon of Thursday 11th March 1920, in Salivahana Saka 1841, in the year Siddharti on Saptami of the dark half the lunar month Phalguna, on the solar date 28th of Kumba, in the constellation Anuradha and the following is the diagram for the time. I hope to live in this work for a long time after my mortal coil passes away, and may Saraswathi bless this undertaking, for the benefit of those who are searching for Truth in the Astrological Sciences.